Dad could play)

the national Anthem

on his nose through

his nose

MODERNIST SURVIVORS

For Senior Project:
Post-modern themes in
Portrait of the Young Artist

Morton P.
Levitt

MODERNIST SURVIVORS

The
Contemporary Novel
in England,
the United States,
France, and
Latin America

Ohio State
University Press
Columbus

The Ohio State University Press, Columbus, Ohio 43210

Copyright © 1987 by the Ohio State University Press

All rights reserved

Printed in the United States of America

Library of Congress Cataloging-in-Publication Data

Levitt, Morton.

  Modernist survivors.

  Bibliography: p.

  Includes index.

  1. Fiction—20th century—History and criticism.

2. Modernism (Literature) I. Title.

PN3503.L378   1987   809.3'91   87-5615

ISBN 0-8142-0420-1

This book is for my father, who
would have enjoyed the notice, for
Paul and Ruth Kovnat, who would
have bought a copy in any event,
and, as always, for Annette, who
sustains me still

CONTENTS

What does our cowardice matter if
  on this earth
there is one brave man,
what does sadness matter if in
  time past
somebody thought himself happy,
what does my lost generation
  matter,
that dim mirror,
if your books justify us?
I am the others. I am all those
who have been rescued by your
  pains and care.
I am those unknown to you and
  saved by you.

—Jorge Luis Borges

"Invocation to Joyce"

ACKNOWLEDGEMENTS No one undertakes a project as ambitious as this one without some awareness at least of the debts he owes to others. No one completes such a project without an absolute certainty of how much he is indebted to how many people. As I re-read this work today, in late July 1986, two years after its completion and more than a decade after I first began to consider it, I realize anew some of my long-standing obligations. But I am certain even now that I cannot give adequate credit to all who deserve it.

To Frank Warlow, who first taught me to read modern novels when I was an undergraduate at Dickinson College in the mid-1950s; to Mitchell Morse, my teacher and doctoral adviser at Penn State in the early 1960s and thereafter my colleague at Temple; to the late Maurice Beebe, my friend and colleague at Temple for many years and my predecessor as editor of the *Journal of Modern Literature:* what I owe them is undeniable (if not always very distinct). Let them stand as well for all the others at these institutions who affected me positively. And to my students, both undergraduate and graduate, at all four campuses of Temple University, at Zagreb University and the Inter-University Centre of Postgraduate Studies in Dubrovnik, at the University of Granada and Concordia University in Montréal, let me offer these belated acknowledgements.

To some people I owe specific debts at specific moments of time: Leon Edel encouraged me to undertake this project at the moment of its inception, and Kimon Friar has been encouraging me for years— throughout the writing of my Kazantzakis book, *The Cretan Glance*—to speak forcefully and in my own voice.

Others—not all of them professors of modern literature—listened to and read about and talked out ideas about novels with me over a long period of years: Max Luria, Bob Buttel, the late Charlie Mauskopf, Phil Stevick, Phil Yannella, Miles Orvell, and Paul Epstein at Temple; Ivo Vidan and Sonja Bašić in Zagreb; Manolo Villar Raso in Granada; Anna Merle d'Aubigné in Paris; and a long list of Joyceans—surely the least specialized and most humane of scholars—Berni Benstock, Shari Benstock, Murray Beja, Fritz Senn, Dick Pearce, Zack Bowen, Ellen Rose, Ira Nadel, Sandy Pinsker, Harry Staley, among many others. Most of all, as always, Annette Shandler Levitt encouraged and listened and mediated and honed, with patience, love, and critical sharpness, through the many years of this project. None of them bears any responsibility for what appears in these pages, but without them it would have been a very different, perhaps a much lesser, book.

I am obligated also to the College of Arts and Sciences at Temple University for the several grants which helped make possible the writing of this book. Finally, several sections of the book have appeared as articles, in somewhat different form, in other publications. For permission to reprint them here, I offer my thanks to the copyright holders: to William T. Stafford, editor of *Modern Fiction Studies*, and the Purdue Research Foundation (for the piece on B. S. Johnson); to A. Owen Aldridge, editor of *Comparative Literature Studies*, and the Board of Trustees of the University of Illinois (Carlos Fuentes); to Randi Birn and Karen Gould, editors of *Orion Blinded*, and the Associated University Presses, Inc. (Claude Simon); to Dorey Schmidt, editor of *Margaret Drabble: Golden Realms*, and the School of Humanities, Pan American University (Margaret Drabble); and to Bradley A. Shaw and Nora Vera-Godwin, editors of *Critical Perspectives on Gabriel García Márquez*, and the Society of Spanish and Spanish-American Studies (García Márquez). Finally, unless otherwise noted, all translations are my own.

MODERNIST SURVIVORS

1 JOYCE VERSUS JOYCE

Moderns and Post-Moderns

You to whom the answers seem easy
do not live in our time.

—Edward Bond, *Restoration*

Only now, when the death of Modernism has been almost universally proclaimed have we begun to be concerned much with the origins of the movement. The problems of affixing a birthdate are obvious. Do we follow Henry Adams, see the year 1900 itself as cataclysmic, and assume that the new literary movement must inevitably follow the new century? Or do we look to some specific event, such as the death of Edward VII or the outbreak of the Great War or the first Dadaist stirrings during the war? One widely admired date is 1922, which saw the publication of *The Waste Land* and *Ulysses*, the principal texts of the period. There was also in that year *Jacob's Room*, which serves as the starting point, in technique and theme, for Woolf's mature fiction, and in the following year *Kangaroo*, so significant a step on the philosophical pathway leading to *The Plumed Serpent*, as well as the first stories of Hemingway. In 1924, Breton issued the *First Surrealist Manifesto*, and *The Magic Mountain* appeared. We might go on, balancing our dates and our documents to fit our critical needs for another decade at least: the posthumous publication of Kafka's novels and of the final volumes of *A la recherche du temps perdu* and the appearance of *Parade's End* in the mid-1920s; Faulkner's creative explosion in the final years of that decade and the opening years of the next; Beckett's first significant efforts in the mid-1930s; the completion, after long years and many revisions, of Kazantzakis' *Odysseia* in 1938 and of *Finnegans Wake* in 1939. And then there is Conrad, whose major works were completed before any of these were begun, or perhaps even contemplated.

It is an intriguing exercise, this effort to date so nebulous an event, and obviously futile. But it appeals to our need for scholarly symmetry, and besides, confident that the period has surely expired, we have the leisure as literary historians to define its boundaries and contemplate its resources. For few of us would deny that Modernism is among the richest of literary epochs and, in particular, the great age of the novel. Yet we are likely to reflect, in sadness no doubt, upon its discontinuity from earlier tradition: what was formerly seen as one of the strengths of the period—its sense that a new age demanded a new art, free of the encumbrances of the past that had sapped both age and art—is now viewed as its major defect. In denying the past, we are told, in elevating the individual artistic performance of the moment over the accumulated heritage of the past, the Modernist artist has cut us off from our history, has sacrificed the communal wisdom for mere technical brilliance, has deprived us of the hard-earned lessons of our humanity. Modernist art, in this widely held view, is distinctively and consciously anti-humanist; for humanism to be resurrected in our time, Modernism as a creative force must be denied. It is a neat formulation, this conviction that we can recover the surety of tradition—that we can regain our humanity—by denying a mere few decades of art (a half century at most)—and just as obviously wrongheaded. Perhaps our concerns should lie elsewhere than with dating; we may well need to reconsider our basic understanding of Modernist forces and effects.

Hardly anyone, a few years ago, used the term "Modernism" to delimit this age. It is a patently inapt term, doubly inapt—doubly ironic—that it should be so widely adopted after the fact, after its inappropriateness had presumably been made clear by the alleged demise of the spirit of the age. What will they call it a century from now? Surely critics (possibly artists as well) will resent an appellation from the past which seems to deny the modernity of their own time. (But, then, they may resolve the problem by naming their age Presentness or the Era of Contemporaneity and letting the twenty-second century fend for itself.) Today, as if to avoid this postmortem problem, we have developed a new term for a new, still undefined era, a literary age in process of formation, more likely a series of separate movements (most of them so individualistic and specialized that they should perhaps be called "moves" rather than "movements" and the whole labeled "gestures" rather than an "age"); an age whose attributes are perceived primarily in terms of what it is not, in relation to its allegedly deceased predecessor, in what seems to me the most negative, stillborn sense of the term: Postmodernism, they have begun to call it; post-Modernism, I prefer to describe its various guises. I hope to suggest by this usage my conviction that, despite the popular wisdom, there is no meaningful movement in the novel which follows Modernism and take its place. The avowedly lesser works of so-called post-Modernist writers—composed in the evident belief that only a reductionist vision and technique could possibly follow in the expansionist Modernist wake—do not, almost by self-definition, constitute a true movement or even a sensibility that will survive.

It is, in part, the growth of this presumed new sensibility which leads us to herald Modernism's demise; in part, as well, it is a kind of historical necessity. For if the Modernist Age was a time of literary giants and of gigantic, often unbearable historical events; and if we live today in a more human-sized world—giantism's inevitable aftermath—yearning desperately for events, historical and literary alike, which we can more comfortably control, then it would seem apparent that Modernist fiction, with its limitless expectations and urges, can speak to us and for us no more. The new sensibility is indisputably in process; the historical necessity seems equally clear, although we may find it deplorable. But the conclusion seems to me not at all so inevitable. My own sense—the major thrust of this book—is that Modernism, in its fiction in particular, is still very much alive, still continuing to change and to grow, and that claims for its demise are a sign of our cultural insularity. I am convinced as well that we are wrong to insist that Modernism represents a break from our humanist heritage. It may be apparent only in retrospect, and we may need to ignore the claims of some of the critics and of some of the Modernists themselves: but from the perspective of the most self-destructive half-century in human history—after Dachau, Hiroshima and My Lai—the Modernist novel seems humanist indeed: accepting human limitations, to be sure, but affirming human potential and dignity; appearing to deny man's most hallowed clichés of self-image, even at times to deny his presence (and the presence of God), but evidencing in

√ | fact great faith in our ability to endure, to prevail, to adapt to the most
| dehumanizing of man-made circumstance and to retain in the process
some at least of our deepest values, the most significant of them. We act
as if it were the Modernist novelist who invented the insane world that
he so well and movingly describes.

II

Artists are not alone in admiring the symmetry and conviction of
symbolic dates and events: how else explain the fixing of Romantic
beginnings by critics to the publication of the *Lyrical Ballads* in 1798
when the unheralded *Songs of Innocence* had appeared almost a decade
earlier? If we need a symbolic moment to posit as the first Modernist
act, I would offer that day in 1909 when James Joyce, shortly after the
birth of his daughter, Lucia—as Richard Ellmann observes—decided to
rewrite *Stephen Hero* and to make of it *A Portrait of the Artist as a Young
Man*. Ellmann points out that the theme of *A Portrait*, "the gestation of a
soul," is consistent with the new facts of the artist's own life; that its
opening images develop directly out of that life; and that Joyce was
"encouraged" in his new state of mind and affairs "to work and rework
the original elements in the process of gestation."[1] I would hazard,
however, another understanding of that act, a rather different symbolic
significance for Joyce and for us, a meaning drawn less from the artist's
own life than from his observation of the life around him.

The narrative of *Stephen Hero*—such of it as survives (its partial
destruction by fire and miraculous salvation is itself a lovely symbolic
event)—is in a form perfectly appropriate to the Edwardian state of
affairs which it describes: an elaboration of late Victorian social views, of
Victorian attitudes toward art and the role of the artist, even of Victorian
omniscience. When the earlier Stephen Dedalus accuses Emma Clery of
betraying him with Cranly, we know that he is wrong. We know this
because the essentially omniscient Edwardian who describes the scene
has informed us that she is innocent: he has shown us already the
attempted public seduction and her inevitable, perhaps wished-for rejection of her would-be lover. There is none of the potential ambiguity
here of the later Stephen's accusation. Even in *A Portrait*, we believe that
Stephen is acting unjustly, that he is fabricating this betrayal—as he will
fabricate others—because of his need to be isolate, to be betrayed, to fit

the Romantic conception of the artist which Joyce always maintained. But in *A Portrait* we are not quite certain; we cannot indisputably contest Stephen's claim because we have been shown no evidence; we must not dispute the artist's essential veracity however much we suspect that he forges his deeds and his words. We understand that he is one of those who will sacrifice his life for his art, that he will demean not merely his friends but himself if it will satisfy the demands of his art, that he will gladly subjugate accepted norms of truth to what he conceives of as a higher truthtelling. Thus we suspect him. But because we are limited to what Stephen himself will admit of his life, we cannot be quite certain. Even on this supposedly higher level of truth, the ambiguity remains.

When the Victorian and Edwardian novelists made use of narrative omniscience, they were reflecting a worldview which harbored few uncertainties. The opening scene of *A Portrait of the Artist as a Young Man*, with its sharply limited perspective, is a consciously symbolic act warning us that that old dispensation has irretrievably altered. The change in point of view is both sign and measure of this change in worldview.

Henry James chose wisely when he adopted the term "point of view" to depict the focal point and lens, the series of refractions and perspectives, and the ordering consciousness which lie at the heart of all narrative technique: the point of view of an age—its basic attitudes toward society, toward art, toward life itself and human involvement in life—is most fully expressed in the narrative points of view which it makes use of in its fictions. Victorian self-assuredness—the self-assuredness, at least, of the Victorian novelist if not always of the Victorian poet and essayist—is perfectly expressed in Victorian omniscience; when there are moments of uncertainty in this view of the world—as there are occasionally in Dickens, for instance—then only are we likely to find variations in narrative technique. Such moments pass quickly: the brief Chancery fog in the opening scene of *Bleak House*, reflective of broad uncertainty about basic institutions of the land; the psychic fog at the start of *The Mystery of Edwin Drood*, an indication of inner uncertainties. But then we remember that Trollope criticized Dickens for being insufficiently omniscient; for betraying his readers' confidence and expectations; in effect, for violating their shared conception of things as they are and as they ought to be shown in art. "Have not often the profoundest efforts of genius been used to baffle the aspirations of the reader, to raise false hopes and false fears, and to give rise to expectations which are never to be realized?" he asks in *Barchester Towers*. "And is there not a species of deceit in this to which the honesty of the present age should lend no countenance? . . . Our doctrine is, that the author and the reader should move along together in full confidence with each other."[2] It is no simplification of the Victorian experience to argue that the world seen by Trollope, if not perfect, is at least perfectible; that none of its facts is unknowable; that no person or event within it is beyond the purview and control of God and his surrogate, the omniscient author. He is social historian, arbiter of morals, carrier of the humane burden for a generation of characters and readers. Neither Stephen nor Joyce nor any of their Modernist fellows is willing to assume such a role, but we are wrong to condemn them or to belittle the very real moral role which they do assume.

The opening scene of *A Portrait* puts us on notice that the comfortable Victorian world is no more. Thrust without warning into a consciousness which cannot order the events it observes, which is incapable of distinguishing among levels of truth or even of sorting out its own sensory perceptions, the reader understands at once that he is in a new world, with changing forces and shifting boundaries, with none of the certainty that Trollope desires and that he himself has long been accustomed to. Joyce's use of point of view in *A Portrait* is not perfect or perfectly consistent; glimpses of omniscience break through even here. But the symbolic import of this narrative act is inescapable: for a new world a new vision is needed, a new lens to penetrate and elucidate the new reality. Yet the change from *Stephen Hero* to *A Portrait* and beyond— from the young Joyce's point of view to the young Stephen's and eventually to Bloom's and HCE's—is both actual and symbolic, reflecting in this duality the dual perspectives of the mature art of Joyce and of Modernism as a whole: these are real people in Joyce's fiction and not merely symbols. We admire Stephen and perhaps despise him; we recognize that the irony is Joyce's irony and not ours alone; we acknowledge the ambiguous stance which we must adopt toward his world. Such ambiguity is the central focus of the Modernist vision and of all Modernist art.

But it was not Joyce or any of the Modernists who invented this state of mind and affairs; the conditions of the world were ambiguous long before the novelists appeared to make them so; Vietnam was hardly the first war to crystallize a civilization in ambiguity. For all of Europe, the Great War—and the chain of events leading inexorably to it and out of it—was a kind of greater Vietnam, destroying expectations along with lives, long-accepted versions of truth along with national boundaries, and seemingly eternal political facts, ideals and visions of man along, it seemed, with humanity itself.

Yet because the shape of man is distorted—as it is in the contemporaneous Cubist painting—because human experience is unlooked for and unhappy, and because man and experience alike are viewed through an unlikely series of prisms and lenses, this does not necessarily mean that the role of man in Modernist fiction has been dehumanized. We react ambiguously to Stephen and to his greater successors, Leopold Bloom and HCE. But we react to them as men, not as mere symbols or forms. No character in literature is more palpable than Bloom. There is none whom we know so deeply and so well, few about whom we care so intensely, few whose humanity so makes us aware of our own. There are times when we scorn Bloom and wish to distance ourselves from him; his is a way of life that most of us would like to deny, with lesser expectations, a lesser sense of achievement. But Bloom retains his dignity and his human concern, even a heroism of sorts, a mythic stature that affixes him in lower-middle-class Dublin at the start of Henry Adams's century and raises him somehow above it. This is not the mythic view of Modernist art as propounded by Eliot—based on irony and scorn for man's present condition, a superstructure of form and control for the artist that is rooted in the past rather than a guide to the nature of man in the present. The Joycean view is more basic, more truly mythic and less brutally ironic, closer to the spirit and intention of the ancient fertility figures whom Bloom at times echoes.[3] That we can see Bloom's endurance, his will to live his life with dignity and even with a certain clumsy grace, his commitment to human needs and involvement: that we can see him as potentially heroic despite the irony and beneath the burden of naturalistic detail, is a sign of Joyce's own commitment to humanism. The times are difficult, to be sure, and man's potential has indisputably lessened: but he remains at the center of Modernist concern, and his values—the old humanist values, altered but still recognizable—are in the end affirmed once again.

III

I have been speaking of Joyce as if his art could stand for all Modernist art. This is not to deny the very real differences—artistic, philosophic, and human differences—which exist between Joyce and Mann, or Joyce and Proust, or Joyce and Kafka. Nor is it necessarily to imply that Joyce ranks unreachably above them as a novelist, that his is the sole meaningful point of view of the age, or that he is more deeply committed than they are to humanist affairs. The glory of the Modernist Age is that it possesses four such masters—and many others, Faulkner, Woolf, Gide, Svevo, Broch, Kazantzakis, and Hemingway among them, who are lesser only by comparison. This diversity may make the period difficult to delimit or to define, but it leaves other, more fruitful tasks to the critic. For it seems indisputable to me that this is the great age of the novel. And Joyce, despite his individuality, is its eponymous hero, symbol (in part because of his individuality) of its artistic and human commitment: the Modernist Age might as tellingly be labeled the Age of Joyce.

In Joyce we find that marriage of sensibility and technique which is characteristic of the period as a whole; he provides in his life the model of the Modernist artistic endeavor; his work makes manifest both the apparent extremes and the actual means which distinguish this age from all others. The developing body of his fiction establishes its critical poles—from the Edwardian *Stephen Hero;* to *Ulysses,* the most representative and, I believe, the major work of the century; to *Finnegans Wake,* which might almost be called the first post-Modernist text. In Joyce we find in detail the most significant Modernist innovations and concerns: the concern for devising a narrative point of view which will most suitably convey a changing worldview (not simply stream of consciousness, as some have claimed, but many other variations of both interior and exterior views); the awareness of time as a phenomenon of the individual mind and not of the clock, as a force which operates in each of our lives and not simply as an objective measure of their passing; the ironic tone which alone can reflect these changing perspectives, another function of point of view; the erection of tight and elaborate metaphoric structures which demand that novels be read as closely now as sonnets alone were once read—and necessitating the rise of a new critical approach to fiction, the New Criticism, so-called; the recognition that in myth we may test out not only our ties with societies of the past but the present status of our own society; the diminished yet central vision of man surviving, of man persisting, a revised yet still powerful humanist vision.

My Joyce, in short, serves in this book as a metaphor, not as a source.

Although I may at times attempt to trace a specific debt owed to Joyce or to one of his contemporaries by one of ours, this book is not intended as an influence study. It is the aura of Joyce that attracts me, just as I believe it compels all those novelists who follow him. For admirers and detractors alike, it is this presence (that is, the continuing Modernist presence which Joyce represents) that may prove to be the central fact in their lives as novelists: a metaphor of the novel's potential as innovative form and humanist vision. Even for those few (mostly British) who would ignore it, it cannot really be denied; and those who best understand the Joycean/Modernist example and its relevance for our time are, not accidentally, our most vital novelists, those who remain most true to their inheritance. These are the Modernist sur- \ V
vivors, and it is their art that will endure, even prevail.

IV

We are all familiar with those graduate-school listings of the characteristics of, say, literary Romanticism. How many of us know much
more than that of the age? It would be simple—and equally useful—to
compile a list of Modernist characteristics[4] and to use such a list to
emphasize the importance of one or another of the novelists of the time
(let us say Joyce) and to preclude some other (Lawrence perhaps).
(Indeed, any approach which cites Joyce as Modernist symbol and
which is concerned more with the characteristic sensibility and technique of the age than with the circumstance of contemporaneous dating
must inevitably deny Lawrence.) Lawrence possesses few of the qualities
noted above (for I would have my listing and abjure it, too); but Joyce
possesses them all, and so, in varying degrees, do Mann, Kafka, and
Proust, as well as Faulkner and Woolf and most of these others. The
listing is as inevitable and useful as it is dangerous and limited. We are
resigned perhaps to offer such lists, but we must not stop there, for it is
obvious that there are other tasks far more telling.

We need urgently, for one, to investigate some of our most hallowed
critical clichés arising from Modernism. We have always assumed, for
example—seemingly with the approval of the novelists themselves—
that Modernist fiction was an elitist activity, designed solely for those
few readers who were willing to fulfill Henry James's implied contrac-
tual obligation and devote to the novelist all the energy and time and

intelligence at their disposal. This is the view which insists—after James and the best of Conrad—that the Modernists have divided the once-unified readership of Fielding, Austen, and Dickens and have created in its stead two distinct and contradictory groups of readers: the elite and the popular, "those who are artists and those who are not," as Ortega y Gasset puts it in *The Dehumanization of Art.*[5] Yet the facts seem to me not quite so clear-cut. There are those, to be sure, who wish only to read Harold Robbins on the subway coming home from work and to shut off their minds; perhaps they might, in another time, have read Dickens. My own teaching experience convinces me, however, that *Ulysses* is accessible to most readers with patience, a moderate experience as readers and a moderate intelligence, a minimum of help from outside and a goodly degree of good will. Parts of the novel, the Stephen parts primarily, are difficult and dense—perhaps, at times, needlessly so. (I have always considered the "Oxen of the Sun" episode, brilliant as it is, Joyce's one great failure.) But there is little about Bloom—his language, his experience, his emotions—that we cannot touch at first hand, that does not touch us. I reject the implicit paradox that this book about the great common man, if you will, is reserved for uncommon men. I have even come to believe in recent years—tentatively, I admit—that *Finnegans Wake*, too, may be more widely accessible than we have realized: one must be struck by the fact that among the world's foremost *Wake* authorities are lawyers, housewives, art dealers and, above all, proof-readers: an elite perhaps, but not a self-anointed academic elite, an elite that many of us can join. It may be most representative after all, this Modernist audience.

Another of the assumed truths about the Modernist novel is the significance of the cool and objective, aloof and distant attitude which we attribute to its makers. "The artist," says the young Stephen Dedalus, following Flaubert, "like the God of the creation, remains within or behind or beyond or above his handiwork, invisible, refined out of existence, indifferent, paring his fingernails."[6] Such aloofness we interpret as a deficiency of ethics, a retreat from humanity. "The world is neither significant nor absurd," says Alain Robbe-Grillet. "It _is_, quite simply," so that a man-centered view can be intended only to shield us from the things which make up our world. The "humanist outlook" he scornfully dismisses as "pre-eminently a pledge of solidarity," out-of-date and out-of-context in this new world of things.[7] Modernist art, comments Ortega, "is an explicit act of dehumanization."[8]

Following Flaubert and eliminating the novelist as a middleman who intercedes between character and event, between character and reader, the Joycean point of view reweaves the fabric of Victorian fiction and fashions a new world from which certainty has fled, in which even objective reality can no longer be unquestioned. The apparent result of Stephen's youthful *obiter dicta*, some half century later, is the feverish perspective of a Robbe-Grillet narrative, his rejection of metaphor because it is centered in man, his denial of humanism. But it is wrong to link Robbe-Grillet too closely with Joyce and the Modernists: his dictates are, in fact, a reversal of their practice; it is unwise as well to identify the young Stephen with the mature Joyce: much of what Stephen says about art in *A Portrait* is repudiated in the novel itself and in the subsequent novels; it is even a bit risky to associate Robbe-Grillet the critic too fully with the novelist Robbe-Grillet: we are far more aware of a fragment of humanity in his novels than he will admit to in his essays.[9] Why should any of the Modernists be bound by their dicta? Why should we, half a century afterwards, be similarly bound? We may take our subjects too readily at their words and not judge them sufficiently by their practice.

Thus when Eliot ordained in "Ulysses, Order, and Myth" in 1923 that Joyce had used myth as "a way of controlling, of ordering, of giving a shape and a significance to the immense panorama of futility and anarchy which is contemporary history,"[10] we assumed that he was speaking for all the Modernists both about necessary artistic technique and about the nature of the world confronting the artist. It seems quite clear today, however, that Eliot was speaking not of *Ulysses* but of *The Waste Land*, that Joyce's use of myth is very different from his and from what he describes in his essay, that the poet's worldview is more conservative, closer to despair and much less humane than that of Joyce and most of the Modernist novelists.

To Robbe-Grillet, not a Modernist at all but one of those who would use Modernist technique in order to repeal its sensibility, "literary revolutions have always been made in the name of realism. . . . out of a concern for realism each new literary school has sought to destroy the one which preceded it. . . ."[11] Man is absent from Robbe-Grillet's realism except as unwitting observer; character, plot, and commitment are among the "obsolete notions" to be implicitly denied by his observation. This is a highly stylized conception of reality, Robbe-Grillet admits. "But to stylize," Ortega contends, "means to deform reality, to derealize; style

involves dehumanization."[12] Trollope smiles, and we assume that on
such extreme poles the Modernist novel as a form has been hoist and
found wanting, as empty within of significance as of expressed emotion.
But there are other means to the Modernist novel within these extremes: "characterization," "plot," and "mimesis" are not synonyms for
"humanism" or for "humanity"; the Modernists in any event do not
abjure these traditional concerns—no character in literature is more
fully realized than Bloom, no day more profoundly chronicled than
Bloomsday; and the Modernist narrator—distant, aloof, uninvolved as
he seems—is by no means unaware of or unconcerned about the
condition of man.

   The author-as-God has indeed been eliminated from the Modernist
narrative; the burden is now on the reader-as-man. He must supply the
narrative answers (if there are answers to be found) or even the
questions once willfully raised by the all-knowing, all-powerful author;
he must collaborate with his author in constructing the framework of
character and event; he must provide with his involvement a human
focus. His is a much less comfortable position than that of Trollope's
reader, his world less predictable and less easily harmonious. But the
Modernist narrative is an accurate reflection of the world beyond fiction
(fiction's goal, after all), and it is not lacking totally in values. For if we
interpret humanism as the willingness to accept responsibility for one's
deeds and even for one's vision of reality, and as the dignity that may
accompany such acceptance, then surely the position of the Modernist
reader—and of Modernist author and character as well—is at least as
humanistic as those of their predecessors.

V

Novelists and critics in Britain—dismissing Modernism as an alien
growth outside the native tradition, as "idle experimentation"[13]—have
reverted in recent years to Edwardian and even Victorian narrative
modes. Through such modes alone, they believe, one can recapture the
humanist past (a past, not perhaps coincidentally, of better times for the
Empire). The reaction among intellectuals in France and elsewhere on
the Continent is to endeavor to progress beyond a Modernist base, to
build on Joyce, Faulkner, and Proust in the novel, and to develop a still
newer critical empire to replace the American New Criticism: hence the

enthusiasm for Structuralism, Phenomenology, and the *Tel Quel* heresies-turned-dogma. In the United States, novelists in the past decade have made significant and varied strides toward the development of a fiction which might truly perhaps be called post-Modernist; critics, more recently, have tried to catch up: this may help to explain the current efforts to foster reader-response criticism as an up-to-date and home-grown replacement for the supposedly outmoded New Criticism.

The novelists' efforts are often interesting and in some cases admirable; the critics are always earnest, at times insightful and in most respects—of this I am quite convinced—superfluous. Robbe-Grillet, for example, will surely be remembered more as footnote than as source, more for the implications of his theory than for its elaboration in fiction, and as far less significant a novelist than his compatriots Butor and Simon. But there is a certain fascination in reading his novels and an awareness that they represent what is for the moment an important intellectual byway. There is even an exasperated interest in reading Margaret Drabble, the contemporary Trollope. Some of the newer critical efforts, however, are far more suspect than these fictions. We well may wonder about the literary implications of Structuralism and its sisters and about their coherence (aside perhaps from Marshall McLuhan, no serious critics seem to write so badly—with so little concern for communicating ideas—as the Structuralists do). I have come increasingly to feel in recent years that the Structuralists, Phenomenologists, and Post-Structuralists are not really interested in literature at all, except perhaps as it may relate to larger structures of social experience. They are essentially technicians, and their value as literary critics, I firmly believe, is minimal at best.

We may question as well whether the reader-response critics in their turn do anything that the New Critics had not already done or, at least, had not fully prepared for. Their efforts seem in some ways a smaller-scale New Criticism, a concern with what might be termed minimalist textual detail. At the Seventh International James Joyce Symposium in Zurich, in June of 1979, I had the pleasure of hearing Wolfgang Iser's brilliant exposition of the role of the reader in *Waiting for Godot*. Yet listening to Iser, one of the major figures of the reader-response school, I could not help realizing that essentially the same critical perspective, using essentially the same tools under different names, had been devised twenty years earlier for a study of *Gulliver's Travels* by a little-known New Critic named Henry W. Sams.[14] The new emphasis on the role of

the reader may well provide new insights into much-read texts. But we
should not forget that New Criticism as it developed in the novel is itself
a response to the Modernist novelists' insistence on reader involvement
in elaborating difficult and ambiguous works. For all its literary appeal,
reader-response seems to me to be little more than New Criticism writ
small. All of these newer schools, in fact, may be doing not much
more—so far as our understanding of fiction is concerned—than changing slightly the emphasis of the New Criticism and changing dramatically its language.

I, for one, am always suspicious of efforts to invent new critical
vocabularies or to offer new definitions for workable old ones. The old
terms, it is true, are rarely very precise. But the new ones are not likely
to be more so—this seems to be the nature and perhaps the necessity of
critical language—and the proliferation of terminology (really of private
vocabularies) will simply confuse matters further. (It is difficult enough
to agree on definitions of such universally used terms as "symbol" or
"stream of consciousness.") And these new vocabularies, I fear, are
intended to make for critics a *fait accompli* of a premise not necessarily
agreed to by novelists: that Modernism in fiction is dead. If it were not,
after all, we might be content still to use its own critical tools; that we
need new tools must be evidence that Modernism is, in fact, dead. The
new critical schools may in some ways be as specious as this circular
reasoning which is implicit in their birth. It cannot be totally coincidental that Latin America in the past decade has produced no new critical
school of note but is the source of the finest fiction of the day, a fiction
closest of all to the Modernist spirit. And it is with the spirit of
Modernism rather than its dating—not a period or style or group of
styles, but an attitude toward life as expressed in technique—that I am
concerned in this book.

The studies which follow thus reject both new logic and new critical
schools. Based on the premise that Modernism—sometimes transformed, sometimes as a residual influence in a new age—remains very
much alive, they make use of Modernism's basic critical tool, what I like
to think of as an eclectic New Criticism which emphasizes the integrity
of the literary text but is willing to employ any additional source—
biography, politics, myth, even art history—which can help us to
appreciate the immediate values and larger contexts of that primary text.
Few critics have ever really practiced—certainly not in the past three or
four decades—that narrowly defined New Criticism which its enemies

attack as "Formalist." Their alleged New Criticism—concerned only with text in the most limited sense and scornful of all further contexts—is simply a straw man and not worthy of argument. As an unreconstructed New Critic—in the more meaningful and accurate sense of the term as I understand it—my concerns here are both with individual texts and with their larger contexts, with the nature of the Modernist literary experience and its continuity within a new age: that is, with a unique sensibility and view of the world, with a powerful fictional technique designed to elaborate that view, and with the moral response implicit within both sensibility and technique. In most cases I begin with technique—and perhaps in the process give some sense as well of the surface of the text—and then endeavor to reach through to the novel's larger, thematic concerns.

I make no claim that this is an all-inclusive summary of contemporary fiction. There are other national literatures and other writers of fiction whom I might have considered. To say that this is a personal reading is accurate but not perhaps adequate as explanation, for there are many other contemporary novelists whose art also appeals to me: Günter Grass, Heinrich Böll, Italo Calvino, Giorgio Bassani, Camilo José Cela, Milan Kundera, Vassilis Vassilikos and Chinua Achebe among them. But I have chosen not to write about German, Italian, Spanish, Czechoslovak, Greek, and Nigerian fiction for the obvious reason that six years is quite enough time to spend on one book. There is clearly another book—or several—to be written on these other novelists, but that will have to wait for another time and perhaps for some other critic.

Moreover, the literatures and novelists about whom I have chosen to write present a critical pattern that I find particularly revealing. At the negative end of the spectrum are the British novelists and critics who have so aggressively denied the relevance (even the existence) of the Modernist example. At the other, affirmative end of the spectrum are the Latin Americans, who have recognized how profoundly the Modernist presence relates to and informs their own experience and who have built their wonderful fictions upon its foundation. At way stations between these poles, as I see them, are certain representative French and North American novelists. The four American novelists whom I discuss here are linked by the innovative uses which they make of myth, that characteristic Modernist method. I might have selected other artists and other techniques, but these particularly interest me, and they are, I believe, particularly indicative of the American reaction to Modernism.

As for the three French novelists about whom I write in this book, they are representative in yet another way: they suggest a range of potential national reactions that I find revealing—about the French and Modernism alike. They are also among my oldest critical acquaintances. I first wrote about their work twenty years ago in my dissertation, and I continue to find them powerful and challenging figures. (And now that Claude Simon has won the Nobel Prize, I take some pride in being one of the first to write about him in English.)

My concern in all of these studies is not to redefine Modernism but to tear away some of the accretion of misunderstanding and critical cliché which has surrounded it from the start and to indicate, at the same time, how this historical force might serve for later generations. I hope, in the process, to throw some light on several of the most exemplary novelists writing today—in Great Britain, on the Continent, in the United States and Latin America—as they reflect the Modernist aura within their separate cultures. For these are the regions most profoundly affected by the major literary force of our time, and they have reacted to it in radically different ways and at different times. Their disparate reactions may speak not only of cultural differences but of the varied, changing yet consistent nature of Modernism itself.

VI

What follows, then, is a very personal reading of the Modernist presence in the novel, of its impact and significance for its own and later generations, and of the work of some of its contemporary heirs. I am not much interested in delimiting the period's dates or in compiling an exhaustive list of its characteristics. That would be at once too easy and probably meaningless to others. The reader anticipating a definition of Modernism (and/or of post-Modernism) will similarly not find it here. That too, I fear, would be too private an exercise. What the reader will find in this book, I trust, is a new appreciation of Modernist art in the novel, its sensibility and its worldview, as well as a firmly held belief in Modernist continuity, its connections to the past, its continuance into the present, its humanist presence.

If this seems today a radical view, it is actually based on a quite conservative premise: my conviction that the Modernist novelists were far more respectful of tradition than they sometimes said or than many of their critics have supposed. It may seem strange to think of *Ulysses*, for example, as a traditional, even a conservative novel. Yet there is a very real sense in which it is. We must not be misled—as so many English critics and novelists have been misled—into mistaking Joyce's fireworks for a revolution devoid of a sustaining context. That context is the very nature and history of the novel as a literary form. There is little in *Ulysses*—little even in *Finnegans Wake*, I suspect—that is not found first (*in ovo*, at least) in *Tristram Shandy*, that has not been prepared for in fact by the whole development of the novel, its themes and techniques, over three centuries. What Joyce was doing, I believe, what Proust, Kafka, and Mann were doing along with him, was building on Lazarillo and Cervantes, on Fielding and Richardson, on Dickens and Dostoevsky and Flaubert—as they had built on their predecessors—to create a novel that would be true both to history and to its own time.

The history of the novel from the first has been a history of adaptation; from its first appearance it has been the literary form uniquely atuned to its time—whatever its time. That is its essence as a form. From *A Journal of the Plague Year* and *Robinson Crusoe*, from *Pamela* and *Shamela* and *Joseph Andrews* and *Tom Jones*, it has demanded by its very nature the new narrative techniques that can best represent and communicate the changing, new times. Continuity in the novel implies, by definition, the flowering of new perceptions and the development of new forms: growing out of old ones, of course, as the point of view of *Finnegans Wake* grows out of "Circe," as the styles and themes of the whole of *Ulysses* develop from such stories as "An Encounter" and "Eveline," as the perspective and sensibility made manifest in *Dubliners* emerge out of Chekhov and late Dickens, out of Jane Austen and Fielding and Richardson and Defoe and, as always, Sterne. The continuity and development within Joyce's own canon mirror those of the novel's history and, in doing so, encapsulate the Modernist experience.

The true radicals, as I see it, are not the Modernist novelists but those who refuse to adapt, who in the name of conserving old virtues—and despite history—insist on viewing both the novel and their time as static. Victorian narrative devices were wonderfully appropriate to the spirit of that age. But the age has changed; no number of omniscient (usually English) narratives will make our time—and the life we must enact within it—any less ambiguous than it is. I would go further. It seems evident to me that to deny Modernism and its alleged "experimentation" in the name of some ill-defined "humanism"—as if humanism were a self-evident function of traditional characterization and plotting and Victorian omniscience—is an act antithetical both to the integrity of the novel as a literary form and to the human subjects whom it would ostensibly defend. In my reading, the Modernists' endeavor to develop narrative techniques which place modern man in his true setting—principally their development of a point of view that removes the omniscient-omnipotent Victorian God at the center of the narrative and replaces him with limited, representative man—such an attempt, in my view, is an act not hostile to humanity but empathetic of our predicament. The Modernist novel, that is, embodies at its core an inherently humanistic approach to art and to life.

"Humanism" is another of those literary terms that the prudent critic might best avoid trying to define with certainty. I would not expect to be much more successful at the task than the opponents of the Modernists have been. But at least I would not presuppose that there is some single, simple, universally agreed upon definition that alone would suffice, on the face of it, to justify a series of negative critical judgments about so positive an age. "Humanism" can never have been an easy term to define, although in an earlier age which never questioned its pre-eminence, it perhaps did not need to be. Today, only the vaguest outlines of the concept are visible. We know that a modern humanism can have little in common with that fourteenth-century Humanism that developed out of Western Europe's discovery of the ancient Greeks. We know as well that no definition can be as secure today as was the Church's pre-Copernican view of a man-centered universe (although certain Fundamentalist groups in the United States have begun of late to attack, with equal certainty, some of their enemies as "Humanists").

But the Modernist novelists have pointed the way to us, if not quite to certainty or even to a definition of the times, at least to an awareness of the potential for humanist activity and concern that survives in our often inhuman world. For there is an order in the Modernist universe in which recognizably humanist values—at least so they have seemed to me and to many of my students over the years—do still pertain. They may appear threatened and fragile. They may well be ambiguous. But in a world as perilous as ours, in which certainty is the final refuge of the desperate, the Modernist example—despite its ambiguity, perhaps even because of it—may seem humanistic indeed.

As I read the novels of the Modernist masters, these values are evoked in various and sometimes surprising ways: through the empathy that we feel for such characters as Joyce's Leopold Bloom and through the emotions that such lives give rise to in our own; as an enactment of the rhythms of nature (as of language and life) accompanying the movement through life of Woolf's Mrs. Ramsay, making us participants with her in the most enduring of rituals, almost as part of the natural process itself. They are evoked also as part of the broader patterning of myth that informs the actions of Mann's Joseph and Kazantzakis's Odysseus and connects us through them to archetypal values and meanings, the most profound link available to us today to our most distant ancestry; and through the sense of responsibility with which Kafka endows all his characters, even those not fully human, recalling that responsibility for our own lives which distinguishes us from animal life (it is this theme, and not simply the character of Bloom, that helps to account for the prevalence in Modernist fiction of metaphors of the Jew). And, finally, underlying all of these themes, the humanist values of Modernist fiction emerge as a result of an intimate and demanding new point of view (enmeshed with a complex subjective time scheme and an intricate imagery, as in Faulkner and Proust), which induces us to participate directly in all of these lives and thereby to assume an added responsibility for them and for our own.

As I understand it, then, and as I believe the Modernist novelists understood it, humanist survival is no easy enterprise in a century such as ours. It can no more be assumed in the novel than it can be taken for granted in life. Whatever its sources might have been in the Victorian era, it must be evident that in ours they cannot simply remain, unthinkingly, unchanged. Perhaps the greatest genius of the Modernist masters was their ability to find stability and meaning in what seemed to some to be chaos, to create new narrative forms that convey dramatically both meaning and chaos, to create, our of change, continuity. Throughout this book, I have used the twin issues of narrative adaptability and humanist concern as a measure of Modernist survival, as a measure of Modernist worth. I apply it not merely to the Modernists themselves but also to their successors in our generation. (I omit here their immediate successors, the generation of Beckett, Nabokov, Greene, Camus, and Bellow: that is yet another book.) There are more of these contemporary successors, in more cultures and languages, than we might expect from all the popular talk about something called post-Modernism. These novelists are endeavoring to expand upon the Modernist example—in technique, theme, and sensibility alike—and adapt it to new situations and cultures. Their effort is in keeping with the novel's history and the Modernist spirit. It is no coincidence that they are the best of our current novelists.

2 THE GREAT TRADITION IN BRITAIN

The (Victorian) Past Recaptured, the (Modernist) Present Denied

I wrote down five verses:

one green,

one shaped like a breadloaf,

the third like a house going up,

the fourth one, a ring,

the fifth one

small as a lightning flash . . .

Then came the critics: one deaf,

and one gifted with tongues,

and others and others:

the blind and the hundred-eyed,

the elegant ones

in red pumps and carnations,

others decently clad

like cadavers . . .

some coiled in the forehead

of Marx or thrashing about in his

   whiskers;

others were English,

just English . . .

     —Pablo Neruda, *Oda a la crítica*

Some years ago, Angus Wilson met with a group of my students at Temple University, shortly before he was to give a public lecture on Dickens, to discuss his own work. For more than an hour, he was gracious, open, even vulnerable in his response to their questions. Then one of the students injudiciously told the novelist the title of the course in which we were reading his work: The New Victorians, I had named it. Wilson was clearly disturbed and disagreed forcefully with our assessment of his work. He spoke, in response, of his respect for James Joyce and indicated that he attempted to make use in each of his novels of at least one new technique that he had learned from Joyce. I felt at the time that I knew something of Joyce, and I had read most of Wilson's fiction, and I could see none of this putative influence. His subject matter, to be sure, like that of the others whom we read in that course—Muriel Spark, Iris Murdoch, Anthony Powell, and Anthony Burgess among them—was clearly contemporary, but in technique he—like them, in most respects—seemed firmly old fashioned. (I have since had to amend this judgment somewhat: *As If By Magic*, on which Wilson was at work at that time and of which he spoke, does indeed make use of certain narrative techniques which might have derived from Joyce. The essential judgment, however, remains.)

Wilson is virtually alone among contemporary British novelists in even caring about such an assessment. Most of the others are more likely to be insulted if we claim that they are connected to Joyce—or, worse yet, to Virginia Woolf; only to D. H. Lawrence would more than a few of them be willing to admit obligation. For the single most dramatic fact about fiction in Britain two generations after James Joyce is that Joyce and his peers have affected it so little. What mark they have left is almost entirely negative: in conscious reaction against the Modernists, fiction in Britain today is not so much post-Modern as pre-.

Speaking primarily of the generation of the 1950s, Stephen Spender distinguishes, in *The Struggle of the Modern*, between "moderns" and "contemporaries," between those who would follow at least in part the characteristic vision and method of the Modernists and those who would deny even their presence in the post-war world. "The contemporary belongs to the modern world," Spender writes, "represents it in his work, and accepts the historic forces moving through it, its values of science and progress. . . . The modern is acutely conscious of the contemporary scene, but he does not accept its values." Where the contemporary is likely to be a social rebel, "a partisan in the sense of seeing and supporting partial attitudes, . . . the modern tends to see life as a whole and hence in modern conditions to condemn it as a whole."[1] The distinction as Spender sees it is largely attitudinal: differing attitudes toward tradition, different ways of viewing the world; he speaks little of differences in technique. But technique and worldview are in the end inseparable; it is impossible to elaborate a mid-twentieth-century perspective using tools more appropriate to the mid-nineteenth century. The "contemporaries" of Spender's formulation are indeed up-to-date in their subject matter and in their knowledge and use of those intellectual forces which have helped shape our world: Freud, Jung, Frazer, Darwin, and Marx variously play prominent roles in their fiction (at least in some of their fiction). But they have consciously and articulately denied those narrative innovations which both characterize and make possible the Modernist vision. "New Victorians" may be too strong a term to label their movement backward; perhaps "New Edwardians" would be more appropriate. There is no doubt, in any event, that as Spender sees it, "a younger English generation of writers such as Kingsley Amis and John Wain, reacting against the modern movement, prefers Arnold

Bennett to Virginia Woolf."[2] A generation younger still appears to feel likewise: Woolf is rejected for "feminizing" Modernism,[3] and Bennett is the subject of a recent biography by the novelist Margaret Drabble. Remembering the old battle between Bennett and Woolf, we cannot help but see the choice as symbolic.[4]

There are British novels of the past decade or so which do show signs of the Modernist example: Anthony Powell's series *The Music of Time* echoes the historical and philosophical rhythms of *A la recherche du temps perdu*, although its tone and technique come more from Huxley and Waugh than from Proust; Anthony Burgess, author of a useful study of Joyce and editor of a not-so-useful abridgement of *Finnegans Wake*, reflects an affection similar to Joyce's for language, music, and Shakespeare in such books as *A Clockwork Orange, MF,* and *Nothing Like the Sun;* in *As If By Magic,* Angus Wilson makes use of a shifting point of view that stays skillfully and unobtrusively inward, avoiding all hints of omniscience, in the service, as he puts it, of "the basic common humanity of Bloom";[5] *The French Lieutenant's Woman,* by John Fowles, both parodies and endorses Victorian narrative omniscience, using Victorian England as an overlay to the modern experience; John Berger's *G.* attempts to blend seeming omniscience with a more limited perspective in a form of reconstruction which loosely recalls Faulkner and the major novels of Claude Simon; the novels of B. S. Johnson are efforts in various ways to open up the form of the novel and to reflect within it the life and personality of the novelist, perhaps even to use the fiction— as Joyce does—as a force which can change this life; Julian Mitchell's *The Undiscovered Country* and Robert Nye's *Falstaff,* even Doris Lessing's *The Golden Notebooks,* take further advantage of the reflexive possibilities of narration and theme which are suggested by *Ulysses* and expanded by Borges and Barth; and Christine Brooke-Rose's *Out* serves as skillful response to Robbe-Grillet's *La Jalousie,* as her *Thru* appears an off-shoot of *Finnegans Wake.*

The evidence of Modernist influence—or at least of Modernist awareness—seems rather persuasive when joined together like this; the evidence, of course, is misleading. Such works are patently outside the main stream of fiction in Britain today. Some seem almost aberrations when compared to the novels of Wain or Snow, of Murdoch or Spark, of Cooper, Drabble, or Lessing. Virtually all are anomalies in another sense as well, outside the more usual pattern of their authors. With the single exception of B. S. Johnson, no British novelist of the post-World

War II era has been willing consistently to utilize and expand upon Modernist technical concerns. And even Johnson denied that he was writing fiction; is it too cruel, too far-fetched, to conjecture whether any of the opponents of Modernism has seen his suicide as a further judgment on that much abused movement? For the contemporary novel in Britain—and contemporary British novel criticism alongside it—is a conscious, articulate, and, I believe, wrongheaded reaction against the Modernist experience: not merely the Modernist literary example but the experience as a whole, as if by repudiating its narrative concerns one could repeal the entire era and all that it signifies. Only so extreme an inference can serve to explain the gross misreadings of Modernism which have been predominant in Britain since the end of the war.

These misreadings relate in the main to the nature of the British novelistic tradition and the relation of Modernist fiction to that tradition. Certain recurrent motifs in the criticism of the past two decades, much of it written by novelists, make it painfully clear that the British have come to see themselves as guardians not merely of a beleaguered realistic tradition but of the voice of humanity in literature. To this singular and inspired end they have been led to reject what they call, in near unanimity, "idle experimentation" (which seems to include all narrative forms devoid of omniscience) and to reinstate traditional (*i.e.,* Victorian and Edwardian) conceptions of characterization and plot. The underlying assumptions here would seem to be that experimentation inevitably negates character and event, that omniscience and old-fashioned characterization are the apotheosis of form in the novel (so that experiment leads inevitably to formlessness), that such form is somehow the equivalent of morality, and, finally, that this view of morality is the only possible valid statement of humanistic concern for the novelist. Opposed avowedly to plot, to characterization, and to moral omniscience, the Modernists on their face must be anti-humanist, a temporary break at best (or at worst) in the major line of Western development since the Age of Pericles. Stated as baldly as this, by an obvious opponent of such reasoning, the neo-Edwardian critical configuration seems utterly preposterous. One must then question the statement; but it is much less unfair than one might expect: the logical connections are not often made quite so openly as this, but contemporary critics and novelists in Britain have been far more extreme in their own comments on Modernism and the great British tradition. Many, I suspect, would be quite content to accept this formulation as it stands.

II

Tradition "cannot be inherited," declares T. S. Eliot in "Tradition and the Individual Talent," "and if you want it you must obtain it by great labour. It involves . . . a perception, not only of the pastness of the past, but of its presence; . . . a sense of the timeless as well as of the temporal and of the timeless and of the temporal together. . . ." It is not an order vast and unchanging but "an ideal order . . . which is modified by the introduction of the new (the really new) work of art" among the monuments of the past.[6] Eliot's formulation seems wonderfully responsive both to the demands of the past and to the needs of the present. As we look closely at the labors of his Modernist co-workers—at Joyce, Proust, Mann, even at Kafka, at their adaptation of literary sources and analogues and their use of myth, at their attitudes toward long-accepted ideas of reality and morals—it is precisely this union "of the timeless and of the temporal" which we see at work. Yet the prevailing critical image is vastly different. Each of the Modernist masters reacts against the history of his or her time, including its literary history, by building upon it, by developing its potential in reactive, often revolutionary ways, but in a general manner that is perfectly consistent with its own prior history and development. Joyce, the greatest of innovators, is careful to name his sources (sometimes inaccurately, as in the case of Edouard Dujardin, the alleged source of the stream of consciousness technique) and to list his supposed Homeric borrowings precisely so that we can trace his ties to his forebears and perceive how he builds upon and against them. Even in the idiosyncratic Kafka we see this same paradoxical union of the acceptance of and reaction against tradition[7]— this most traditional of all literary activities, which characterizes all significant new literary eras. This seems a truism, yet much of the reaction against the Modernists, notably in Britain, presupposes that they deny tradition completely, apparently so that they can be repudiated completely by contemporary critics. The balance of Eliot's formulation has been widely ignored in Great Britain, and the "pastness of the past" has become virtually a rallying cry, for and against, in this most bloody of critical battlegrounds.

In 1919, in the seminal essay called "Modern Fiction," Virginia Woolf appeared to speak for all the Modernists (she was still calling them "Georgians" as late as 1924) in rejecting the stultifying influence of the recent, Edwardian past and breaking loose, it would seem in the process, from the whole of the novelistic tradition. Her words reflect the revolutionary task which she and her contemporaries were undertaking at that time. They are not a precise measure of Modernist fiction in general, however, or even of Woolf's fiction alone: they were written, after all, at a time when *Ulysses* was appearing still in separate chapters in the *Little Review* and before any of Woolf's mature fiction had been conceived. They have come to stand for some, nonetheless, for the entire Modernist creative endeavor.

For the writer enslaved to tradition as the Edwardians conceived it, Woolf wrote three years before *Jacob's Room*—the writer "in thrall to provide a plot, to provide comedy, tragedy, love, interest, and an air of probability embalming the whole"—for such a writer the most apt similes are from architecture and tailoring rather than from history or life. His is the province of matter, the surface of things, and not that of the spirit. "There is not so much as a draught between the frames of the windows" in the fictional house constructed by Bennett and his Edwardian fellows, "or a crack in the boards. And yet—if life should refuse to live there?" If Bennett's figures "were to come to life they would find themselves dressed down to the last button of their coats in the fashion of the hour. . . . [Yet] is life like this? Must novels be like this?"[8]

Woolf's repeated demand—repeated throughout her essays and novels, throughout her career—answers itself: life, especially life as perceived by a survivor of the terrible Great War, is beyond the reach of such artificial conventions. But Woolf answers it nonetheless, inverting question into answer and unwittingly providing in the process ammunition for two generations of detractors; her rhetorical question and answer become the basis of the rhetorical warfare directed against her as a symbol of a feared and difficult time. "If a writer were a free man," she writes in challenge, "and not a slave, if he could write what he chose, not what he must, if he could base his work upon his own feeling and not upon convention, there would be no plot, no comedy, no tragedy, no love interest or catastrophe in the accepted style, and perhaps not a single button sewn on as the Bond Street tailors would have it. Life is not a series of gig lamps symmetrically arranged; but a luminous halo, a semi-transparent envelope surrounding us from the beginning of consciousness to the end."[9] "No plot, no comedy, no tragedy, no love interest," presumably no characterization:[10] these seeming strictures resonate in the responses of the modern British enemies of Modernism, sometimes sneeringly, occasionally with regret, throughout

Leavis and Snow, Cooper and Wain, Amis, Bayley, Bradbury, Drabble, and the others. Almost universally, they have looked to Woolf's words rather than to her works or the works of her contemporaries: the "luminous halo," the "semi-transparent envelope" of consciousness have come for virtually all British critics to represent the Modernist reaction against character and plot, against reality and morality, against life itself as it is lived by the mass of men and women and as it must be portrayed by the mass of novelists. It seems a most elaborate structure to be erected on so slim a foundation, on so fundamental a misunderstanding.[11]

This misunderstanding about the intentions and results of the Modernists is so gross at points as to seem almost intentional: some quality in the fiction of Joyce and Woolf is evidently so threatening to the British sense of tradition that it must be denied regardless of logic or the evidence of their work. The Great English Tradition, opened by F. R. Leavis to the foreigners Conrad and James and to the radical Lawrence, is irrevocably shut against the far more alien Woolf and Joyce. Woolf argues in "Mr. Bennett and Mrs. Brown" for a narrative method which will make characterization more viable; she is accused of forsaking character completely. She complains about the "indecency" of Joyce and the "obscurity" of Eliot and is accused herself of being both overly delicate and overly obscure. She speaks for moderation and a marriage of subject and form and is accused of a revolutionary disregard for the facts of our lives, of an inherent anti-humanistic bias. " 'What is it, life?' Virginia Woolf is continually asking. . . . She creates because she is unable to be, and her creations cannot therefore, to most persons, appear as an adequate representation of being."[12] Yet the rhythms of her prose and of the lives of her characters—her own life aside—surely celebrate the natural process and man's role in that process. Even the death of Mrs. Ramsay in *To the Lighthouse* is announced—preceded by images of the waves and the wind inexorably in motion, of leaves turning and flowers fading, of light coming on and being extinguished— as a function of nature. This is not, as has sometimes been said, a giving in to death but, in "the profusion of darkness" enveloping the house, it is an affirmation of the rhythms of life, which include death within them.[13] Ironically, Woolf warns her own creation, Orlando, against just such an abstraction from life as she is accused of: the function of the artist in *Orlando* (as in *To the Lighthouse*) is to learn to live, to observe life truly and to represent that life truthfully within his/her art: hardly the fearful, form-ridden, life-denying bias of which Woolf is so often accused.

This misunderstanding—about Woolf in particular, about Joyce, about the Modernists in general—is sadly pervasive, sadly destructive. I have no desire here to attempt to uncover the causes of this mistrust: the fall of Great Britain as a world power, its social breakdown and economic decline may or may not be related to its fearful rejection of Modernist influence. Perhaps the cause is mere chauvinism, or some newly enforced insularity; perhaps the roots are purely literary, as its proponents have implied, and not related at all to contemporary circumstance. My concern is simply with the literary results of this situation, and it seems quite clear to me in this context that the sad, reactionary state of fiction in Britain today can be traced directly to this willful confusion, to the almost universal denial of the most significant of the century's literary movements.

Yet there is a certain sense in which this profound misunderstanding is really quite understandable: Woolf herself as badly misunderstood and misinterpreted the work of Joyce. Here too, unfortunately, her comments have been allowed to stand as if they were definitive. The Modernists have not simply permitted their enemies to assume the mantle of the protectors of reality, of characterization, of humanity in the novel. They have provided them with their most damning rhetoric. "In contrast with those whom we have called materialists," Woolf writes in "Modern Fiction" in 1919, "Mr. Joyce is spiritual; he is concerned at all costs to reveal the flickerings of that innermost flame which flashes its message through the brain, and in order to preserve it he disregards with complete courage whatever seems to him adventitious, whether it be probability, or coherence or any of these signposts which for generations have served to support the imagination of a reader. . . ." *Ulysses* fails, she believes—writing, remember, three years before the novel had appeared as an entity—"because of the comparative poverty of the writer's mind," because of its "indecency," because of "some limitation imposed by the method as well as by the mind. Is it the method that inhibits the creative power? Is it due to the method that we feel neither jovial nor magnanimous, but centered in a self which, in spite of its tremors of susceptibility, never embraces or creates what is outside itself and beyond?"[14] Woolf tempers her judgment somewhat when she writes again of *Ulysses*, now two years after its publication as a book, but even here her discomfort is readily apparent: "Mr. Joyce's indecency in *Ulysses* seems to me the conscious and calculated indecency of a desperate man who feels that in order to breathe he must break the windows. At moments, when the window is broken, he is magnificent. But what a waste of energy! And, after all, how dull indecency is. . . ."[15]

These are hardly the reactions of a co-conspirator; they confirm what every serious reader of the Modernists must already know: that this is no unified movement, that its major practitioners may share certain qualities but that they are wonderfully and disturbingly individualistic, that any simple and linear critical positions regarding their work will inevitably prove simplistic and foolish. Still, Woolf's complaints about Joyce, tinged as they are with a certain admiration and respect, have persisted to this day among critics and novelists in Britain. The still-prevalent view of Joyce in Britain, alone among the regions of the world in which he is read, is that he is concerned more with technique than with substance (no matter that the technique is brilliant), so obsessively self-involved that he seems to disregard the humanity outside his books (thus ignoring the wealth of humanity within them), lacking in joy and humane magnanimity (managing somehow to overlook Bloom) and a rebel against all narrative tradition ("or any of these signposts which for generations have served to support the imagination of a reader"). The charge of indecency no longer seems to apply. Even when it can accept the power of his work and perceive its humor and humanity, British criticism is unable still to overcome these initial simplifications. "Of all modern authors," John Bayley admits, "the closest to Shakespeare is certainly James Joyce, but for all its marvellous and intricate power to move us *Ulysses* is leaden with its own art, sunk in its richness like a great plum-cake."[16] Even so sensitive a critic as Bayley seems blinded by the stereotype to this foolish self-contradiction in his words. It is not accidental that there are so few Joyceans of note in the British Isles (even if we include Ireland), that even in the 1980s many of the best known British Joyceans are foreigners, that the most useful British study of Joyce (S. L. Goldberg's *The Classical Temper*) treats of him as if he were, in fact, D. H. Lawrence. The most influential and, arguably, the finest writer of the century has been cut out of the British tradition almost entirely. Yet that is not all; the full effects of this operation are still wider, still worse. Through a paradoxical process of critical expansion, these observations, so inappropriate to Joyce, their putative subject, are made to stand for—to stand against—the Modernists as a group. Half a century of literary history—and, one might argue, the finest half

century—is neatly excised from the British experience.[17] Two generations of critics in Britain have been ensnared by this foolishness; two
generations of novelists are similarly imprisoned.

III

Modernism, in the prevailing British critical view, is (a) an alien
growth,[18] (b) a transient growth,[19] (c) a radical,[20] anti-rational,[21]
apocalyptic,[22] explicitly cancerous growth which in its innate disease is
(d) cut off from, perhaps hostile to, the phenomenal world[23] and the
human beings who inhabit it. It is, moreover, (e) rigidly formalist and,
most significant of all, (f) unmistakably, irretrievably dead.[24] The
charges are interconnected: to label the Modernists "formalists" is not
simply to condemn them as idle experimenters and opponents of
traditional characterization; it is to insist as well that they are inherently
anti-humanist.

Britist critics have consistently reacted to the Modernists as if their
endeavor were a purposeful attack on British literary culture. (American
critics who have spoken of Modernism's demise have done so, on the
whole, regretfully and certainly without any sense that their own
cultural identity was threatened by the movement or was at stake in its
passing.) Hence, the British critical emphasis on "tradition" and the
insistence that the Modernists are somewhere outside this tradition and
inimical to it. Hence, also, the renewed effort to define—or perhaps
redefine would be more accurate—that great and hallowed tradition.
That Modernism in Britain is dead is undeniable. But it is dead not of its
own failure or because it outlived its usefulness in a new age; it died in
its flowering youth in Britain, creator of a handful of masterworks but
with no new generation to follow after it, an allegedly alien plant in soil
turned suddenly sterile, rejected, ironically, in the very place whose
tradition should have been most open to it. Its early death is a sign of
the current frailty and insularity of the literary culture which continues
to reject it. It is not the tradition of British fiction itself which warrants
our scorn; its greatest strength from the start has been its responsiveness
to new influences and forces (from the picaresque and its parody in the
eighteenth century to naturalism and psychological investigation in the
late nineteenth). The culprits are the narrow defenders of a straitened
tradition who would legislate against the alien and threatening; their

actions over the past few decades violate the very spirit and sense of the uniquely developing, uniquely receptive literary tradition which they purport to defend.

James Joyce, for one, surely believed that he was working within such a tradition. The readers of Richardson, Fielding, Sterne, Austen, and Dickens can easily find in their fictions many of the roots of *Ulysses* and *Finnegans Wake*. Joyce and his critics have spoken often of his indebtedness to such Continental writers as Flaubert and Ibsen, but his native debts, if less dramatic perhaps, are equally evident; Joyce names his forbears, major and minor, native and foreign, throughout his novels. In order to write Joyce out of the tradition, and to disenfranchise Woolf at the same time, the tradition itself must be rewritten, its storytelling, character-developing, morally-centered aspects emphasized to the exclusion of all others. The subjective narrations of Richardson and Sterne and the inner time sequences of *Tristram Shandy* must be ignored, the ambiguities of even Fielding and Dickens conveniently forgotten. And surely we must assume—we must assume it because a responsive reading of their novels would disprove it at once—that Joyce and Woolf and their Modernist fellows are uninterested in telling stories or in developing characters or in creating recognizable moral centers, those allegedly unique British fictional activities. We must emphasize as well the elitism and internationality of Modernist fiction as further signs of its alienation from the popular British tradition, neglecting to note that all literary movements of any significance are international in scope (Modernism no more so than the ones which link Boccaccio and Chaucer, or Rousseau, Goethe, and Wordsworth) and that the expectations of Joyce and Woolf regarding their readers are not so very different after all from those of some of their predecessors and their lesser contemporaries (remember Thackeray and Dickens being criticized by Trollope for misleading their public, or Bennett deriding the people, who "simply don't know from one day to the next what will please them," and extolling the "passionate few" who "are always working either for or against the verdicts of the majority").[25] That Bennett is seen as securely within the tradition and Joyce and Woolf are lodged firmly without is a commentary more on the viewers than on the novelists themselves. One suspects that Bennett is included largely because or his argument with Woolf, as a tool for excluding her.

In *The Great Tradition*, that seminal and controversial work, F. R. Leavis posits an historical, literary, and moral continuity which extends

from Austen and George Eliot through to James, Conrad, and Lawrence:
Joyce, he derides; Woolf, he ignores; Bennett, he does not much like,
although it is his formulation which makes it possible for succeeding
critics to list Bennett among the greatest of modern novelists.[26] The
great novelist, says Leavis, "the few really great—the major novelists
who count in the same way as the major poets, . . . not only change the
possibilities of the art for practitioners and readers, but . . . are significant in terms of the human awareness they promote; awareness of the
possibilities of life."[27] They are, of course, "all very much concerned
with 'form.' . . . But the peculiar quality of their preoccupation with
'form' may be brought out by a contrasting reference to Flaubert," by a
contrasting attitude toward life. Leavis at this point cites D. H. Lawrence,
who "adduces Flaubert as figuring to the world the 'will of the writer to
be greater than and undisputed lord over the stuff he writes.' . . .
Flaubert, he comments, 'stood away from life as from a leprosy.' "[28]
From Lawrence also comes Leavis's final word on the novelist's necessary attitude toward his art and toward life: " 'One must speak for life
and growth, amid all this mass of destruction and disintegration.' "[29]
Ulysses ("a dead end, or at least a pointer to disintegration")[30] evidently
does not speak for life and growth as Leavis perceives them; *The Plumed
Serpent* presumably does. Viewed through Lawrentian lenses, the Modernists Joyce and Woolf seem fated for exclusion from the great
tradition.

   Leavis's concern for tradition extends beyond the tradition of the
novel. It would appear, indeed, that the function of the novelist in
Leavis's scheme—as of the critic—is essentially extra-literary, that he is
responsible above all else for transmitting meaningful values to an age
that appears to lack meaning (precisely the priestly role which the
Modernists are so often accused of attempting to fill). These are the
values of the so-called "organic community," of an idyllic earlier time,
"that is, the agrarian socio-economic system that preceded the Industrial
Revolution, and survived in a few isolated pockets till the end of the
nineteenth century, to be totally submerged in the mechanized mass
society of the twentieth century. In the organic community, so the
theory ran, labour was not alienated but a fulfilling exercise of genuine
craftsmanship, life and death were made meaningful by an instinctive
connection with the soil and the rhythm of the seasons, and if most of
its members were illiterate, they nevertheless had their own folk art and
a richly expressive oral tradition which nourished the roots of higher

culture."[31] This theme is sounded throughout Leavis's canon, over two decades of the issues of *Scrutiny,* which Leavis founded and edited with his wife, Q. D. Leavis, and others (it was in *Scrutiny* that most of *The Great Tradition* originally appeared), and in such works as *Culture and Environment,* which he wrote with Denys Thompson.[32] It is a controversial theory, much attacked over the years.[33] Whatever its value or practicality, it is clear that this is a sense of tradition very different from Eliot's: Leavis's view is intentionally inflexible, avowedly ingrown, proud of its turning back to the past. We can understand, within this context, why Leavis would include Austen and George Eliot in the great tradition and omit the urban Dickens, why he would value James (seemingly the preserver of old values), the conservative Conrad (he seems not to notice much the innovator Conrad), and especially Lawrence over Joyce and Woolf. There can obviously be no room for the great Modernist novelists, so determined to create the literary future, in such a scheme as this.

Yet Woolf too has yearnings for the pastoral rural past of England— surely this is a major theme of the opening sections of *The Waves*—and her characters too are seeking constantly for union with the natural and social forces which surround them and dominate their lives. She does not fool herself, however, into believing that the past can so easily be revived, or even that such a revival would inevitably be desirable. As for Joyce, if there ever was an "organic community" within British culture, it can certainly not be found in the chaotic urban life of Leopold Bloom's Dublin. *Ulysses* would seem by definition to be beyond Leavis's purview. Yet there is a sense of community—even of what might be called organic community—within Bloom himself, in his relation to his own (Jewish, archetypal) tradition.[34] Bloom too, however—however much he may wish to escape some of the facts of his daily life—is no such escapist as to attempt to repeal two centuries of history. We may disagree with his glorification of progress; it is difficult to disagree with his recognition that we must learn to live in the present. In its relationship to life and to literary tradition—both Continental and British, earlier and to come—it is *Ulysses,* along with those other Modernist masterworks which it represents, which has come in this half-century to define the tradition of the novel. To ignore it, as Leavis does, is really to repudiate the tradition.

The debt to Leavis of those who follow him—and not merely of his followers—is enormous, and too often unfortunate. Even those who disagree with his reading of the great tradition, or with his attitudes toward the moral role of literature in society at large, are likely to accept his view of Modernist fiction. Building to a certain extent on the misleading dicta of the Modernists themselves and utilizing Lawrence— not a Modernist at all, I would think, and an avowed enemy of Joyce and Woolf—to point out the flaws of their enterprise, it is Leavis who has delimited the Modernist novel for the modern British critic. Reading the novels of Snow and Cooper, of Lessing and Drabble, it is apparent that the same view prevails for the modern British novelist as well. Much that is wrong with their work can be traced to this willful misunderstanding.

The bitter argument between Leavis and C. P. Snow is too familiar to need recounting here. What is less familiar perhaps is the essential agreement of their positions vis à vis the state and demands of contemporary fiction. Snow, in effect, has written the novels called for by Leavis in *The Great Tradition* and elsewhere. That he has written them badly, that his thought is murky and his sense of humanity confused, that Leavis has seen fit to attack his work—none of this is quite coincidental. There are significant differences between Leavis and Snow—the "organic community" v. "The Two Cultures," the demands for a high-toned old excellence as opposed to the insistence on the popular taste; but it is fair to say, I believe, that the novels of Snow are the logical fulfillment of Leavis's strictures, the inevitable result of their joint repudiation of the infinitely greater Modernist tradition.

As a critic, Snow has led the assault on the Modernist "experimental" novel, on an allegedly cold "formalism" that is aloof from humanity. "Looking back," Snow wrote in 1953 from the heights of the literary paleontologist, "we see what an odd affair the 'experimental' novel was. To begin with, the 'experiment' stayed remarkably constant for thirty years. Miss Dorothy Richardson was a great pioneer, so were Virginia Woolf and Joyce: but between *Pointed Roofs* in 1915 and its successors, largely American, in 1945, there was no significant development." The sweep of Snow's line is breathtaking: *Ulysses* and *Finnegans Wake*, the entire mature canon of Woolf, all the volumes of *A la recherche du temps perdu* after *Swann's Way*, *Joseph and his Brothers* and *The Magic Mountain*, virtually all of Kafka—not to speak of Faulkner, Nabokov, Hemingway—eliminated in a single sentence from the useful history of the novel. Their work, we see, is 'experimental,' a pejorative term, and outside the slow and steady, predictable development of fictional form as measured by Snow and by Leavis as well. As Snow concludes, "In fact there could not be [further "experimental" development]; because this method, the essence of which was to represent brute experience through the moments of sensation, effectively cut out precisely those aspects of the novel where a living tradition can be handed on. Reflection had to be sacrificed; so did moral awareness; so did the investigatory intelligence. That was altogether too big a price to pay and hence the 'experimental' novel . . . died from starvation, because its intake of human stuff was so low."[35] There can be few comments in the history of novel criticism over the past two hundred years as arrogant as this, or as stupid. Only the mediocrity of his own fiction can serve to justify Snow's view. Yet it is a view which has been widely echoed in Britain.

Thus, Kingsley Amis: "The idea about experiment being the life-blood of the English novel is one that dies hard. 'Experiment,' in this context, boils down pretty regularly to 'obtruded oddity,' whether in construction—multiple viewpoints and such—or in style; it is not felt that adventurousness in subject matter or attitude or tone really counts. Shift from one scene to the next in midsentence, cut down on verbs or definite articles, and you are putting yourself right up in the forefront, at any rate in the eyes of those who were reared on Joyce and Virginia Woolf and take a jaundiced view of more recent developments."[36] One wonders whom this jaundiced Joycean audience might consist of: surely there are few novelists or critics in Britain who over the past two generations have taken such a novel position. Perhaps the enemy is the French "New Novelist" or the American followers of Joyce and his followers. In any event, since Amis wrote these words in 1955, it is clear that his battle, however unreal, has long since been won, his victory a national victory. The novelist William Cooper, a disciple of Snow, emphasizes the nationalistic aspect of the battle against "Experimentalism": "Aren't the French wonderful!" he writes. "Who else in these days could present a literary *avant-garde* so irredeemably *derrière? Avant-garde*—and they're still trying to get something out of Experimental Writing, which was fading away here at the end of the thirties and finally got the push at the beginning of the fifties. What a *garde!* . . . The point not to miss is this: not only are these anxious, suspicious, despairing French writers nullifying the novel, but they are weakening the intellectual world as a whole, by bringing one part of it into disrepute. The impulse behind much Experimental Writing is an attack from the inside on intellect in general, made by intellectuals so decadent that they no longer mind if intellect persists—in fact some of them sound as if they would be happier if it didn't."[37]

It is the British, in this widely held British view, who continue as the defenders of the liberal humanist function of the novel: "formalist" Modernist art is opposed to this function;[38] it is an art marked "by a kind of formal desperation"[39] in technique, by an overturning of traditional concepts of the self in theme;[40] even the criticism designed— by Americans—to explain this art, the still so-called New Criticism, is a sterile "formalist" form.[41] (Much the same has been said of Modernist painting and art criticism as a "formalist" enterprise.)[42]

The mass of accusation is so widespread, so strong, that one hesitates to reply to it. An American, in particular, may fear that his response may be unknowing and narrow, alien to the history and needs of a culture which he can only obliquely observe. Yet this British depiction of Modernism—so terribly close at times to hysteria—has little in common with the actual novels of Joyce, Proust, Mann, Kafka, Woolf, and Faulkner, et al. This American critic hesitates still to seek reasons to explain this dichotomy either in the current state of British society or in some psycho-social conception of "the British mind." But hesitation ceases at the point of literary judgment: the British view of Modernism, to my mind, is grossly mistaken, with certain of its pronouncements so extreme as to appear irrational; and the new-old fiction which results from this view, I firmly believe, is not merely retrograde and out of tune with the world it endeavors to capture—it is often quite bad. That the critics continue to value such fiction, that such fiction continues to be produced, says something of the health of the literary culture. The cycle is seemingly endless, self-serving, self-destructive.

IV

"I would not say, as William Cooper sometimes seems to say, that modernism does not count; and I would certainly deplore an evident slackening of scale that became part of the climate brought about by feelings of this sort. But we should also remember that this sort of statement is a statement on behalf of the humanist powers of art and their connection with life."[43] Along with John Wain and Kingsley Amis, Cooper is frequently credited with inaugurating the anti-Modernist movement in post-war British fiction.[44]

With its title derived from George Eliot and its setting in the provinces and the lower middle class, William Cooper's oft-cited first novel, *Scenes from Provincial Life* (1950), invites comparison with Turgenev and Chekhov, not to speak of the Joyce of *Dubliners*. The results of such a comparison, unfortunately, are ludicrous. In reacting against the self-conscious artistry associated with the Modernists and certain of their Continental predecessors, Cooper creates scenes lacking not only artistry but interest, characters without depth, language with no real verbal skill. His intention is to trace the understated growth of a young man from the provinces, working slowly as man and as novelist toward maturity. Like the heroes of Wain's *Hurry On Down* (1953) and Amis's *Lucky Jim* (1954), Cooper's protagonist appears to reject the values of the University, of the city, of the established and striving bourgeoisie. This appearance, however, deceives: in *Scenes from Married Life* (1961), the sequel novel, Joe Lunn, science teacher and novelist—the perfect young Snow man—has emigrated to London, has moved up through the bureaucracy, has become a novelist of some note. Like Wain's Charles Lumley, having scorned in his youth bourgeois expectations, he is quite willing now to accept the pleasures of life in the urban middle class (as Jim Dixon becomes One Fat Englishman). The real provinciality of these novels is thus not social but intellectual.

Joe Lunn's older mentor, Robert, skilled scientific bureaucrat and novelist (C. P. Snow himself?), calls his friend's new book " 'the most original book to come out since the war. And it may well be the progenitor of a whole series of similar books,' " he adds.[45] And so it has been. These post-Modernist novels are "original" because they stay on the surface of things, because they subjugate the creative intelligence to practical concerns (novel writing is a job like any other; there is as much pleasure in revising to satisfy the censor as in creating to satisfy oneself), because they are unfailingly, if not very convincingly, omniscient. Three decades after *Ulysses,* is there perhaps a better term than "original" for so retrograde a reaction?

Each of these novels is essentially omniscient, even those with a first-person protagonist serving as narrator (Joe Lunn is indistinguishable from his creator and speaks not as his reliable spokesman but with the same voice) or those utilizing a central intelligence (we remain totally outside Charles Lumley, perhaps because there is so little inside him, because he has so little intelligence to be conscious of). Each is full of exposition and informed commentary from without and devoid of ambiguity; each would seem to endeavor to fulfill Trollope's strictures on keeping faith with the reader, in other words, to reduce the burden of interpretation placed on him by the Modernists. Yet we may suspect that the choice of point of view by Cooper, and by Wain and Snow as well, may have something to do with reducing their own burden: there is no convincing quiet contemplation in any of these books, no significant moral insight, none of the worldly wisdom that such proximity and authority are supposed to provide; there is only the ease of omniscience. Their collective voice, which consciously avoids both distance and irony (those Modernist vices), is uncertain yet in no way ambiguous, reflecting not a view of a changeable world but a simple lack of depth and narrative skill.

If we are aware, when we read Henry James, of the voice of the master in the background beyond his centers of intelligence, we understand that this is not really inapt. These lapses into omniscience are distracting in James but not destructive; they hinder his planned movement toward ambiguity (as in *The Golden Bowl*), but they do not significantly undercut character and theme. James, we realize, is a nineteenth-century novelist writing of a changing, but still nineteenth-century world. (His sometime contemporary Conrad, to the contrary, becomes a twentieth-century novelist devising radically new narrative tools in order to depict a radical, new reality.) From James we cannot expect a mid-twentieth-century perspective. His narrative art is the culmination of the old form (as Conrad's is the beginning of the new), the highest degree of development of which an essentially omniscient form was capable. It allows for distance and irony and for some ambiguity, but it is rooted still in authorial certainty. In these contemporary novels, however, there is the force neither of the nineteenth- nor of the twentieth-century modes, little of the conviction that the authorial voice can provide for the Victorian world and none of the ambiguity that the modern world appears to demand, nothing, in short, of either James or Conrad. These are mediocre, anachronistic, lazy fictions, supported by passion-filled rhetoric but cut off from the real world of passion and intellect.

It is curious—since this "original" new mode so prides itself on its return to the basics of plot, characterization, and humanity—that each of these novels offers so little in the way of discernible plot (only some desultory movement toward self-recognition by a series of desultory protagonists), or of character development (these characters are so thin that we not only cannot identify with them, we can in some cases barely remember them), or of humanistic insight or concern (perhaps because they internalize so little, the characters appear to be moved by events rather than to move them, and we see little that they learn about either the events or themselves). These failures are related to the failure of point of view: because we see these characters and events only from outside, and then often with uncertainty, we are shown no development within them; we are merely told that they change. And yet we are insistently informed by the critics that this—and not what happens in Joyce or in Woolf—is true characterization and plot, the product of a true humanistic tradition.

When C. P. Snow speaks of the Modernist novelists' sacrifice of "reflection" and "moral awareness" and "the investigatory intelligence," he is referring, obviously, to their rejection of the simple and unassuming prerogatives of Victorian fiction. That is, of authorial omniscience in the full Trollopian mode: omnipotence as well as omniscience, an author who not only knows all and tells all but who manipulates all as well; in short, the author as God. Had he the skill, Snow would be another Thackeray as Manager of the Performance, dangling his puppets, providing their reason and their action, intruding constantly between them and his readers, benignly overlooking all from his authorial Olympus. It seems not to matter to Snow and his fellows that the world has changed since Trollope's and Thackeray's time, that we may no longer be able to accept such a view of a managed universe quite so trustingly as could the Victorian reader.

The reader reared on the Modernists has come to consider himself both participant in and co-creator of the fictional world in which he is asked to believe. Modernist technique, its use of point of view in particular, mandates such a role. Even the moderately informed reader of the mid-twentieth century is likely to demand more participation than Snow et al. will allow. Some readers may desire to escape temporarily from the world around them by reverting to the more passive Victorian role; few are likely to believe that we can so simply move back into the narrative past and recapture old values. Yet this is precisely what such novels as those of William Cooper in the 1950s and of Margaret Drabble two decades later expect us to believe. At the chronological poles of the anti-Modernist movement in British fiction, these representative texts indicate forcefully the failures of that inherently negative movement.

Speaking in a voice indistinguishable from Cooper's in the two volumes of *Scenes from Life*, Joe Lunn, himself a novelist, explains to his readers something of the parameters of his art; his comments, devoid of discernible humor or irony, deal more with the failings of the novel form than with its potential. In Cooper-Lunn's eyes, it is a most limited genre, unsuited for political discussion, for psychological analysis, for philsophical inquiry. In Cooper-Lunn's hands, it is more limited still.

Thus, Lunn on the political novel: "Unfortunately it is very difficult to write about politics in a novel. For some reason or other political sentiment does not seem to be a suitable subject for literary art. If you doubt it you have only to read a few pages of any novel by a high-minded Marxist. However I am writing a novel about events in the year 1939, and the political state of the world cannot very well be left out. The only thing I can think of is to put it in and get it over." What follows upon this subtle preface is not politics at all but self-serving, romanticized commentary on himself and his friends, offered in total seriousness and lacking the irony that might have redeemed it: "Robert, Tom and I could be called radicals. . . . Though we were three very different men, we had in common a strong element of the rootless and the unconforming. We had not the slightest doubt that were some form of authoritarian regime to come to our country we should sooner or later end up in a concentration camp" (p. 8). We must presumably take his word for their nonconformity since we are shown no such quality.

But then we see little of any of the characters except for what we are told: Lunn's characterization is consistently at several removes. "For the sake of describing myself completely," the narrator admits of friends who are not characters in his story, "I should have to explore the lot. Let me give prompt assurance that I do not intend to do so." To justify this perhaps surprising omission, he cites the ultimate authority: "Trollope discourses somewhere upon the difficulty that arises in novel-writing of disentangling men and women from their surroundings in order to isolate them as literary characters. A novel cannot contain everything" (pp. 52–3). The narrative is filled with similar omissions: "The conversation went on a little further. I could hardly have been more inept, so I will not record it" (p. 41); "Tom and I exchanged our interpretations of the latest European events. I will not record them because they will make you think us feebler prophets than we really were—this may be called omission of true facts in the cause of art" (p. 69); "Pureness of heart is an odd thing, rarely comprehended by the righteous. I could write a lot more about it" (p. 82); "But, a veil over *cris-de-coeur!* They were embarrassing" (p. 94). In a fiction allegedly devoted to old-fashioned characterization and plot, there is surprisingly little dialogue in *Scenes from Life*, few explicit acts, and no effort at all to root beneath the surface of things. Perhaps the reader, after all, is expected to fill in the gaps: "You, no doubt," he confides in us à la Trollope, "could have offered me a dozen suggestions . . ." (p. 56).

The discovery of sexual activity is similarly reticent and arcane, as explicit as anything in Howells (think of the revelation of pregnancy in *A Modern Instance*): " 'What's the matter?' I asked. Myrtle looked at me. 'Darling,' she said, *'you* know.' My knees knocked together. 'Oh!' I cried. I knew exactly what she meant" (p. 95). But Myrtle is evidently not pregnant after all, and Lunn's response is evidence of the depth of his psychological analysis: " 'I'm glad,' I said. Yet I knew that I felt as if something had been lost. These things are very strange" (p. 99). Strange, too, is the treatment of existential choice in this proletarian novel: " 'Exercise of moral choice is one of the perks of the leisured classes,' " the "mature" Lunn expostulates; " 'it often seems, to people who aren't preoccupied with it, to come pretty close to self-indulgence' " (p. 302).

And yet Cooper-Lunn does purport to seek universality in his fiction. "I will not describe our clock-tower in detail," he comments at one point, "because I feel that if you were able to identify our town my novel would lose some of its universal air" (p. 167). His friend Tom (who vanishes totally from the sequel) serves as a kind of clock-tower among the characters—"Tom was a revelation to me, and through him others were revealed. Only through observing Tom, I decided, could one understand the human race" (p. 132). Yet we see virtually nothing of Tom, whose role is filled by Robert in *Scenes from Married Life;* of him, too, we see virtually nothing beyond secondhand observation. Perhaps, somehow, this procedure is intentional, a part of Cooper-Lunn's repudiation of Modernist technique and perceptions. At least this seems, at one point, to be the point of it all: if Modernist fiction is built around an elaborate metaphoric structure, then this newer fiction must abjure metaphor, and perhaps structure too; characters and events must exist for their own sakes and not as part of some larger meaning: "Sometimes I tried to link the disintegration of our private lives with the disintegration of affairs in the world. I saw us all being carried along into some nameless chaos. Yet it rang false. In spite of what the headlines told me every morning, in spite of what I reasoned must happen in the world, I was really preoccupied most deeply with what was going on between me and Myrtle and between Tom and Steve. People can concentrate on their private lives, I thought, in the middle of anything" (p. 112). Lunn's private life is presumably interesting at least in part because he is an artist ("though we looked startlingly alike," he says of his publisher, "I was an artist and he was a business-man"—p. 331) yet one who is thoroughly professional, rejecting the mystique of the artist as ultimate creator (proud of his "literary carpen-try," he wishes that others might edit as well: "Would that more novelists, especially American naturalistic writers who produce 900 pages of 'total recall,' would discover this innocent professional plea-sure!"—p. 348).

Cooper-Lunn wittingly avoids the larger structure of metaphor and symbol, yet fails to convince us of the smaller world of character which he purports to describe. Witlessly, he confuses authorial statement with proof of characterization. Rejecting politics, psychology, and philosoph-ical depth, he clings relentlessly to the surface of things, relentlessly names them for us, and assumes that he has shown us convincing slices of life. That he writes so badly, with such superficiality and so little sense of the nuances and rhythms of the language, that he is so smug and self-righteous in his rejection of those allegedly Modernist concerns, does not of course disprove his critical position. The Modernist novel cannot stand alone on the inadequacy of the novels which follow it and claim to replace it. But can work such as Cooper's survive merely on opposition to the Modernists?

When Bradbury and others speak of "the humanist powers of art and their connection with life," for which Cooper allegedly stands, what precisely is it that they have in mind? Can novels as badly written as Cooper's, with so little depth of characterization or intellect, whose only conceivable interest is their opposition to a literary movement which never really took root in Great Britain, can such works actually be valued by critics who are normally astute? At an early point in his narrative, Joe Lunn comments on his disagreements with his superior: "Bolshaw merely wanted me to behave like a schoolmaster," he writes. "He wanted me to conform. You may ask, who was he to demand conformity? The answer is, Bolshaw" (p. 23). Must we too, as critics, conform to similarly held beliefs about the novel? Can we take any novelist, or school of novelists, seriously when he can write such sentences as these?

V

Margaret Drabble is a better writer than Cooper, less jejune and simplistic than he in her view of the world, less impassioned than he in his
anti-Modernist crusade. Yet her novels fail for much the same reasons,
for her work is founded on the same unyielding belief that Modernism
is rightfully dead and that an earlier fictional form is most appropriate to
convey the nuances of contemporary life. Failure for the anti-Modernist,
post-Modernist novelists of Britain may well be inevitable, built into the
core of their cause.

If Joe Lunn, scientist-bureaucrat-novelist, can be said to fulfill the
program of The Two Cultures, then Margaret Drabble's searching and
demanding female protagonists can be seen as the manifestations of
another admirable force of another generation. The literary results of
both movements, however, are less than admirable. If critics can so
easily confuse intent with result in the case of Cooper, and value his
novels despite their evident mediocrity, then we may face the same
danger with Drabble: it would be too easy to misplace our sympathy for
her feminist-humanist goals. Like Doris Lessing, who is similarly admired, Drabble is not a good novelist. Her prose is less flat and banal
than Cooper's (or Lessing's); she does have some sense of humor and
awareness of irony; her subject matter is certainly contemporary. But
she too insists on using, even on flaunting, an antique omniscience that
simply cannot convincingly communicate her uncertain contemporary
worldview—that blurs her worldview. There is simply no way in which
an essentially Victorian narrative mode can be made appropriate (without a massive infusion of irony) to so contemporary a subject and
resolve.

"I see my characters as glued together by personality," Drabble has
said.[46] "I feel myself to be and I often think that surely it would be
more dignified to fly into a thousand pieces in this situation and give
up. But in fact I'm incapable of it. I will go on relentlessly to the end,
trying to make sense of it, trying to endure it or survive it or see
something in it. I don't divide. I often wish I could." This divisible
world, in each of Drabble's novels, is seen from an essentially unitary
vision; the self torn between vision and self, ready "to fly into a
thousand pieces" yet somehow "glued together by personality," is seen
through a single, undivided, unambiguous lens; the subjectivity which
links Drabble to her characters, the objectivity with which she views

herself, are both lost in the totally omniscient narrative perspective through which she views characters and self, the world without and the world within. Her words speak of a worldview that is surely appropriate to a post-Modernist writer; the points of view of her novels are deliberately and grossly pre-Modernist. Her sense of irony is at no time directed at this paradoxical split—it is never even seen as a split; she refuses, unlike Lessing, to make use of the reflexive potential within such a frame of contemporary characters, contemporary awareness, and Victorian voice (no narrative sin in itself, to be sure, yet Drabble seems sometimes to raise reflexive possibilities in order to ignore and reject them); she denies all claims that her technique might well be influenced, however indirectly, by the Modernist example;[47] she wills to out-Trollope Trollope. Her characters, as a result, fail to convince us that they are capable of speaking on their own or of leading lives of their own, independent of their creator, and that we should be concerned about such voices and lives.

The Waterfall (1969) is that rare Drabble novel in which the protagonist appears to speak for herself. Jane Gray's narration begins in the third person, with seeming objectivity, often concerned with memories of her past, and then shifts suddenly to the first person, as she presumably grows more willing to deal with her subjective needs in the present. Yet the third-person account is not really objective ("She felt so strongly about the child: she loved him, and yet she knew that because he was hers he was doomed. She had felt this before he was born . . ."—p. 92),[48] and the first-person narrator may not really be Jane ("How I dislike Jane Austen. How deeply I deplore her desperate wit. Her moral tone dismays me. . . . Morals and manners: I leave it to Jane Austen to draw those fine distinctions."—pp. 65–7). Underlying all, first-person and third-, intensely involved and purportedly aloof, is the omniscient voice of Margaret Drabble, merely pretending to speak through her heroine.

Although there is nothing in the account of her life to indicate that Jane Gray is a professional novelist—indeed, nothing suggests that she is capable of any act of willed creativity—we are evidently meant to assume that she is the one who is writing this novel and commenting on it throughout. But we recognize that the novelist's voice in *The Waterfall* is that of the novelist, Drabble. It is she who confides in the reader directly about her technique, who admits deception in speaking of this life, who explains, finally, the shift from third-person to first-person narration and back. "Lies, lies, it's all lies. A pack of lies. I've even told lies of facts, which I had meant not to do. Oh, I meant to deceive, I meant to draw analogies, but I've done worse than that, I've misrepresented. What have I tried to describe? A passion, a love, an unreal life. . . . Reader, I loved him, as Charlotte Brontë said" (pp. 98–9). "I began the last paragraph with the word 'firstly,' so I must have been intending to begin this with 'secondly,' but I can't remember what it was or if I can it was too embarrassing and I've repressed it. Anyway, I'm tired of all this. It has a certain kind of truth, but it isn't the truth I care for. (Ah, ambiguity.)" (p. 156). "There isn't any conclusion. A death would have been the answer, but nobody died. Perhaps I should have killed James in the car, and that would have made a neat, a possible ending. A feminine ending?" (p. 280). She has omitted; she has distorted; she has attempted through this fiction to find some meaning in life and then has rejected that meaning: "the only moral of it [a weekend with James in Yorkshire] could be that one can get away with anything, that one can survive anything, a moral that I in no way believe (and if I did believe it I couldn't tempt providence by asserting it)" (p. 286). She is in control of her material, yet not quite in control.

She has endeavored to seek objectivity but has given it up ("I tried, I tried for so long to reconcile, to find a style that would express it, to find a system that would excuse me, to construct a new meaning, having kicked the old one out, but I couldn't do it, so here I am, resorting to that old broken medium"—p. 51); yet even subjective narration does not quite serve when the subject is too intimate, its psychological potential too threatening: "I am getting tired of all this Freudian family nexus, I want to get back to that schizoid third-person dialogue" (p. 155). No matter in which person she speaks, Jane Gray speaks with the voice of Drabble, a ventriloquist's dummy.

But this is hardly unique and hardly reprehensible in itself. Why, then, the labored pretense that the protagonist writes her own story? Why create such an elaborate reflexive frame if no use is to be made of it? We recognize that Jane Gray is more than reliable spokeswoman yet less than autobiographical creation; her story, we assume, is a fiction and not an account of Drabble's own life, although its theme (of an emerging female consciousness) is obviously important to Drabble. All of this would be clear without the mass of reflexive references. Why is it necessary to rub our (Modernist) noses in such a mass?

Reflexivism, when it works (as in Gide, Borges, Nabokov, and Barth), can offer a rich potential of insight and discovery into the nature of identity in general and of the novelistic identity in particular, of the interaction between fiction and life, of the act of writing and the act of living a novel about a novelist's life. We discover at the close of *The Counterfeiters*, for example, that Edouard the novelist, who is a totally reliable spokesman for Gide when he speaks of the art of the novel, is another of the false-moneyers who is not to be trusted emotionally. This is not simply one more manifestation of the central theme of human and artistic integrity—and of their absence. Because Edouard is so closely associated with Gide, because he is at work on a novel to be called *Les Faux-Monnayeurs,* this ironic discovery serves as central proof of that theme: the good artist is not inevitably a good man; humanity and art are not inevitably linked. Similarly, the interaction between Borges the character and Borges the writer, between story and life (as in "Pierre Menard, Author of the *Quixote*" or "Tlön, Uqbar, Orbis Tertius"), serves as the central focus, realistic and metaphysical, of the stories of Borges. Art for Borges (the character who is also a a writer) may well be an escape from life, and Borges (the writer who creates the character and serves as his model) enables us to judge his withdrawal from life. In Nabokov's *Pale Fire*, there are novels (and a poem) within novels and various potential creators within the primary act of creation, reflecting on characters, on art, on language, and on life. The reflexive roots of Barth's *The Sot-Weed Factor* are Borges and an eighteenth-century poem called *The Sot-Weed Factor;* of the "Dunyazadiad" they are Scheherazade and *The Thousand Nights and a Night* (with Barth himself playing the genie); of the stories of *Lost in the Funhouse* they are the stories of Joyce and the career of John Barth. At their weakest, these are provocative, entertaining and witty narrations; at their best, they provide profound insight into the nature of narrative creation for a writer post-Joyce who is determined to build upon the Joycean example. There is nothing of this, obviously, in *The Waterfall.*

It is a highly subjective mode, this reflexive technique, an outgrowth of the intensely self-aware Modernist use of point of view. It is the sole Modernist technique which has been substantially expanded in this period post-Modernism. Drabble appears to know the vocabulary, and she evidently believes that its use will help lead her character to some sort of increased self-awareness. Yet she makes no real effort to facilitate that process through the reflexive technique, and we get only the vocabulary and none of the substance: no new discoveries about art or life or their interconnection; no new knowledge (or self-knowledge) concerning her characters; no relation at all to the development of character or theme. Behind her elaborate reflexive frame, Drabble coyly reverts to her role as omniscient/omnipotent author; Jane Gray, her puppet, is no more capable of writing her life than she is of acting it.

Hers is one of those lives in which a woman meanders—lazy, desultory, a presumed victim of fate—through marriage, through motherhood, through a strangely uninvolving affair with the husband of her closest cousin. Throughout her life Jane Gray has emulated, in a determinedly lesser way, the life of her cousin, Lucy Otford. When James Otford brings her for the first time the possibility of passion, she responds for the first time—so at least she tells us—with passion. Having lost control of her life for no discernible reason, she is said to re-assert it for no better reason. Yet we are shown no truly passionate acts; we are shown virtually no acts at all. We must presumably accept her word and that of the author: a toy of fate, in her own mind, she remains a toy of her creator. We acknowledge the significance of the theme of the emerging female consciousness in a world long dominated by males, the central theme of all Drabble's work, but we are totally unmoved by this coyly omniscient account of this desultory, passionless life. Drabble's omniscience is but one more assertion of Jane Gray's dependence. It is not merely inappropriate in a general way to the contemporary setting; the omniscient technique of *The Waterfall* specifically and directly contradicts and undermines the intended theme of the novel.

It is a problem that we meet in all of Drabble's fictions, although in somewhat different forms. In *The Realms of Gold* (1975), for example, there is none of the reflexive vocabulary, no pretense at all that the protagonist is concerned with writing her own story. Drabble does not lurk now in the background of characters and events; she is present at the center, all-knowing and all-powerful, manipulating her people and their lives and endeavoring as broadly to manipulate us as well. Her narrative is filled with parentheticals setting forth the true facts: "(The true explanation never crossed her mind)"—p. 76; "(She did not succeed. She had too strong a sense of reality)"—p. 77. She juggles her characters and our ability to view them: "Remember him, for it will be some months before he and Frances Wingate meet again" (p. 51); "They had never met, and were not yet to meet" (p. 99). She speaks directly to us, in her own voice, of her plans for her characters and their lives and of her own evaluation of them as characters: "The truth is that David was intended to play a much larger role in this narrative, but the more I looked at him, the more incomprehensible he became, and I simply have not the nerve to present what I saw in him in the detail I had intended. On the other hand, he continues to exist, he has a significance that might one day become clear, and meanwhile he will have to speak, as it were, for himself" (p. 176); "And that is enough, for the moment, of Janet Bird. More than enough, you might reasonably think, for her life is slow, even slower than its description, and her dinner party seemed to go on too long to her, as it did to you. Frances Wingate's life moves much faster. (Though it began rather slowly, in these pages—a tactical error, perhaps, and the idea of starting her off in a more manic moment has frequently suggested itself, but the reasons against such an opening are stronger, finally, than the reasons for it.) Because Frances Wingate's life moves faster, it is therefore more entertaining. We will return to it shortly, and will dwell no longer on its depressing aspects. It is depressing to read about depression" (p. 175).

Drabble assumes—and she assumes that we will assume—that this is merely a fiction, not to be taken too seriously, surely not a substitute for and rival to life. Thus she is willing to rest the resolution of her action on the coincidence of a lost and then suddenly found postcard. ("And to those who object to too much coincidence in fiction, perhaps one could point out that there is very little real coincidence in the postcard motif, though there are many other coincidences in this book"—p. 218). She is willing too, in a pretty pink bow of a Dickensian final chapter, to take us some years into the future to keep track of her characters. Her omniscience is so obtrusive at times as to appear almost parodic. But the sense of self-satire which works so well in a similar situation in *The French Lieutenant's Woman* is absent here. There is humor here and self-awareness, but no parody. ("It is depressing to read about depression.") We are meant to take the technique seriously, as if, somehow, we were Victorian readers and Drabble were truly Dickens or Thackeray or Trollope—but, of course, with much less naturalness and a greater sense of tradition, since she has obviously read Dickens and Thackeray and Trollope, and she is obviously not of their time. The effect is terribly disjointing. Thematically, *The Realms of Gold* is concerned with a changing Britain, with a kind of cultural progression in which generations, classes, and sexes confront one another, effect some change, but as yet reach no resolution; technically, it would obviate all change, a self-satisfied return to tried and presumably true and sorrowfully inapt narrative modes.

It is clear by the time of *The Ice Age* (1977) that there is a basic Drabble mode which allows only minor variations and whose development is limited to thematic issues. There are, on the surface, however, some changes: the protagonist of this book is a man; the concern with the moral state of Britain is still more pronounced ("A huge icy fist, with large cold fingers, was squeezing and chilling the people of Britain, that great and puissant nation, slowing down their blood, locking them into immobility, fixing them in a solid stasis, like fish in a frozen river. . . . The flow had ceased to flow"—p. 50); the problems of individual identity are restricted no longer to women but are extended also to men, indeed, to the nation as a whole. But the coy Victorian narrative tricks remain. The omniscience is still ostentatious; whatever irony there is, like point of view, is imposed from without; technique by now seems totally mannered: "It ought now to be necessary to imagine a future for Anthony Keating. There is no need to worry about the other characters, for the present. Len Wincobank is safe in prison: when he emerges, he will assess the situation, which will by then have changed, and he will begin again. He will make no more such mistakes. As he will say to the prison governor on the day of his release, I have learned my lesson. Max Friedmann has been, throughout, dead; Kitty Friedmann will not alter. . . . Evelyn Ashby, who has not been allowed to appear, will not remarry; she will grow eccentric and solitary . . ." (p. 205).

In this sad, almost will-less moral state, most individuals seem incapable of change, whereas change for the people as a whole—as exemplified in a series of old houses and new housing developments (the metaphor of *Brideshead Revisited* updated)—is likely to be deleterious, although positive change is seen as possible for some individuals and even perhaps, in the future, for the nation as a whole. Drabble offers no monolithic view of affairs, private or national, and no simplistic thematic solutions. Yet her technique could hardly be more simplistic. In each of these novels, she has something challenging to say about the nature of human relations—about the changing attitudes and roles of women, in particular—in a world that is most uncertain. But her technique speaks of a world that is almost totally at odds with her theme, that could not be more certain. Unlike William Cooper, Drabble is surely not unaware that the world will never again be as simple as it may have seemed in Victorian and Edwardian times. She seems far less concerned than Cooper with simply reconstituting the past[49] and with waging war on the Modernists. But her point of view is painfully similar to his—it may even be worse since her voice seems so much more conscious and knowing. Perhaps she desires to contrast the certainty of an omniscient point of view with the instability of contemporary life and misjudges the effects of her technique; perhaps she is simply a lazy writer who wishes to avoid the strain of writing through more limited narrative perspectives. It is difficult, whatever her reasons, to justify so incongruous a usage: that narrative technique, like theme, should be appropriate to its time seems not to concern Drabble at all.

The Modernists believed that the novel was a significant art form and its practitioners dedicated and professional craftsmen. Many contemporary British critics and novelists reject this approach as elitist; they would appear to opt for a kind of amateur author, for whom the novel is but one human activity among many. At the end of *The Ice Age,* we are shown a vision of this ideal post-Modernist novelist: the hero is in an East European prison, where he has found both his God and his art—neither, perhaps, to be taken too seriously, since he knows so little about either and since the narrator is silent on our expected response: "Anthony Keating is writing a book, while he is in prison. He is not the first prisoner to spend his time in this way, and will not be the last. . . . Anthony's book is not very well written because he is not a very good writer. But he writes for himself. He has lost interest in any market" (p. 247). Perhaps intended as commentary on the supposedly solipsistic Modernist author, he speaks, in fact, for the anti-Modernist, post-Modernist school: an imprisoned amateur, without audience, without skill, without a subject that he understands very well or that we are likely to be concerned much about, very likely without a narrative technique that deserves consideration: what more fitting image could Drabble give us of her fictional generation?

VI

The occasional exception to this post-Modernist rule serves primarily to prove it. There are British novelists of the past decade or so who are in no sense Victorian but who endeavor instead, actively and with creative intelligence, to utilize Modernist advances and insights. This is true to

an extent of certain members of that older generation which first
followed the Modernists, such as William Golding and Graham Greene.
It may be said as well of some younger novelists at work in the age of
Leavis and Snow, among them Julian Mitchell, Robert Nye, Christine
Brooke-Rose and, especially, B. S. Johnson. But the writer most com-
monly linked with the Modernists, and in particular with Joyce, is
actually not very Joycean at all. The misleading public image of
Anthony Burgess is further proof of the rule that Modernist influence in
Britain has been terribly tenuous and that fiction has suffered as a result.

Burgess himself has noted frequently his connections to Joyce: "I can
think of no other writer," he says at the start of *Re Joyce,* begun on the
anniversary of Joyce's death, "who would bewitch me into making the
beginning of a spell of hard work into a kind of joyful ritual . . ."
(p. 17);[50] "Joyce continues to set the highest standards of any author
except Shakespeare, Milton, Pope and Hopkins to those who aspire to
writing well," he writes at the end of his book (p. 348). Joycean themes
and motifs have served as starting points for one of Burgess's finest
novels: the Shakespearean biography of *Nothing Like the Sun* (1964)
derives directly from Stephen Dedalus's theory of Shakespeare as martyr
(in "Scylla and Charybdis"), and the lives of Stephen and Bloom
provide further elaboration for this fictional life. Ann Hathaway's marriage bed recalls Molly's; the cuckolded poet's conjugal life ceases after
intercourse with his wife at the window, as Bloom's does (not watching
dogs copulate, however, just an old witch being beaten during a
drought); his son, too, dies at eleven, destroying his hopes for posterity.
Burgess's Shakespeare has the intellect of Stephen and the sensibility of
Bloom. ("[W]e, if not Stephen, are beginning to find [Bloom] Shake-
spearian. Stephen is concerned only with his theory"—pp. 163–4).

To both Burgess and Joyce, language is infinitely expandable—not
merely as a tool for communicating ideas and events but as a force with
a value and significance of its own, an end in itself as well as a means
to one. Joyce's linguistic example is apparent in such Burgess works as
M.F. (1971), in which he combines Welsh, Maltese, Anglo-Saxon, and
Yiddish with rare English words in exotic contexts, and *A Clockwork
Orange* (1962), with its rhyming slang and its Anglicized Russian idioms.
For Burgess, like Joyce a musician manqué, music too can serve as more
than mere literary accompaniment. "When can a machine be also a
living organism?" he asks of the "Wandering Rocks" and "Sirens"
episodes of *Ulysses.* "When it is a piece of music" (p. 173). In this sense,

Joyce helps point the way to the *Napoleon Symphony* (1974). (Burgess has also composed a yet unproduced musical comedy version of *Ulysses.*) Joyce, for Burgess, all in all, is "a major prophet, one who foresaw the 'abnihilization of the etym' without living through it. He is a modern novelist who has equipped our minds with the words and symbols we need in order to understand the contemporary world, and he will still be waiting to help when the fearsome future rolls in."[51]

Yet for all this uniquely (in Britain, that is) high praise, Burgess's knowledge of Joyce is in many respects surprisingly superficial. *Re Joyce* might have been written by almost any perceptive and well-read layman with a special sensitivity to music and language. It is liable in other areas to the usual popular misconceptions of Joyce and his work: an exaggeration of the importance of the Homeric myth in *Ulysses,* a simplification of Joyce's connections to such literary forebears as Blake, an undue emphasis on the symbolic content of the work, among others. These are hardly heinous misreadings; we no more condemn Burgess for them than we would an absolute layman. But the superficiality of much of his reading of Joyce (in areas other than the musical and linguistic) may induce us to look more closely at Burgess's novels, so strongly influenced, allegedly, by Joyce. Here, too, we discover that the acclaimed connections are very selective indeed, often more apparent than real.

Burgess's narrative technique—his use of point of view, his understanding of the nature of time, his handling of metaphor and myth, his ironic outlook—owes virtually nothing to Joyce's. His point of view is less limited in perspective than Joyce's—observed more from outside—influenced more by James than by Joyce; his sense of time is more fanciful and less psychologically rooted; his reading of myth is more personal and less universal (he makes little use of metaphoric structure); his irony is derived from a very different exile's life and a very different reaction to his Catholic upbringing. His themes and his view of the world are different as well. "I've never seen any great fault with the church's conception of man as a rather sinful creature," Burgess, a self-proclaimed "old Catholic," has said.[52] We can hardly imagine the creator of Bloom and HCE in essential agreement. The Malayan Trilogy (*The Long Day Wanes*) derives more from Waugh, Orwell, and L. P. Hartley than from Joyce; the Enderby novels, seemingly so Bloomian, would probably have been written had Bloom never lived (the schlemiel hero is a product of the age and not just of Joyce, although his humanity, in *Ulysses* and afterwards, is profoundly Joycean). Joyce, we suspect in the end, serves more as analogue for Burgess than as source, as a reinforcement of already chosen interests and themes. The self-proclaimed disciple would likely have written the very same novels if the putative master had taken his wife's advice and become a famous musician and not just a novelist.

Of course, there is no reason, beyond his own claims, to expect Burgess to know Joyce more intimately than he does or to use him with greater success in his fiction. One might even argue that it is better for the fiction not to follow Joyce more closely. "But Joyce can't really be imitated," Burgess has said.[53] "If you write in Joyce's style you end up with Joyce's content as well, and one *Ulysses* or *Finnegans Wake* is enough." The conclusion is arguable (as is the minor premise); what is certain is that, in the end, beneath the apparent Joycean flash of his fictions, Burgess adopts neither Joyce's content nor his style, neither the Modernist vision of the world nor the unique composite technique designed to elaborate that vision. He is less Modernist in this sense, surprisingly, than either Golding (with his daring use of point of view, his pervasive ironies, and his sense of human responsibility and worth) or Greene (with his meticulous metaphoric structures, his own ironic sense, and his insistence on responsibility in the midst of sin and guilt). Still, it may be quite enough, in the anti-Modernist context of current British fiction, that a serious novelist such as Burgess, one worthy of critical respect, chooses at least—and so firmly—to acknowledge the example of Joyce. A true believer in Joyce and the Modernist example cannot help wonder, however, how much more substantial his fiction might have been had Burgess gone beyond the linguistic and musical analogies and made more use of the style and content of Joyce, of his Modernist substance.

VII

A few younger novelists, less avowedly than Burgess and with less specific reference to Joyce, have made far more effective use than he of Modernist technique. The results, in several cases, are really quite admirable. Yet we realize that such writers are at work in a literary vacuum, at odds with most of their colleagues and with prevailing critical thought, with little support from without to develop a consistent,

Modernist-influenced perspective in technique or in theme. We must speak, then—with the single significant exception of B. S. Johnson, whose brief career is marked throughout by the damned "experimental" urge—of what are essentially isolated phenomena, of individual works by individual novelists.

In his wonderfully rich and reflexive *Falstaff* (1976), Robert Nye makes use of the ambiguities which are inherent within Modernist point of view as a means of enhancing the humanist potential of his notorious subject. Falstaff, who appears only indirectly in *Nothing Like the Sun*, is now at the center, dictating in one hundred installments his story of his life. Shakespeare himself does not figure at all in this account—naturally enough, since, as we are told, Falstaff dies in 1459, the year of his narration. But the Shakespearean echoes which we hear throughout (phrases, characters, and events) are so varied and convincing that we may be inclined to believe that the *Acta domini Johannis Fastolfe* served alongside Holinshed and Plutarch as source for the plays. In this case, Nye (and Shakespeare as well) has captured admirably the spirit of the age and of the man: raunchy, hyperbolic, close to but extended from historical truth in the fifteenth and sixteenth centuries. Yet it is often difficult to tell whether Falstaff is telling the truth—even to ask the question is to imply that he is indeed an historical figure. (Sir John Oldcastle, on whom Shakespeare's Falstaff is purportedly based, passes through this narrative in a minor role, suggesting perhaps that they are jointly historical personages.)

The ambiguities are heightened by the narrative technique: Falstaff dictates his memoirs to several scribes, of differing personalities and varying styles, at least one of whom constantly questions his veracity and refuses at times to take down his "lies" (although somehow we manage to read these episodes, too). Our affection for Falstaff grows along with our awareness of his isolation and his own awareness of his approaching death; it increases despite, almost because of, the ambiguity which is built into his narration; our understanding of his basic humanity is a natural function of his own point of view: we, too, become actors in his tale, involved more closely with his life than we would have imagined. "Fact?" he confides in the reader. "My belly gives me license to give imaginative body to what is essentially sparse, even skeletal material: memories, biographies, jokes, histories, conversations, letters, images, fragments. I make patterns of my fragments. . . . But I give you also the fragments . . . untrammeled by *my* pattern—so that

you, the reader, are free to put upon them your pattern . . . ,"[54] and we
are inclined to agree that somewhere in the flux of these patterns,
created equally (and reflexively) by Falstaff, Shakespeare, Nye, and
ourselves, perhaps beyond the narrowest limits of historical truth (a
result of Modernist ambiguity), is the more significant human truth
represented by Falstaff.

VIII

Julian Mitchell's *The Undiscovered Country* (1968) confronts directly some
of the major narrative issues of the Modernist/post-Modernist controversy as it has developed in Britain. Rooted in the more or less conventional yet flexible frame of the novel within the novel, with both
narratives throwing light on both narrators, it attempts to reconcile
Modernist involvement with integral form and the current British
obsession with characterization and plot; it is also imaginatively reflexive. Julian Mitchell the protagonist, not necessarily to be identified with
Julian Mitchell the novelist (other characters are similarly based, among
them Bernard Bergonzi at Oxford and various students of Leavis at
Cambridge), publishes here a novel by his friend Charles Humphries, an
admitted pseudonym and a suicide. Is there a model for Charles among
Mitchell's (the novelist's) friends? Is *As Far As You Can Go*, a novel by
Julian Mitchell the character, the title of, or based upon, an earlier novel
by Julian Mitchell the novelist? In the reflexive spirit of the enterprise,
we assume that all this may be so but resist the temptation to find out
for certain.[55] "I am a minor novelist," Julian the character writes,
"telling the literal truth. I am a character in one of my own books. Yet I
feel I am really a character in one of his. He never wrote it; and I don't
know what to do or say" (p. 79).[56]

The one book which Charles presumably does write, the book which
Julian includes here in his own, is *The New Satyricon*, which draws
almost equally on Petronius, Freud, and *Orlando*. The outer narrative,
Julian's account of his long friendship and rivalry with Charles, owes
more to *Brideshead Revisited*. The interaction between the two, each
writer's commentary on his own work and on his friend's, provides
insight into the nature and primary concerns, artistic and human alike,
of *The Undiscovered Country:* " 'Your novels,' [Charles] said one day, 'are
piss-awful.' I had published four by then, and was thought by some to
be 'promising.' 'You've deliberately excluded all feeling, all passion, all

personal emotion. . . . If you're determined to write about the uncertainty in the world, and it's a perfectly good subject, I agree, you've got to do it from a definite standpoint. . . .'

"I defended myself by saying that my own standpoint was implied. There being no such thing as absolute truth. I tried to show situations which seemed to me to have significance beyond themselves from several possible viewpoints . . . but by choosing the ones I did, I was in fact showing how I felt about the situations myself. . . . A writer shouldn't necessarily appear in his own work, I admired impersonality in art" (p. 157).

As a student at Cambridge, Charles might be expected to reflect, however indirectly, some of the strictures of Leavis. Yet he rejects traditional plotting (" 'Why tell people how A got from B to C? Why not just have characters and scenes?' "—p. 175), while he exaggerates in his picaresque novel the godlike role of the author ("I used to argue for the illusion of realism through the elimination of the author from his work; Charles said that the only honest thing for a writer to do was to display himself in and through his book. 'I don't give a damn about stories,' he said. 'Not in themselves. But I'm always interested in the people telling them' "—p. 177). Denying the extremes of such as Robbe-Grillet and the unique accomplishment of a Joyce,[57] attempting to adapt within these separate yet linked narratives the conflicting contemporary reactions to Modernist fiction, *The Undiscovered Country* has it both ways: both objective and subjective, both a limited point of view and omniscience, both an unblinking affirmation of literary tradition and its scornful rejection. The dual narratives of the novel are not fully integrated, and its full reflexive potential is never quite realized. But in one respect at least the human and artistic goals of Charles Humphries and Julian Mitchell are very well effected: out of the latter's objectivity and concern for form emerge powerful emotions; within the former's passion is a commendable sensitivity to form. In the best Modernist manner, feeling and form in *The Undiscovered Country* are coordinate, each one developing because of the other.

IX

In an early novel, *The Dear Deceit* (1960), Christine Brooke-Rose recreates an Edwardian social and intellectual milieu, but with occasional hints in the narrative of potential, post-Edwardian ambiguity. In a later novel, *Thru* (1975), she attempts to evoke the linguistic richness—although she misses the depth—of *Finnegans Wake*. Her work is obviously derivative, just as obviously an effort to evolve new meanings out of old forms. This is most apparent in *Out* (1964), in which Brooke-Rose makes her most important commentary on Modernist and post-Modernist fiction.

In the tradition of *1984* and *Brave New World* (set in the future, in Africa, in the aftermath of nuclear war), *Out* is an allegory of racial upheaval (radiation deprives its victims of color: color in this new society is a sign of health and hence of social significance).[58] But its real roots are not so much Orwell or Huxley, its prevailing theme not really racial tolerance or strife. The central source and concern of *Out* is as response to the principal post-Modern adversary of Modernism, Alain Robbe-Grillet. *Out* is virtually a line-by-line parody of *La Jalousie*, an evocation and exaggeration of its already heightened form (which develops out of Modernist form, especially in its metaphor and point of view) but a repudiation of its explicitly anti-Modernist theme (denying the significance of metaphor, denying human significance). To many British critics, Robbe-Grillet is identified totally with Joyce and his fellows; Brooke-Rose perceives that he is, in fact, their enemy. Her work can be seen, then, as a kind of reaffirmation of basic Modernist forms and concerns.

The view in *La Jalousie* (published in 1957, seven years before *Out*) is from the plantation house out toward the regular rows of banana trees; the view in *Out* is reversed (in social perspective as well as color), from the plantation shacks toward the big house. There are no workers in Robbe-Grillet, no buildings which might even house workers, no politics, no sense of history or of human identity beyond the observer's immediate needs. This unnamed viewer is probably psychotic (certainly obsessed with his own emotional concerns), a potential (or actual) murderer, a denier in his person and point of view (and in the persons and points of view of every Robbe-Grillet protagonist who follows him) of simple, basic human concerns (except for the most brutalized and degrading). His obsessions are repeated in *Out*, but here the purpose is to parody them, to place them within a radically new context and thereby to counter the anti-humanist, anti-Modernist vision of Robbe-Grillet.

The opening image of the fly on the narrator's knee recalls the ubiquitous centipede of *La Jalousie*; the obsessively observed and ob-

sessively repeated physical detail of the earlier book is present here, too;
this observer is also a geometrician, perceiving objects as geometrical
constructs and defining his perceptions through scientific terminology
(the botanical terms, which are absent in *La Jalousie*, remind us
nonetheless that Robbe-Grillet was trained as a tropical agronomist);
shadows move similarly here as an (unreliable) measure of time, and
rows of trees are seen similarly as a (misleading) measure of space; Mrs.
Mgulu, mistress of the big house, sits at her dressing-table combing her
hair, as A . . . , the protagonist's wife, does in the central scene (in fact
or in memory) in *La Jalousie*. But Mrs. Mgulu is black, and this observer
is aware not only of social change but of his own place in the process.
The meticulously reported detail, the repetition of actions and memories
(and of scenes that are perhaps merely imagined), the confusion of time
and space are not intended here, as they are in Robbe-Grillet, as screens
against self-realization. A full human personality is at work here,
acknowledging its human-ness; depressed perhaps and diseased (color-
less), the viewer of *Out* confronts his problems and admits his failings.
He sees things much as the jealous husband does in *La Jalousie*, but he
is conscious of what he is doing, and he endeavors to understand the
implications of his actions as viewer.

He is aware of his body ("It is important to believe in the bowl of
steaming gruel. A microscope might perhaps reveal animal ecstasy in the
numerable white globules that compose the circle, but the gruel tastes
hot and salty on the soft palate at the back of the mouth and flows
hotly down the digestive track to the duodenum"—p. 84),[59] aware of
himself ("The body lies under the army blanket, as close to its objective
self [at 5:00 a.m.] as it is possible to be, listening to the lack of dialectic
that strengthens it from within . . . comfortably enclosed in the absolute
knowledge that it lies under the army blanket in the dark on a large
square mattress on the floor of a small rectangular room . . ."—p. 103);
body and self are never separated in his dialectic, as they continually are
in Robbe-Grillet. He can comment on politics and the world outside
("Oh, we brought you syphilis and identity and dissatisfaction and other
diseases of civilization," he says to an Indian. "But medicine too, and
canned ideas, against your own diseases"—p. 83); he can comment
ironically on his own obsessive observations ("The number of the
vehicle [frequently cited] is 24. 81. 632. There is no numerical significance in such a number"—p. 40); he can ask challenging questions of
himself and his way of living, questions that seem directed at Robbe-

Grillet and his viewer ("Through all the false identities that we build, the love-making, the trauma-seeking, the alchemising of anecdote to legend, of episode to myth, what really happened to us?"—p. 120).

Speaking, one might argue, on behalf of those faithful to the Modernist vision, Brooke-Rose in *Out* confronts directly the post-Modern, anti-Modern strategies of Robbe-Grillet and refutes them directly. The human is present in Robbe-Grillet by implication; his is the selective, observing eye and consciousness, and his emotions can be discovered and named. But he himself refuses to name them, refuses in the process to admit his humanity. Brooke-Rose shows us that this is never enough, that we cannot function as things or as mere observers of things, that no matter how brutalized our world we must never forget that we are human. In their concern with form and a world that is seemingly formless, this is the primary message of the Modernists, too.

X

In 1973, the year of his death by suicide, B. S. Johnson published a strange little volume entitled *Aren't You Rather Young to be Writing Your Memoirs?* consisting of nine varied and moderately interesting stories and a most revealing critical essay. The stories, written between 1960 and 1973, add little to our knowledge of this prolific and imaginative writer, but the introductory critical comments can serve as a primer not only for Johnson's own use of the novel as form and experience but for the entire area of fiction post-Joyce. It is a quite extraordinary essay, not so much for what it says as for the fact that it needed to be written at all. Less forward-looking and more personal than Woolf's "Mr. Bennett and Mrs. Brown," which attempts to develop a universal rationale for new fictional forms and perceptions, these comments are written with an eye on the present and recent past, in anger and wonderment, at opportunities willfully lost and a literary tradition unwisely distorted. Johnson's observations, half a century after *Ulysses*, point up starkly the condition of the novel in Britain today, the almost undisputed realm of what he calls the "literary flatearther" (p. 11).[60] They explain as well how his own work came to develop out of his life and his times. For these are not really memoirs, and, in the final months of his life, their creator seems not so young after all.

"It is a fact of crucial significance in the history of the novel this century," Johnson begins, "that James Joyce opened the first cinema in Dublin in 1909. Joyce saw very early on that film must usurp some of the prerogatives which until then had belonged almost exclusively to the novelist" (p. 11). The novelist, conversely, must now learn to make use of the possibilities of technique opened up by the film and by other media as well—hence, Joyce's development of the interior monologue. (For the film, while "an excellent medium for showing things, . . . is very poor at taking an audience inside characters' minds. . . .") "But how many have seen it, have followed him? Very few. It is not a question of influence, of writing like Joyce. It is a matter of realising that the novel is an evolving form, not a static one, of accepting that for practical purposes where Joyce left off should ever since have been regarded as the starting point" (pp. 12–3).

To this point, Johnson sounds somewhat like Burgess: both acknowledge the mastery of Joyce; both insist that he is not to be copied. For Burgess, however, this is at times an excuse to revert to old-fashioned narration, strong on an expansive Joycean language, to be sure, but equally strong on characterization and plot for their own sakes. Yet "Life does not tell stories," Johnson contends. "Life is chaotic, fluid, random; it leaves myriads of ends untied, untidily. . . . The novelist cannot legitimately or successfully embody present-day reality in exhausted forms." Still, for some reason, the "neo-Dickensian novel" remains paramount among writers and critics in Britain today. "No matter how good the writers are who now attempt it, it cannot be made to work for our time, and the writing of it is anachronistic, invalid, irrelevant, and perverse." All this at a time when the other arts in Britain, particularly the drama, are vital and increasingly attuned to the times. "Why then do so many novelists still write as though the revolution that was *Ulysses* had never happened, still rely on the crutch of storytelling? Why, more damningly for my case you might think, do hundreds of thousands of readers still gorge the stuff to surfeit?" (pp. 14–6).

To reject "the crutch of storytelling," however, is not to abjure characters and the stories of their lives; to refuse to honor the ancient union of totally controlled and developed plot lines, fully rounded characterization and an all-knowing narrative technique is not to deny the humanity of characters' lives. Post-Joycean novel making, as Johnson understands it, is—like each of its predecessors—an effort to capture, perhaps to comprehend, and even, in some sense, to master reality. "Present-day reality is changing rapidly; it always has done, but for each generation it appears to be speeding up. Novelists must evolve (by inventing, borrowing, stealing or cobbling from other media) forms which will more or less satisfactorily contain an ever-changing reality, their own reality and not Dickens' reality or Hardy's reality or even James Joyce's reality" (pp. 16–7): a truism prehaps, but one not discoverable in the works of Cooper or Snow or Drabble or Amis or Wain.[61]

Reality, for Johnson, is highly personalized, yet not simply an out-growth of the facts of his life (as Proust and Joyce use their lives as starting points for their fictions), nor merely a reflexive account of the use of his life in the act of writing about it. The living of the life and the writing are virtually interchangeable in Johnson, influencing, reinforc-ing, even, in a way, creating each other. His is the most reflexive of all fictions: it makes the new term "reflexive" seem strangely inadequate; it explicitly denies the old term "fiction." "The two terms *novel* and *fiction* are not, incidentally, synonymous, as many seem to suppose in the way they use them interchangeably. . . . The novel is a form in the same sense that the sonnet is a form; within that form, one may write truth or fiction. I choose to write truth in the form of a novel" (p. 14). In some other voice, this might be pure, prattling pretentiousness; but Johnson is willing to pay the price of his claim: his final novel, *See the Old Lady Decently,* is an attempt to reconstruct the early life of his mother, begun shortly after her death. Shortly after the novel's comple-tion, her son was dead. He seems to have believed, in truth, that his novels are life and not fiction.[62]

"With each of my novels there has always been a certain point when what has been until then just a mass of subject-matter, the material of living, of my life, comes to have a shape, a form that I recognise as a novel" (pp. 23–4). I, for one, am unwilling to determine to what extent these novels are, in fact, autobiographical, unwilling to attempt to ascertain, that is, how closely the events of the life of the historical Bryan Johnson coincide with those of the characters who people his novels. Such an investigation seems intrusive even with an author who publicly proclaims that it is his life—his motivations, his failures, his private connections—of which we read. (The protagonist of *Albert Angelo* is murdered in the dreamlike Coda by a group of his students: this is surely not, historically, the fate of B. S. Johnson the novelist, even if he too did serve as supply teacher in London slum schools—an aspiring artist who spent most of his nights in pubs away from his desk

and who visited each weekend with his parents [did he?]—even if he
may have envisioned such an end for himself.) A more pertinent
objection to such an inquiry is that the literal historicity of these novels
has little to do with their worth, or even with their "truth." What is
significant about these novels is their continuing, developing, determined effort to evolve a form (or series of forms) appropriate to their
actions and to express through such forms the essential human quality
of the people who live and create them. We are struck in each of
Johnson's novels by his imaginative use of technique and by his ability
to move us.

In *Travelling People* (1963), Johnson devises different forms of narration to serve different functions, from intrusive, seemingly Victorian
comments on his characters' actions ["Henry's heart pumped faster and
louder (fear not, reader! It is mere arrythmia!")—p. 278],[63] on his own
art ("Boswell likened this attenuated style of writing to 'portable
soup' "—p. 179), on his control of his characters' lives ("Part of me
would like to have her bereft her maidenhead on the same inebriated
occasion, but, in a way, I am too fond of her for that. Let her lose it at
her leisure"—p. 247), to interior monologue and stream of consciousness. Between these extremes he makes use of objective narrative
from outside, first-person commentary by the protagonist, the central
intelligence, journal entries by the protagonist and a letter of his to a
friend, a film scenario and typographical formats derived from both
Joyce (suggesting the interior monologue of "Circe") and Sterne (pages
which grow gray as a character suffers a heart attack and which blacken
as he dies). The authorial intrusions are part of the social comedy (more
self-aware and much funnier than superficially similar comments in
Drabble), part also of the reflexive strategy which is explained in the
opening pages: "Dr. Johnson's remarks about each member of an
audience always being aware that he is in a theatre could with complete
relevance be applied also to a novel reader, who surely always knows
that he is reading a book. . . . From this I concluded that it was not only
permissible to expose the mechanism of a novel but by so doing I
should come nearer to reality and truth . . ." (pp. 11–2).

But there is far more to *Travelling People* than this technical invention
and playfulness: characters' lives touch and break apart; people fearful
of emotions and of making commitments love each other briefly, with
tenderness, and then, in unison, step back. We are moved by their need
to love and their ability to love, moved even more by their failure to

make more than a tentative, touching commitment. They do not pretend to speak for their whole generation or even very coherently for themselves. But the central metaphor of travelling and rootlessness permits us, in control of our part of the enterprise, to read into and beyond these individual lives: "Travelling itself was important, of course, thought Henry, but the most important thing was the going and the coming and the having been. . . . Especially the having been. In fact, anything was all right as long as it had passed. All's well that ends" (p. 300).

Although Johnson admitted to being "embarrassed" by *Travelling People* (because it is "part truth and part fiction") and refused to allow it to be reprinted (*Aren't You Rather Young*, p. 22), we can see in these people, rootless in home and emotion, the essential seriousness and continuity of all of his later work. Henry Henry, the protagonist, has no real background, but we can infer that he, like all of Johnson's heroes who follow him, has somehow been wounded by life and somehow cherishes that wound. It is difficult, despite our reticence, not to read his final words ("Especially the having been.") into his creator's suicide, a decade afterwards. But these words might more pertinently serve for any of Johnson's travelling people, just as the inventive, variable narrative technique of this early novel can serve to predict the imaginative and multiple forms of the novels which follow it.

Thus, in *Albert Angelo* (1964), in which "I really discovered what I should be doing" (*Aren't You Rather Young*, p. 22), we encounter a five-part dramatic (and musical) structure and a broad variety of narrative devices: the dialogue form of a play ("Joseph said: . . . , Luke said: . . ."); essays written by Albert's students about their school lives prior to his appearance and later about their reactions to him (an assignment to defuse their hostilities); various external documents which he has read and which he shares with us (a letter from a student's mother, a spiritualist's ad, excerpts from architecture and other texts); a true stream-of-consciousness rendering, including objects observed and the raw, unmediated thoughts themselves (with intruding dialogue in capitals); a recounting on opposing pages of classroom noises (heard or not heard by Albert) in roman type and, in italics, his internal monologue; a poem of Albert's about an idyllic earlier time spent in Ireland; and open slits in several of the pages so that we can look ahead into the future.[64]

In the fourth section, called "Disintegration," Albert breaks down (or is it Johnson?), admits that he has been writing a novel, and explains his narrative strategies; he breaks down emotionally as well. "—fuck all this lying look what im really trying to write about is writing not all this stuff about architecture trying to say something about writing about my writing in my hero though what a useless appellation my first character then im trying to say something about me through him albeit an architect . . . through the objective correlative of an architect who has to earn his living as a teacher" (pp. 167–8).[65] He becomes a character in his own fiction, B. S. Johnson and Albert Angelo blurred, a strange, compelling mix of objective and subjective, of commentary on art and emotion and of emotion itself: this book "Is about the fragmentariness of life, too, attempts to reproduce the moment-to-moment fragmentariness of life, my life, and to echo it in technique . . ." (p. 169); "And also to echo the complexity of life, reproduce some of the complexity of selves which I contain within me, contradictory and gross as they are . . ." (p. 170); "Faced with the enormous detail, vitality, size, of this complexity, of life, there is a great temptation for a writer to impose his own pattern, an arbitrary pattern which must falsify, cannot do anything other than falsify: or he invents, which is pure lying. Looking back and imposing a pattern to come to terms with the past must be avoided" (p. 170).

He goes on then to explain the changes which he has made in his story—the name of the girl who has betrayed him from Muriel to Jenny ("you can't call a girl in a book Muriel, now can you?"—p. 171), the place of their best loving (and of his poem) from Scotland to Ireland. Four years after she has abandoned him for a cripple who needs her more than he does (changed from the original epileptic), he aches still over her betrayal. But what is life and what fiction? "I have this other girl, Virginia, now, at the time of writing, very happy too, but who knows what else will be shifted by galleyproof stage, or pageproof stage, or by publication day, or by the time you are reading this?" (p. 172). *Albert Angelo* is dedicated "for Virginia"; Albert Angelo is dead, his murder and funeral seen through the eyes of his students; B. S. Johnson is also dead, his life and dying seen through his own eyes, clearly but not quite directly, coolly, intellectually, but with feeling. "[T]he novel must be a vehicle for conveying truth," Angelo-Johnson declares (p. 175), and for character and novelist alike the truth is more in the telling than in the tale. "Im trying to say something not tell a story telling stories is telling lies and I want to tell the truth about me about my experience about my truth about my truth to reality about sitting here writing looking out across Claremont Square trying to say something about the writing and nothing being an answer to the loneliness to the lack of loving" (pp. 167–8).

The Unfortunates (1969) consists largely of separately bound folios four to twelve pages in length, one entitled "First," one "Last," but the others unnamed and otherwise unconnected; and it comes in a box. Imprinted on the inside of the box is the newspaper article whose commissioning serves as *donnée* for the book: "Sub inspires City triumph, from B. S. Johnson, City 1   United . . . . 0," and a note: "If readers prefer not to accept the random order in which they receive the novel, then they may re-arrange the sections into any other random order before reading." The result is a narrative not quite as random as Marc Saporta's *Composition No. 1* (1962), not quite as planned as Julio Cortázar's *Hopscotch* (1963).[66] The randomness, that is to say, the particular randomness with which I first read the novel, does not always work. There seems little point, for example, in seeing the narrator search for the Football Special bus long after we have seen him riding on it. But the simultaneity created by such a reading is often revealing and moving: hearing Tony's realization that he will never see his son grow up and then reading that his wife, June, is pregnant, or hearing officially of Tony's death after we have witnessed his burial, or only then appreciating the irony of Tony's being told that he has been cured of cancer. This is the sort of simultaneity experienced in the narrative by the narrator himself and, in life, by the reporter who serves as his model (both, of course, named B. S. Johnson). The randomness of the reading is designed to recreate the randomness of memory, of a particular Saturday, two years after his death, in the city in which Tony had lived (Nottingham) and of other times spent with Tony, in that city and elsewhere, recalled to memory on that one day, recalled in the random, spontaneous manner in which such memories recur: "The mind is confused, was it this visit, or another, the mind has telescoped time here, runs events near to one another in place, into one another in time." An unbound, boxed book seems a suitably ironic memorial for Tony, Ph.D. in English, dead at twenty-nine, "who had helped me with my work when no one else was interested" (*Aren't You Rather Young*, p. 24), deprived by his illness "of his ability to read, as he had always read so much, the way he read, the way he held a book, turned over its pages, was so practised, so professional, so dedicated, reverent almost,

but familiar, at the same time, the way a craftsman holds his tools. . . ."
The irony is an appropriate balance to Johnson's fear that he "sentimen-
talizes" Tony's death, but it does not negate the sentiment. Returning to
London, he thinks of his own death. All's well that ends.

House Mother Normal (1971), subtitled "A Geriatric Comedy," seems at
first to be pure fiction (and hence less than "truth"), to derive from
outside the author's immediate experience. But the connections to
Johnson's life and art (the art by now being part of the life and not
simply its vehicle), to what we might call his imaginative experience,
again are present. This is yet another attempt to recreate imaginative life
through a reconstruction of the novel's form (recalling in its method
Michel Butor's *Niagara*, which similarly endeavors to use the written
form itself as a means of representing the varied states of inner
consciousness).[67] And its theme—the effects of old age, the continuity of
memory and experience, the human persistence in the process of
dying—has clear personal overtones, which become clearer still as
Johnson's career reaches toward its climax. The sudden reflexive appearance of the author, near the end of his narrative, reinforces this
point. The scene is a small nursing home, with eight aged patients and
their head nurse; the scene is inside their skulls. We are first given their
vital statistics, objectively, as from a hospital chart. We then listen to
precisely twenty-one pages of text from each patient, including occasional direct speech (in italics), many memories of the past and separate
reactions to present events (arranged in identical positions on the page),
with typographical layouts that are representative of their individual
states of mind (the pages for a senile patient are largely blank). We
conclude in the mind of their house mother, purportedly normal, who is
brutally frank about her little dishonesties, her strong sexual urges, and
the combination of cruelty and pressure with which she keeps her
house functioning. She alone is aware that we are listening; she
addresses us directly as "friend" (a little ploy, perhaps, to involve us in
her dealings?); her narration covers twenty-two pages ("outside the
convention"). "Thus you see I too am the puppet or concoction of a
writer," she advises us on that extra page, "(you always knew there was
a writer behind it all? Ah, there's no fooling you readers!), a writer who
has me at present standing in the post-orgasmic nude but who still
expects me to be his words without embarrassment or personal com-
fort.   So you see this is from his skull. It is a diagram of certain
aspects of the inside of his skull!   What a laugh!"[68] Because these

aspects seem less immediately personal, more anticipated perhaps than actual, the situation of *House Mother Normal* is less involving than those of Johnson's earlier novels. The technique is imaginative and skillfully attuned to its subject, but because the subject itself is more distant from Johnson's and from our own experience, we stand aside too much, judge both technique and subject too much from a distance. Perhaps there is something after all, at least where Johnson is concerned, to his seemingly academic distinction between "novel" and "fiction," between felt and imagined experience, in the capability of the novelist to involve us through his technique in the lives of his characters.

We perceive something of this same emotional distance in *Christie Malry's Own Double-Entry* (1973), where again the author takes us inside his skull, shows us its mechanisms at work, yet leaves us somehow aloof, as he too seems aloof. There is an advance here in the reflexive technique, but a step backward in felt emotion—on the characters' part, on the author's, on our own. The plot and surface theme seem simple enough: a young man feels society's evils and, after learning double-entry bookkeeping, decides to balance them with his own. And then, suddenly, he dies of a cancer which may or may not be related to his excessive, vengeful activities. Christie Malry is pointedly the creation of an omniscient, omnipotent author who seems so unconcerned about psychological verisimilitude and so involved with characterization, plot, and conventional morality that he informs us at each step of his own role in his characters' lives: it is at once a reflexive ideal and a parody of the New Victorianism, which utilizes their characteristic concerns and techniques at their most extreme. The author speaks unashamedly and often of his narrative role: "For the following passage it seems to me necessary to attempt transcursion into Christie's mind; an illusion of transcursion, that is, since you know only too well in whose mind it all really takes place" (p. 23).[69] He will do only so much personal research—willing to check the height of Claremont Square in Finsbury in a text but refusing to go out "with theodolite and mate" (p. 155). He questions the wisdom of the realistic approach: "Oh, I could go on for pages and pages about Christie's young life, inventing and observing, remembering and borrowing. But why?   All is chaos and unexplainable" (p. 82). Even his characters speak of themselves as characters in a novel—"am I not overdrawn," Christie wonders—and criticize the art form itself: " 'The writing of a long novel is in itself an anachronistic act: it was relevant only to a society and a set of social conditions which no longer exist'" (p. 165). "Aaaaer,'" declaims his girlfriend's mother, "'it was worth it, all those years of sacrifice, just to get my daughter placed in a respectable novel like this, you know. It's my crowning achievement. And with only one leg, too!'" (p. 156). The author himself appears as a character at Christie's deathbed, "And the nurses then suggested that I leave, not knowing who I was, that he could not die without me" (p. 180). Christie dies as suddenly and inexplicably as Tony does in *The Unfortunates,* but we feel at his death primarily humor and relief. Christie is so far removed from realism that it is impossible to identify with and feel much for him. But we can glimpse behind and around him a wounding, festering, familiar world: "you know the ways in which we are all diminished: I should not need to rehearse them further" (p. 116). What Johnson does rehearse here, and with great skill and effect, is the narrative technique on which he has labored since *Travelling People,* the tools which were imperfect still by the time of *The Unfortunates* but which finally, by now, can fulfill "the need to communicate with myself then, and with such older selves as I might be allowed, on something about which I cared and care deeply," in the hope "that the novel will communicate that experience to readers, too" (*Aren't You Rather Young,* p. 26). Only in his next novel, his final novel, does that technique work in near-perfect harmony with that searing personal vision of a wounded and wounding world.

See the Old Lady Decently (1975) is the first volume of a projected trilogy, *The Matrix Trilogy,* intended to recount the early life, maturity, and death of Bryan Johnson's mother, Emily, the decay of Britain, the mother country, and the processes of growth, decay, and renewal inherent in all life. The second and third volumes, planned but never written, were to be called *Buried Although* and *Amongst Those Left Are You,* the three titles meant to be read as a single, continuous statement. Inspired—impelled, perhaps, is more accurate—by the death of his mother from cancer in 1971, this first volume does indeed see the old lady decently buried, although her son was left alive for only a few weeks after its completion. *See the Old Lady Decently* serves as memorial for both mother and son.

From old photographs and letters, family legends, the recent testimony of his father and his own memories of the older woman, the author attempts to reconstruct the early life of his mother, culminating in his birth, an Rh-negative, destined-to-be-only child. Balanced alongside this maternal account are the modern history of Mother England

and of her dwindling Empire, derived from guidebooks and old texts, and references to Great Mother archetypes, drawn from Erich Neumann's great work. Also included in this account are original poems, from limerick to sentimental to concrete, and a photostat of an old family document, the official notification of the death in battle of his mother's father in 1918. The result is not so much a history as an imaginative reconstruction, at once inventive and unknowing, with certain passages (italicized) seen from Emily's point of view but with as many unanswerable questions about her: his sympathy can take him only so deeply into her life.

The author thus becomes a participant in the act of creation, a character based both on fiction and on his own life: his conception becomes blurred with that of Rudy Bloom at the window opposite (p. 125);[70] his intra-uterine development and birth echo Tristram Shandy's (pp. 129–39). The process of reconstruction at work in this novel—even to the author seen at his desk, in his home, amongst his family—recalls the similar efforts of Claude Simon. For Simon's author, however, tortured and lyrical and still a survivor, the reconstruction is largely implicit; his model is Proust's Marcel reconstituting the courtship and disillusionment of Swann in Love. For Johnson the process is actual, explicit, occupying a central role in his narrative and in the life which serves as his model. He speaks directly to his reader, tells us frankly of his methods and limitations, notes the interruptions caused by his research (going, for example, to visit the house where his mother was once in service) and by visits to his study by his own daughter. These lives are intimately interconnected—Emily's and Bryan's, father and daughter, the man and the writer—linked far more closely than Proust's and Marcel's, or Marcel's and Swann's, or Simon's and those of his at least partly fictional protagonists.[71]

Yet B. S. Johnson the author is not quite the same as Bryan Johnson the man. However autobiographical these events, however rooted they are in "truth," the fact that the author must himself become a character in his novel changes of necessity his angle of vision, changes his view of the man that he is, changes the man himself in the act of creation. We are compelled by circumstance (if not by wisdom) to look beyond this narrative, to fill in, as it were, the two unwritten volumes of the trilogy: thus the terrible irony of his mother's yearning to have her child grow up with a father, since she had no natural father, balanced against our knowledge, from outside the text, that this work was undertaken shortly after her death and that her own son's suicide, leaving his children fatherless, followed soon after its completion. "And what is it that I am saying in all this? That this is how people live, die, suffer? Is that all there is?" (p. 112). The technical complexity and inventiveness of *See the Old Lady Decently* undermines the customary line between subject and object. In its reflexive use of the author as character, it is intensely personal; yet the apparatus of reflexivism serves as a screen against subjectivity: author and character remain separate so long as the author can keep them separate, so long as we can recognize that life and art, however interconnected, are not quite the same. Framed by its two tragic deaths, in its union of function with form, of feeling with technique, *See the Old Lady Decently* is a brilliant and moving celebration of life.

In *Aren't You Rather Young to be Writing Your Memoirs?* only months before his death, Johnson speaks of his reasons for writing: pride, a joy in language and creativity, the need to fill in the gaps in his private conversation, the need to understand who he is and what he has done. "And I write especially to exorcise, to remove from myself, from my mind, the burden having to bear some pain, the hurt of some experi-ence: in order that it may be over there, in a book, and not in here in my mind" (pp. 18–9). What rich material he provides for the psycholog-ical critic, for the biographical critic and the critic of society, for the critic who believes with Lawrence in trusting tale rather than teller, for the New Critic who seeks in the text for patterns of structure and meaning and who might find critical truths of beauty and significance both in these complex tales and in their multiform teller. The temptation is strong to make metaphors of Johnson's final novel and his final act, to impose our order (Neo-Victorian or Modernist) on his seeming chaos, to create, as the narrator of *Albert Angelo* warns us, "an arbitrary pattern which must falsify, cannot do anything other than falsify." It would be so neat and convenient to find a larger literary moral in Johnson's career, cut off at precisely the moment that he seems to have finally, ironically, found a form to suit his subject and a subject worthy of his imaginative form: surely the New Victorian critics and novelists cannot have welcomed his work; surely it is not too extreme to view his death as a judgment on the state of the contemporary novel in Britain.

Yet the very neatness of the formulation offends. We can hardly avoid being suspicious of such convenient rubrics, even when they are our own, especially, perhaps, when they are our own. What is certain is that with Johnson's death Britain has lost its sole significant novelist who had been influenced by Joyce from the start and had proudly proclaimed and demonstrated that influence from the start, the one serious novelist of his generation who had been fearless of "experiment"[72] and of being linked with the Modernists, the creator of a developing canon who almost alone in the land had shown promise of further and challenging development. This is not to suggest, obviously, that Johnson's narrative path is the only or even the best path for contemporary novelists to follow. But it is one which follows imaginatively, in its handling of the novel's form and its attitude toward man its subject, in the spirit of the Modernists. Albert Angelo is dead, and his creator is dead, victims, in a sense, of their hostile surroundings. But the Neo-Victorian novel of Britain, in the third decade now of its dominance, appears to live on, its critics, practitioners and audience still unaware, it would seem, that it was stillborn.

3 HONORED PAST? FEARSOME PRESENT?

Pynchon, Coover, Doctorow, and Barth and the American Rendering of Myth

"Better this present than a past like that. . . ."
—Robert Browning
" 'Childe Roland to the Dark Tower Came' "

I realize only too well that I am losing my faith in the possibility of a rational organization of the world, that old dream of the millennium, in which peace and harmony should rule, has grown pale. . . . How totally different did the world appear to mediaeval man!

—C. G. Jung
Modern Man in Search of a Soul

The Modernist novelists were hardly the first to build their fictions from the myths of the past. Milton, Vergil, probably Homer himself, even the writers of Genesis preceded them. Yet myth is inevitably associated with them; both in its natural function and its myriad forms, it remains integral to their work as it does not, for example, to that of the Romantic and Victorian poets. It is, with point of view, their most characteristic technique, and it reflects their most basic concerns. Serving as ironic commentary on the present state of human affairs, as continuing proof of the difficult survival of human values, as bond to the past, at once ironic and affirmative in its implications, myth is central to our understanding of the Modernist literary experience. There is no single attitude toward or rendition of myth in which all the Modernist novelists share: the fertility archetypes of *To the Lighthouse* and *The Waves* (of flora and the sea: feminine images) differ markedly from those of *Ulysses* and *Finnegans Wake* (mixed images of sleep and dream and procreation and warfare: at once masculine and feminine); Mann's use of Jewish lore and the Old Testament is more direct and explicit but less felt than Kafka's; Faulkner's history is only in principle like Proust's. For them all, however, it is not individual myths but the mythic mentality, not illustrative narrative acts but the rhythms and forces of natural process and of man's place in the natural order, that is significant. Compare to this the mythic tourism of Shelley or Tennyson, whose exposition of the (usually Greek) past is not unrelated to or much more profound than the nineteenth-century British idealization of Greece and support for Greek independence. (The name and character of Stephen Dedalus function on a comparable level; but Joyce would do better.) I do not mean to belittle the Romantics and Victorians because they were not Modernists. Their use of myth may be occasional and somewhat superficial, but it is not their central concern, and it accurately reflects their needs and their view of the world; at the same time, myth remains a necessary, organic aspect of the Modernist vision of modern experience.

Unlike those British novelists who have rejected mythmaking along with the rest of the Modernist baggage (although there are some exceptions, as in Iris Murdoch's *A Severed Head*),[1] unlike the Latin American writers of the so-called Boom, for whom myth appears to be a natural, inevitable function of their lives on a distant, new continent (although it is not), certain contemporary North American novelists have consciously and wholeheartedly adopted Joycean mythopoesis. They have done so, however, at a certain remove: as a means of commenting both on our own age and on the modernists themselves, as a means of using the Modernists as commentary on our age. In the complex process, they both pay homage to and repudiate (at times, simultaneously) the Modernist literary example and the Modernist vision of life. Their myths may also promise sustenance, but they will likely not provide it; they may also be ironic, but they may undercut that irony, too; they are a means of measuring—as they are for the Modernists—human endeavor, human potential, and the extent of humanist survival in an increasingly inhumane world.

Perhaps the most hallowed critical cliché of Modernism, going back to Eliot's famed essay "Ulysses, Order, and Myth" in 1923, relates to the centrality of myth in Modernist fiction. Half a century later, it becomes increasingly clear that Eliot was speaking then not of *Ulysses* but of *The Waste Land* and that his strictures as applied to the novel are incomplete and perhaps incorrect: the mythic method is more than a means of "making the modern world possible for art," as Eliot puts it,[2] of providing form to evident formlessness; the Modernist attitude toward myth is not so very different after all from Classical attitudes, for it too strives to attain what one scholar has termed a "retrospective vision"[3] as a means of understanding our present predicament. Yet Eliot is surely correct in his belief that the essential aim of the mythic method is moral—although Modernist fiction may offer a vision radically different from the one that he would expound—and we can begin to recognize today that the Modernists' perspective on myth, "their attempt to understand and to express our human situation by means of myth,"[4] is perhaps their central link to the humanist tradition. We can recognize as well that the use of myth is one of the few Modernist techniques to survive unchanged by American novelists in this period of post-Modernism, although again attitudes have changed: Pynchon, Coover, Doctorow, and Barth are closer than Joyce ever was to the bleak moral vision of Eliot.

The Joyce of *Ulysses* offers a prospect of mythic potential that his contemporaries could not always recognize. Jung, for example, despised what he saw as the literary and moral morass of the novel—"a positively brilliant and hellish monster-birth," he called it[5]—although it is the Jungian approach to myth which can most clearly reveal the ultimate fertility of Leopold Bloom and his ties to the humanist tradition.[6] Despite the diminution of each facet of his life, in the midst of the irony of Homeric myth which acts at times as counterpoint to his life, Bloom perseveres, and he does so accompanied by a complex of images from nature and fertility myths which provides a view more affirmative by far than that of Eliot or Jung. It may take the perspective of half a century for us to perceive it, but Bloom is a hero of sorts, and Joyce holds out through him the possibility of continuity at least, if not quite of renewal.

For the Americans Pynchon, Coover, Doctorow, and Barth, however, myth is the primary sign in our times of discontinuity, of the disruption of tradition, and of human values and life. Inverted, distorted, pushed to its logical conclusions and found inherently illogical, myth in the post-Modernist American novel is both result and representative of its age. It is an age, moreover, which these novelists see as peculiarly American in its expectations and in its failure.

Myth, of course, is not the only way of measuring Modernist survival, and these are not the only novelists currently at work in the United States who make use of myth. Others might equally be called Modernism's heirs, and other attitudes and techniques might be singled out as its legacy. What is significant about these novelists—what is representative in their efforts—is their willingness to confront their forebears directly, their awareness of and receptivity to (even when they may deny its conclusions) Modernism's example. Like those American critics who praise the Modernist endeavor even as they regretfully announce its demise, they recognize that it is impossible to be a novelist in this presumably post-Modernist world without some acknowledgement at least of the Modernist masters: that it is not enough simply to write works of fiction with contemporary subjects but that, in order to meet the needs of the present—as the tradition demands, as the Modernists do—we must understand and respond to the lessons of the past. But these Americans go further: by treating Joyce and his epic work not simply as a source of mythmaking technique but as himself a figure of myth, by reacting to him as Joyce once reacted to Homer, they become mythmakers themselves. They advance beyond Joyce by using his example, and, in the process, they create their own new, literary mythology.

II

If Leopold Bloom is eponymous hero for the Modernist Age, offering a surprisingly affirmative view of human endeavor, then Thomas Pynchon's protagonists are his antithesis. Where Bloom blunders ironically toward some sort of mythic continuity and fulfillment merely by following the erratic course of his life—by living as a man as he understands that term, with unconscious dignity and pride—they are willful seekers after salvation, puzzled wanderers determined to discover the source of their personal bewilderment, would-be mythmakers who fail to comprehend their own goals. Their careers are a parody of the archetypal myths of nature—of rebirth, redemption, and eternal return—and, more directly, of the national myth of American innocence, as it has progressed from Benjamin Franklin to Henry James to F. Scott Fitzgerald. Reflecting the chaos of the post-Modernist world which they inhabit, their narratives are a strange and compelling mixture of literary forms, of the spirit of science and seance, of an encyclopedic knowledge of history and of modern life. The pattern is established as early as *V.* (1963), a novel both of and against its time.

If we did not know for certain that the second half of the twentieth century was a time egregiously unfit for allegory, with a characteristic quality of mind and sensibility and a faith—or lack of faith—grossly unsuited to the needs of the allegorist, we could swear that *V.* was allegorical. Its opening scene is set in a Dantean bar called the Sailor's Grave; not merely the owner but two of her barmaids are named Beatrice. Its protagonist, Benny Profane, as his name announces, is a son of the people, an Everyman on a level far more vulgar than Dante's. The world through which he wanders as a Pilgrim—aimlessly, without goal, in a conscious denial of goals—we would surely call Purgatory if it did not seem so much like Hell: urban and godless, open-ended and ambiguous, with no symbol of light and no hope of redemption. In this post-Modernist world, Benny Profane is a type of universal Everyman-Pilgrim, echoing ironically both old allegorical quest heroes and new.

Benny Profane travels through the streets, subways, and sewers of New York City much as Leopold Bloom meanders through Dublin. Part-Catholic, part-Jew, like Bloom; cut off, like Bloom, from conventional family ties; an aggressive failure as economic man, a victim of others' desires and of his own and yet a survivor, Profane follows closely in the tradition of Bloom, his spiritual schlemiel father. In the peopled but solitary landscape through which he travels, Benny Profane, like Bloom, is constantly "in alien country." Bloom lives with some grace in this country. But "Profane was afraid of land or seascapes like this, where nothing else lived but himself" (p. 12).[7] His land is unremittingly a waste land. For much has happened since Bloom's time in 1904, and the purposiveness of Bloom's life—his social and political concerns, his familial obligations and guilt, his tenaciously sought goal, above all—is tenaciously lacking in Benny's. Poldy and Stephen urinate at the moon in a fertility paean to Molly, the moon goddess above them. Profane pisses at the sun. "It went down; as if he'd extinguished it after all and continued on immortal, god of a darkened world" (p. 17).

The mythic potential of man in Modernist fiction, as exemplified by Bloom, is diminished, to be sure, yet capable still of fertility; Joycean man remains potentially in Bloomtime. The eighteen hours of 16 June 1904 are crowded and comic; its actors are lifesize and smaller, its hero only ironically Odyssean—hardly a situation suitable for fertility myths, one would think. Yet Bloom walks through his city (imagining the history of his people and their ideal/probable future) and remembers his own past (accepting the seedcake from Molly on the Hill of Howth) and drifts into sleep (with unconscious echoes of mythic deities in his mind) as if myth might resonate still, productively still, in his life. The Modernist perception of myth is surely ironic, but it allows at least for the possibility of redemption for individual man in the present through connections with our collective, myth-filled past. Joyce's use of myth in *Ulysses,* centering in Bloom (and discounting the superficial structure of Homeric myth), is surprisingly traditional in many respects.

In Pynchon's universe, however, traditional myth is inverted, a further and forceful sign of man's modern degeneration. Myth, for Pynchon, with its ancient echoes and humane ties, has been replaced by recent history, by the debased deeds of an inhumane century. Some of his characters, almost unknowingly, continue to seek for mythic connections; for them, in a further irony and betrayal, what had once been the collective fertility of myth becomes the source of current collective paranoia. On another level, myth provides the structure of novels which may, at first, seem unfinished and structureless. Both the structure and themes of *V.* and of *Gravity's Rainbow* derive from this disillusioning vision of a civilization no longer capable of productive life. The allegory is more telling and ironic than we might have realized.

The action of *V.* takes place within the context of history but is somehow beyond history. Its events are easily datable—often to political crises—but it strives for a universality beyond dates and events, a continuum of history and of myth. Thus the uncenteredness of life in New York City in 1956 is not simply for Pynchon the embodiment of the contemporary age; it is also in some strange but inevitable way the result of the Fashoda crisis in the Sudan in 1899 and of the massacre of the Hereros in German Southwest Africa in 1904. In *Gravity's Rainbow,* published a decade later, such events achieve the level of metaphor; here they are merely a part of a larger pattern of social and moral sterility. *V.* offers, in this sense, a history of the West from the non-peace preceding World War I to the restless decade following the Second War, itself an historical episode " 'fundamentally no different from the Franco-Prussian conflict, the Sudanese wars, even the Crimea' " (p. 431), linking the events of that earlier century to those of our own, joining the present to our past and future alike. The continuum is established in *V.* and expanded in *Gravity's Rainbow.*

Benny Profane has no concern for history and no confidence in myth, but he allows himself to be caught up in Herbert Stencil's obsessive search for the woman called V., so redolent of both history and myth. V.

becomes for Stencil (whose name may suggest another, more mechanized sort of Everyman), and perhaps for the reader as well, at once a
mysterious woman and the female principle, a character in a melodramatic and improbable tale of international espionage and the heart of
the mystery. " 'Most of what he has is inference. He doesn't know who
she is, nor what she is. He's trying to find out. As a legacy from his
father' " (p. 140). It is possible for us to piece together the puzzle of V.'s
mysterious career, as Stencil pursues her (as his father had once pursued
her), from its start in Egypt at the time of Fashoda (she is at this point
Victoria Wren, eighteen-year-old Englishwoman, named for her queen
and for the architect of her nation's harmony and greatness, on the
periphery of the intrigue) to its grotesque and brutal ending on Malta
during the Second Great Siege (known now and disguised as the Bad
Priest, perhaps a spy for the Nazis, she is set upon by a band of children
during an air raid, the star sapphire in her navel and her clockwork
artificial eye removed with a rusty bayonet, leaving behind but a tattoo
of "suffering Christ foreshortened on the bare skull, one eye and one
socket . . . a dark hole for the mouth, stumps at the bottoms of the
legs"—p. 322)—sad state indeed for a fertility goddess. But we are
uncertain still that this is Stencil's V.

Her other manifestations during the intervening decades (identities or
apparent identities) include various women (Vera Meroving, Hedvig
Vogelsang and Veronica Manganese, among others) and places (Valletta,
Vesuvius, Venezuela, and the perhaps apocryphal Vheissu), forms human
and inhuman (a recurring V-shaped stain on a dish, the delta of Venus),
concrete objects and abstract concepts (volcanoes, the viola da gamba,
vision, venality, a sewer rat named Veronica, the Machiavellian virtú).
Foreshadowing *Gravity's Rainbow,* she may echo also the development of
Vergeltungswaffe Eins und Zwei, the rockets V-1 and -2. "V. by this time
was a remarkably scattered concept" (p. 364). It is even possible that
Stencil is right, that she remains somehow alive even after Malta, as if—
as once before—"she saw herself embodying a feminine principle,
acting as complement to all this bursting, explosive male energy" (p.
192), as if she were indeed immortal. As Stencil perceives her, she is a
function of universal needs and desires and of our fears, source of every
man's infinitely duplicable quest for the female. Is she the White
Goddess herself? The very fact of Stencil's search appears to suggest that
she is.

V.'s country is Old World Europe and older still Africa (despoiled by

Europe) and, by implication, the New World as well. " 'V.'s is a country of coincidence,' " says Stencil, " 'ruled by a ministry of myth. . . . If the coincidences are real then Stencil has never encountered history at all, but something far more appalling' " (pp. 423–4). It is fitting that the novel should end—although the search goes on—on female Malta (" 'She's restless. She will find ways to reach out from Valletta, a city named after a man, but of feminine gender, a peninsula shaped like the mons Veneris . . .' "—p. 438). Malta: "serene in her own past" (p. 446), yet somehow beyond that past ("alienated from any history in which cause precedes effect"—p. 460); all conspiracies, real and imagined, come together "in Malta where all history seemed simultaneously present" (p. 452). The disparate characters, themes, and techniques of Pynchon's narrative similarly merge here. History and myth (the birth of Venus and the Suez crisis of 1956), New World and Old, the detritus of obscure events and literary antecedents, coincidence, conspiracy, incipient paranoia—once emanating from the island, now again culminate on Malta and environs. " 'The Middle East, cradle of civilization, may yet be its grave' " (p. 363). V., immersed in it all, is somehow aloof from it all. Its unarticulated lessons are directed at Profane, the experienced yet naive, representative American.

In America, where inanimate objects are loved more than people, Profane seems irretrievably out of place: "being a schlemihl, he'd known for years: inanimate objects and he could not live in peace" (p. 28). Yet he fears loving people as well and cannot begin to: " 'I don't change,' " he contends. " 'Schlemihls don't change' " (p. 359). His characteristic pose is one of the first in which we find him—"straddling a spar," looking down on a party-turned-riot on his Navy ship, concerned for his friends but distant, not quite aloof but unable to be involved, observing Dante-like from on high (pp. 21–2). Searching with Stencil for V., who partakes of both animate and inanimate (like some figure in Yeats's "Byzantium"), seems an appropriate act for Profane, an American act, demanding interest more than involvement, yet threatening involvement. The roots of such acts go deep in the American experience: to the search for self-knowledge in the wake of history, as in Faulkner; to the American confrontation with Europe, as in James; to Franklin's provincial in search of success; to the Puritans' quest for their God. "Work, the chase—for it was V. he hunted—far from being a means to glorify God and one's own godliness (as the Puritans believe) was for Stencil grim, joyless; a conscious acceptance of the unpleasant for no other reason than that V. was there to track down" (p. 44). " 'In this search,' " says Stencil, " 'the motive is part of the quarry' " (p. 362); in this search, American Profane may hope to find himself and his national ethic, but finds neither. The search itself has become its own cause and justification. Perhaps that is all that remains of the American myth and identity.

As for Stencil, "he would dream perhaps once a week that it had all been a dream, and that now he'd awakened to discover the pursuit of V. was merely a scholarly quest after all, an adventure of the mind, in the tradition of *The Golden Bough* or *The White Goddess*" (p. 50). Yet he cannot withdraw from his quest, as he cannot fulfill it. The road is too well taken, the quest too often tried. Franklin and James and Faulkner, and Jung as well,[8] have all become stereotypes in Pynchon's scheme; themes of initiation and *rites de paysage* have turned, like the tango, to "a dance for automata" (p. 376). Ours is a civilization capable only of aping the ancestral patterns of myth, the events of *V.* seem to warn us. Myth itself can no longer provide certainty and value to our lives; compulsively copying its now sterile forms is a further sign of our own degradation. Hunting for alligators in the sewers of New York—another of Profane's itinerant tasks—is no substitute for the enactment of fertility rituals;[9] the fear of conspiracy may replace the logic of myth in our lives, but it can hardly revivify us.[10] Even the irony of Joycean myth is for Pynchon inadequate statement of the depth of our loss. V. herself, the no-longer White Goddess, whoever she may be and whatever it is that she may represent, is surely the spirit of our age, as he sees it. The ongoing quest for her identity—the closest we can come, it seems, to mythic fulfillment—is a mark of our barrenness, of our conscious removal from the connections provided by myth to our past and to ourselves. The same mythic process which once defined our humanity has become, for Pynchon, a key to our loss of humanity.

There is much in Pynchon's novels to make us think of Joyce. Yet the universe of *Gravity's Rainbow* (1973) is radically different from that of *Ulysses* or *Finnegans Wake*. Joyce's Modernist world, even in dream, is solid, substantial, coherent, a place of evident cause-and-effect: a world of little heroism perhaps, but one in which some at least of the old values remain. In Pynchon's scheme, to the contrary, little of the traditional order remains, and what we can find to replace it offers us not much solace: more clues than there are answers, an infinite search without a discernible goal, a growing sense that the clues exist only to lead us to continue to search, to lead us to learn that there can be no reachable goals any longer. It is a world of science and seance, in which metaphors from physics, mathematics, and the behavioral sciences co-exist alongside the uncanny, in which, indeed, they may be identical; a world in which the manic map of a young American's sexual conquests in wartime London exactly parallels—even predicts—the pattern of V-2's rocketing down on the city; in which an octopus trained by a colleague of Pavlov suddenly appears on a beach in France, copying King Kong, to kidnap a beautiful blond spy and through her to entrap the innocent American; in which goldfish swim in Pisces-sign conforma-tions, and we wonder whether the sign is in their eyes or in ours, and what if anything it all has to do with this newest victim of the forces that be; a world not quite surreal because it threatens to make too much sense, but one whose meaning is hidden from reality-bound Leopold Blooms, from most of Pynchon's readers, that is.

This is not mere ambiguity that Pynchon creates, not simply an open-ended Modernist world devoid of the pretty pink bow of a Dickensian ending, or even of the certain knowledge of what it is that will happen on 17 June 1904—the day after Bloomsday in Joyce's *Ulysses*—or of what it was that HCE did that terrible day in the Phoenix Park, in *Finnegans Wake*. Pynchon's world is as different from Joyce's as Joyce's ambiguity is from the omniscience of Dickens. There is no ambiguity about this inability to know—it is clear-cut, definitive, the only certainty in a mass of persistent, unprovable possibilities. *Gravity's Rainbow* is set during the final months of the Second World War in Europe, but its vision is a post-war perspective, growing out of Modernist insights perhaps but advancing beyond them, repudiating whatever order re-mains in the Modernist universe. Pynchon is as funny as Joyce, as addicted to music and especially to popular songs (most of which he writes himself), as seemingly anarchic and yet as intensely organized and controlled. (The word "Control," in fact, is one of the recurrent motifs of the novel, occurring only slightly less often than, and regularly linked to, the ominous "They.") But the brief glimpses which we get of the characters who populate this world—the multitude of grotesques in London and Berlin and in the so-called Zone between East and West—provide not a sense of ultimate order, as they do in Dublin on that fine spring day in 1904, but of absolute, functioning disorder. It is a world, as the title of Book One puts it, "Beyond the Zero." "Toto," says

Dorothy arriving in Oz, in Pynchon's epigraph to Book Three, "I have a feeling we're not in Kansas any more" (p. 279).[11]

Pynchon has learned much from Joyce about narrative technique, has found in *Ulysses* and especially in the *Wake* models for his own encyclopedic interests, has used Bloom's Odyssean quest as the starting point, charged with irony, for those of his own, homeless heroes. Joyce's creation functions as a metaphor of sorts in *Gravity's Rainbow*, reminder of a worldview that is relevant in this post-Modernist world only as metaphor.

If Joyce's view of Europe after World War I is ironic, then Pynchon's vision of the end of the Second World War and the start of the Atomic Age is surely paranoid. But it is a paranoia full of real and not simply imagined enemies—at least they seem more real than imagined. In the syllogism which begins, "Even paranoics have enemies," we go on to discover in the minor premise that "All men have enemies" and therefore conclude that we too are paranoid—not good logic perhaps, but excellent paranoia. In *Gravity's Rainbow* "They" pursue without passion and manipulate without evident cause not only the naive American hero but the British spy who pursues him, his Russian counterpart, Black rocket engineers from West Africa, and all those others who populate the Zone—German black marketeers, Dutch whores, and, of course, the refugees and the Jews; all equally are "Their" victims. "They" appear to be some new international cartel, not all of whose members are knowable. General Electric and I. G. Farben obviously, the Masons to a certain degree and the followers of Pavlov and Wernher von Braun: but who else? And what reader in his right mind can accept so conspiratorial a view of the universe? At a time when we suddenly discover that international corporations have loyalties irrespective of national boundaries, that chiefs of state may be as bad as the most venal of those whom they govern, that genocide has become almost a banality of national policy on several continents, in such a time we may all be capable of a certain belief. Perhaps the syllogism is not so insane after all.

As idiosyncratic as it may be, as closely (if negatively) linked as it is to Joyce and to Modernist perceptions, *Gravity's Rainbow* is nevertheless an inherently American work, product of three centuries of American experience and filled with echoes of American history and American writing. It is a retelling, in a very real sense, of Benjamin Franklin's *Autobiography*, an Atomic Age American Dream, its dark vision long inherent in Charles Brockden Brown and Herman Melville, in Hawthorne, Twain, and Fitzgerald, even in Irving and James. The Pynchons, we recall, are the accursed occupants of the House of the Seven Gables, and one William Pynchon was denounced as a heretic and exiled from Massachusetts colony in 1652. Like Hawthorne's young heroes, like James's Americans confronting the experience of Europe, Thomas Pynchon's protagonists retain a certain innocence even as they discover their own potential—as men, as Americans—for evil.

Tyrone Slothrop, hero of *Gravity's Rainbow,* is an archetypal Jamesian naïf thrust into the European Zone of history and morals, and scion of a family that could serve as national symbol: among its ancestors are "a mess cook or something" on the Puritan flotilla of 1630 (p. 204) and a witch hanged at Salem (p. 329), a participant in Shay's Rebellion (they would soon become Establishment themselves) and the author of the Slothrop Heresy, which spoke for the sanctity of those passed over in the race for salvation, those "without whom there'd be no elect. . . . Could he have been the fork in the road America never took, the singular point she jumped the wrong way from?" (pp. 555–6). The uncertain Slothrop experience is ingrained in our heritage: " 'These early Americans,' " we are told, were " 'in their way . . . a fascinating combination of crude poet and psychic cripple' " (p. 738); even paranoia, our contemporary state, is seen as a "Puritan reflex" (p. 188).

Much of the action of *Gravity's Rainbow* is set in a Dantean place called the Zone. It is a region between East and West, aloof from politics, removed from time, offering shelter for the moment to victim and persecutor alike. Although rooted in the history of the final days of the European campaign and linked to the *Inferno,* the Zone too is an American export, another product of the American literary experience. Its prototype is the countryside beyond Sleepy Hollow, the site of the vision of Ichabod Crane. During the Revolutionary War, this was the region separating British and American lines, "the scene of marauding," Washington Irving describes it, "and infested with refugees, cow-boys, and all kinds of border chivalry. . . . There was a contagion in the very air that blew from that haunted region; it breathed forth an atmosphere of dreams and fancies infecting all that land."[12] "So generation after generation of men in love with pain and passivity serve out their time in the Zone"—this is Pynchon speaking again—"silent, redolent of faded sperm, terrified of dying, desperately addicted to the comforts others sell them, however useless, ugly or shallow, willing to have life defined for them by men whose only talent is for death" (p. 747). We have come a long way from Franklin's optimistic American Dream, although the darkness may have been there from the start. Like Hawthorne, Pynchon reacts against, yet works out of, his Puritan ancestry. *Gravity's Rainbow* is not only a repudiation of Slothrop's spiritual forebears; it is also an elaboration of some of their most basic attitudes.[13]

Slothrop comes from an America secure in its purity—the time is 1944–45, before Hiroshima, long before Vietnam, a time "when the land was still free and the eye innocent, and the presence of the Creator much more direct" (p. 214). He persists to the end in trying to return to America, to recapture its innocence, in believing that "there's a way to get back. . . . Poor asshole," says the author, "he can't let her go" (p. 623). His search, Pynchon tells us, is "our basic search" (p. 348); Americans today, like Slothrop, are condemned to seek for a world free of the old entanglements, "without elect, without preterite, without even nationality to fuck it up" (p. 556). No such world exists, of course, although America may once have seemed such a place.

The vision of America as a new land free of the encrustations of the old, that vision of a human Eden which served Europe as a symbol of renewal for over four hundred years and which in some ways serves it still (if only in disappointment and outrage) is, after all, a European invention, and its betrayal, at least in part, is European also. As Hugh Honour writes in *The New Golden Land*, "the relationship between America and Europe has always been a 'special' one. From a very early period America seemed almost a creation or extension of Europe—in a way which Asia and Africa could never be. And with time this relationship became ever more involved as Europeans increasingly tended to see in America an idealized or distorted image of their own countries, onto which they could project their own aspirations and fears, their self-confidence and sometimes their guilty despair."[14] The discovery of America, one of Pynchon's characters proclaims, " 'was a gift [to Europe] from the invisible powers, a way of returning [to innocence]. But Europe refused it. It wasn't Europe's Original Sin . . . but it happens that Subsequent Sin is harder to atone for. . . . Now we are in the last phase [of colonialization]. American Death has come to occupy Europe" (p. 722). New World and Old, in this post-Modernist view, are not so very different after all. Tyrone Slothrop's experience only ironically recalls Christopher Newman's. "He is growing less anxious about betraying those who trust him. He feels obligations less immediately. There is, in fact, a general loss of emotion, a numbness he ought to be alarmed at, but can't quite . . ." (pp. 490–1). The metamorphosis is not just Slothrop's but his nation's. An American M.P. has accidentally killed Anton Webern in a black market raid. " 'Do you know what kind of myth *that's* going to make in a thousand years?' " (p. 440).

The American experience in Europe in this American Century— emerging from an America no longer immune to the lessons of history, in a Europe rather different from James's: this is only part of the mythmaking of *Gravity's Rainbow*. As an aspect of Pynchon's en-cyclopedic approach, in which all knowledge is potentially usable as matter for fiction, the mythic method, too, may be encyclopedic. The mythic referrents of *Gravity's Rainbow* are thus derived not merely from the customary sources (the *Nibelungenlied*, for example),[15] but also from literature (Dante, Borges, and Günter Grass, along with Joyce), from science and psychopathology (Newton and Einstein, Sacher-Masoch and Pavlov), from history itself. These are not just analogues or influ-ences. They serve, as traditional myth does in Modernist fiction, as a means of making connections between societies and epochs, as a measure of our own time in terms of the past, as a test of our continuing humanity. Dante, for example, appears in the hellish move-ment of souls within the Zone, Borges in the Argentine obsession (among the myriads of souls in the Zone is an Argentine submarine crew) " 'with building labyrinths, where before there was open plain and sky. To draw ever more complex patterns on the blank sheet' " (p. 264), Grass in the nightclubs "catering especially to guilt enthusiasts" (p. 453), as in *The Tin Drum*. They function collectively as signposts of where we have been, of literary and moral imperatives which we can no longer attain. Coming from a nation that has never been very proficient at creating viable myth—Davy Crockett and Daniel Boone, George Washington and his cherry tree, even John Kennedy and Camelot, hardly achieve the stature of Odysseus or Moses, of King Arthur or even of Bloom—Pynchon expands the potential subject of mythmaking and then goes further still: in *Gravity's Rainbow*, it is the mythic process itself that is under assault. Pynchon uses this diversified, encyclopedic basis of myth as a means of refuting the Modernist insistence that we may retain in our day meaningful connections to our past, that even in this century the humanist potential inherent in myth remains present in human lives. The connections present in *Gravity's Rainbow* point determinedly to our dehumanization.

"The primitive mentality," writes Jung, "does not *invent* myths, it *experiences* them. Myths . . . have a vital meaning. Not merely do they represent, they *are* the pyschic life of the primitive tribe, which immediately falls to pieces and decays when it loses its mythological heritage, like a man who has lost his soul."[16] Pynchon's use of myth suggests that we must invent myths today, often outrageously, precisely because we can no longer experience them, that we have lost our mythological heritage because we have lost our souls.

"It was nice of Jung to give us the idea of an ancestral pool in which everybody shares the same dream material," proclaims Pynchon's narrative voice. "But how is it we are each visited as individuals, each by exactly and only what he needs?" In the end, the collective unconscious seemingly refuted, "one of these archetypes gets to look pretty much like any other . . ." (pp. 410–11). Yet Pynchon's archetypes have a look all their own, as the forces of paranoia and science in *Gravity's Rainbow* invert and distort the familiar patterns of nature, altering patterns of myth which once seemed universal. A new kind of fertility myth is erected around the phallic rocket which hovers over the Zone, with new festivities and new gods. "Soon it will come to the folk-attention how close Wernher von Braun's birthday is to the Spring Equinox, and the same German impulse that once rolled flower-boats through the towns and staged mock battles between young Spring and deathwhite old Winter will be erecting strange floral towers out in the clearings and meadows, and the young scientist-surrogate will be going round and round with old Gravity or some such buffoon, and the children will be tickled, and laugh . . ." (p. 361). The rocket at its birth is compared to Jesus, " 'a baby Jesus, with endless committees of Herods out to destroy it in infancy' " (p. 464); the test stands of its maturity are called "stations of the cross" (p. 502); pilgrims collect its fallen parts on its penultimate journey as if they were sanctified relics (p. 391). But here there will be "No return, no salvation, no Cycle . . ." (p. 413). Reality itself in this world becomes a futile night-sea journey, initiation without end, without purpose. Slothrop, "or Rocketman, as he is soon to be known" (p. 359), will not reach his goal in the Zone, may never come back to America.

The myth of the eternal return has aborted. A woman looks into the water " 'at the edge of one radioactive night.' " What she sees in her mind is " 'One of those children—preserved, nourished by the mud, the radium, growing taller and stronger while slowly, viscous and slow, the currents bore him along underground, year by year, until at last, grown to manhood, he came to the river, came up out of the black radiance of herself to find her again, Shekhinah, bride, queen, daughter. And mother. Motherly as sheltering mud and glowing pitchblende—' " (p. 479). Science, Pynchon indicates, has changed the Mother Goddess herself. Even the seasons are reversed (p. 373) on this ravaged earth, this once again "Pre-Christian earth" (p. 465). We move not simply "from chaos to cosmos," as Mircea Eliade describes the myth of Creation,[17] but back once again to chaos. The traditional patterns of myth and of human life are destroyed—victims each of the great conspiracy which pervades *Gravity's Rainbow* and, Pynchon would tell us, each of our lives. Our long-standing vision of our own humanity falters, and the Zone is the ultimate, inevitable result: "To expect any more, or less, of the Zone is to disagree with the terms of the Creation" (p. 729).

Such is the possibility of order which slothful, anarchic Slothrop slowly begins to discover, "an order whose presence among the ordinary debris of waking he has only lately begun to suspect" (p. 202). It is the order, of course, of the paranoid. However frightening such an order may be, however insane it may strike us, it may well be preferable to the lack of order, to simple anarchy. "If there is something comforting— religious, if you want—about paranoia, there is still also anti-paranoia, where nothing is connected to anything, a condition not many of us can bear for long" (p. 434). Victim and persecutor alike are necessary to the compound system: " 'For every They,' " Slothrop is told, " 'there ought to be a We. . . . Creative paranoia means developing at least as thorough a We-system as a They-system' " (p. 638). The primary source of these systems in our time—it is Pynchon's great paradox—is science, the technological revolution of the modern age and its romantic sister, turning inward into the mind.

Cut off from the ancestral order which is both symbolized by and encapsulated in myth, contemporary man, in Pynchon's scheme, falls back for a substitute on the newer forces of science and psycho- pathology—on science, that is, and seance. They function for us as myth once functioned for Jung's primitive man. As such, they are a sign of human advancement and a sign of our loss. Science in *Gravity's Rainbow* is throughout an ambiguous force.

Thus, in this view, even the Second World War is Their product. "[T]his War was never political at all, the politics was all theatre, all just

to keep the people distracted . . . secretly, it was being dictated instead
by the needs of technology . . . by a conspiracy between human beings
and techniques, by something that needed the energy-burst of war . . ."
(p. 521). Gravity, our basic law,[18] is Their ultimate symbol. Its invariable
force in nature becomes almost magical within the novel, a kind of
witchcraft even, as we discover with Slothrop "that Gravity, taken so for
granted, is really something eerie, Messianic, extrasensory in Earth's
mindbody" (p. 590). It is gravity which binds us (metaphorically, also)
to earth; most of our efforts to ascend from this earth are "betrayed to
Gravity. But the Rocket engine, the deep cry of combustion that jars the
soul, promises escape. The victim, in bondage to falling, rises on a
promise, a prophecy, of Escape" (p. 758). At the heart of the technological conspiracy of *Gravity's Rainbow* is its potential counterforce, a
conspiracy to build the ultimate rocket, a conspiracy which seemingly
slips from the hands of its makers and creates in their stead new
conspirators to persecute them (or is this, too, part of the plot?). The
great rocket which is fired at the end of the novel is propelled and
guided by the *Schwarzkommando*, black rocket engineers from West
Africa, ostensibly in the employ of the Nazis, theoretically at the service
of Them, and yet in the end perhaps on their own, serving their own
destinies as exiles, striving perhaps to escape their hateful lives on this
earth. It is in their cause that Slothrop is hounded into the Zone, and
yet their cause may some day be his salvation as well. For science is at
once threatening and preserving: it would enslave and destroy us; it
might save us from ourselves.[19] In the open-ended closing to Pynchon's
narrative, we do not know what happens to Slothrop or to the
Schwarzkommando or even to the great phallic rocket as it begins its
descent.

Perhaps in this seeming ambiguity we may discover some hope.
Despite history, despite our collective paranoia, we are tempted to find,
in the midst of what threatens us, the potential source of salvation, the
vaguest possibility of human ennoblement in place of certain despair. To
do so, however, we must repudiate Pynchon and turn back to Joyce.
Looking back to *Ulysses* over the past half-century of our history, we
may well find dignity and even ennoblement. In the continuing everyday affairs of its persistent protagonist—in Bloom's insistence on main-
taining his belief in the community of men although everything about
him would seem to indicate that community is no longer possible, that
humanism is dead—in Bloom we find evidence that we are capable of

more than our history would indicate, more than just Dachau or Hiroshima or My Lai. Looking directly ahead at *Gravity's Rainbow,* however, we are bound by our history as by gravity itself; in *Gravity's Rainbow,* we find only despair: great, comic, prophetic, inventive, disturbing, but despair nonetheless. Slothrop may eventually escape from the Zone, but it would be only to enter another one; if somehow he does reach America, it will have become the Zone. The *Schwarzkommando* may foil their destiny and live on as a race, but to do so they will need to surrender their racial identity, the individuality which they have so tenaciously guarded and which has kept them intact until now. The rocket may some day break through gravity's force, but whatever new world we ascend to, They will surely make like our own. Joyce, at the close of the terrible First World War, in the midst of his irony, allows us to hope; hope, to Pynchon, is sentimentality. When he paraphrases Joyce to describe his hero—Slothrop, like Bloom, is the "Last of his line, and how far-fallen" (p. 569)—he is parodying in turn the prevailing humanism of the Modernist novel, its belief in the essential worthiness of man which persists despite the evidence of events.

It is not enough for Pynchon to proclaim the death of the humanist spirit in our own troubled time; he must argue as well that it has never lived truly, never been more than an illusion, that our sense of our mastery of the universe of nature and of our individual lives has from the start been deception. The Puritan vision of Slothrop's ancestors (and of Pynchon's, as well)—that hateful vision of universal sin, devoid now even of an Elect—wins out after all. Our fates seem predetermined, yet we must bear the onus of freedom and individual responsibility. Paranoia is total. Defeat for mankind's most ancient pretensions—tied to myth, affirming humanity—is total. Still, Slothrop persists in his search, and the rocket blasts off in the final chapter to find . . . what new worlds? Is is perhaps, despite all that has happened, a force for renewal as well as destruction?

For Pynchon, finally, is capable of parodying even himself: it is when he seems most omniscient that he may, in fact, be most uncertain. Functioning as puppeteer in the manner of Thackeray, manipulating the lives of his people as They do, speaking directly to us and for us, an omnibus American voice out of an innocent yet Puritan past, looking back on the events of a prior generation from the perspective of the Revisionist present, seemingly in total control of characters and time and events, he is in fact as much Their victim as we are. What does he fear?

No more than we do. Slothrop, his hero, awakens from a continuing
dream in which he fears that at the end of his search, he will find only
himself. "Perhaps you know that dream too," the author confides.
"Perhaps It has warned you never to speak Its name. If so, you know
how Slothrop'll be feeling now" (p. 287). We do know how
Slothrop[20]—how Pynchon—must feel: in a world without such order as
we have customarily known, a world devoid of humane values, their
fear may be our only certain reality. The mythopoesis of Pynchon's
fictions suggests that it may be our fear as well.

III

In a fearful, deflated world void of mythic potential, the characters of
Robert Coover endeavor to create their own new mythologies. Their acts
are inventive, creative, distinguished by a language and wit and excess
that are uniquely American, destined too for a notably American fall;
they possess the rhythms and mannerisms of myth, the regular patterns
and heightened attitudes which from the most ancient times have
demarked the relationship of the individual to nature and to his own
society. But nature seems far distant now, and society's values—especially in America, their creator would tell us—are indistinct and
uncertain. By allowing his characters to substitute their own temporal
constructs for ancient archetypes, Coover furthers the process begun by
Pynchon of undercutting the mythic venture itself: as if—in this world
at least, for Americans at least—there were no longer the potential for
creative renewal and spiritual regeneration, as if, somehow, the endeav-
or to preserve humanistic ties through newly made myth has actually
hastened the process of disintegration.

From his earliest work, Coover inverts the functions of mythmaking
as a means of demonstrating both our contemporary needs and our
failures. *The Origin of the Brunists* (1966) is a burlesque not so much of
New Testament Christianity or its modern derivatives as of our inability
today to emulate old myths successfully or to create lasting new ones of
our own. The inversion is irreverent (" . . . the only consolation for
those who might have guessed the true state of affairs being that which
the risen Jesus centuries ago offered to his appalled disciples. . . . 'Come
and have breakfast.'"—p. 512);[21] it is funny (the Presbyterian minister
and his wife, "both students of *The Golden Bough*," celebrating Easter in

their private ritual of rising and falling—p. 394); and it is deadly serious. Whether Giovanni Bruno is inspired or insane, reborn in the mine disaster from which he alone escapes or so deprived of oxygen that his brain has been damaged, there is surely no salvation here, neither for those fools who follow him nor for those who reject him. The Brunists' attempt to create new myth is testimony to their desperate need to renew their society. But their circumstances—and ours too, Coover suggests—are inimical to true mythmaking.

The Universal Baseball Association (1968) serves as a shield against the workaday world for J. Henry Waugh, its proprietor; in the end, it cuts him off from even the possibility of communion with others. The game developed by the middle-aged accountant—"The game? Life? Could you separate them?" one wonders (p. 171)[22]—starts out as baseball, a game played with dice and actuarial charts, and becomes at last a ritual of life and death, of imposed guilt and imagined redemption. Waugh becomes himself a subordinate actor in this "ancient yet transformed ritual" (p. 146); it dominates his life too and offers him nothing more positive than escape from office routine and the human disorder of the streets outside his room. " 'We are mere ideas,' " one of the players complains, " 'hatched whole and hapless, here to enact old rituals of resistance and rot. And for whom, I ask, for whom?' " (p. 165). Not for their creator certainly, for he has vanished completely from the final chapter depicting the rites, is living now through his imagined surrogates alone. His association is universal only in name: its enactment is no true myth but a substitute for life, a highly ordered, highly self-conscious structure which denies the real substance of mythmaking—union with the processes of nature, union with the past and present of one's own society, union with self.

But perhaps even the original myths are less fruitful than they once seemed. The writers of Genesis, borrowing from Babylonian sources, had made the story of the Flood into a moral paradigm, reinforcement of the new world myths of Adam, Abraham and Lot, and foreshadowing, as some would have it, of that of Jesus. They had provided the moral imperative which was absent from their source: in the Babylonian tale, the flood is sent by a god angered because the noises of mankind deprive him of sleep; its victims are the good and evil alike; its sole survivor is the favorite of another of the gods, a man decent enough but not notably pious, a man saved by circumstance and not by good deeds. Compare this to Noah, "a righteous man" who "walked with

God" in an age of corruption and lawlessness (Gen. 8:9–10) and who offers to those who follow renewed possibilities of life.

But Coover has a different sense of the Patriarch Noah—a reading at best implicit in Genesis and its Babylonian source—as he is seen through the eyes of one who fails to survive the Flood. In "The Brother," one of the "Seven Exemplary Fictions" of *Pricksongs and Descants* (1969), we see the results of God's act directly, as the younger brother of Noah experiences it. He is a common man of his time: a farmer, a husband, a soon-to-be father; mildly blasphemous; moved by familial obligation. And so he aids his " 'old fool' " (p. 92)[23] of a brother in building his ark: "God knows how *he* ever found out to build a damn boat lost in *his* fog where he is . . ." (p. 93). As the rains begin and the water rises, he seeks admittance into the ark for himself and his pregnant wife: "still he don't say a damn word he just raises his hand in that same sillyass way . . . and right then right while I'm still talking he turns around and he goes back in the boat and I can't hardly believe it me his brother but he don't come back out . . . and I can see my brother's boat is floatin and I wave at it but I don't see nobody wave back and then I quick look out towards my own place and all I can see is the top of it and of a sudden I'm scared scared about my wife and I go tearin for the house swimmin most all the way and cryin and shoutin and the rain still comin down like crazy and so now well now I'm back here on the hill again what little there is left of it and I'm figurin maybe I got a day left if the rain keeps comin and it don't show no signs of stoppin and I can't see my brother's boat no more gone just water how *how* did he know? that bastard and yet I gotta hand it to him it's not hard to see who's crazy around here I can't see my house no more I just left my wife inside where I found her I couldn't hardly stand to look at her the way she was" (pp. 97–8). "Never again," says the God of Genesis (Gen. 8:21), "will I doom the world because of man, since the devisings of man's heart are evil from the start."

In this post-Modern rendering of ancient myth, in what seems a direct response to Eliot's moral strictures on the nature of myth and literary form, Coover posits a form of divine selection which would appall Leopold Bloom and perhaps even Eliot. Man's role in this divine scheme of things is so diminished that humanism seems inconceivable now. Even when we are capable of creating new myth, Coover suggests, we cannot create a new world; and our world simply cannot sustain, will necessarily undercut—in the midst of its vitality of imagination and language—the creative potential of traditional myth. It is a terribly bleak vision that we find in "The Brother," one that is incapable perhaps of being sustained for long, one that is surely incapable of sustaining us.

Yet the mythmaker's own vitality in the midst of this deflated world—as a consequence, perhaps, of this deflation—appears to expand, almost as a literary substitute for the vitality once provided to all men by myth. Coover's mythic concerns in *The Public Burning* (1977) are more ambitious than in his earlier work and more narrowly and particularly American. These new myths of his are no longer the products of individual characters and their states of mind. It is not the gamesman J. Henry Waugh, nor Giovanni Bruno or his fellow townsmen, nor uncaring Noah or his unconcerned God who erects the elaborate structure of myth in this fiction; this is the construct of history itself and of the American character: the characters and events, the attitudes and tone, the very extravagance and excess of *The Public Burning* are American. Still, Coover suggests, the principal failure elaborated here may once again be more than national: for a people not very skilled at effecting true myth, this is creativity—Coover's creativity and that of our history—that seems fully consonant with the most rigorous demands of the ancient mythmaking process. The failure here may again be inherent within the process and the life which it celebrates, as it is within our history and national character.

The subject of *The Public Burning* is the Rosenberg spy trial of 1951 and its judicial and mythic aftermath. Its sources, noted meticulously in the text, include the Archives of the United States, the *Congressional Record*, the *New York Times*, the newspaper of record, and Henry Luce's *Time* magazine, as well as the Rosenbergs' letters and certain other items of popular culture. Its characters include the Rosenbergs, their accusers and judges—but not their children; President Eisenhower and his Cabinet, the Congressional leadership, including Joe McCarthy, and the justices of the Supreme Court; Uncle Sam himself, godlike yet comic, a creature of history and of the folk imagination; and those other folk figures J. Edgar Hoover and Betty Crocker, Jack Benny and Rochester, the Marx Brothers and General of the Army Douglas MacArthur; and a strangely sympathetic Richard Nixon. Their linking, surprisingly, appears à propos. We are not even shocked, within so special a context, at the incipient affair which Coover uncovers between Ethel Rosenberg and Nixon: the national character is perhaps more embracing and paradox-

ical than it seems from the papers of record. Also unnoted therein is the
sole complete union brought about in this narrative, the passing of the
spirit from Uncle Sam to Richard M. Nixon, which event takes place on
Times Square on a June night in 1953, close to the summer solstice, the
fourteenth anniversary of the wedding of Ethel and Julius Rosenberg, at
their public execution. " 'It ain't easy holdin' a community together,' "
Uncle Sam comments, " 'order ain't what comes natural . . .' " (p.
559).[24]

Little comes natural: Under Sam's spirit is passed to Nixon—the final
step in his initiation to power—in a graphically detailed act of sodomy.
As Ike, Uncle Sam's "current Incarnation" (p. 87), he had previously
passed the word to Nixon at the Burning Tree golf club—Nixon calls it
the Burning Bush—outside Washington. But it is only on Times Square
that Nixon knows at last that he is the Chosen One and, in considerable
embarrassment and pain, can acknowledge his love. This Uncle Sam
whom he fears and loves is no mere national spirit but an actual
character, Sam Slick the Yankee Peddler, one-time Inspector of Government Provisions, now a "figure gaunt and grand . . . , the emptiness of
ages in his face, and on his back the burden of the world. He winks and
Albert Einstein, no longer with the angels, comes down with the flu. He
tugs at his balls and cargo transports airlift the heaviest tonnage of the
year" (p. 67). He is at once a comic Local Color hero out of the mid-
nineteenth century and "the American Superhero" (p. 76), a most
contemporary figure, and he is simultaneously possessed of the marks of
each of his previous manifestations—" . . . Washington's rhinoceros
teeth and smallpox scars, F. D. R.'s shriveled legs, Cleveland's vulcanized
rubber jaw, Abe's warts, and Jim Polk's spastic bowels . . ." (p. 182). He
has been particularly drawn to Ike: "only Uncle Sam knows why this or
that receptacle is chosen to receive the Host, but one thing is clear:
Uncle Sam moved toward Dwight Eisenhower with more conviction and
gusto than toward any other Incarnation since the Father of the Country
himself" (p. 171).

There are those, however (underlings, usually), who cannot even see
Uncle Sam (p. 82), those rebels who know him but "who do not wish
to surrender to the Incarnation, . . . to be possessed by Uncle Sam, be
used by him" (p. 276), and those who might have been chosen but who
simply lack all respect for him and his various manifestations—" 'that
goofy knuckle-headed Incarnation of yours.' " Justice Douglas calls Ike
(p. 81). Nixon, of course, is a true believer, and for him, as for Uncle

Sam, the Rosenbergs and their public burning are but one more act in
the eternal conflict with the Phantom. (In these days of Cold War, the
Phantom is cast as Uncle Joe Stalin, but he too has his manifestations,
even domestic ones; he was deeply involved, for example, Uncle Sam
suggests, in the administration of Ulysses S. Grant—p. 352.) Theirs is a
contest of light against dark, of accumulated past virtues opposed to
present, continuing wickedness, a true mythic confrontation. Nixon's
private *rite de paysage* is played out against this backdrop of politics and
history and myth.

Yet this America of his seems from the first a nation devoid of history;
only Uncle Sam provides continuity. " 'This here's a country of begin-
nin's,' " he says, " 'of projects, of vast designs and expectations! It's got
no past; all has an onward and prospective look!' " (p. 218). Nixon
would agree that this is good, and so too would many of us. Even Julius
Rosenberg, in a sense, concurs: he too is opposed to "all this irrelevant
history" (p. 204); his need is "to destroy all this so-called history so that
history can start again" (p. 205). The idealistic, naive Julius, however,
continues to believe. Perhaps this is why he seems so dangerous.
"[E]ven that yellowed newspaper copy of the Declaration of Independence that he kept taped up on his cell wall, presumably to demonstrate
his undying patriotism, was just one more sign of his alienation: the
Declaration was never part of the mainstream either" (p. 194). Julius is
the child of immigrant parents, a New Yorker and a Jew (even worse, a
renegade Jew), and his outsiderness, in this contest of mythic forces and
wills, after "over two years of exemplary Anglo-Saxon jurisprudence
and liturgy" (p. 69), ensures his destruction. "In a very real sense,"
Nixon concludes, "Julius Rosenberg was going to the electric chair
because he went to City College of New York and joined the American
Students Union when he was sixteen. If he'd come to Whittier instead
and joined my Square Shooters, worn slouch sweaters and open collars
with the rest of us, it wouldn't be happening. Simple as that" (p. 197).

Nixon finds it easy to identify with Julius in his own passage rite, his
prototypically American need to rebel and yet to belong, his self-seeking
yet idealistic belief in and recapitulation of the American Dream. (A
truism: the dream seems to mandate acts, so Coover suggests, that are at
once idealistic and self-serving; that is its point and uniqueness. No
other nation, after all, has a Dream named for itself and known to all. It
may even be our substitute for history.) And so Nixon contemplates
leaving Pat, who no longer kisses him goodbye in the doorway each

morning, and joining with sensuous, exotic Ethel, in part as an act of mythic renewal: "Maybe Uncle Sam even liked it that way, a source of energy and renewal: keep the Incarnation's pecker up" (p. 217). Certainly Uncle Sam himself, in his various guises, has known the loss of power and the need for regeneration (as Herbert Hoover "confessed to me what it felt like, that awful day in 1932, when he first felt the power going out of him. The strange hollowness, the painful deflation as his body closed in upon the void . . ."—p. 274); as the mythic king who must die and be reborn in order to ensure the fertility and life of his people, Uncle Sam experiences within himself the poles of the mythic cycle. ("After all, look how many of the poor misused bastards had been physically destroyed by the travail of transmutation: one Roosevelt had been brought to his knees, the other blinded, . . . they'd nearly all got shot at and some hadn't made it through at all, while others—Jackson, for example, Coolidge—had been left a little batty when it was all over. I'd seen Hoover up close, and there was something in his eyes that worried me, too"—p. 358). Still, Nixon persists—out of that special sense of American idealism and mythic compulsion—in his attempt to fulfill for himself the traditional configuration of the myth.

His initiation is harsh and demanding: "Of course I expected to be tested like this, expected it and welcomed it, knew it to be part of the sacred life . . ." (p. 88). The roles of this life are long established, the actors responsible but not entirely free: "Not only was everybody in this case from the Judge on down . . . behaving like actors caught up in a play, but we all seemed moreover to be aware of just what we were doing and at the same time of our inability, committed as we were to some higher purpose, some larger script as it were, to do otherwise" (pp. 122–3). The play, as it were, continues, and we all play our parts: that seems the nature of ritual and myth in this land outside history and hostile to myth, where nevertheless, " 'we cannot escape history' " (p. 8) and where we manufacture our myths to suit our contemporary, our passing needs.

Uncle Sam is thus a master of ritual, and the Rosenbergs serve as his exemplary archetypes. Their execution takes place on Times Square, "long associated with festivals of rebirth" (p. 4), "the ritual center of the Western World" (p. 176), beneath the Times Tower, known for "its perennial charm against death and entropy" (p. 177): our site of record. "Many believe . . . that such a communal pageant is just what the troubled nation needs right now to renew its sinking spirit. Something archetypal, tragic, exemplary" (p. 4). The mistress of ceremonies is Betty Crocker, "everything one would want in a Holy Mother" (p. 479). Many of the witnesses have gone first to Bedloe's Island, in order to re-enact "the traditional birth voyage" and, at the Statue of Liberty, "to enter into the Mighty Lady" (p. 336). But her flame has passed westward now to Yucca Flat, home of the new holy light, the Atomic Bomb, "a white-hot kernel of manifest destiny: a spark from the sacred flame!" (p. 521). It is in its service that the Rosenbergs are burned, in this New World auto-da-fé. Henry Wallace, we are told, once "got too near the sacred fire and went berserk" (p. 319), but Ethel survives the first surge of electricity and must be re-charged. "[I]t's hard to tell who gets his hands on [the switch] first, maybe the Vice President with his head start, maybe [Executioner] Francel himself, or young Senator Kennedy, more athletic than most, or perhaps all of them at once, but whoever or how many, they throw themselves on it with such force they snap the thing clean off! . . . Ethel Rosenberg's body, held only at head, groin, and one leg, is whipped like a sail in a high wind, flapping out at the people like one of those trick images in a 3-D movie, making them scream and duck and pray for deliverance. Her body, sizzling and popping like fire-crackers, lights up with the force of the current, casting a flickering radiance on all those around her, and so she burns—and burns—and burns—as though held aloft by her own incandescent will and haloed about by all the gleaming great of the nation—" (p. 546).

It is an image at once telling and gross and telling in its grossness. There is little of this final scene to be found in the public record of the Rosenberg case, yet it seems somehow apt. Coover's inventiveness is perfectly consistent in spirit, in image, even in tone with the official and popular attitudes of the time and with the mythic possibilities which underlie the record. Part history and part imagination inherent within that history, set deeply in both the atmosphere of its time and in the national spirit and need which created that atmosphere, *The Public Burning* evokes not merely the troubled 1950s but the deeper failures of American history and American will. Envisioning the execution of the Rosenbergs as a national carnival set on Times Square simply encapsulates in a single scene the frenzied air in which the case was conducted and acts out dramatically our desperate search (in history and fiction) for a truly functional mythic resolution.

Questions of guilt or innocence aside—and only Nixon of the major characters in the book seems much concerned with such questions—

there can be little doubt that the Rosenbergs were burned (the historical act, that is) to fulfill certain national mythic needs: as scapegoats for our losses in the Cold War; as Jews, paradoxically, to expiate our guilt over our negligent role in the Holocaust; to make possible a new symbolic beginning—new life for the people, fertility for our leaders, an uplifting from the morass of spirit into which we had fallen. As archetypes of our national terror and of our need for certainty in a time of great trial—this is not Coover's creation but that of our government and people just one generation ago—the Rosenbergs function, as in true myth, as manifestations of our deepest fears and desires. They too die, ironically, so that the people may live, as the king must die in all fertility myth. That they do not work as intended—that the Cold War does not end, that there are no new beginnings, that we are troubled to this day not only by questions about their guilt but also by the certainty that their case was mishandled: that this is not, after all, true myth—is but one more sign of our failure.

We failed in the 1950s, history suggests, and we are likely to continue to fail (of this, Coover seems certain) because we still do not understand the nature and function of myth and its significance for modern individuals and societies alike, and because, even after three centuries, we continue to distort the mythic possibilities inherent in our own history. We are a people not competent at mythmaking but facile. Although we manufacture new myths quite easily and freely—perhaps because we do so—we still cannot quite comprehend (witness Uncle Sam) that they must be integral to and not grafted upon existing social and human structures, that myths can be meaningful only when they evoke not fictions or lies but a deeper, more fundamental state of truth. We forget Jung's dictum that myths are to be experienced and not simply invented. We fail because we confuse the substance of mythmaking with its manifold forms ("form, *form*, that's what it always comes down to! In statesmanship get the formalities right, never mind the moralities—why did I keep forgetting that?": Richard Nixon being schooled by Uncle Sam—p. 96). We fail because we believe that myths, like technology, will inevitably attest to our mastery of nature and of the world. ("This is a misrepresentation," says Joseph Campbell, "the dominant motive in all truly religious . . . ceremonial is that of submission to the inevitables of [nature] . . . : the rites dedicate the whole people to the work of nature's season."[25]) We fail, finally, because in our chronic exaggeration of individualism we nonetheless undervalue individual worth and misread the changing relationship of individual and society.

In the past, myth and ritual served to integrate the individual into his society and, at the same time, to give him a sense of personal stature; the early Modernist novelists, utilizing myths (and despite Eliot), accomplished much the same end. Witness the series of myths which became Homer's *Odyssey* and Joyce's reaction to them in *Ulysses:* both Odysseus and Bloom, in their very different ways, are outsiders, yet each manifests the most significant virtues of his society (different as they are), and each is able to determine his own identity and worth. It is their reaction to myth, in large part, which defines their humanity: the elaboration of myth, in the past, has been virtually synonymous with the humanist endeavor.[26] As Coover uses myth, however—and as Pynchon does—it is a means of demonstrating our human and historical failures, our potential but missed connections. Today, as *The Public Burning* demonstrates so well, there may be no communal will to which the individual can join himself and few individuals who are able to define their own values vis à vis their societies. We are a long way from Campbell's unified and "mythologically instructed community."[27]

If we can understand a people best through their elaboration of myth—through their own reading of their history and through their symbolic constructs of societal and individual worth—then we can view them as intimately in these fictional structures in which they react, at a distance, to their own mythology. Coover may thus be as significant for us as Parson Weems and Davy Crockett and those others, like Bret Harte and Mark Twain, who created and undercut the myth of the American West. We read Coover not merely as historical footnote, moreover, or to delimit his connections, through his use of the mythic method, to his Modernist precursors. Reading Coover, we perceive that in our society individual and national values are at war and humanism is in retreat, that recent history is no substitute for myth and the mythic method itself may lead us, seductively, astray, that the difference between inventing myths and living them is profound indeed.

IV

The Rosenbergs' children never appear in *The Public Burning*. In E. L. Doctorow's *The Book of Daniel* (1971) they are at the center. Daniel Isaacson, whose parents have been executed as spies for the Russians, is the narrator of this book about their lives and deaths, about his subsequent life and his younger sister's seemingly preordained death. As Daniel, he writes of a time of trouble for individuals and for the nation; the prophecy of a better future, however distant it may be, is at best implicit—and limited—in his narration. As Isaac's son, he is both Esau the outcast and Jacob, called Israel, who would some day father a new people; he is also, as Isaac's son, the child of one who is offered as sacrifice for the people. The implications of Doctorow's title and names are pervasive. On the immediate, personal level, problems of fathers and sons run throughout Daniel's narrative; more generally, the interconnected issues of Jewishness, history, and myth permeate his life and those of his other subjects; these themes, on a still broader level, speak again to the nature of the American character and of the modern experience, for Daniel Isaacson, as his mutli-faceted name suggests and despite his particular history, is spokesman for universal instincts and concerns.

Daniel's book is an account of a new Babylonian Exile: the rule of fear and conformity which held Americans captive throughout the 1950s (not a time about which to be nostalgic, after all). He is both participant in and objective viewer of these events which he describes. The Isaacsons' children had been used by the Communist Party in their parents' defense; his sister, years afterward, would be destroyed by these events; and Daniel would be concerned to justify her life and their parents' and to prove them all worthy and innocent. But he is also an historian (a graduate student at Columbia University, ostensibly writing his dissertation),[28] and he brings to these characters and events—as to his own character and acts—an admirable but passionate distance. His historiography is Revisionist but unresolved: his parents' innocence cannot be proven, his sister's agony not undone. He is no Daniel to save his people, but perhaps, he comes to realize, he can save himself and his own wife and son.

Daniel writes, then, as an historian, but this past of his is not quite comprehensible, and he cannot quite limit himself to the past. Present and past, public and private co-exist in his narration: his problems with his father (well-meaning, ineffectual, yet strangely brave) and with his own infant son (how will he react to his father's capriciousness?), and the nation's problems as well (demonstrations on behalf of the Isaacsons-Rosenbergs blur into the peace demonstrations of the late 1960s in which Susan, his sister, is actively involved). Past and present come together, finally, in two funerals, one, his parents', in memory (standing at their graves, "I think if I can only love my little sister for the rest of our lives that's all I will need"—p. 316),[29] the other, this last day, his sister's ("She died of a failure of analysis"—p. 317). The failure is not simply psychiatry's, he knows, but his as well. He has been too preoccupied with the past to live well in the present. Daniel writes, finally, as more than historian.

Writing in the first person, in his own voice, in the present, Daniel Isaacson, not unlike his predecessor the Prophet Daniel, speaks in fact in several voices. He has the ability to view himself both subjectively and objectively, both in the present (as husband and father, brother, historian) and in the past (as a child on the fringes of a major historical event)—to see himself in both sequences as "I" and as "he." He can also endeavor to see as others may have seen, to extend himself, for example, into the minds of his parents in prison—to speak for them too in the third person and as "I." He jokes in the intensity of his search about "The novel as private I" (p. 285), but he is capable of viewing even certain scenes in which he is an actor with near-total objectivity, as if he were merely a dispassionate eyewitness and not a participant with vital interests at stake. He shares, he admits, in " 'the fucking family gift for self-objectification' " (p. 93), the ultimate historian's gift, it would seem. Yet we perceive beneath the objectification, in the midst of the most apparently neutral scenes, an intensely subjective, passionate involvement. He is self-consciously aware that he is writing both history (announcing his sources, documenting his research) and a novel, both for himself and for the world. "Who are you anyway?" he asks his audience. "Who told you you could read this? Is nothing sacred?" (p. 72). Yet like the Underground Man (the source of similar complaints) that he might have become, he is compelled to go on—to continue to feel, to endeavor to understand the source of his feelings, and to share them with us. The death of his sister recalls their parents' deaths and brings to the surface emotions long unacknowledged. As a child, he had learned not to show his feelings to outsiders or even to admit them fully to himself; as an adult, although he may still not articulate them fully, he learns during the course of his writing at least to acknowledge his feelings and to begin to confront them. Daniel's most powerful gift, beneath the self-conscious objectification, is his ability to feel and to make his readers feel with him.

Daniel's difficulties as an adult and Susan's destruction arise directly from their being the children of figures of myth—in what may be the

most revealing of all modern American myths. His historical search is
designed to uncover the truths underlying that myth, truths which
neither the Government nor the Communist Party has seemed much
concerned with: each has in the myth precisely what it requires
(conspirators or martyrs), and each therefore ignores the humans Paul
and Rochelle Isaacson (and, of course, their children). Daniel knows
them as people, attempts to understand them as figures in myth, learns
through his search for his parents to begin to articulate and perhaps to
resolve some of his own human needs. But he can never determine
with certainty their innocence or guilt. Knowing that the Government
has treated them unjustly, knowing that the Party has similarly distorted
the meaning of their lives, knowing now what the price of their loss has
been for him and his sister—knowing all this, that they have been
forced into pre-established mythic forms with no concern for those
deeper truths which are the heart and function of true myth, of abiding
fertility—Daniel can still not reach the ostensible goal of his search:
none of this speaks to the specific question of innocence or guilt. Even
tracking down his parents' principal accuser does not help, for Selig
Mindish, their former mentor and friend, a grasping, coarse man whom
Daniel even as a child had distrusted, is now thoroughly senile.

> The whites of his eyes were discolored. He needed a shave. . . . His jaw
> moved up and down, his lips made the sound of a faucet dripping as they
> met and fell apart. But there was still in him the remnant of rude strength I
> remembered.
>   I said, "Hello, Mr. Mindish. I'm Daniel Isaacson. I'm Paul and Rochelle's
> son. Danny?"
>   . . . He struggled to understand me. . . . He smiled and nodded. Then as
> he looked in my eyes he became gradually still, and even his facial palsy
> ceased, and he no longer smiled. . . .
>   "Denny? . . . It's Denny?"
>   For one moment of recognition he was restored to life. In wonder he
> raised his large, clumsy hand and touched the side of my face. He found
> the back of my neck and pulled me forward and leaned toward me and
> touched the top of my head with his palsied lips. (pp. 308–9)

For Daniel, even hatred cannot hold. He must learn to live outside myth
and with ambiguity.

In *Gravity's Rainbow* and *V.* and *The Public Burning,* the traditional
functions of mythmaking are intentionally distorted. The preponderance
of mythic forms in these works serves initially to mask but finally to

accent the loss of true mythic substance: of those ties to natural process and to past human experience which are represented in myth and which have served throughout history (and probably prehistory as well) to denote continuity and affirm our humanity. By accenting the forms, and thereby the absence of substance, Pynchon and, especially, Coover demonstrate the apparent failure in our time of the mythmaking process itself and the concomitant disruption of those universally shared values and norms which are traditionally associated with myth. By substituting the facts of history—in particular, those of recent American history—for myth, they indicate in addition the narrowing expectations and goals, the lessening fulfillment of which we are capable today: our ties, such as they are, are to a most restricted past and to a straitened sense of historical process. There is something of this in *The Book of Daniel* as well: it is no coincidence that Daniel Isaacson's confrontation with Mindish takes place in Disneyland, "shaped like a womb," expressing "the collective unconsciousness of the community of the American Naïve," where Americans are invited "not merely to experience the controlled thrills of a carny ride, but to participate in mythic rituals of the culture" (pp. 301–3). Doctorow's Disneyland would seem the perfect symbol of our human and mythic loss.

But there is something more here, some surviving sense of human potential, a pervasive theme allied to myth that distinguishes *The Book of Daniel* from *Gravity's Rainbow* and *V.* and, especially, from *The Public Burning*. Richard Nixon's Rosenbergs are executed because they are Jews; Doctorow's Isaacsons-Rosenbergs, like the originals, are Jews victimized by other Jews serving as over-zealous prosecutor and hanging judge, Jews who have been foresworn by their compatriots in order to prove to the community at large that Jews are citizens as much trustworthy as potentially perfidious (a fact which the McCarthyite gentiles, with their Cohn and Schine, already know). The child of a public sacrifice, Isaac's son, Daniel is a representative Jew (even if unobservant) in the same sense as the Prophet Daniel and that later prophet, Leopold Bloom: as aliens in their native lands, as threatening and threatened outsiders. Yet like his namesake and Bloom confronting their nationalist lions, Daniel in a strange way is preserved, even dignified by his Jewishness. He speaks, as a Jew, for continuity; he speaks for the stranger in us all.

Jews have always served—even at the time of their ascendancy, one would think—a specialized function within the myths of others: they, in myth, have been the other, the frightening, if weak, persisting outsider. Greeks and Turks, Irish and English, Southerner and Northerner may see one another as the enemy and thereby accord one another a certain limited mythic status. But Jews alone seem to serve as outsider for virtually all other peoples—even for those few with whom they have not come in contact: witness the United Nations action equating Zionism and racism. This is particularly true in the Christian West, with its literary Hugh of Lincoln and Blood Accusation (witness Stephen Dedalus and Bloom), its religious image of Jews as Christ-killers (fulfilling the ambiguous role of the Serpent/Lucifer/Prometheus in the Creation myth), its political fear of Jews as radicals challenging the established order.

The senior Isaacsons—those pre-eminent threats to order—are not very good Jews. But their political ideals somehow evolve from their Jewishness. Ascher, their lawyer, understands "how someone could foreswear his Jewish heritage and take for his own the perfectionist dream of heaven on earth, and in spite of that, or perhaps because of it, still consider himself a Jew" (p. 134). Daniel's grandmother, a survivor of Cossack pogroms, is appalled at her daughter's Americanization—"the thankless child who . . . forsakes [the old] ways and blasphemes and violates the Sabbath to be a modern American" (p. 78), who even changes her name from Rachele to Rochelle. But Daniel himself easily equates his parents' idealistic politics with their religious heritage. As he remembers his grandmother praying over the Sabbath candles, "When she lowered her hands, her eyes . . . were filled with tears, and devastation was in her face. That was my mother's communism. It was something whose promise was so strong that you endured much for it" (p. 53). More significantly, perhaps, the radical Isaacsons must be seen as Jews because everyone assumes that they are: the attackers of the bus bearing them back from a Paul Robeson concert need ask no questions before yelling " 'Kikes!' " (p. 61)—as if "radical" and "Jew" were necessarily synonymous. Their Jewishness, then, may have—must have perhaps—both positive and negative results.

As he watches over his dying sister, Daniel, with no preparation or apparent context, thinks suddenly of Bloom: "Mr. Leopold Bloom ate with relish the inner organs of beasts and fowl" (p. 224): the (slightly misquoted) introduction of Bloom into *Ulysses*. Homey, mundane, realistic, these words, like their subject, offer a sharp contrast to intellectual, impractical, aloof Stephen Dedalus. But they note similarities as well.

They announce at the start, and with humor, Bloom's apparent alienation from his own, Jewish tradition (he eats pork kidneys for breakfast).
Cut off from his heritage by distance and time, by imperfect knowledge
and by lack of belief, Bloom nonetheless is viewed by all as a Jew
("though in reality I'm not").[30] Why did Mr. Joyce make his hero a
Jew? Not simply because he was, as Joyce has answered, but because in
a world cut off from its roots—the obvious lesson of Homeric myth in
Ulysses—Bloom's Jewishness provides virtually the sole surviving measure of continuity and human worth. This and not Homer is the central
mythic and metaphoric pattern of *Ulysses*. Ignorant as he is of his
tradition (each of the two-hundred-odd Jewish references in the novel is
marked by error or incompleteness or both), alienated as he is by some
of its precepts and customs,[31] Bloom still brings with him into the
gentile world a sense of history, an affirmation within history of the
individual's responsibility for his own acts and thereby of individual
dignity and worth: tenets as central to Jewish history and life as the
belief in the One God. This heritage of Bloom's, truncated as it may be
in his life, serves in *Ulysses* as reminder of or supplement to or substitute
for a humanist tradition presumed otherwise dead. It is Bloom's major
link to the mythic past and, through him, it may be ours, his readers', as
well. Daniel's sudden reference to Bloom attests to the centrality within
his world of a similar vision of Jewishness, of myth, and of humanity.

In their "refusal to be victim" (p. 43) yet their impulse toward
victimization; in the lifelong innocence of his father (p. 51) and sister (p.
291)—as contrasted to Linda Mindish's trendy "alienation" (p. 287) and
his own too easliy avowed "Hard corruption" (p. 291); in their concern
for suffering humanity and in their own suffering, the Isaacsons act out
the literary myth and metaphor of Jewishness as enunciated by Bloom.
They never question their responsibility for their acts; they achieve
dignity because they assume that they possess it as humans; they act out
in their lives—idealistic and involved if perhaps misguided—the humanistic values of their people's ancient tradition. Searching through
their lives for the meaning of his own, Daniel discovers the validity of
two clichés of Bloom's: it is not merely history, "the irreparability of the
past,"[32] which governs their lives—his parents', his sister's, his own; he
can also find in them, in writing about them, "the eternal affirmation of
the spirit of man in literature,"[33] a synthesis of history and myth.

History, for Daniel, is thus more than a means of observing the past
and applying its lessons to a troublesome present. It is an active,

pervasive force in his life, revealing, inexorable. ("It is History," he
thinks through his father's thoughts, "that pig, biting into the heart's
secrets"—p. 115). It is because he has thought of himself and his sister
as characters in history that he has lost sight of her—as of himself—as
people who must live in the present. His problem is that of the nation at
large, as we struggle, too, to come to terms with our history: Daniel's
concern with comprehending his past is not so very different from
Pynchon's use of his Puritan heritage in *Gravity's Rainbow.* What is
different is the intimacy and immediacy of these events—both for Daniel
and for his readers. Here there are none of the distancing devices of
Pynchon's narrative; we are not merely allowed but consistently induced
to react to Daniel as humans reacting to a fellow being. His use of myth,
his Jewish heritage, his reaction to history all affirm his humanity and
ours. He will not claim to believe, as does his Marxist father, "in the
insignificance of personal experience within the pattern of history" (p.
43). His narrative proves—both his writing and our involvement—that
the humanist impulse is alive still in post-Modernist fiction. The book of
Daniel, as he comes at last to acknowledge, is his life.

V

The American novelist closest to Joyce in his understanding of myth as a
literary device is undoubtedly John Barth. It is not simply that Barth
adopts in his fictions the mythic techniques of *Ulysses:* one of his finest
books, the subtly connected collection of tales called *Lost in the
Funhouse,* is an homage to and updating of *A Portrait of the Artist as a
Young Man,* suggesting that, for Barth at least, Joyce's work too has
attained the stature of literary myth. But Barth goes well beyond Joyce
in his belief that the mythmaking process is itself central to the writer's
craft—not just a tool for his use but a key to his identity as artist. The
sustaining potential of myth and mythmaking—not so much for individual characters, as in *Ulysses,* or even for entire societies, as in Homer,
but for the artist himself—is the prevailing concern of virtually all of
Barth's fiction.

   No novelist of our time has recognized more surely than Barth that it
is the literary function of each age not merely to expose its failing
present by means of the myths of the past, as Eliot dictates; or to
destroy the old and create in its place a unique new national mythology,

as Pynchon and Coover attempt to do; or even to find in modern events a sustaining mythic pattern of human emotions and acts, as Doctorow does; but that each age is obliged to restore and adapt the old myths as well—to devise, in effect, new Homers and even new Joyces, new archetypes of fertility (or of infertility) and new renditions of national legends and history to suit the new sensibility and state of life. But Barth's concern for the mythmaking process per se, and for the reflexive attitudes framing his myths, has led him at times to subordinate the human needs of his characters to his own needs as an artist.[34]

The protagonist of *The End of the Road* (1958) fails in his prescribed "Mythotherapy," obscures his own identity, disrupts the lives of those whom he touches. His is the modern disease: ambivalent and passionless, he is capable of playing various roles but unable to assume responsibility for any. The catatonic state in which he ends this adventure is almost a symbol of the times: the humanizing quality of myth is beyond his comprehension or reach. He has sought for myths within himself as a means of ordering his life (with references to Freud, Sartre, Heidegger, Beckett, Korzybski) and has found both myths and life to be inadequate ("my limbs . . . bound like Laocöon's—by the serpents Knowledge and Imagination, which . . . no longer tempt but annihilate"—p. 196).[35] His failure presages those of later Barth heroes who would seek unsuccessfully for their mythic truths within history or who are themselves figures in myth and therefore unable to define themselves (or to be defined by their creator) as humans. As Jacob Horner's quack psychoanalyst tells him, " 'not only are we the heroes of our own life stories—we're the ones who conceive the story, and give other people the essences of minor characters. But since no man's life story as a rule is ever one story with a coherent plot, we're always reconceiving just the sort of hero we are, and consequently just the sort of minor roles that other people are supposed to play" (p. 89). That the Doctor speaks here for Barth as well—for his interests and problems as the creator of characters and their stories, with self-knowledge and irony—becomes increasingly apparent in the later fiction.

The Sot-Weed Factor (1960) is at once profoundly original and highly derivative, although both originality and sources are not quite what they seem. *The Sot-Weed Factor* (1708), "A Voyage to Maryland, A Satyr. In which Is Described, The Laws, Government, Courts, and Constitutions of the Country; and also the Buildings, feasts, Frolics, Entertainments and Drunken Humours of the Inhabitants of that Part of America. In

Burlesque Verse," by Ebenezer Cook, purportedly an Englishman returned from America, and published in London, would seem Barth's
primary source. Ebenezer Cooke, after all, is his hero, even if he is an
American, and Barth's prose suggests throughout the rhythms and forms
of the Hudabrastic verse of the original. The narrator cites as additional
sources two still-earlier documents, one of them Captain John Smith's
Secret Historie of the Voiage Up the Bay of Chesapeake, a work not otherwise
found in Smith's voluminous canon but one that seems perfectly
consistent with his frequently apocryphal writings and life. As stories
themselves and as documents, they too become a concern of the
narrative; they help to distance us still further from Barth's protagonist.
Self-proclaimed poet and virgin—Poet Laureate of Barth's native Maryland, another Candide in the New World—Ebenezer Cook(e) discovers
new modes of life in the unsettled regions of the Chesapeake Bay and
new possibilities of human behavior in the unknown territory within
himself. His is another of those books embodying the European myth of
the New World. ("In the beginning," says John Locke, "all the world
was America."[36]) He too discovers in this garden not innocence but the
roots of future disillusionment. Distanced as we are from him, however,
by intervening manuscripts and stories, we are less moved by his plight
than we are perhaps intended to be.

Barth's version of American colonial history antedates Pynchon's by
more than a decade, is equally inventive, comic, even manic at times,
equally serious and ultimately far more complex and under greater
control. Its borrowings, moreover, are not scientific but literary: the wit
and game playing of Sterne, the Juvenalian satire, even the coprophilia
of Swift, Rabelais' bawdiness, and the philosophical iciness of Voltaire,
all are reflected here—in addition to Ebenezer Cooke. Barth's primary
source, however, is the more modern fiction of Jorge Luis Borges,
author of such rich and intricately reflexive tales as "Pierre Menard,
Author of the *Quixote*" and "Tlön, Uqbar, Orbis Tertius," stories in which
new worlds are created by authors within old ones, fictional worlds
which soon take the place of their originals and from which human
emotions seem to have vanished. In "Pierre Menard," a twentieth-
century Frenchman endeavors to create out of his own experience a
modern *Don Quixote*—not a copy of the original or a translation but a
literal rendering, independently arrived at, in antique Spanish. How
much more difficult his task than Cervantes': "to go on being Pierre
Menard and reach the *Quixote* through the experiences of Pierre Menard.

. . . To compose the *Quixote* at the beginning of the seventeenth century was a reasonable undertaking, necessary and perhaps even unavoidable; at the beginning of the twentieth, it is almost impossible."[37] His success is small but spectacular; he has left only a fragmentary manuscript behind him, yet, as his editor points out, "Cervantes' text and Menard's are verbally identical, but the second is almost infinitely richer."[38] So must it be—at least it seems logical here—the creation of a seventeenth-century Spanish world drawn from the life of an early twentieth-century French writer. The editor himself, the persona of Borges, writing in the Americas, labors through Menard's notes and attempts to build further on them. "Unfortunately, only a second Pierre Menard, inverting the other's work, would be able to exhume and revive those lost Troys. . . ."[39]

The writer's task seems at first less demanding in "Tlön, Uqbar, Orbis Tertius." Uqbar is a world discovered within a pirated and corrupt edition of the *Encyclopaedia Brittanica;* Tlön is its illusory "third world," which supplants its creator in the minds of its readers and comes to dominate as well the reality outside them both, the tired, embattled reality of the Western World just after the Second World War. The world recoils from the disorder of our history and reaches out instead to fantastic Tlön. Reality shifts; languages alter; science and history are "reformed": "already a fictitious past occupies in our memories the place of another, a past of which we know nothing with certainty—not even that it is false."[40] The narrator meanwhile, as a new order vanquishes the one he has known, in the midst of this turmoil and change, goes his own scholarly way. "I pay no attention to all this and go on revising, in the still days at the Adrogué hotel, an uncertain Quevedian translation (which I do not intend to publish) of Browne's *Urn Burial.*"[41] Immersed in the literature of the past (whose subject is immortality), in a foreign language and provincial town, writing in an "uncertain" style which would seem to mandate satire but in which satire seems absent, remaining personally aloof and seemingly uninvolved, the Borges persona expresses no emotion as the world he has known dissolves around him. We are induced to name and to experience his feelings. And we understand that they must be profound, that his lack of expression makes our perception of them still more profound. Barth's persona, the omniscient Author of *The Sot-Weed Factor,* perhaps the second Pierre Menard for whom the Borges persona appeals, expresses a rather different, more intellectual irony at the end

of his task. "[Ebenezer's] complaint that Maryland's air . . . ill supports
the delicate muse was accurate, for to the best of the Author's knowledge her marshes have spawned no other poet since Ebenezer Cooke,
Gentleman, Poet and Laureate of the Province" (p. 806).[42] Barth's
reflexivism develops from that of Borges, his author's world as remote as
what passes for the real one in Borges, but his wit and self-irony are
only partial substitutes for a more telling statement, even a more telling
inference, of his hero's emotions.

This is not to suggest that there is no feeling or emotional force in
Barth's fiction. The impact of Ebenezer's discovery of evil in the New
World is powerful indeed, and we are not left distant in our own
involvement. The pivotal scene of the novel is a mass rape—extending
into the rigging—on board the ship carrying Ebenezer to America; it is
so outrageously funny as seen through the eyes of this innocent that,
knowing the subject, we may nonetheless laugh aloud at its enactment.
Only much later, when the results of the rape are revealed in terms of
human lives and symbolic events, do we perceive its full significance
and the import of our laughter. For this is the original sin in the garden,
and we are privy to its commission and infected by its results. The
mythic and historical construct of *The Sot-Weed Factor* suggests that all
America is equally diseased, that our disillusionment may be inherent
within the myth of America itself: it will need far more than an ocean
voyage, no matter how arduous and long, to justify such expectations of
a new beginning in a world removed from European tradition. The
effect of Barth's humor and irony here, at the heart of the myth, is to
heighten our complicity and emotional concern. Too often, however, our
involvement is with Barth the Author and not with his people.

This is, of course, the traditional—and misguided—complaint against
Joyce: that our feelings for his characters and their acts are diminished
by the humor which surrounds them, by the rich and varied and intense
language, by the often elegant and sometimes gross wit, by the complexity of the movement of the plot and (in Barth's case) by the
complexity and depth of his philosophical concerns. The complaint is
demonstrably wrong in Joyce's case (with the sole exception of the
"Oxen of the Sun" episode of *Ulysses,* in which style may well obscure
content), and so we should be suspicious of it as applied to Barth. But
there is one instance at least in which Barth's post-Modernist usage goes
well beyond Joyce's: this is the reflexivism which he has learned from
Borges.

In a sense, we can speak of Joyce's reflexivism at the end of *Ulysses*. At the end of the novel, we know, Stephen Dedalus, having discovered at last his subject in Leopold Bloom, will go off somewhere to write the novel of Bloom's life in Dublin, the novel which we know as *Ulysses*. To the extent that it deals with its own creation, *Ulysses* may be thought of as self-reflexive. But this is quite simple when compared to Borges's practice or to Barth's. Joyce's reflexivism, such as it is, is a simple extension of the Romantic poet's accustomed self-involvement: the concern, above all else, for the artist as creator and for the personal implications of his creativity (the sense that he is separate from others and superior to them, yet incapable of living normally alongside them. Stephen Dedalus is so quintessentially a Romantic in this sense that he might almost be the creator of "Kubla Khan.") Yet it is Joyce's irony— the distance which he studiously maintains from Stephen—that helps make possible post-Modernist reflexivism. That distance is greatest from Stephen as artist: he is presented to us as sensitive but immature, self-involved and committed to art but lacking a subject or theme or knowledge of the world, a Romantic in sensibility and language but not yet an artist (witness his juvenilia in *A Portrait*). Joyce is thus glorifying Stephen and, at the same time, warning us of his limitations; but the emphasis remains on Stephen, his youth, his emotions, his life. A comparable, perhaps more telling distance develops in *Finnegans Wake*, in which the artist is viewed from the perspective of his mortal enemy, the man of affairs, his twin. Among the most compelling passages of *Finnegans Wake* is Shaun the Post's derisive yet moving account of the process by which Shem the Penman transmutes his flesh and his blood, quite literally, into substance for art ("brought to blood heat, gallic acid on iron ore, through the bowels of his misery . . . the first till last alshemist wrote over every square inch of the only foolscap available, his own body . . .").[43] For all its power and insight and its echoes of the creative process for Joyce himself, this too remains a Romantic conceit (with further echoes of Blake, the poet and engraver): the emphasis is once again on the artist and not on his art.

For Barth and Borges, however, it is not so much the artist as the work of art that matters, not the implications for him of the artistic process but the process itself. The artistic sensibility is not at issue in their art except insofar as it is revealed in—and helps to reveal—the act of creation. Their goal is not to trace the development of the artist per se but rather to show him at work: the piece which they present us is as likely to be his creation as theirs. Building on Joyce's irony and distance, they station themselves still further away from the artist, the Romantic hero, and address themselves to the reader—force him to acknowledge that this is not life he holds in his hands but artifice, not a recreation of some objective reality but the artist's rendition (Borges's or Barth's, Menard's, or Cooke's) of that fictive world. Artists have always been concerned, of course, with art as a theme (see Plato in the *Ion*), even with reflecting themselves and their craft in their work (Velasquez in *Las Meninas*). The artist who appears as a character in his work, interacting with his creations, has long been a feature of the popular arts as well (as in the vaudeville-based comic strip *Mutt and Jeff*). Today, the practice seems everywhere, in films (François Truffaut's *Day for Night* and Paul Mazursky's *Alex in Wonderland*) and in music (Tom Johnson's *The Four-Note Opera* and Alvin Lucier's "I Am Sitting in a Room") as well as in fiction. It is Brecht's "epic theatre" brought to the page, Plato's parable of the cave objectified, the work of art holding itself up to a mirror—a hall of mirrors—and reflecting not so much the figure seen there but his role as creator and his creative work. It is the most significant addition by the post-Modernist sensibility to the Joycean legacy and not always a fortuitous one. For it may lure us to process and away from humans. Ironically, this post-Modernist practice may prove in the end more self-involved even than the Romantic, more self-indulgent as well.

In Borges this practice may lead us back to the artist's emotions: witness the end of "Tlön." In Barth, more likely, it will direct us to his intellect. This is no insignificant accomplishment, but it is, I believe, inherently limiting. When applied to myth—as Barth so often applies it—it works against the larger humanistic impulse which has always been associated with myth. Thus, in *The Sot-Weed Factor*, brilliant as it is, we are too often directed to Ebenezer Cooke the author, to Barth's persona the Author, to Barth himself as creator of them both, and distracted from Ebenezer's life and the mythic core of that life. By building on Borges's reflexive concerns about writers, the act of their writing and the interior worlds from which and of which they write— we might almost speak in this sense of Jorge Luis Borges, author of *The Sot-Weed Factor*—Barth has increased our wonder and perhaps lessened our commitment. This post-Modernist rendering of myth, in the end, as subtle and sophisticated and challenging as it is as literary tehcnique, is not quite what Joyce and the Modernists meant by myth.

The tension between teller and tale, between mythmaker and myth, is central to the stories of both *Lost in the Funhouse* and *Chimera*. The writer's preoccupation with the act of writing and with its manifold implications—for art, for the world, for the artist as man or as woman who must live in the world—is still more pronounced in these works, almost obsessively so at times. It is also tied more directly to myths of creativity. Barth seems determined to play out this dual reflexive theme as far as it will go, beyond predictable results, beyond reason it seems in some cases. These re-versions of myth, as a result, are always inventive, always witty and challenging, but only occasionally moving; their sometime coldness reflects the barren, obsessive, post-Modernist world from which they emerge.

"Hate love!" cries the hero of "Night-Sea Journey," mythic prologue to *Lost in the Funhouse* (1968), at the end of his terrible *rite de paysage*. He has witnessed the holocaust of his fellows and questions his own right to survive. He has passed through all the steps of the initiation of the hero who will lead or even form his society, but he rejects that path and society as well. His cry is an elegy to all our Modernist lives. "I have seen the best swimmers of my generation go under. Numberless the number of the dead! Thousands drown as I think this thought, millions as I rest before returning to the swim. And scores, hundreds of millions have expired since we surged forth, brave in our innocence, upon our dreadful way. 'Love! Love!' we sang then, a quarter-billion strong, and churned the warm sea white with joy of swimming! Now all are gone down—the buoyant, the sodden, leaders and followers, all gone under, while wretched I swim on" (p. 4).[44] His greatest fear is that his voyage of initiation—almost a literal enactment of what Joseph Campbell has termed "the monomyth"[45]—will be not just without meaning but opposed to meaning, that its sole significance is survival itself and survival of the least fit at that. He questions his sanity, questions the reality from which he has emerged and which he has come, he fears, to represent. "Perhaps, even, I am drowned already. Surely I was never meant for the rough-and-tumble of the swim; not impossibly I perished at the outset and have only imaged the night-sea journey from some final deep. In any case, I'm no longer young, and it is we spent old swimmers, disabused of every illusion, who are most vulnerable to dreams" (p. 10). Abused, disillusioned, embittered, he leaps nonetheless into the final void, " 'the Shore of Light' " (p. 6), and calls out to his listeners his final, awful legacy: "It is *not* love that sustains me. . . . What has fetched me across this dreadful sea is a single hope . . . that You may be stronger-willed than I, and that by sheer force of concentration I may transmit to You ["You who I may be about to become"], along with Your official Heritage, a private legacy of awful recollection and negative resolve. . . . [M]ay you to whom, through whom I speak, do what I cannot: terminate this aimless, brutal business! Stop your hearing against Her song! Hate love!" (p. 12). It is a strange invocation indeed to the Muse.

The voice of "Night-Sea Journey" is that of the last surviving sperm, "tale-bearer of a generation" (p. 9). His immediate offspring is Ambrose, the young artist figure of "Ambrose his Mark," of "Water-Message" and of the title story, "Lost in the Funhouse." But he is progenitor as well of all those creators and heroes of myth who distort mythic meaning by substituting the narrative process for life: the "I" of "Autobiography" and the "He" of "Life-Story," the tape-recorded "printed voice" of the "Menelaiad" and, above all, "the first person anonymous" speaker of the "Anonymiad." Yet all these narrators, even those who precede him in historical time, even those who are not quite human, are manifestations of Ambrose: *Lost in the Funhouse* is best understood as a unified work, a *künstlerroman,* and its frequent references and allusions to Joyce indicate clearly that its model is *A Portrait of the Artist as a Young Man.* "If the night-sea journey has justification," the progenitor has said, "it is not for us swimmers ever to discover it" (p. 5). It is the task of Ambrose and his fellows to find and elucidate such meaning; following their forebear's example, however, and ignoring Joyce's, they choose the art of narration over that of living and thus perhaps distort what meaning they do find.

Honey-tongued Ambrose, as uncertain as he is glib, is himself a character on the fringes of myth: he is one of those singled out as an infant by a swarm of bees (joining Plato, Sophocles, Xenophon, and that early Christian enemy of Arianism, Bishop Ambrose of Milan); the bees settle, however, not on his mouth, as is customary, but on his eyes and ears—an ironic fate for a would-be narrator perhaps, but one which may recall the emphasis on the senses in the opening sequence of *A Portrait.* The choice of his name indicates that he will be neither philosopher nor tragedian nor historian or man of action; he seems destined instead to be a fighter for a particular faith, a maker of spurious hymns, yet one who may nonetheless " 'see things clear' " (p. 34), himself a drone bee. His fear of bees reminds us of Stephen Dedalus's fear of dogs (both potential images of creativity); his rivalry with his brother echoes that of Stephen with Maurice (especially in *Stephen Hero*) and that of Shem with Shaun (in *Finnegans Wake*)—both on behalf of their art; his adolescent romanticism and the places in which he plays as a child, his love of words and his immature theory of narrative art (p. 78), are further parallels to the young Stephen destined to be an artist. Ambrose quotes Joyce directly when describing the ocean at Ocean City, Maryland ("The Irish author James Joyce, in his unusual novel entitled *Ulysses*, now available in this country, uses the adjectives *snot-green* and *scrotum-tightening* to describe the sea. Visual, auditory, tactile, olfactory, gustatory"—p. 74). In another of his manifestations, as the "I" of "Autobiography," he paraphrases both the end of *A Portrait* (Stephen's reverential "Old father, old artificer"[46] becomes his "Wretched old fabricator"—p. 38) and the end of the cyclical *Wake* ("my last words will be my last words"—p. 39—he says without end punctuation, suggesting that they may also be his first).

Yet the "I" of "Autobiography" is not the author but the story speaking itself, a true auto-biography, and this is decidedly not Joycean: nothing heroic here, not even the joy of creation; this narration is mere necessity, compulsion even, a complaint of existence that ignores not just human creativity but human existence as well. It is to Joycean technique that Barth acknowledges his debt in *Lost in the Funhouse* and not to Joyce's vision of man in the world, Joyce's sense of narrative creativity carried, in one way, to its final potential development and Joyce's sense of the artist's commitment to life avoided, even denied. Barth's acknowledgement, that is, is to the immature Stephen of *A Portrait of the Artist as a Young Man*—idealistic, Romantic, and not yet an artist—and not to the Stephen of the end of *Ulysses*, who has found a mature subject at last and who now bears the responsibility of mature creation.[47] Thus the uniqueness of Barth and what may be his ultimate failure. The ambiguity is most apparent perhaps in the concluding story of *Lost in the Funhouse*, the post-Modernist epic called for its hero "Anonymiad," in which prose fiction replaces myth and narrative supplants life, which seems to speak against human involvement yet which is at times profoundly involving and moving.

The speaker of the "Anonymiad" is an unnamed poet on an unnamed Greek isle. Once he had been attracted to the world of affairs and honored to be a trusted member of the court of King Agamemnon in Mycenae; he has now been marooned by Aegisthus, who wants merely to be alone with Queen Clytemnestra during her husband's absence in Troy. Thrust back on his solitary art, he invents writing, invents fiction ("abandon[ing] myth and pattern[ing] my fabrication on actual people and events: Menelaus, Helen, the Trojan War"—p. 193), attempts to reproduce the rhythms of human speech in his prose, begins his epic in the middle of events. He has learned that one need not be a witness to great events in order to create great art; he has lost the need for an audience or for the possibility of future influence or fame. He casts his creation upon the waters but anticipates no reader and demands no response. (Perhaps it is one of his missives, changed over the years and oceans, that Ambrose comes upon in "Water-Message.") His art exists for itself. His art, too, is reflexive, for it reproduces the epic which it describes, is in fact that same epic; it depicts the development of the hero as artist and at the same time is a step in that development. The anonymous poet's anonymous epic denies Romantic conceptions, even the Romanticism of artistic discipline (a paradox which Joyce knew well). Yet at the same time it glorifies—reproduces, indeed—the Romantic vision of the isolated artist dedicated to his art despite society, outside the world. He is no Homer perhaps, but he is content in his art: his art is his life, quite literally. It is a moving predicament which he details, yet he denies us the emotion which his predicament may arouse, as, caught up in his art, he denies himself all those aspects of his humanity beside his art.

" 'Every writer,' " Barth says that "Borges says in his essay on Kafka, 'creates his own precursors.' "[48] Reading "Kafka and His Precursors," the critic senses that Borges is actually saying that the writer-critic creates after the fact those precursors whom he needs for his own work. Thus, Borges is claiming Kafka, and Barth is claiming both Borges and Kafka as precursors. That Robbe-Grillet too can claim Kafka as precursor suggests something of the latter's viability as metaphor, if not of his literary uniqueness: it would be difficult to imagine—even for Borges to imagine—a writer more unlike Borges than Robbe-Grillet. Precursorship in this sense, then, is a strangely variable, often useful condition. And so it seems perfectly natural for Barth, who has already indicated his admiration for *The Arabian Nights* of Sir Richard Burton, to create to his own specifications another forerunner of modern (*i.e.*, Barth's) narrative art. Again, he begins with Borges: "one of his frequenter literary allusions is to the 602nd night of *The 1001 Nights*, when, owing to a copyist's error, Scheherezade begins to tell the King the story of the 1001 nights, from the beginning. Happily, the King interrupts; if he didn't there'd be no 603rd night ever, and while this would solve

Scheherezade's problem—which is every storyteller's problem: to publish or perish—it would put the 'outside' author in a bind. (I suspect
that Borges dreamed this whole thing up: the business he mentions isn't
in any edition of *The 1001 Nights* I've been able to consult. Not yet,
anyhow: after reading 'Tlön, Uqbar,' etc., one is inclined to recheck
every semester or so.)"[49] Of course, Barth offers no sources for Borges's
comment. Had Borges not made such a comment, Barth would surely
be willing to invent it—or its maker. In the "Dunyazadiad," he is willing
even to invent John Barth.

The "Dunyazadiad," first of the three mythic novellas which constitute
Chimera (1972), is named for and in part told by the younger sister of
Scheherezade, for whose ostensible sake the one thousand and one
stories are to be told (or at least to be completed), listener along with
King Shahryar to these wondrous tales, our sole surrogate within the
narrative. Here she tells her own tale (to Shahryar's brother, Shah
Zaman), a tale, of course, of listening, of tale-telling, of authorial
sources; the tale which she tells is of the Genie who inspires her sister
and who, in turn, is inspired by her (by both sisters, that is). The Genie
is Barth—there is no mistaking his physical appearance and artistic
predicament at the time of this writing. As character, Barth the Genie
consults with Scheherezade on the power of the imagination in fiction,
on the comparative realities of fiction and fact, on the relationship
between narrative and sexual artistry, and for some three years he
provides her nightly with the stories which she must tell to keep herself
and her sister alive. His source, obviously, is the original *Thousand Nights
and a Night,* which he, as a twentieth-century man, has read, but which
she, as a character in a twentieth-century fiction, cannot even begin to
recall. But the true hero of this Borgesian tale is Dunyazade. She is
Barth's tribute to the active and imaginative reader, the Modernist ideal.
(If there were more like her, Joyce and his contemporaries would seem
no more elitist today than Dickens and his.) She is the listener/reader
become so involved in working through the narrative that she herself
has become a narrator; passive recipient (the Victorian model) become
active collaborator in fiction; a figure on the fringes of myth turned, like
Ambrose, into its center. At a time when the Genie's "own pen . . . had
just about run dry," she represents the possibility for him of a new
creative beginning: "he wished neither to repudiate nor to repeat his
past performances; he aspired to go beyond them toward a future they

were not attuned to and, by some magic, at the same time go back to
the original springs of narrative" (p. 17).[50] Those springs are in myth,
and in the recreation of myth: Barth's characters, in his re-vision of the
myth of the thousand and one nights, opt for love and commitment
beyond the narrative performance. The omniscient Genie, however,
turns inward and reverts, like a Borgesian narrator, to old obsessions:
"The Book of the Thousand Nights and a Night," he concludes, "is not
the story of Scheherezade, but the story of the story of her stories . . ."
(p. 63).

His is demonstrably one of the voices also of the "Bellerophoniad,"
third of the novellas in *Chimera,* a tale as unwieldy in structure and
theme as in its title, a narrative so clever and contrived, so rich and
contradictory in plot and potential meaning, so filled with references to
the author's own canon (to *The Floating Opera, Lost in the Funhouse,*
"Anonymiad," "Dunyazadiad," *The Sot-Weed Factor, Giles Goat-Boy,* even
to *Letters,* which would not appear for almost a decade), that it is
impossible to take seriously the hero and his predicament. Building once
again upon Borges, Barth in the "Bellerophoniad" goes far beyond
Borges, but in his inventiveness, unlike Borges, he loses sight of his
human concerns. Here, again, he retells a myth in accord with the
mythic Pattern, with a hero unsure of his identity outside the Pattern.
" 'A passionate lack of alternatives,' " Proteus describes him; " 'not so
much an absolute apprentice hero as absolutely nothing else instead, if
you see that I mean' " (p. 195). Eventually the narrative devolves into a
course on mythology—"the Distinguished History of Bellerophon the
Mythic Hero . . . in the University of Lycia's newly established Depart-
ment of Classical Mythology," a required course, to be sure (pp. 205–6).
As Bellerophon cuts himself off from the family he loves in order to
fulfill what he believes to be his mythic imperative—to return in middle
age to being a hero of myth—so Barth in his urge to fulfill his narrative
mandate (an elaborate Borgesian construction depicting a world in the
process of deconstruction) cuts himself off from his hero's human
predicament. The empathy which we may feel for Bellerophon and his
family is quickly lost in our wonder at (and our labor in the unraveling
of) the complex narrative threads which depict and determine his fate.
We are left not with a man at all but with a disquisition on narrative
and myth, another course, as it were, with surprising ties to new
fictional forms. For Polyeidus, Bellerophon's tutor, who wants desperately to get "out of Greek myth altogether—that tiresome catalogue of

rapes, petty jealousies, power grabs; that marble-columned ghetto of immortals" (p. 307), this new fiction will be "written (so help me Muse) in 'American'" (p. 312), product of a people who "speak more or less in English, and have a literature (which no one reads) but no mythology" (p. 317). This is meant to be that mythology. Yet Barth, like his hero, seems "'bogged down more than immortalized'" (p. 303), a prisoner of the process which has become his (narrative) life.

Only the "Perseid" seems relatively free of this narrative obsession, and only Perseus of the mythic heroes of *Chimera* approaches some resolution of the problems of his life. Here the elaborate form works for and not against the reader's involvement: Perseus, too, is concerned with the dual exigencies of myth and narration, but he learns something as well of human commitment. It is a different quality of myth that Barth endeavors to form in the "Perseid," not one whose purpose is to explore and expand "the original springs of narrative," as in the "Dunyazadiad" and "Bellerophoniad," but a myth in the nature of Joyce's mythmaking, one more responsive to human needs in our a-mythic time: a myth ultimately, like traditional myth, of human responses to and involvement in the world and not merely of national or narrative urges.

The "Perseid," as its title indicates, retells the myth of Perseus and Medusa, using several known variants of the original and some potential variants as well. Thus Perseus tells the story of his life to Calyxa, priestess of a temple dedicated to him in Egypt; as source material, more even than on his memory, he relies on a series of biographical panels painted by Calyxa to Athene's dictation—"to learn about life from art," as he puts it (p. 70). Two motifs dominate in this first part of his narration: his frequent references to Medusa, "my true adversary and chief ally" (p. 86), and his near-obsessive concern that the adventures of his life conform to the "archetypal pattern for heroic adventure" (p. 88); even so late in his life, he is still clearly more hero than man. Calyxa, his lover and critic as well as his source ("explication only after forn" is her critical motto—p. 94), comments admiringly on his narrative technique—"'I could listen all night to the way you talk,'" she tells him (p. 89)—but she misses much of its meaning. She is willing but shallow: enthusiastic as a lover and friend, perceptive as a critic of literary form but unable to appreciate the human implications of his narration. Or is it simply that it is through Perseus' eyes that we view her and that he himself is too shallow at this point to perceive the significance of all that

he says? (Maybe he simply distrusts textual critics: "I don't mind
sleeping with a critic now and then," he tells Calyxa, "but I wouldn't
spend eternity with one"—p. 136.)

The intricate patterning of Perseus's tale reveals possibilities of human
behavior that he does not yet comprehend. We develop them with him
as we work our way through the narrative maze: Perseus, we learn, has
been speaking all along not to Calyxa but to another, repeating verbatim
to her what he has said earlier to the priestess in Egypt. Calyxa is
merely a memory now; his true audience is Medusa herself, a reader of
the old myths in her own right (her favorite, of course, is the "Perseid"),
even an artist of sorts (sculptured happenings, we might call her
creations). Her greatest art, however, is her ability to feel and to make
Perseus feel. The combatants of the old tale have here been transformed
into lovers, and a local Greek myth which spoke once of economic and
territorial expansion, of the ways in which ambition and pride may lead
us to overcome our deepest fears, speaks in this new version of Barth's
of more basic concerns: of the human capacity for self-hatred and self-
love, of our desire for continuity and fame and our urge toward self-
annihilation, of our need both to achieve the rewards offered in this life
and to repudiate them, to progress somehow beyond the limits set out
for us all. It is mythmaking in the truest tradition of myth.[51]

Perseus and Medusa, through a process that neither quite understands, have now become stars—yet stars who retain at a distance their
human needs and desires. Their greatest need is everyone's need: to be
understood, to be loved, to understand and to love. And so each night
he tells her this tale, as they try to comprehend now that they are
immortal the processes which once made them human. "Half of each
[night]," Perseus declares to his love, "I'll unwind my tale to where it is
ours"—the repetition of the narrative to Calyxa—"and half of every
we'll talk. There's much to say" (p. 134). No longer does he worry
about "archetypes [or] stereo-types" (p. 137); no longer is he obsessed
by the traditional patterns of heroic activity or the emerging new
patterns of narrative technique. Now he is concerned with his actions as
man. His goal is both mythic and narrative and simply human as well:
"to be the tale I tell to those with eyes to see and understanding to
interpret; to raise you up forever and know that our story will never be
cut off, but nightly rehearsed as long as men and women read the
stars . . ." (p. 142). Even so, their story—like all of our stories—is finite:
"But even our stars' nights are numbered, and with them will pass this

patterned tale to a long-deceased earth" (p. 67). With Calyxa in Egypt, Perseus attempted to learn about life from another's art; among the stars with Medusa, he learns from his own narration, learns that it is less important to live as a hero of myth for the ages than to live now as a man. He has learned through myth to seek no longer for ultimates in fiction or life.

Jacob Horner, in *The End of the Road*, is warned by his quack psychoanalyst never to engage his emotions for fear that he will lose control of his life; he does so nevertheless, and, as a result, becomes spiritually and emotionally bereft. He is the obvious ancestor of Ebenezer Cooke in *The Sot-Weed Factor* and his American offspring, of the speaker of "Night-Sea Journey" and his narrator-descendants, of Bellerophon, the author of the "Dunyazadiad," and their fellow creators. Creators and characters alike, they have become so caught up in form that they lose much of their ability to feel. When Barth speaks of " 'the literature of exhausted possibility,' " he is speaking—perhaps more than he intends to—of human as well as narrative limitations, of his own failings as well as others'. Only occasionally, as in the "Perseid," does he manage fully "to accomplish new human work": not just to erect new narrative forms from the frame of old forms, but to devise new forms which can manage still—as he says of Borges and Beckett—"to speak eloquently and memorably to our still-human hearts and conditions, as the great artists have always done."[52] Always inventive, always witty and intellectually engaging, sensitive to the conditions of his characters and to the demands of myth, Barth nonetheless too often fails his own test. Too often he uses myth to limit rather than to expand human potential. And so he frequently seems to support in practice the mythic perspective of Pynchon and Coover. Yet there are moments when Barth's use of Joyce and his narrative model is not ironic, when, as Doctorow does in *The Book of Daniel*, he is able to suggest that transcendence of the human condition, that affirmation of humanity even in our age, which is possible only through myth. This is surely what happens in the "Perseid."

If humanism can be defined as the knowledge of and concern for man and his condition—his connections to the past, to present society, to God, to nature, to self—then there is no better source of humanist understanding than the myths created over the time of man's existence, as man, on earth. It is not toolmaking but mythmaking which heralds our rise to humanity; we became fully human only when we learned to create myths as manifestations of our connections to the otherwise incomprehensible world. Myth may be said to equal humanity. From Homer on, writers have perceived this connection. Even after the devastation of life and expectation of the First World War, something of this usage survives for Joyce in *Ulysses* and for that Modernist vision which he serves as metaphor. Even inverted, it may suggest our essential, continuing humanity.

To Pynchon, Coover, Doctorow, and Barth, however, as different as they are, myth can no longer function as a means of revealing man's closeness to divinity or to the cycle of nature or even to his own past. This new fiction of theirs, "written (so help me Muse) in American," may more readily depict the absence of those forces in our lives, the reflection of a renewed fall—and a fall, ironically, in what was to have been the new garden of the world. Their use of myth as a literary device and as moral measure demonstrates both the ties and disjunctions between contemporary American fiction and its Modernist forebear, demonstrates, above all, the radical change in American perceptions of life between Joyce's age and ours. The old retrospective vision provided by myth no longer works in post-Modernist America; the past has been dishonored as a model for our lives in the present, and the present, devoid even of the ironic yet moral center of Joyce's vision of myth and mankind, appears fearsome indeed.

4 ROBBE-GRILLET, BUTOR, AND SIMON

French Responses to the Modernist Presence

It is not possible that a piece of sculpture, a piece of music which gives us an emotion which we feel to be more exalted, more pure, more true, does not correspond to some definite spiritual reality. It is surely symbolical of one, since it gives that impression of profundity and truth.

—Marcel Proust, *The Captive*

The writer himself, despite his desire for independence, is situated within an intellectual culture and a literature which can only be those of the past. It is impossible for him to escape altogether from this tradition of which he is the product.

—Alain Robbe-Grillet, *For A New Novel*

When the Nouveau Roman first came to public notice in the late 1950s, it seemed to many to promise a continuation, even an expansion, of Modernist interests—in technique especially but also potentially in theme. This was, after all, just a few years after Harry Levin in America had first lamented the death of Modernism and the New Victorians in England—Cooper, Snow, Amis, and Wain most prominent among them—had gleefully announced the passing, without issue, of Joyce and Woolf and their troublesome fellows and their own movement backward to earlier forms and simpler times. In such a context as this, a forward-looking movement calling itself the New Novel, with awareness of and implicit respect for Modernist concerns, even if centered in France, seemed especially welcome. In the end, of course, the Nouveau Roman proved to be not a new movement at all and not much more than a public relations phenomenon. As Vivian Mercier suggested in 1971,[1] one major element which bound these disparate writers together and made them seem, for a moment, a unified enterprise was the fact that most of them were published by the same firm, Les Éditions de Minuit. Beyond this trivial business circumstance, Robbe-Grillet,

Butor, Simon, Sarraute, Duras, Pinget, and Claude Mauriac were linked only by their shared perception that a changing reality demanded changing narrative techniques: a truism known to all novelists since Richardson and Fielding (if not since Cervantes) and somehow forgotten in post-Modernist England.

In the past decade or so, their alleged movement dispersed, several of these novelists have moved outside the novel altogether, into film in particular, but also into other forms of prose—memoirs, literary theory, travel, even radio scenarios and opera libretti. One might argue, perhaps, that their abandonment of the form is proof of the Modernist novel's demise: the evil influence, presumably, of those who would extend safe old forms in radical, even dangerous new ways. Yet there are clear ties to (Modernist) tradition in the work of these post-Joycean French novelists, and a certain consistency and development as well. Moreover, the best of their efforts are wonderfully able to stand by themselves, not merely as a part of literary history, independent of their sources. If they do not quite represent the expansion of the Modernist presence that we once thought them to, the New Novelists, so called, do attest to the central Modernist beliefs that technique both follows and precedes theme, that new historical periods mandate new fictional modes but that it remains possible still, through innovative narrative techniques, to affirm the human condition even in inhumane times.

It is perhaps true that Alain Robbe-Grillet, Michel Butor, and Claude Simon cannot today be called Modernist or even Modernism's heirs. But it is certain that each of these writers—who as a group constitute the spectrum of reactions in France to the Modernist example—continues to define his own art in terms of the art of his greater ancestors: ·Simon, creating for two decades in the path of Proust, Faulkner, and Joyce (and, more recently, more limited efforts in the side track of current critical theory); Butor, continuing to adapt Modernist fictional forms—even now, outside the novel—to a continually varying world (so that his non-novels need to be read as if they were novels still); and Robbe-Grillet, most paradoxically, repeatedly and forthrightly denying the relevance for us of the Modernist example and in the process continuously affirming it.

At one end of the spectrum, Robbe-Grillet has seemed to me from the first to be more interesting as a theorist on the state of the novel and of the world than as a novelist (or filmmaker). It is the aridity and harshness of his fictions that convince me that they will not survive—

except perhaps as manifestations of his theory that because life in our time is arid and harsh it is, of necessity, dehumanized. His perception of the world is thus, as I see it, antithetical to that of the Modernist novelists, although it is Modernist narrative technique that he utilizes—for he does have a sense of humor and paradox—to elaborate his vision. He has been consistent throughout his career in denying the relevance of the Modernist presence in our post-Modern time.

Butor, at the center of the spectrum, began his career as a novelist with a distinct and evident debt to the Modernists and then turned gradually to other, related concerns. That is, he can no longer be thought of strictly as a novelist, although his more recent nonfictional works grow clearly out of his early novels and are themselves novelistic (as *Finnegans Wake* has helped us to understand that term). The development and consistency of his entire canon merit our respect: in turning away from the Modernists and the novel he has been following what he sees as the Modernist way. And so, in the spirit of the later Joyce, he has become a true post-Modernist. Yet it is still to his Modernist novels, I must admit, that I turn for more than intellectual sustenance.

Finally, at the nearer end of the spectrum, Simon remains one of the most powerful and demanding novelists of his generation. Not since Faulkner, I believe, has a novelist so effectively yoked technique to theme in a series of interconnected, ascending fictions. If his most recent work has been somewhat too indebted to literary theory for my tastes, it too is informed by an unmistakeable humanist presence, at once disturbing, informing, and profoundly moving. Although this work looks also to the present, it remains, in my view, inherently Modernist.

Together these novelists present a diverse national reaction to Modernism that may lack the inventiveness of North American or the brilliance of Latin American reactions, but that is surely more positive, more in keeping with the novel's inherently progressive tradition, than the virtually unified British negation. They attest—with all their limitations—to the potential vitality of the Modernist presence even in a post-Modernist age. And they speak as well to the nature of the age.

II

In his well-known essay on "Nature, Humanism, Tragedy," written in 1958 (included in *For a New Novel: Essays on Fiction,* published in 1965), Alain Robbe-Grillet assaults several traditional notions, relating both to technique and to theme, that have long been regarded as central to the novel as a literary form. To many critics, he seems in the process to set the pattern for all the French novelists of his generation. He argues, for example, against the persistent use of metaphor, so important to the structure of Modernist fiction, because it "is never an innocent figure of speech," and its very presence presupposes "a constant relation between the universe [of things] and the beings who inhabit it" (pp. 53, 54). Robbe-Grillet's point is that the Modernist novel, like all its predecessors from at least Stendhal on, is inherently humanistic, determining all values according to the human presence which regards and orders the objects of the world, which makes metaphors of mere things. But the world which Robbe-Grillet sees around him is not humanistic at all, not at all informed by the clichéd (as he views them) old humane values; his world is unmarked by a significant, ordering, evaluating human presence. And so he would deny metaphor—a technique—in order to deny its underlying theme of humanist affirmation.

As Robbe-Grillet sees it, this is a simple realistic observation, for the world itself, in the wake of two world wars, is devoid of a significant, continuing humanist presence. It is in the name of realism, then, that he would conduct his revolution; all literary revolutions, he assures us, are carried out in its name. As he concludes in "New Novel, New Man" (1961), one of the pieces in *For a New Novel*, "Forms live and die, in all the realms of art, and in all periods they have had to be continually renewed." In the old order, before the world wars, "Man was the reason for all things, the key to the universe, and its natural master . . . " (pp. 135, 140). But all that has changed along with the harmonious, orderly old human-centered world which made it possible. Robbe-Grillet's new order consists of objects viewed objectively, without human intervention, with neither affirmation nor explicit negation: a world not of humanism but of *chosisme*.

It can hardly be surprising that so radical a vision disturbs so many of its viewers. As Wayne Booth has said of *The Voyeur*, with its ambiguous point of view and uncertain morality, "is this really what we go to literature for? . . . is there no limit to what we will praise, provided it is done with skill?"[3] Such judgments have been carried over by other critics (notably the English) to Robbe-Grillet's entire generation: to them, he is not merely the principal spokesman for the so-called New Novelists but also their representative figure. And so, by extension, they may all be considered enemies of humanism—although Robbe-Grillet has warned us that they are not a cohesive group and that even his own body of work is not as uniform as it may at first seem. Even if his novels do not survive, as I suspect, we must continue to read his critical words carefully and not leap to overly easy conclusions.

Robbe-Grillet's essays are filled—like Joyce's novels—with references to the literary tradition from which he evolves. Flaubert, Dostoevsky, Kafka, Mme. de La Fayette, Joyce, Proust, Faulkner, Svevo, Beckett, Camus, Sartre, and Borges are among those of whom he speaks knowingly and to whom we might find connections in his novels. His assault on "the novel of characters," on the act of "telling a story" and the relationship it presupposes between storyteller and reader ("their ready-made idea of reality"), on political "commitment" (known, "in the East . . . , with more naive colors, as 'Socialist realism' "), his defense of "formalism" as the necessary union of content and form, make of his essay "On Several Obsolete Notions" (1957) another "Mr. Bennett and Mrs. Brown." But the Second World War which Woolf so feared has of course intervened, and that aloof vision of art and life which Woolf was wrongfully accused of advocating, Robbe-Grillet adopts with assurance. So much have sensibility—and the world— changed. But even here he is not quite as single-minded as he may seem. He can perceive ambiguity and make use of paradox; he is even capable of humor. He knows that his critical theory and his fiction may at times be contradictory; he knows, in "A Future for the Novel" (1956), that narrative objectivity—"total impersonality of observation—is all too obviously an illusion" (p. 18); he rejects despair along with hope ("the world is neither significant nor absurd. It *is*, quite simply"—p. 19).

Yet he seems to suspect that the traditional humanist perspective is not so easily denied, that perhaps even his own novels might somehow affirm it. "The humanist outlook," he tells us, "is pre-eminently a pledge of solidarity" (p. 53), but in "The Use of Theory" (1955 and 1963) he advances his own allegedly a-humane thesis on grounds that seem suspiciously human-centered: "the systematic repetition of the forms of the past is not only absurd and futile, . . . it can even become harmful: by blinding us to our own real situation in the world today, it keeps us, ultimately, from constructing the world and man of tomorrow" (p. 9). Implicit in Robbe-Grillet's rejection of metaphor and humanism is the understanding that the Modernist novel, erected on an elaborate super-structure of metaphor, is inherently and necessarily humanistic: he need not even argue the case against Modernism's detractors. He advances Modernist technique in his novels—including the elaboration of potential metaphors that are, ultimately, devoid of meaning—as a means of denying the Modernist vision. But he seems to perceive that the paradox may not end here, that by denying the Modernists through the use of their own narrative tools, he may indeed be affirming their vision in the face of their mutual enemies. The ambiguity is apparent in the particular ancestor whom Robbe-Grillet has chosen for himself above all others, that idiosyncratic Modernist Franz Kafka.

Kafka, for Robbe-Grillet, serves as exemplar of the demanding and difficult "creative consciousness" at work, of the role played in artistic creation "by will, by rigor." He is also, along with Flaubert, a primary source of the "new realism," this "realistic style of an unknown genre" which Robbe-Grillet is endeavoring to bring to fruition in his essays and fictions ("The Use of Theory," pp. 11–14). Kafka's characters in their anonymity and apparent lack of a background demark the end of the "novel of characters," a mode which "belongs entirely to the past, it describes a period: that which marked the apogee of the individual" ("On Several Obsolete Notions," p. 28). His life and work thus provide a model of the changing nature and position of man in the modern world, framing concepts which are central to Existentialist thought. Through all this, Robbe-Grillet insists, Kafka remains essentially a realist: even in his diaries, "when the writer notes down what he has noticed during the day in the course of a walk, he retains merely fragments. . . . Partial objects detached from their use, moments immobilized, words separated from their context, or cross-conversations, whatever rings a little false, that lacks 'naturalness'—it is precisely this which rings truest to the novelist's ear" ("From Realism to Reality," 1955 and 1963, p. 163).

Yet Kafka has had the "misfortune" to be read as an allegorist. "This *realistic* author (in the new sense which we are trying to define: creator of a material world, of a visionary presence) is also the one who has been most charged with meanings—'profound' meanings—by his admirers and exegetes. He has quickly become, above all in the eyes of the public, the man who pretended to be speaking about things of this world, but with the sole purpose of revealing the problematic existence of a beyond" ("From Realism to Reality," p. 164). His is a realism in truth, we are told, without signification, beyond metaphor, freed of the demands of a human presence and its attendant history. "In the whole of Kafka's work, man's relations with the world, far from having a symbolic character, are constantly direct and immediate" ("From Realism to Reality," p. 165). In short, Robbe-Grillet finds in Kafka precisely that ancestor that his own work demands: the observance that he describes in its "naturalness" is his own; its meanings and lack of meanings are his as well.

Robbe-Grillet's Kafka is more conventional than he might realize, however. For all those who would make of Kafka an allegorist, there are as many readers for whom he is more truly a "visionary presence" heralding a new world; for those who contend that he must be read as a Juvenalian satirist of bureaucracy and the diminished modern condition or as an explorer of the uncharted depths of the troubled psyche or as an individual who reverts always to his own life in his work, there are those others for whom his work exists principally on the level of observed reality—so that the Castle is simply the dominant structure at Zurau, where he lived for a time with his favorite sister, Ottla, or perhaps the Hradschin of his native Prague, and not a metaphor of bureaucratic indifference, or "the heavily fortified garrison of a company of Gnostic demons,"[4] or "a symbol of woman and mother,"[5] or " 'The Castle of Despair.' "[6] What all such readings may have in common— what they may share with analogous readings of Joyce and Woolf (and Beckett and pre-Nobel Faulkner and sometimes Proust as well)—is their underlying conviction that Kafka (like most of the other Modernists) denies most of the time that presence and set of values that we commonly call humanistic. And so Gregor Samsa and Joseph K. and the Hunger Artist and the Country Doctor and all their fellows, ostensibly animal and allegedly human alike, are seen as unmistakable proof of Kafka's rejection—for whatever reasons, private or metaphysical—of the humanist tradition. Robbe-Grillet clearly has no difficulty at all with the results of such readings, however antagonistic he may be to their methods.

At the risk of compounding the issue further, I would posit a rather different Kafka and a different tradition against which to read and understand his work. For it seems evident to me that Kafka's protagonists are no more a manifestation of Modernist dehumanization than is Leopold Bloom. My Kafka is as much humorist as satirist (remembering Max Brod's story of Kafka's laughing "quite immoderately as he read aloud the first chapter of *The Trial*"[7]); a writer whose power arises precisely from the tension between matter-of-fact, naturalistic statement and extraordinary, almost surreal, potentially metaphysical event; not the sado-masochist that Robbe-Grillet's later fictions give evidence of, but a caring, concerned, strangely affirmative presence.

It is not the fact that his humans become animals that interests us, but that his animals function as if they were humans: animals or humans, they are never so debased by the difficult conditions of their lives that they are freed of responsibility for what they have made of their lives or deprived of the dignity that comes with responsibility. The quality of observations that seems so strained in Robbe-Grillet comes naturally to Kafka, for he is inevitably the outsider who has long since learned to see with intensity. His tradition, like Bloom's, is that of Middle European Jewry, on the fringes still of the ghetto (abolished only a generation earlier: we tend to forget that ghettos were created for Jews), only superficially integrated into the general society, anticipating the Holocaust. "In us all it still lives," says Kafka of the former ghetto of Prague, "the dark corners, the secret alleys, shuttered windows, squalid courtyards. . . . Our heart knows nothing of the slum clearance which has been achieved. The unhealthy old Jewish town within us is far more real than the new hygienic town around us. With our eyes open we walk through a dream: ourselves only a ghost of a vanished age."[8]

The extraordinary outpouring of creative energies which accompanied the granting of civil rights to Jews in mid-nineteenth-century Europe—a cultural explosion comparable to the results of the Crusades (whose principal victims were Jews)—is both a manifestation and a source of Modernism. It is no accident that Joyce made his hero a Jew (or that Proust and Kafka were Jews, or that Mann and Woolf were linked to them, or that Beckett has sometimes been mistaken for one, or that Kazantzakis and Borges have claimed to be Jewish) or that Jews have become subjects for much of the best Modernist fiction. In a world from which humane values appear to have fled, the Jews have provided for Modernist novelists an alternate tradition: with a sense of continuity of its own, an inbred awareness of the extremes of the human condition, a long history of belonging and alienation, an ethic in which the individual is valued both as a member of the community and as an individual, a profound conviction of human responsibility and worth. It is a history and ethic not simply human-centered but human-revealing, far older than Renaissance Humanism or its Classical sources, inherently humanistic however we define that term.[9] And it is in this context, I believe, and not in the tenuous frames provided by Robbe-Grillet and the exegetes whom he abhors, that we must read and appreciate Kafka. Such a context makes even firmer Kafka's position among the Modernists and the disjunction between them and Robbe-Grillet: it is not only

Balzac and the Realists against whom Robbe-Grillet rebels; his principal enemies are the affirming Joyce and his humanist fellows and even that Kafka whom Robbe-Grillet singles out as an ancestor.

There are parallels between Robbe-Grillet's world and Kafka's, to be sure, even what are probably conscious borrowings; but they are similarities more of surface than of substance. Thus, K. of *The Castle* may be said to serve as a model for the actions of Robbe-Grillet's protagonists. His alleged occupation of land-surveyor predicts the ostensibly scientific preoccupations of the doctor of *In the Labyrinth,* the plantation owner of *La Jalousie,* the watch salesman of *The Voyeur,* and his contrasting inner confusion anticipates theirs. K. continues to believe unyieldingly in himself and his ordained role despite the contradictions in his account (he arrives without his instruments or proof that he has been engaged as a surveyor, even that he is a surveyor), just as the jealous husband of *La Jalousie* refuses to envision the scene of his wife's evident murder, and the suitor of *Last Year at Marienbad* insists on envisioning a scene of seduction which may never have taken place— their need to believe is so strong that it imposes itself on whatever may have been actuality. K.'s single-minded point of view prepares us for the naturalistic detail and psychotic assurance of Robbe-Grillet's viewers; yet fact and vision become so confused for K. that it is even possible for him to believe at one point that " 'the appearance does really correspond to the reality,' "[10] as for Mathias of *The Voyeur* a recently veneered door "imitated the veins and irregularities of wood to a fault. Judging from the sound of his knock, there could be no doubt that under this deceptive layer the door was really a wooden one" (p. 26).[11] Even the blurring of appearance and reality becomes blurred for them. K. seeks compulsively for entry into the Castle but passes over those possibilities which are opened to him; and Robbe-Grillet's characters erect layers of seeming metaphor which lead to no possible conclusions.

Beneath these similar appearances, however, there are fundamental distinctions between the meanings and values of Robbe-Grillet's world and those inherent in Kafka's. For Robbe-Grillet's people, there is no reality beyond this tangible and evocative, if misleading, world and no responsibility (as if they were Naturalistic heroes) for their actions within it. As things—the most imprecise and impersonal word in the language—they can, of course, bear neither responsibility nor the human dignity which flows from it. But Kafka's characters, charged by the very different milieu from which they emerge, are made to seem responsible (not guilty, but responsible) for their vision, their obsessiveness, their acts. Although none of them is identified as a Jew—the word "Jew" appears nowhere in these fictions—although each of them appears to exist outside time and in no particular place, we recognize in each of Kafka's characters the presence of his background: the Jewish experience in history is made to serve here as the modern experience. Whatever the specific facts of their lives may be, whether animal or human, these characters of Kafka carry with them the dreamlike memory of the ghetto of Prague: uncertain, equivocal, neither quite part of nor fully removed from the larger society, but informed still by abiding values and standards. They are all unmistakably human, and as they emerge from this long and difficult, Jewish tradition, they make a powerful statement of the surviving humanist potential in the most difficult of our lives. For Robbe-Grillet's characters there is no memory; there are no standards; there can be no potential and no humanity. It is not just Joyce's affirmation that Robbe-Grillet assaults, but his ancestor Kafka's as well. This is evident in each of his novels.

The Voyeur (1955), for example, is the story of a man who rapes and kills a thirteen-year-old girl, or who sees someone rape and kill her, or who thinks he has committed the crime, or who thinks he has seen someone else do so. It is possible, moreover, that his account of the crime is prospective rather than retrospective, that the ferryboat on which he is traveling at the end of the narrative is taking him to and not away from the island on which the rape and murder ostensibly take place, so that they exist as yet only in his mind and not in some objective reality. And although the victim is given a name, Jacqueline Leduc, she is confused in his account with other potential victims: a girl on the ferry, a bargirl, a girl glimpsed in a window on the way to the ferry that morning, a girl whose "tragic fate" is depicted in a newspaper clipping which he carries for some reason in his wallet (p. 61), even a dressmaker's dummy ("smaller than normal"—p. 57) of a girl. There are more than a dozen of these potential victims, all of them viewed with the same intensity, the same strange mix of close observation and wild imagination, all interchangeable. We can never learn definitively who the victim is and who the culprit, or whether the crime has even taken place; we know only that Mathias, the viewer, who never indicates his own last name, is capable of such an act, that he is a psychopath with a fetish for the nape of a woman's neck, and that any victim of his on this day must be a young girl, for on the island where the crime may have taken place, mature women wear high-necked dresses. Because we are limited to Mathias's point of view, however, because he is so disturbed that he cannot be certain who his victim is, or whether he has yet (or again) committed the crime, or whether he has merely witnessed (or imagined) it, we too cannot be certain. This is the ambiguous moral situation which Wayne Booth so deplores.

It is essentially this same situation that we find in Robbe-Grillet's other early novels: in *The Erasers* (1953), his first work, a detective sorts through a pattern of clues related to the Oedipus myth, unravels the crime he has been sent to investigate, and then turns out himself to be the murderer, perhaps of his own father; in *La Jalousie* (1957), a jealous husband appears to have killed his (probably innocent) wife, whose death he refuses to visualize, turning instead in his mind to the images and events of the day preceding her death (including vivid if unsorted memories of still earlier days), awaiting her return and perhaps her murder; in *In the Labyrinth* (1959), a wounded soldier, in his delirium, identifies with a soldier in a painting on the wall of his doctor's office and takes up a role in the painting, a role assumed after his death by the doctor, who is presumably not wounded and feverish. The same basic pattern prevails in *Last Year at Marienbad* (1961), the film which Robbe-Grillet wrote for Alain Resnais, and in *L'Immortelle* (1963), which he directed himself. None of his early protagonists is able to distinguish between what appears to be fact and what passes for imagination or memory. Each is an acute if limited observer of the things that he finds around him, yet each is uncertain of their meanings (if any) and of his own place among them. And each is the sole viewer of this world of things, so that the reader too is limited inevitably to what he can show us and interpret for us—or induce us to interpret for him.

The literalist Mathias would seem at first glance, like his compatriots, the ideal observer of a Realistic narrative. He turns inward all the observations of his voyeurism, as might a Modernist observer, but he expresses them in strictly objective terms. There is no internal mono-logue to denote the surface of his mind, no stream of consciousness suggesting the flow of his thoughts, no sense at all of a sensibility at work: only the recorded images of his sense perceptions, memories, and imaginings—recorded as it were on a surface innocent of personality or past—totally undifferentiated. And yet we understand that this seeming-ly objective presentation is, in fact, the subjective state of his mind. We are left—induced is perhaps more accurate—like good Modernist readers, to interpret what Mathias cannot, to read not so much the concrete images themselves as the consciousness and worldview hidden behind them.

Thus, when Mathias sees things not merely scientifically—that is, concretely and with seeming dispassion—but as a mathematician might, even as a geometrician, we conclude that this is all part of his effort to force order on the disorderly world surrounding him. But, of course, nothing is in order for him. Although he calculates carefully all the events of his stay on the island—the time of day (he is a watch salesman, but he is always late), the proceeds from his sales, the ratio of visits to successful sales ("he must omit nothing, leave nothing to chance, if he wanted to sell eighty-nine wrist watches to slightly less than two thousand people"—p. 22), the precise number of minutes he can devote to each sale (four) if he is to reach his self-imposed quota and meet the last ferry back to the mainland—although he pays careful attention to these details, he misses the ferry and loses sight of his sales. And although he views all objects as geometrical constructs—a landing slip appears to him as a rectangle cut into two triangles by a shadow (p. 7), a shadow on the street as "two horizontal planes in sunlight alternating with two vertical planes in shadow" (p. 59), a milestone on the road as a complex of rectangles, squares, half-cylinders, and half-circles (p. 163), even the humans he encounters are likely to be viewed geometrically—the mastery over reality that such constructs promise is not his after all. They serve momentarily to mask his confusion but thereafter to heighten it. He wants so desperately to order his reality that he inevitably distorts it still further.

There is even a certain sense in which he acts as a symbolist in his attempt at ordering and controlling his life; at least he provides the data for patterns we may be tempted to view as symbolic. For it cannot be simply coincidence that leads him to see everywhere around him the vertical figure eight, the mathematical sign of infinity. He finds this sign in a piece of rope (p. 4), in the irregularities of a wooden door (p. 26), in some iron rings on the quay (p. 112), in the claws of a crab (p. 118) and the eyes of a boy (p. 183), even in the spiraling smoke of a cigarette (p. 152). But no meaning is attached to this pattern. We may be tempted to wonder, when Mathias does, "if they used handcuffs on the island, and how long the chain linking the two rings would be" (p. 195) and to ask if this can be the sole end of this intricate pattern: as a clue in a mystery, hinting to others of the culpability of one who is not certain himself of his role in a crime? Or does it lead somewhere toward infinity? Of course, we cannot be certain; we cannot even conjecture with confidence. We can know no more than Mathias, and he is a prisoner already of his consciousness.

In a technique borrowed from filmmaking, whenever life seems particularly threatening Mathias is likely to view others (a scene in a barroom—p. 45, the interior of an island home—p. 80, the passengers on the ferry and those waiting on the quay—pp. 3, 5, 137) within a "frozen" frame, "as though unexpectedly recorded on a photographic plate" (p. 30), and he is likely at such times to adopt for himself what might be called a frozen attitude: motionless, silent, unfeeling, only his disturbing consciousness continually at work. For all the objectivity of its language and line of vision, his point of view is ultimately highly subjective, an obvious, outward manifestation of a distorting inward state.[12] It is a state, Robbe-Grillet tells us throughout his early work, that is characteristic of the post-Modernist human condition.

The quasi-scientific perspective from which each of these protagonists views life, the geometrical patterns in which he places everything that he sees around him, the images that threaten to turn into metaphors for him but never quite do so, the frozen attitudes which he naturally assumes as the things around him grow difficult to manage—as if he, too, had become lifeless, like one of them—simultaneously establish the appearance of an objective reality and undercut it. Limited as we are to the point of view of the convinced, compelled, disturbed protagonist, who views other people (and himself) as he views his things, we recognize that there is no certain truth for him after all and that for us there may be no objective reality. Robbe-Grillet thus willfully accomplishes what Woolf and Joyce were wrongfully accused of: he destroys the conviction of realism that lies at the heart of the Realistic novel. In the process, he denies the humanist worldview which persists throughout the Modernist novel. And he does so, self-consciously, by a heightening of certain of the narrative techniques perfected by the Modernists themselves. With certain changes only, it is a pattern which continues in his later work as well.

These later novels of Robbe-Grillet's assume our knowledge of his earlier work. *La Maison de Rendez-vous* (1965), *Project for a Revolution in New York* (1970) and *Topology of a Phantom City* (1976) are filled with echoes and images derived from *The Voyeur, La Jalousie, In the Labyrinth,* and *Last Year at Marienbad:* the frozen attitudes, the confusion of realities, the action which continues beyond its logical conclusion, the point of view whose intense observation only weakens our confidence in its reliability, the strong hint of sexual violence. The dressmaker's dummy of *The Voyeur* appears again in *Topology,* as do the theatrical performance within the performance of *Marienbad,* the bloodstain on the floor of *La Jalousie,* and the confused military mission of *In the Labyrinth;* there is even an explicit reference here to *The Erasers,* "the first novel I published."[13] These later novels are also mystery stories whose search for reality and the truth are more likely to create than to solve mysteries. This, of course, is their point: in a world in which meaning is so distant and reality so uncertain, the detective's search for truth seems the perfect metaphor—and his failure to find it the ultimate truth.[14] The recurrent images and techniques of these novels provide the sole stable reality (in their very instability) of Robbe-Grillet's world. The human-focused world of the Modernists has been shuttered; this objectified, thing-ridden, arid universe of Robbe-Grillet's is now the setting for whatever human events may remain and the norm against which they are now to be judged.

Certain human possibilities do remain in *La Maison de Rendez-vous.* One reasonable solution to the mystery of its narrative is that it is simply a fabrication, built on the details of a dying old lady's dwindling life, a game created by the narrator to brighten her final days. That it entraps the narrator himself—that he goes on with his tale (of exoticism and intrigue in Hong Kong) even after her death (probably in a home for the aged that is not in the Orient)—may be a sign not only of the same narrative compulsion that drives the doctor of *In the Labyrinth* after the death of his patient, but also of human concern and involvement. Robbe-Grillet has by now made it impossible for us to accept such easy, human-centered conclusions—indeed, to reach any conclusions at all in his narratives; but the narrator's compulsiveness does suggest his genuine emotion at Lady Ava's death, and we may feel with him something of his loss. At the other, more familiar extreme of Robbe-Grillet's canon is *Project for a Revolution in New York,* a cold, consistent, obsessive narrative whose only games are sexual and political, the sort of Sadean pseudo-metaphysics that only the French can take seriously and that to others may seem more suitable to pornography (of the sadomasochistic, non-erotic sort) than to literature or life. The only human awareness here is the awareness of dehumanization. Such a work may make us suspect, for a moment, that Wayne Booth might not be so wrong after all.

There is a scene in Virginia Woolf's *The Years* (1937) that almost seems the *donnée* for a Robbe-Grillet narrative, perhaps for *La Jalousie*. A woman is looking out through a window at the vineyards around her, removed from the life outside, her activity directed inward: "Maggie, standing at the window, looked down on the courtyard, and saw her husband's book cracked across with shadow from the vine above; and the glass that stood beside him glowed yellow. Cries of peasants working came through the open window." The jealous husband of *La Jalousie* peers through a window at his wife as she reads a book, crossed by shadows, with unheard peasants at work in the background. He is removed from her, from the workers, from all life outside him. But the sun beats down on these fields of Woolf's in the South of France, connects them to fields and moors in England and to man-made images, the buildings of London, the trains which reach out from London through all the country: "Off the trains swung through the public gardens with asphalt paths; past the factories; into open country. Men standing on bridges fishing looked up; horses cantered; women came to doors and shaded their eyes; the shadow of the smoke floated over the corn, looped down and caught a tree. And on they passed."[15] The scene is set in 1911, at the height of the peace, before the outbreak of the war, and it connects to a similar scene set in 1937, at a similar moment in time. The world will soon erupt into darkness, and Woolf herself will not be present to see it. Her protagonists are similarly always set apart at pivotal moments from the life around them, and life always passes on. But none of them is ever removed from life, dispassionate about it, or untouched by it. All are connected, as in this scene in *The Years* (as in a similar scene in Wordsworth's sonnet on "Westminster Bridge"), to nature, to other human beings, to other times. They affirm life's glories even as they testify to its pains. Apart as they may stand at times, they speak always to human connections.

Leopold Bloom, too, this alien in the city of his birth, this telling symbol of our own alienation, affirms life in everything he does; even as he witnesses betrayal and remembers death, even as he acknowledges his isolation in space and in time, even as he testifies to the lessening expectations of our age, Bloom reminds us in his dignity and heroism of the worth of human life. Set himself in the long line of an ancient tradition (although also outside it), he establishes a new one for his descendants in fiction and for us as well. Even Kafka's ambiguous heroes, self-isolates, self-victimized, affirm the value of their lives—and ours—when they accept responsibility for their acts.

Robbe-Grillet is right, of course, when he speaks of humanism as "pre-eminently a pledge of solidarity." It is such a pledge that these Modernist novelists make in their art. In assaulting their values so vigorously, Robbe-Grillet paradoxically—as he recognizes—seems himself to affirm their potency and perhaps also their continued survival.

III

The novelist Michel Butor is as much essayist as novelist, an eminent and early New Novelist who in recent years has seemingly abandoned the novel form and written instead unconventional travel books, highly personal literary biographies and critical studies, radio scripts and open-ended opera libretti and poems. Yet all of his works are infused with the spirit and technique of the novelist, and all of his novels are, in a sense, imaginative essays: there is a wonderful consistency in Butor's changing and developing career. That he has stopped writing recognizable novels, however, and that the novels he has written show evident ties to the Modernist novel are signs, I believe, of the state of the novel—and of Modernism—in contemporary France. Butor's career is testimony both to the endurance of Modernism in post-Joycean France and to its current metamorphosis.

One of Butor's earliest essays, written some six years before the publication of his first novel, written evidently when he should have been preparing for his Agrégation examination (which he duly failed), is modestly entitled "Petite croisière préliminaire a une reconnaisance de l'archipel Joyce" (1948). It is an essay more descriptive than evaluative, an appreciation of the master by a perhaps-not-yet-aspiring young novelist rather than a major critical assessment, but it is significant both because it comes relatively early in the French criticism of Joyce and because of what it tells us about Butor. For his Joyce is truly—as he names him—an archipelago, embracing in his sea many tributary islands, among them *Passing Time (L'Emploi du temps), A Change of Heart (La Modification),* and *Degrees (Degrès).* When the young Butor speaks of the revolutionary narrative techniques at work in *A Portrait, Ulysses,* and *Finnegans Wake,* of their organizing patterns of imagery and metaphor and myth, of their recurrent theme of the search (often futile) for meaningful connections among humans, he is anticipating the central concerns of his own future fictions. A second essay on Joyce, "Esquisse d'un seuil pour Finnegan" (1957), written a decade later by the mature novelist, predicts the new Joycean route that he will follow beginning with *Mobile* in 1962; it represents a transition comparable to that which Joyce made between *Ulysses* and *Finnegans Wake*, the first movement beyond literary Modernism to forms that might be considered post-Modernist.

Ulysses is a work of evident order and control, more closely linked to its antecedents in the history of the novel than its early readers could possibly realize. With the sixty years of hindsight available to us, however, we can see for ourselves that what seemed so radical in 1922 is, in many ways, surprisingly traditional. It is not simply that Joyce points to his predecessors in his text; much of the narrative technique of *Ulysses*, its organic structure of metaphor and myth, the development of its characterization and plot and theme is derived from Joyce's forebears, most notable among them Sterne's *Tristram Shandy* (paid homage to throughout Joyce's canon) and the later novels of Conrad (who is nowhere mentioned but who is the precursor of all the Modernists) and including, among many others, Rabelais, Cervantes, Defoe, Richardson, Fielding, Swift, Dickens, Dostoevsky, Flaubert, Lewis Carroll, Meredith, and James. Joyce's genius in *Ulysses* is to build on these disparate sources from the past and to create from them a new entity fit to a radically new era. The fit is so close that to many of his contemporaries it seemed that he had created the era. His is the task reserved not simply in the history of the novel but throughout human history (and probably prehistory as well) to the true creative spirit: to consolidate our experience from the past and to make possible—to make inevitable—our great leap forward into the future. The primary accomplishment of *Ulysses* is that it maintains past values so well as it shapes the new sensibility—that it affirms so powerfully the humanity of Bloom (and therefore of his readers) while leaping forward in narrative technique: that it utilizes technique as a means of affirming humanity.

Finnegans Wake clearly grows out of *Ulysses*, yet it is a work of a different order and a different reality. Some four decades after its publication in 1939, there remain about it many unresolved questions; we are just beginning to learn some of the questions to ask. But we have understood from the start that Joyce, having made one great leap forward in *Ulysses*, makes a second, perhaps greater one in the *Wake*. The new sensibility of the post-war era is first defined in this novel which appeared on the eve of the war. Reading the "Circe" episode of

Ulysses, however, with its nonlinear narrative form (looking like a play but clearly not a play, or at least a different kind of play), with its outer reality and internal logic derived from dreams and the preconscious, with its conjoined psyches and mythos and times and its suggestion of an identity beyond the individual, we can discover the roots of *Finnegans Wake:* the new sensibility is perhaps not so radically new after all. If indeed there is a coherent post-Modernist sensibility, it is Joyce, eponym for the Modernists, who in his last work is its first exponent. In its heroic effort to create an integral and recognizable universal human experience, its encyclopedic knowledge and sense of history, its new language designed to dramatize images and events never before put into words, its conviction that language and psyche and history and myth are ultimately one, *Finnegans Wake* builds on *Ulysses* as *Ulysses* built on its tradition. *Finnegans Wake,* says Butor, "is a dream about language," "a common dream," and "so for each one of us it's an instrument of inward understanding, because the portrait of myself that I discern there is not the one that I would have drawn before reading it."[16]

In moving from the traditional Modernist forms of his early novels—marked by narrative and metaphoric constructions suited to a world in which certainty is constantly sought for but little can ever be known for certain—to the nonlinear, other-orderly realm of those later works that can no longer be simply called novels, in moving away from the evident influence of the Ulyssean Joyce, Butor continues to manifest the master's presence. The forms of Butor's work, like Joyce's, have developed continually, but his major thematic concerns—like Joyce's again—remain essentially unchanged. He is consistently involved with the problem of our finding our way and knowing ourselves in a threatening, ambiguous world, with the problem of developing narrative forms appropriate to such a search, with the overriding problem of defining and comprehending our humanity, and he works throughout his changing canon under the aura of Joyce. Butor responds to Joyce, as he once told an international audience of Joyce scholars and enthusiasts, "not as an author of earlier times but, if I dare say it, as an author of today and even of tomorrow."[17]

The protagonists of Butor's early novels, who strive like Bloom to maintain their presence and dignity in an uncaring world, inherit only part of his Modernist legacy. Possessors of a vision intense but limited, they seek after certainty but are consigned, at best, to ambiguity; constructors of elaborate patterns of imagery and metaphor that briefly give promise of meaning where there seems to be none, they create instead intensified confusion; inveterate mythmakers, they possess no real ties to the past or to future human endeavors or values. Put like this, then, they seem little different from Robbe-Grillet's characters. Yet like Bloom they do reach affirmatively beyond themselves toward some potential universal, humanistic meaning. The intensity of their search, however—perhaps the very fact of their search—makes inevitable their failure. They are unmistakably Blooms's heirs, but they lack his balance and his roots (where Robbe-Grillet's characters lack his humanity). Their post-war world is also more dangerous than his, and their failure more threatening.

For Jacques Revel, the French clerk who labors in the English industrial city of Bleston in *Passing Time* (1956), the searches after meaning and the failures to find meaning are interconnected and many: Who is it, he wonders, who has attempted to murder his friend George Burton, the well-known writer of mystery stories? Is he related in some way to the arsonist setting the fires that besiege the city? What clues to his identity—or to his motives—are to be found in *The Bleston Murder*, Burton's mystery, or in the film about the burning of Rome (looking strangely like Athens or Knossos) that is shown at the Royal Cinema, or in the Theseus Tapestries at the Museum of Fine Arts, or in the so-called Murderer's Window (with Cain dressed as Theseus) in the Old Cathedral? Alone and uneasy in this alien city, Revel works desperately to construct a pattern of meaning and purpose that will provide some certainty, however burdensome it may be, however artificial, in this strange and rootless new life of his. What emerges from his labors is a labyrinth, recalling that of Theseus, "the labyrinth of my days in Bleston, incomparably more bewildering than that of the Cretan palace, since it grows and alters while I explore it" (p. 195).[18] It is a labyrinth not of outward events, we suspect, but of his own construction, as he plays unwittingly on the ironic possibilities of his name, abandons his friends and his chance for normal life, and immerses himself, more and more deeply, more and more compulsively, in the journal designed to solve the mysteries and resolve the problems of his own identity. His narrative method reveals nothing new, merely deepens his confusion, makes certain his alienation.

Beginning his journal several months after his arrival in Bleston and thus after the events it describes—in May he writes of the previous October, in June of November, in July of December—Revel tries desperately to bring his account up to date before his year in the city has ended. But he cannot ignore contemporary events and includes them in his journal as well: and so in June he writes also of June, and in July of July. Although Revel carefully dates both entries and events and is acutely conscious of the time which has elapsed between action and reporting, he is not always certain of his dates and cannot always distinguish between present and past, or between events in his narrative (subsuming that other narrative, *The Bleston Murder*) and events in his life. Moreover, in July he begins to re-read his earlier entries and often to re-interpret them in the light of more recent events or more recent entries. Past and present and distant past and the past revisited thus merge in his consciousness, distort further his reality, deflect him from the identity he so anxiously seeks. At the height of his uncertainty, his year in Bleston suddenly concluded, he as suddenly abandons his journal and search and returns to his native France to resume his familiar, unthreatening, non-narrated life, this past year testimony to the dangers of travel and narration alike.

For Léon Delmont, the creating consciousness of *A Change of Heart* (1957), the journey is both shorter and potentially more lasting in its effects. On his overnight train trip from Paris, the city in which his home, family and business are located, to Rome, city of "radiance" and "mythos" (p. 243),[19] he undergoes in his mind a journey of passage and writes there a chronicle of its symbolic events. This is the first draft of a novel that he may or may not afterwards complete; its subject is his putative transformation, its imagery and myth drawn from the journey's (largely inward) events. Traveling in a third-class compartment because he has decided impulsively to make this trip, traveling just two days after his forty-fifth birthday, traveling in order to bring his mistress back to Paris with him, tired and discomfited in these unfamiliar surroundings, in his excitement and agitation at the prospect of a changed lifestyle in middle age, Delmont creates an imaginary new life from among the sourcebooks of the old. In the timetable which he periodically opens and closes and briefly scans,[20] in the *Guide Bleu* to Rome which he remembers from an earlier trip (his honeymoon, in fact), in his fellow passengers and their imagined lives, in the unopened novel which he holds on his lap and its imagined hero ("this book which you bought so that it might distract you and which you haven't read precisely because during this journey you wanted, just for once, to be wholly involved in your action"—p. 169), in these, Delmont finds images of himself and the roots of the narrative of his own condition. And in a figure from French mythology, the Grand Veneur, Master of the Hounds of the Forest of Fontainebleau, whom he sees from his window riding alongside the train, he sees both himself and his inquisitor: "and you even fancied you could catch that famous wailing cry, *'M'entendez-vous? Do you hear me?'* " (p. 95). "Qui êtes-vous? Who are you?" (p. 181). Delmont knows none of the answers. But at least on this journey he has begun to learn some of the questions that he must ask: of Rome, of his mistress, of himself.

"Standing with your left foot on the grooved brass sill, you try in vain with your right shoulder to push the sliding door a little wider open" (p. 1). From his opening sentence as he enters the compartment in the Gare de Lyon, Delmont refers to himself as "you," implying a sense of detachment, an ability to stand apart from himself and judge himself objectively. Under the pressures of his difficult journey, however—anxious, fatigued, increasingly confused, and unable to separate dream from wakefulness, imagination and memory from present events, or characters in myth from his own life—his detachment and objectivity break down. He continues to think of himself in the second person in his narrative, but it is the most subjective "you" in modern fiction. As he leaves the train in the Stazione Termini, he is certain only of his plan for his book: "This book should show the part Rome can play in the life of a man in Paris; the two cities might be imagined one above the other . . . with communicating trap doors which only a few would know, while surely nobody could know them all, so that to go from one place to another there might be certain short cuts or unexpected detours, so that the distance from one point to another would vary according to one's knowledge, the degree of one's familiarity with that other city, so that every man's consciousness of place would be twofold, and Rome would distort Paris to a greater or less degree for each individual, suggesting authentic or misleading parallels" (pp. 243–4). In Rome, Delmont may or may not see Cécile, his mistress; he may tell her the truth about his journey but will probably think of some lie; his life may well change but may also go on as before. And he may never write the final draft of this novel of his. His hard-earned journey and narrative have brought him that possibility of self-realization that Jacques Revel so desperately seeks for himself. But there is no certainty that Delmont will be able to achieve what his predecessor has missed. In daylight, rested and shaved, his clothing changed, his hunger satisfied, his spirits renewed, he may forget all that he has learned of himself, ignore his still-to-be-written book, continue to travel unknowingly.

For Pierre Vernier, instructor in history and geography at the Lycée Taine, self-discovery entails not a physical journey but a symbolic lecture on the discovery and conquest of America. His book is *Degrees* (1960), the meticulously compiled chronicle of his class. He abandons his task long before its completion; his research is so consuming that it destroys his life. He has built into it, however, a kind of continuity, so that it proceeds beyond the limits of his strength, beyond even his lifetime perhaps, into the next generation.

"I began writing up these notes about our class, which are meant for you, Pierre, though not as you are today . . . which are meant for you when you will finally be able to read them, for that Pierre Eller who will apparently have forgotten all about this October 12, 1954, the events which occurred on it, the knowledge that we attempted to give you on it" (p. 46).[21] Pierre Eller, the "you" of the narrative, is Vernier's nephew, the second son of his sister and a member of his eleventh-grade class. This is one of the degrees of his title, one of the seemingly coincidental relations in the class and school that have led Vernier to undertake his project. There are many others: Pierre Eller's paternal uncle, Henri Jouret, teaches Greek and French literature at the lycée; his friend Alain Mouron is the nephew of the English teacher, Monsieur Bailly, and the cousin of Michel Daval, who is also in the eleventh grade; another classmate is Denis Regnier—who should have been a senior this year—the nephew of both Monsieur Hubert, the physics and chemistry instructor, and Monsieur Bonnini, who teaches Italian. Sometimes, however, apparent relations prove illusory: Jean-Claude Fage is not the brother of Henri Fage, not even his cousin; Jean-Claude's brother, Bertrand, is in the same senior class as Denis Eller, Pierre's older brother. Where no relations are visible, Vernier seeks them out; he is even willing to help construct them himself, usually in triads: "Monsieur Hutter, the German teacher, is at the other end of the floor, with his tenth-graders. I now know his degree of relationship with his homonym, Francis Hutter, in the first row in front of me, besides Alain Mouron, in front of Michel Daval. One must go back rather far; Frederic Hutter, grandfather of Monsieur Alfred Hutter, had a first cousin, Émile Hutter, great-grandfather of Francis. They had never seen each other before meeting in class" (p. 29). Through Vernier they learn of their kinship. With them, arbitrarily, he links the student Jean-Pierre Cormier, although, he admits, the connection "remains vague and is perhaps even illusory" (p. 54).

Vernier's chronicle attempts to reveal every interrelationship in the school, to cover the entire school year from the perspective of Tuesday, October 12, Pierre Eller's fifteenth birthday. His method, at first, seems omniscient: he reflects not only the events in his classroom, but also those on the other side of the blackboard, in Henri Jouret's Greek literature section—their major work for the term is *The Odyssey*—as well as those down the hall: at 2:00 p.m. on this Tuesday, at the precise moment that Vernier begins his lecture on Columbus's discovery of America, Monsieur Hutter is reading *Egmont* to his seniors, Monsieur Hubert attempting to explain vectors and initial forces, and Monsieur Martin (he is new to the Lycée Taine, and Vernier sometimes forgets his name) teaching his ninth-graders how to draw. The historian knows also what his students do after school—in Alain Mouron's apartment, the members of the Chamois patrol are planning their scouting activities for the new season—and he follows closely the personal lives of his colleagues—Monsieur Bonnini is deeply concerned about his wife's poor health; Monsieur Bailly fears that his wife will leave him for a younger, more successful teacher from Orleans; Monsieur Hubert's wife is about to give birth to their first child. Not merely omniscience, a kind of simultaneity suggests the chronicler's guidance of events as well as his total knowledge of them. But Vernier is no god manipulating his creations; he is merely a conscientious plodder who seeks out every available source of information, an historian who endeavors to reconstruct in full a moment of history, a symbolist who recognizes in that moment a personal allegory akin to the discovery of the New World. His apparent omniscience is merely a function of his familiarity with the routine of the school day, with the curricula and methods of his colleagues and with the reactions of his pupils. He goes further by consulting the class lists of Monsieur Bonnini, asking Monsieur Bailly for information about his nephews, reading all the other assignments of his students, consulting his own nephew. Despite his conscientious research, however, he cannot possibly unearth all the relevant details.

Some of his colleagues are beyond the reach of his study. He cannot, for example, penetrate Monsieur Tavera's Spanish class: "though I can read English and Italian, though I know a few words of German, I don't know any Spanish, and consequently it's very difficult for me to reconstruct the way it's taught" (p. 55). And as for Monsieur Moret, the gym teacher, "I know in advance that I have too few sources of information concerning him ever to manage to find out exactly where he is during this second hour of the afternoon, on Tuesday, October 12" (p. 79). Almost from the start, the historian recognizes the impossibility of his task. He wishes to be a neutral observer, perfectly aloof and objective: his notes, he hopes, "will be a literal description, without any intervention on the part of my imagination, a simple account of precise facts." The job of the historian is also to interpret facts and, at times, to reconstruct them imaginatively: literal description alone "wouldn't have permitted me to give an adequate representation, for . . . it is necessary to imagine a quantity of other events impossible to verify" (p. 46). His task is so demanding, the dual pressures of research and interpretation such a "terrible, oppressive burden" (p. 88), that the shape of Vernier's life is distorted. His teaching suffers because he has no time for preparations; his students come to distrust him because of his apparent favoritism toward Pierre; his private life virtually ceases. Even so, he cannot fulfill his plan; to be the complete historian, "I would have to write down everything . . . and I cannot even write down everything I know I might need for this narrative" (p. 104).

On Tuesday evening after class, in the apartment which he shares with Pierre's parents, Vernier has shown his nephew the first pages of his study and enlisted his aid. In the second part of his narrative, Vernier has become the "you" and Pierre the ostensible speaker. Yet neither suspected at the time of their agreement "that you were going to introduce me into it in this new manner, making use of me as a narrator, and this by making not the Pierre Eller who I was on that day, who certainly wouldn't have been able to express himself in this way, but the Pierre Eller who I might be in a few years, do the writing" (p. 132). The historian has been so devoured by his task that he has had to alter dramatically its perspective.

On that Tuesday of Pierre's birthday, Vernier takes his nephew to dinner, allows him for the first time to order for himself, buys him a beer and even a cigarette. Through his chronicle he hopes to help bring him to maturity, "to help you realize what you yourself have been, in other words, where you come from, in other words where you are going" (p. 104). He recognizes that his lecture on the discovery and conquest of America can serve as a metaphor of the knowledge and mastery of the self, but he directs his reading only to Pierre; he does not seem to recognize that it can apply as well to himself, that he may need the lesson more than his young student. He is willing to "make a great imaginative effort of reconstruction, . . . put myself in your place, try to see myself through your eyes and consequently let you speak, thereby destroying the equilibrium of the narrative" (p. 104). But he is not willing to look directly at himself, to risk his own equilibrium. And so his project will fail.

Pierre as (alleged) speaker concentrates on the activities of his class-mates and introduces sources of information unknown to his uncle. He follows carefully the latter's deterioration as a result of their project, "that demon which was gaining more and more control over you as the written pages accumulated on your desk" (p. 218). He records as well the effects of his new role on his own relations with his peers: his inquisitiveness, his secrecy, and the seeming favoritism of his uncle have led his friends and brothers to distrust him and to draw away. Thus he breaks with Vernier. It is soon after "that terrible conversation" whose details neither speaker will reveal (p. 327) that Vernier suffers a break-down. He leaves his sister's apartment to recuperate at the home of Henri Jouret, returns to work, and has a relapse. He is in the hospital now, watched over by his friend Micheline Pavin, who had encouraged him to begin his project and who has left her job to act as his nurse. But his task continues. In Part III of the narrative, the voice is that of Henri Jouret, also speaking to his nephew Pierre. "Your Uncle Pierre will not write any more. . . . I am writing; I am taking up where he left off; I shall shore up this ruin a little" (p. 330).

Monsieur Bonnini's wife has died; Monsieur Bailly's wife has sued for divorce; Madame Hubert has given birth to a son; Pierre Eller, who has resigned from the Chamois patrol, will not invite his Uncle Pierre to his sixteenth birthday party. It is October 1955, and Henri Jouret has begun to read all of his students' other assignments and to be late with some of his own. For the first time, from the teacher of Greek literature, we hear the details of the historian's lecture on America, delivered that fateful Tuesday to his eleventh-grade class, cornerstone of his unfinished guide to maturity. He had spoken that day not only of the discoverer Columbus and the conquerors Cortez and Pizarro but also of Marco Polo and of Montaigne's essay "On Coaches," which begins, "Our world hath of late discovered another (and who can warrant us whether it be the last of his brethren . . .)" (p. 286).

Just as the obscure manuscript of Marco Polo, rejected by his contemporaries, is said to have come into the hands of Columbus (p. 350), so Vernier's work has at last found its true believer. "Your Uncle Pierre will not write any more. How long will it be before you read the ruin of his book?" (p. 346). "Your Uncle Pierre will not write any more; I am the one who will tell you that this text is for you, and it is Micheline Pavin to whom I shall entrust it" (p. 351). Along with Vernier—and perhaps some day Micheline Pavin as well—like their predecessors Jacques Revel and Léon Delmont, Jouret in his narration will point the way for others to that self-realization which he himself will never attain. None of the protagonists of Butor's novels achieves the maturity, the sense of self-worth, the conviction of mastery of self and surroundings that he so fervently seeks; each becomes a victim of the narrative method—increasingly elaborate and seductive, increasingly misleading—that he devises in order to orient himself within alien realms. In the end, all places for them are alien, especially those of their own devising. Together, they offer a vision of disoriented modern man grasping for meaning in a world without seeming order or ultimate significance, and together they bear responsibility for their role in its creation. It is a distinctly Modernist vision that Butor develops in his novels, and a distinctly Modernist technique that he uses—that he entrusts to his narrators—as a means of invoking it. The vision remains constant in the books to follow—they can no longer be confidently called novels—and, in a sense, so does the narrative technique. But their forms will be new, owing more to the radical example of *Finnegans Wake* than to the surprisingly traditional *Ulysses*. Their newness is usually apparent in their subtitles.

Growing out of Vernier's lecture, *Mobile, Study for a Representation of the United States* (*Mobile, étude pour une représentation des Etats-Unis*, 1962) is the journal of a more or less alphabetical trip across the United States, with brief stopovers in towns of similar names if different geographical regions. Thus, Sunday night in Cordova, Alabama, is followed by Monday morning in Cordova, Alaska, close to Russia, and then by Douglas, Arizona, where it is again Sunday night. In the course of his two days' journey, the traveler returns repeatedly to the Monticellos, the Mount Vernons, the Edens and Washingtons of the nation. His theme is not so much the materials of American society—glimpsed fleetingly as if through the window of a moving bus—but the American consciousness: the settlement of the continent by Europeans, the displacement of the native Indian, the enslavement of the Negro. The traveler is never individualized—the snatches of conversation and the letters home, the glimpses of dreams, the brief readings of historical documents may not even be his—so that he becomes a kind of everyman. The meaning of America, in the eyes of Butor's European traveler, is the universal guilt of Western man.

Réseau aérien, texte radiophonique (*Aerial Network, Radiophonic Text,* 1962) is a series of dialogues among several groups of passengers on different airplanes, flying at the same moment throughout the world. As they cross at random all the time zones of the world—not just the few of *Mobile*—all times merge into one; the collective myths which link the passengers are those which all men create, in dream and in wakefulness, in an effort to give meaning and order to their lives; the voices too blend into one, speaking the universal human language of our hopes and fears.

The radio play *Réseau aérien* was followed by an opera *Votre Faust, fantaisie variable genre opera* (*Your Faust, Variable Fantasia in the Operatic Genre,* 1962), done in collaboration with the serial composer Henri Pousseur. Its first act is based loosely on the Faust legend and is more or less closed in its form, as the Faust figure contracts reflexively with the devil to compose an opera based on the Faust legend. In the open-ended (and open-sided) second act, Mephistopheles, the producer-director, consults with the audience on the fate of his actors. There are many alternative actions and more than two dozen endings to choose from, so that no two audiences are likely to participate in the same work.

Also meant to be heard, with full audience participation and all the freedom of the written page, is *Niagara*, published originally as *6 810 000 litres d'eau par second, étude stéréophonique* (1965). Looking like a McLuhanesque scheme, complete with directions for stereophonic speaker systems, *Niagara* asserts the supremacy of the book and thus denies McLuhan's basic premise. In some ways, the text is predictable: we visit Niagara Falls at various times of the day and year and overhear the stereotyped conversations of the typical tourists, the newlyweds, the disillusioned old married couples, the old madams and young gigolos, the vile seducers and their easy prey; their names change throughout the months, but their initials and identities remain constant, testimony to the mundane and unchanging nature of North American culture. Predictable, too, is the look of the text, with the Falls announced in bold type, the Reader in italics and the various characters balanced in different positions on opposing sides of the page; eventually they speak not only to each partner but to every other participant as well, and they speak, surprisingly, with a certain power if not with individuality. *Niagara* concludes where *Mobile* begins, as an outsider's view of America: in his last line, Butor cites the lyrical description of a pristine Niagara in Chateaubriand's *Atala, or the Love of Two Savages in the Wilderness*, and we are left to judge for ourselves about the nature and meaning of the change in our time.

Butor is willing, however, to explain his own change, the "search for new novelistic forms" which characterizes all his books after *Degrees*. It is, he says, echoing Robbe-Grillet, an effort to refine "our consciousness of reality. . . . The novelist who refuses to accept this task, never discarding old habits, never demanding any particular effort of his reader, never obliging him to confront himself, to question attitudes long since taken for granted, will certainly enjoy a readier success, but he becomes the accomplice of that profound uneasiness, that darkness, in which we are groping for our way. He stiffens the reflexes of our consciousness even more, making any awakening more difficult; he contributes to its suffocation, so that even if his intentions are generous, his work is in the last analysis a poison. Formal invention in the novel, far from being opposed to realism as shortsighted critics often assume, is the *sine qua non* of a greater realism."[22]

Constant in Butor's changing canon is the need to involve us in the characters' predicaments, to lead us to see our own need for self-awareness. Through dreams and myth, through the creation of a universal human time and a universal human voice, through the strange mix of objectivity and subjectivity which characterizes his narrators—that is, through traditional Modernist devices—Butor has made us all participants in this difficult and dangerous task of knowing ourselves and our world. In a note to his strange little book called *Histoire Extraordinaire: Essay on a Dream of Baudelaire's*, the author advises us, echoing Joyce with Bloom, "Some may consider that, intending to talk about Baudelaire, I have succeeded only in talking about myself. It would certainly mean more to say that it is Baudelaire who was talking about me. He is talking about you."[23]

IV

There was a time, not many years ago, when Claude Simon seemed the ultimate Modernist novelist, acknowledged heir of Proust, Faulkner, and Joyce, a survivor—in an age given over to a new, post-Modernist dialectic—who continued to believe in and practice the fictional and human values of the old. Critics might reasonably complain that Simon's work had become anachronistic, but it was difficult not to be drawn by the rhythms of his prose, by our own intense involvement in the lives of his characters, by his gradually expanding personal universe, built, so we felt, of the bricks and blood of his own experience. Even those raised in the New Criticism and scornful of the biographical approach were attracted to his Proustian "reconstitutions" of this experience, the "magma" (another of his favorite words) of an inchoate world which afforded to the creator almost endless possibilities of giving life. But his was more than a private vision. It was Simon who helped us to see—in that remarkable series of novels beginning with *The Wind* in 1957 and continuing through to *Histoire* in 1967—that the Modernists had not repudiated the legacy of humanism, as early readers had felt, but had placed it at the core of their work: hidden by irony perhaps, diminished because the world had diminished, but somehow raised precisely because creative potential seemed less certain in their time than it had in Homer's or Milton's or even in Tennyson's. From Joyce's Bloom to Simon's (the Blum of *The Flanders Road*), the Modernists saw heroic potential in the man who merely survived, who continued to act on the humane values at a time in history when all value had seemed to vanish.[24]

Critics today speak of a new Simon. His style has changed: "No longer do we have in his later novels long, intricate sentences, replete with parentheses, dominated by present participles. Instead . . . we read rather short statements, minimally qualified, impersonal";[25] there has been a shift in reader involvement from his characters to his text: "By challenging the reader to examine carefully what is signified by a text, [these last works] lead him further and further down a path along which it is difficult for him to retrace his steps. He may indeed, if he follows the arguments scrupulously, be led from a study of the text ["the one personage who is undeniably true and present and verifiable"] to a reconsideration of his relationship with the world";[26] his universe has expanded geographically (the action of *Conducting Bodies* takes place entirely in the New World) but has contracted in all other respects. Simon appears in his latest books to have abandoned the Modernists and their basically humanistic concerns and to have followed Robbe-Grillet and Butor into the post-Modern era, with its radically different critical interests.

The early novels of Simon[27] are written under the influence, almost with the explicit guidance of Joyce, Proust, and Faulkner: a rare instance of interplay among the three generations of Modernists. In the subtleties of his narrative technique, in the rich rhythmical flow of his prose, in his vision of man adrift in an uncaring universe—of man cut loose from historical community but a prisoner of the past nonetheless, of man struggling to comprehend his perilous new role and somehow, with some dignity, to endure—in vision and art alike, Simon in these early works echoes and recalls and builds upon the worldview constructed by the Modernist masters. An act of homage, to be sure, his is still a profoundly original creation. His myth is as forceful and at least as accessible as are those of his predecessors, and the demands of human response to his heroes' condition are equally pressing. The development throughout these novels is both circular (repeating characters, feelings, and events, although often in new contexts) and linear (explaining the familiar obsessions and enriching them through these new contexts). Myth and emotion alike are the functions of a private history, almost, we are tempted to say, of autobiography.[28] But it is an autobiography rather different from those transformed into art by Joyce, Proust, and Faulkner: fragmentary, elusive, achingly personal yet universal in its implications; a life story, in an exploding world, that is suggestive of both continuity and change.

The regional history begins to take shape in *The Wind* (1957), set in the country around Perpignan in the southwestern corner of France, the home country where Simon still lives for part of each year. It is a region where the wind blows steadily, threateningly, throughout the spring months and then grows still in the summertime; the wind serves in the novel as source and symbol alike of that preternatural force in human relations which is inimical to lasting connections and exposed emotions. It is implicit, in a sense, in all the subsequent fiction. The unnamed narrator of *The Wind*, a Parisian history professor who spends only his summers in the town, tells a tale of betrayal, of love gone awry, of lost opportunities for communication and understanding. In endeavoring to reconstruct this petty history out of the multiple sources available to him and his own knowledge of the participants, he is reminiscent of Proust's Marcel. His protagonist, one Montès, is a lineal descendant of Leopold Bloom: heir to his alienation and sense of humanity. Scorned by his neighbors and deprived of his inheritance, an outsider in the place where he was conceived, he is the fool who emerges somehow as a man of great sensitivity and decency. But he is viewed largely from the outside, although sympathetically; he will serve as model for each of Simon's suffering protagonists, but each of them we will view, ultimately, from within.

The Grass (1958) narrows the narrative focus to the members of a single family. Under different names and in various guises, they will appear and reappear through the remaining novels of the canon. The setting now is no longer the town but an old farm, ancestral seat of the family, where the narrator, Louise, awaits in stillness the death of the old woman who lives there, the spirit of the place. Hers is an account derived from old journals and photographs, built upon conjecture and rooted in a past of small economies, unspoken emotions, and familial self-sacrifice. In the present is her estranged husband, Georges, who has mismanaged the farm, mismanaged his marriage, wasted his life. He is as much the prisoner of the past as his dying aunt. He has been raised as its servant: his father, the child of peasants, is a professor of history; his mother, descendant of the noble de Reixachs, is a kind of family historian. Yet, as viewed by Louise, he lives not only with little grace or strength but with almost no self-knowledge: as she sees him, he is unable to assess the lessons of the past or to comprehend their significance for himself—and his wife—in the present. These are lessons that we ourselves comprehend only in part and only in the succeeding volume, in which Georges himself is the narrator.

This is *The Flanders Road* (1960), perhaps the most powerful and compelling of all Simon's fictions. Based loosely on *Absalom, Absalom!* it details the uncertain and painful process of reconstruction by means of which Georges attempts to understand certain events from his past, to master, by extension, the history of his age. These are events from the war: the death in battle of Captain de Reixach, his company commander; his own internment in a prisoner-of-war camp; his survival while those around him fail to survive. It is obvious, as he proceeds, that Faulkner's novel serves more as analogue than as source, that Simon had long been working toward such a fusion of prose style, of emotion, of a questioning protagonist who endeavors to reconstitute the past in order to comprehend its effect on his life in the present. This is a process of which his wife knows nothing; his narration is directed not to her but to Corinne de Reixach, widow of his commander, his own cousin and youthful love. They are lying in bed in a country inn, and Georges speaks of the captain's suicidal charge on horseback against a machine gun emplacement and of his own efforts and those of his comrade, a little, cynical, questioning Jew named Blum, to reconstruct the rationale of this death. He speaks of an unfaithful wife and her servant lover; he speaks as well of a family legend, whispered over the years by his mother: the legend takes the form "of one of those prints called The Surprised Lover or The Seduction that still decorated the walls of the room: the valet leaping up at the sound of the shot and running in, dressed haphazardly, his wide shirt half hanging outside his breeches pulled on as he jumped out of bed, and perhaps behind him, a servant girl in a night cap and almost naked. . . . "[29] The master, home unexpectedly from the Thirty Years War in Spain, has been killed—inadvertently? Blum wonders—by his wife or her servant lover. His great-grandson, more than a century and a half afterwards, appears to have died in a similar way. Corinne leaves the room in rage, but Georges goes on speaking, without pause, confirming what all along he seems to have known: that he has been speaking not to her but to Blum, long since dead in the prisoner-of-war camp. Within the multiple prisms and layers of his narrative, in the rich complexity of his search and his prose, Georges reveals himself finally as far more compelled and compelling than the fragmented figure seen by his wife: as a searcher after meaning in a world without meaning; as a naïf whose idealism has been slain by an insane world but who continues to seek for ideals; as a worthy descendant of Montès and Leopold Bloom. Knowing that his search must fail—that there is no more coherence in history than elsewhere in life—Georges continues to search, made to look foolish perhaps but given dignity as well by his failure. Accepting responsibility for what he has become, he affirms, like Bloom, his humanity.

The unnamed protagonist of *The Palace* (1962) travels for the first time beyond the borders of France—to Spain, to fight for the Loyalists in the Civil War. But that was when he was younger and, presumably, more readily disillusioned. He returns now in middle age to Barcelona, that peaceful and prosperous city from which all outward signs of the war have long since been removed, a city which seems to have forgotten its past. Only the pigeons of the city remain unchanged: the Frenchman's story opens with the rush of their wings and virtually closes with them. They serve for him as a metaphor of time, attesting to the continuity of past and present, to the inescapable burden of history for those condemned to bear it. Sitting on the square in front of the bank that was once Loyalist headquarters, he remembers his part in that past, reliving in his mind those acts of betrayal, of political and personal disloyalty, in which he was innocent but for which he assumes responsibility still.

After five years of near silence,[30] Simon published in 1967 the last of his novels which can be thought of as unmistakably Modernist. *Histoire* is the culmination of his long-building concern with the intricate and uncertain affairs of this ill-defined provincial family, with Proustian reconstitutions of history, rich in the possibilities of point of view and the handling of time, with demands for the reader's emotional involvement in the lives of these people. It is the culmination as well of a characteristic style of prose, recalling Proust and Faulkner and certain moments in Joyce, a style built upon a continual and perilous accretion of language and detail, on rhythms which are seductive and endlessly involving, suggestive of the human situation of character and reader alike, a style which in itself is emotionally, as well as intellectually, demanding. Thus, the narrator of *Histoire* recalls his invalid mother, long since dead, as she has appeared to him over the years: "as if something in her fate had irresistibly dedicated her to these terrible and migrating multitudes endlessly swarming across the surface of the earth wandering from East to West through time and space trailing from one holy place to the next fanatic nightmarish with their rheumy eyes their ulcers their twisted limbs their anger and their despair the ragged troops of paralytics starvelings the blind and the lame and the deformed jostling each other in the deserts the passes the wild mountains the pestilential and empty cities in the hope of impossible miracles dragging themselves limping carted in a clatter of crutches invalid carriages carrioles rattletraps litanies hymns begging bowls and imprecations spattered pell-mell from toothless mouths with the sticky fragments of countless kinds of food rice crusts of bread wafers or sandwiches Able to see. . ." (p. 190).[31]

His inheritance subverted, his own life deformed by his losses, the narrator himself has traveled far from this town in search of a cure—to Greece on his honeymoon, to Spain to fight in the Civil War, to other unspecified and distant places. He has returned now to the ancestral house—brought there by the death of his Oncle Charles, his surrogate father, the final survivor of the family's older generation—in order to settle the estate and to begin to settle accounts with the past. His focus throughout the one day of his narration is on familial relations, especially on those unarticulated and misunderstood. He begins also to name some of his familiar obsessions.

He finds in the house, in the mass of postcards collected by his mother over her lifetime, all that he has ever known or will know of his father. Once arranged chronologically and tied in bundles, these cards are as disorganized now as time itself, "representing, with certain variants of detail, the same repetition of rubble, of debris (something with the look of detritus rather than of ruins . . .)" (p. 84), depicting in their variety "all He created all that flies breathes flutters sways rocks rivers cities all that runs crawls moves builds collapses rots butterflies caymans palm trees . . ." (p. 314). His father appears to have been a professional soldier who visited French installations throughout Africa, Asia, and the Middle East (or maybe he was merely escaping from an invalid wife) and who sent back on these cards the briefest possible record of his travels. He was killed, this modern Ulysses, in the First World War. And so his son, his Telemachus, can discover him neither in fact nor in memory; he is reachable only in this unsorted mass of personal history. But this cannot be a reliable source, the son thinks: the pictures must have been posed, the sort of fake local color that is everywhere arranged for visiting foreigners, and the native women in them must surely be prostitutes. But he cannot be sure. The narrator's preoccupation with images of duplicity and false appearances—with masks and mirrors and the armored carapace under which men so frequently hide—suggests that he does not really expect even now to find his rootless father, and also, perhaps, that he will never discover his own identity.

The record of the distant past is thus closed to him; his own memory, the key to more recent events, is similarly selective, similarly untrustworthy. Yet it is only in memory that he can reach for Hélène, who was once his wife. He remembers, for example, their honeymoon in Greece, at the ruined citadel of Mycenae, remembers too leaving behind his pregnant wife to go off to Spain, to fight, he insists, for his ideals. Like Bloom, however, he will have no heir; he must be his own Telemachus and search for himself. For Hélène, abandoned, sees his departure as an act of betr—he will not permit himself to think the word—and kills herself by leaping from a fourth-floor window. At least it would seem that she has, for the narrator refuses to visualize her death. But an incomplete headline flashes continually across his mind—"THROWS SELF FROM THE FOURTH STO . . .", it may read, or "KILLS SELF BY JUMPING FROM A . . . ." This may be no more than a story glimpsed in a newspaper as he eats lunch, but its variant forms suggest that he is the author. The restaurant in which he eats leads him to think of a terrace café in Barcelona, where he witnessed another act of betrayal, a political assassination in the bloody contest between Loyalist factions. The décolletage of the waitress recalls the blue-veined breasts of Hélène, and memories of her lead him inevitably to Corinne, the cousin with whom he grew up and by whom he still seems obsessed. She is now the Baronne de Reixach, widowed in an ambush like the one in Barcelona, and he has sent her today some documents relating to Oncle Charles's estate.

All of his activities on this summer day are related to the estate; all lead him inexorably back to the past, to memories of Corinne and Hélène, of Oncle Charles and Maman, of Mycenae and Barcelona, to thoughts of betrayal. Even the election posters along the road—puffing Lambert, his childhood friend—resurrect memories of self-betrayal to a more assured and aggressive companion. That night he looks again through the accumulation of postcards and photographs, like Bloom sifting through the artifacts of his past. In this empty and silent house, relic of a dying family tradition which he strives implicitly to revive, repository of disillusionments and betrayals far more ancient than his own, it is simple to recapture the past but difficult indeed to comprehend it. And so the narrator undertakes a kind of constructive recreation of the past, an effort to understand those events which took place before his birth in terms and images derived from his own experience. It is an effort which recalls Proust and which, at the same time, goes much beyond Proust.

In the bottom drawer of his mother's chest—the one item in the house which he refuses to sell—there is an old photograph of Oncle Charles in which the narrator reads his own fate. Taken many years earlier in the studio of a Dutch artist resident in Paris, it pictures the artist's model, a visiting friend—"a supernumerary in a rattan armchair" (p. 224)—and a triple exposure of the artist himself, caught most likely by a time exposure before he can regain his place. Attempting to reconstruct the scene as it must have occurred, the narrator imagines the Dutchman (Van Velden?) alone with his model in his cluttered studio, setting the timing mechanism on his camera, when his unexpected visitor "dropped in (what to imagine?: idleness, or on the pretext of one of those reviews those descriptions of an exhibition he was writing for some magazine, or simply a book to return or borrow—after all it doesn't matter)" (p. 229). But it must matter, for his interest now shifts to the visitor: this is Oncle Charles as a young man—it almost seems to be his father—a real image "and not the vaguely mythical person as I had imagined him for years" (p. 224). Attempting still to reconstruct the scene, he identifies with his surrogate father and sees himself in the group picture, seated leisurely in the rattan chair. In a later novel, he (or someone much like him) will pursue the identification further, and Charles's betrayal by the artist and his model-lover will become his own. Now, his eyes "furiously peering for the thousandth time" at the photograph, he searches it still for meaning: "But what else? Nothing but skin, hair, mucous membranes? But what else? What else? else? else?" (p. 238).

The lack of apparent meaning in a metaphor which hints repeatedly at hidden truths, the merging of places and times and identities in a unique kind of multiple exposure, the effort to reconstruct the past as a means of understanding the present, of discovering himself—these are the unarticulated strategies of the unnamed narrator. But through them he will find only further betrayal: his failure is ordained by the rules of his search, rules he himself has established. It is the search that is meaningful for him and not its would-be resolution. And so he remembers Barcelona not as he knew himself but as it appears in an old aquatint in Oncle Charles's office, the view shifting continually as he moves away from it in space and in time. So also he views Oncle Charles, the only father he has known, not as the bookish, quixotic old man with whom he lived for so long but as an allegorical figure in Renaissance portraiture—a Prince of the Church or of the Government, painted perhaps by El Greco: "an image which for years I substituted for his when he was no longer there, as if each time he returned to Paris at the end of the vacation the being I knew underwent a kind of metamorphosis, was reincarnated somehow in an external aspect stamped with a remote somewhat arrogant gravity matching those premises which had no reality for me except what I had made out on a few postcards . . . and where I knew vaguely that he gave himself up to activities which also lacked all reality for me such as writing and frequenting artists . . ." (pp. 68–9).

So the narrator invariably sees in his cousin Paul's young daughter, also named Corinne, the re-creation of her aunt; so he finds himself caught up in the family postcard mania and inexplicably sends one to the elder Corinne; so he views all the acts of betrayal in his lifetime and earlier as if they were one and as if he were responsible; so he merges all women—both Corinnes, Hélène, the waitress, the artist's model, his

mother—in his search for a single woman, both loving and motherly; so
he confuses his uncle, his father, even his schoolboy friend and himself
in a search for his own identity. It is a search that cannot succeed. His
narrative ends, as it began, with the image of a fluttering bird in a tree.
But this is not the bird-filled tree beyond his bedroom window; it is not
even a bird, but a birdlike fetus, himself in the womb of his long-dead
mother. And the tree becomes a palm tree in the Seychelle Islands, the
picture on a postcard sent by his mother, perhaps on her honeymoon.
He imagines her writing the card, bent over a table, "her mysterious
bust of white flesh swathed in lace that bosom which already perhaps
was bearing me in its shadowy tabernacle a kind of gelatinous tadpole
coiled around itself with its two enormous eyes its silkworm head its
toothless mouth its cartilaginous insect's forehead, me? . . ." (p. 341).
Even in the desired security of the womb, he cannot recognize himself
truly.

Covering the events of a single day, cyclical in its movement, and
dreamlike in its action—growing out of Joyce, Proust, and Faulkner—
Histoire is about history and itself is history. It is appropriately named
not only because it deals with the accumulated details of a family
history in provincial France, or even because its form suggests the
processes by which such a story develops: *Histoire* also enables us to see,
more clearly than ever before, that all of Simon's work during this
major phase deals with history, with the burden of the past on the
present, with the larger significance of those who bear this burden. We
perceive that each narrator is a prisoner of the past, even when it is not
his own that entraps him: that each—however futile his own life may
be—is a kind of Everyman who suffers for all men, who bears sym-
bolically the burden for an entire generation whose ideals have been
betrayed by its history.

The narratives which follow *Histoire* are perceived through a lens
which is radically new: enlarging details, almost to giantism at times,
but narrowing the focus. They are more superficially personal but more
abstract than *Histoire* and these other earlier works, more obviously
obsessed with the most intimate issues (such as jealousy and love) at the
expense of these broader historical concerns. Yet they are, in fact, much
less immediate and much less demanding; even the rhythms of their
language are colder and less involving. They are more obsessive and less
humane, attesting to an enlargement of petty human details at the cost
of true human commitment: in short, they are perfect post-Modernist

works. One must assume that Simon, having reached a Modernist peak in *Histoire*—in its creative development of narrative sequences, in its union of function and form, in its persistent humanist concern—has followed the critics heralding the new post-Modernist modes, has repudiated his history and gone on to newer, if lesser, concerns. The formulation is comfortable and neat. Yet the discontinuity may well be less great than it has seemed to the critics.

The turning point would appear to be *The Battle of Pharsalus* (1969). Themes, images, even characters and narrative patterns are familiar here, but there is a new dynamic operating as well: the author's own self-conscious involvement with the process of writing as process, with the literary text as a manifestation of a reality ostensibly more basic than that of love or politics or betrayal, with the reconstitution of a text as if it were life. The obvious analogies are to Robbe-Grillet's denial of metaphor and his repudiation of humanism and to Butor's abandonment of narratives based on myth and psychological motivation and his adoption in their stead of open-ended, experimental constructions ordered only by internal structural demands. In each case, the movement is away from man-centered celebrations of inner life, as in the best Modernist novels, and towards a fiction which plays on the technical advances made by the Modernists and abjures their human concerns: a fiction made to order for that new school of critics who write as if fiction were no more than anthropology.

The Battle of Pharsalus is, in a sense, Simon's *Mobile,* the book which marked a major change in direction long before its readers could detect that change. As Butor's prior novels had dealt with the psychological disintegration of their protagonists, this transitional work was itself disintegrative, destructive of the very form on which those earlier works had been built. It was logical, when *Mobile* first appeared in 1962, to trace its connections to *Passing Time, A Change of Heart,* and *Degrees.* Today we can see that, connections aside, Butor had already progressed into the new sensibility: he is perhaps the best single example of a Modernist writer moving willfully and articulately into the post-Modern age. Simon appears now to be making a similar transition. The parallel with Butor seems instructive.

We may be even more struck, however, by the specific comparisons between Simon's present work and that of Robbe-Grillet, who once seemed his opposite pole among the writers of the so-called Nouveau

Roman. Most evident is the stylistic change from the richly expansive, Faulknerian diction of Simon's major novels to a prose that is very nearly as reductionist as Robbe-Grillet's. But there are other parallels as well: images that seem to be drawn from Robbe-Grillet, for example, the torn series of circus and movie posters in *Triptych* (an image that can also be found in Butor), palimpsests of experience which come alive for their beholders; here, too, are images which promise to grow into metaphors but may never quite do so; some of the acts of love in *Triptych* are described in geometrical terms, as if they were being perceived by the (dis)ordering consciousness of an early novel by Robbe-Grillet; the obsessive jealousy of the protagonist of *The Battle of Pharsalus* seems worthy of the hero of *La Jalousie*; scenes are suddenly frozen, and we may suspect the presence of the same camera eye that orders *Last Year at Marienbad* and *The Voyeur*; external objects obtrude into the perceiving consciousness and threaten to usurp it, as if they all along had been the source of the vision, as in *Project for a Revolution in New York*; even the sad, old, cuckolded Picasso king of *Orion aveugle* (*Blind Orion*) and *Conducting Bodies* may have his origin in the mad, old king Boris of *La Maison de rendez-vous*. The evidence, at first glance, seems highly persuasive. It may also be highly misleading. For Simon is no Robbe-Grillet, nor even a Butor. His artistry has certainly altered in these last books—the discontinuity grown greater, the point of view more diffuse, the self-concern still more obsessive. But the continuity with his major works is equally undeniable; the humanist Simon continues to function even as he seems to become a post-Modern artist. The opening image of *Orion aveugle*—a drawing by Simon himself—is of the workplace of the writer: his desk, the postcard lying on his dictionary, his cigarettes and matches, some extra pens, his manuscript being revised by his hand. It is the same image as at the end of *The Battle of Pharsalus:* the artist observing himself, the man of feeling using his own experience, his own emotions, as the basis of his art, both subject and object of a narrative trick done with multiple mirrors: the reflexive Modernist artist whose obsession with his own task provides technique and theme for one of the central post-Modern subjects. But there is more. In both novel and drawing, the window in the room opens outward, away from the desk and the self-involved writer, into the world.

Part III of *The Battle of Pharsalus*, "Chronology of Events," begins with an epigraph from Heidegger announcing a change of technique and intention. The change of technique is immediately apparent in the jarring new prose style which marks this section: simple declarative sentences, conventional punctuation and syntax, an almost total avoidance of the lush rhythms which characterize Simon's previous prose. The old tool spoken of by Heidegger is presumably no longer usable, and so the author endeavors to forge here a new piece of equipment, a new language and consciousness through which to approach a new-forming world. As a result, the viewer in *The Battle of Pharsalus* is more self-consciously concerned with his role as viewer, as creator, than are any of his predecessors. This much is clear. The change of intention, however, is less easily perceived, for the major theme—the relationship between technique and theme—is unchanged. These events are no more chronological, no less subjective in presentation and effect than comparable events in earlier novels, and their emotional demands are much the same.

Simon's subject, again, is history, more specifically the interconnection of past and present, the Proustian lesson that we are beings constantly in process, autonomous products both of our youth and our maturity, responsible for our lives even when we do not quite comprehend them. The narrator of *The Battle of Pharsalus* is as tied to his past—it is virtually the same past—as are Montès or Georges or the student of *The Palace* or the unnamed narrator of *Histoire*. Their creator too, despite this newly fashioned equipment of his, is himself tied to the past. Thus throughout the novel, even in Part III, we hear echoes of earlier works: familiar patterns of imagery and metaphor, the same literary sources and analogues, even aspects of narrative technique that we have long been accustomed to. Simon fills his novels with revealing signs of the continuity which in his work must accompany change.

And so *The Battle of Pharsalus* begins with the open window and the wings of a bird: the same bird seen through the window in Barcelona at the start of *The Palace* and heard through the window in the provincial French town in the first scene of *Histoire*. It closes with the narrator-author as he sits at his desk, watching through his window as "a pigeon passes in front of the sun," writing the first sentence of the novel that would eventually become *The Battle of Pharsalus*. "O. feels the pigeon's shadow pass rapidly over his face, like a sudden touch. He remains a moment in the same position. Then he lowers his head. Now only the upper corner of the page is in shadow. O. writes: Yellow and then black in the wink of an eye then yellow again" (p. 187). [32] Having built on the presumed facts of his life as a man, Simon gives us now, through his persona, his life as an artist.

The development is organic, emerging naturally from within the life and the art. But it is also conscious, intentional, derived in part by external analogy to other Modernist works. The novel's reflexive concern with its own creation, for instance, finds contemporary parallels in Beckett, Borges, and Barth, among others, all of them rooted ultimately in *Ulysses*. Its variable chronology, recalling Cortázar's *Hopscotch*, provides limitless possibilities of structuring time but virtually no possibility of certainty. An unread book on a train journey through Italy somehow becomes the source of subsequent events, a separate perspective into reality, as in Butor's *A Change of Heart*. And, peering down through his window at the world outside, like the protagonist-author of Claude Mauriac's *The Marquise Went Out at Five*, Simon's narrator, called simply O., becomes one of the world outside, looking upward now to the window and imagining the occupants within, making them part of his projected fiction; he himself becomes in the process not merely the jealous lover but the woman who is the cause of his jealousy, also called O., and even her new lover, his friend and betrayer. Time sequences blur; objective reality dissolves; even individual identity grows ambiguous as Simon continues to reflect, in this transitional novel, the major technical and thematic concerns of his Modernist forebears and contemporaries.

What little apparent stability there is in this narrative comes, ironically, from that paragon of uncertainty, the jealous lover who knows in his heart that he has been betrayed but who remains unsure to the end if his jealousy is justified, Proust's Marcel. Simon uses Proust much as Eliot once claimed that Joyce had used Homer; as an established pattern designed to give order and form to uncertain events in a chaotic time. Proust functions, then, as a kind of myth for Simon, a universally accepted norm of technique and behavior, an affirmation that events in the present are allied to and evolve from the deeds of the past, deeds which may now seem exemplary indeed. Marcel provides as well the inevitable moral judgment to be drawn from such a mythic perspective; here, as with Bloom, that judgment is largely ironic. Bloom seems diminished in contrast with Ulysses; O. learns from Marcel only to follow in the path of jealousy and betrayal, to intensify his master's example. For Proust speaks, finally, as all myth does, to our deepest fears and desires. And for O. that is the fear, and perhaps in a strange way the desire, of betrayal.

Leopold Bloom, the modern Ulysses, does not read Homer. O. appears almost never to be without his Proust. The names of Marcel, Oriane, Albertine, and Odette ring with surprise throughout his narration; his childhood memories—arriving, for example, with his mother and grandmother at a hotel in Lourdes (p. 83)—recall those of Marcel at Combray and Balbec; we can almost trace his jealousy to its roots in Swann and Marcel. The name "MARCEL" is "scratched in pencil" alongside the door at which the narrator listens for the sounds of his lover's betrayal (p. 11), his "Seeing ear" (p. 13) creating what he cannot experience at first hand; her full first name, we discover eventually, is Odette (p. 132). Most of his narration, like Marcel's, proceeds from heightened sentence to heightened sentence, charged with meanings that he can only partially grasp "(like those magic-lantern images sliding from right to left then from left to right, one driving out the last . . ." (p. 44). Part of his narration comes directly from Proust—especially as he turns the pages of *A la recherche du temps perdu* in search of a half-remembered phrase about jealousy—as if he can define his own existence only by reference to Proust and those other lives which he has created. Swann's jealousy serves him explicitly as metaphor of his own; reading about Swann's distorted love for Odette intensifies his love. Proust even appears himself in a photo which recalls Charlus (p. 108).

Marcel, let us remember, does not write of the events of his life until some time after he has lived them. At this late point, the act of writing itself becomes an implicit event in his account. (The sole exception to this narrative and psychological process is the action of "Swann in Love," events occurring before his birth which he reconstitutes many years afterwards from the several sources available to him and from his own conjecture.) Swann's affair with Odette surely helps shape Marcel's own relationship with Albertine. But since he does not begin to write of Swann and Odette until long after he has known and lost Albertine, we might reason that in a circular manner it is Marcel's own affair which influences his account of that earlier affair; life imitating art; art, in this reflexive account, infiltrating life. O. similarly finds analogues to his state in the characters of Proust. And perhaps, too, he models his state after those of Marcel and Swann. Perhaps he needs Proust even to name his state, as if the mythic source alone can give stability to his life and to his art.

We can follow this process further in the lovemaking scenes which O. recreates behind the locked door and window. For the images which he envisions—images so intense that he appears to be acting not merely as voyeur but as each individual participant as well—are drawn only in part from his own experience and his knowledge of the participants, as similar images are derived in Proust; for O. they come largely from his imagination and from external, almost scholarly sources. Simon in this way goes beyond his model, building on Proust in a manner perfectly consistent with Proust, furthering the potential of jealousy and suffering. Thus, the opening image of the passing bird, barely registered on the retina, brings with it "a recollection (warning?) a recall of the shadows . . . the air rustling or perhaps not heard perceived merely imagined bird arrow . . . like the one in that painting (where was it?) some naval battle between Venetians and Genoese . . . the feathered arch humming in the dim sky one of them piercing his open mouth just as he rushed forward sword raised leading his men transfixing him stabbing the shout in his throat" (p. 3). The uncertain "he" merges with a character from a passage in Caesar's *Gallic Wars*, translated with his uncle many years earlier, in which Crastinus, who casts the first lance at Pharsalus, is killed in the battle. "Plutarch, Caes., LXIV, gives the details: 'He received in the mouth a thrust of the sword so violent that the point emerged at the back of his neck' " (p. 163). The red spear becomes the man's thrusting penis, the mouth and vulva an open wound, sex and warfare united.

The process is compounded as the image blends with other paintings and pieces of sculpture whose subject is warfare or love (Polidoro da Caravaggio, Cranach, Poussin, the elder Brueghel, Piero della Francesca, and Uccello, among others), with a series of photographs, some of them quite old—part of the inheritance of *Histoire*—and with other strange and surprising sources: a catechism illustration and an ad for farm machinery; a comic strip, postage stamp, matchbook cover, and Gauloises wrapper; a box of paper clips, some coins, a few foreign bank notes, and a series of postcards of art reproductions. Each separate picture becomes a work of art to be judged critically; each provides analogues to "his" fate. O.'s betrayal, in the process, merges with the imagined one, in an earlier generation, of his Oncle Charles. Betrayal, too, seems an inevitable part of his inheritance.

Do the imagined lovers reflect the paintings he has seen, or are they themselves some sort of Ur-painting, source of all those other illustrations of warfare and lovemaking? He is clearly of two minds about them. On the one hand, each is viewed from the perspective of the art critic and historian, as if it were part of an essay that he is constructing;

on the other hand, each feeds his obsession. From the old photo of
Charles in an artist's studio, he recreates his uncle's presumed betrayal
by his friend, the artist; upon this scene—like Marcel with Swann—he
erects the elaborate structure of his own betrayal by his artist-friend, the
Dutchman Van Velden, whose model Odette has become his mistress. He
becomes himself a participant in the act of betrayal, perhaps even its
inventor (like Swann, like Marcel, like Bloom), reacting with passion
and yet with a certain cool objectivity, as if this scene too were part of
his essay. He chooses continually to link the facts of his life with his
reactions to art. Like each of his predecessors he is unable to express or
confront his emotions except indirectly (one of the functions of his art
criticism); the reader again is forced to fill in and deal with the
emotional details. We see this especially in his trip to Pharsalus, in
northern Greece.

O. goes to Pharsalus for the same reason that the narrator of *The
Palace* returns to Spain: to uncover past history, to find his own past as
well. The history of the race, for Simon, is individual history, each one a
reflection and source of the other. This is why his fiction is so intensely
personal and at the same time so closely tied to historical events. In the
lesson of past civilizations, conned long before with his uncle in that old
Latin text but never learned truly, O. seeks to discover the source of his
own betrayal. But he finds no Jungian truths about himself or mankind;
he cannot even locate the site of the battlefield with certainty: only a
soccer game at modern Pharsala, a folk memory of a medieval battle
against the Turks on a nearby hill, his own memories of World War II.
In the process, however, he may teach us something about the state of
humanity.

"I didn't know yet," "I was suffering like"—these refrains sound
throughout O.'s narration. What he comes to know is riding to war and
betrayal; he suffers like a man, justified perhaps by his suffering.
Inexpressive he may be, yet as art historian and critic he easily finds
metaphors to communicate his feelings. Thus, the dead horse passed
and repassed alongside the Flanders Road becomes in this narrative the
grim shell of a McCormick reaper, Heidegger's equipment made manifest, "rusty lying on its side a tangle of plates wheels and gears bristling
with broken rods Like some wreck cast up by the sea stranded after a
flood . . ."(22). A symbol of natural decay, remnant of "antediluvian"
times, the reaper is linked somehow to the imagined, yoked lovers (a
modern variant of the beast with two backs) and to his own childhood

memories—a brief masturbatory scene with an older boy (Lambert?), a voyeuristic scene as they spy on lovers in a barn—played out near a similar shell. O.'s memories of the war constitute a reprise of the battle scenes of *Histoire,* where we learn for the first time some of the details of the terrible cavalry battle fought at the start of the Second World War in *The Flanders Road;* the lovers in the barn look ahead to *Triptych.* One battle scene, one pair of lovers, overlays another; the thrashing legs of horses in battle mix with those of soccer players and lovers; imagination, memory, and physical perception are indissolubly joined; all times merge into one time; all metaphors coalesce. In front of the House of Parliament in Belgrade—seen on his trip to Greece—stand two bronze statues, "each representing a man supporting the legs of a rearing horse over his arms." Even to an ex-cavalryman, he admits, "The meaning of this allegory is obscure. The naked, muscular men seem to belong to that race of creatures doomed to superhuman and endless tasks, ceaselessly repeating the same gestures . . . combating an invisible enemy ceaselessly vanquished and ceaselessly reviving" (p. 167). We suspect that he knows all too well what the allegory means and how it applies to his life.

The Pharsalus for which Simon's hero searches is no different essentially from the palace in Spain or the prisoner-of-war camp or his native town: "not a country: a place, something apparently unknown to geographers" (p. 93), a place, that is, where the blind man can seek for himself through space and through time. The ultimate metaphor for Simon's questing hero is another work of art, "the extraordinary *Blind Orion Searching for the Sun* precipitating the spectator precipitating himself . . ." (p. 111). For his search, in the end, is our search as well, and the sun endlessly recedes from the blinded seeker of light.

   Conducting Bodies (1971) consists in large part of that work of art criticism researched and written by O. in *The Battle of Pharsalus* and published by Simon under the title *Orion aveugle* (1970).[33] Combining the texts of these separate works shows us for the first time the actual images—drawn from painting, engraving, collage, and photomontage; symbols of contemporary culture, an old map of the heavens, several charts of the human body—which serve as source of the narrator's imaginative life and become finally the metaphors by which he implicitly defines himself. Poussin's "extraordinary" *Blind Orion Searching for the Sun* is at the center of his quest. Pictures of the conquistadors and of modern political violence point up its moral. The charts of the body encapsulate his physical disease. These are the visual images of *Orion aveugle* and the root of the actions of *Conducting Bodies*. The temptation is great therefore to read *Orion aveugle* not merely as sourcebook for and gloss upon *Conducting Bodies* but virtually as the identical work, less complete perhaps (if any of Simon's open-ended books can be called complete) but even richer because of its illustrations and the presence of the author's revealing preface. Simon the art critic speaks in his preface of Simon the novelist, providing the evidence for the new text-laden approaches to his latest books: the revealing physical presence of the artist at work at his desk, writing in his own hand, and speaking directly to his readers of the artistic process, what in the old New Criticism would have been discussed in terms of point of view ("omniscient" on the one hand, "reflexive" on the other), or what in the language of art criticism would be called "painterly."

Surely the preface encourages such a post-Modern, text-oriented approach. Seen through the eyes of the art critic and historian Simon, the novelist Simon seems almost a passive participant in the artistic process, creator of a text which exists apart from its creator and his intentions. From his starting point—"an unformed magma of sensations . . . of memories accumulated more or less in fragments"; to his basic equipment, the incantory power of words which are separate from the objects and acts they are meant to represent—"Not one drop of blood has ever fallen from the tearing of a page on which is written the body of a person"; to his ultimate, unreachable goal—"the singular adventure of the narrator who never stops searching, gropingly discovering the world *in and through the act of writing*" [italics added]—Simon speaks as if preparing a text were a reflexive act that virtually produces itself, as if art criticism and fiction were one, as if, implicitly, the reading of *Conducting Bodies* were really no different from that of *Orion aveugle:* the perfect post-Modern statement. And yet, at the same time, he speaks of these acts as some sort of Odyssean initiation rite—"the exhaustion of the voyager exploring that inexhaustible landscape"—as if protagonist, writer, and reader alike were engaged still in a traditional Modernist quest. How are we to reconcile this evident dichotomy?

The point is, of course, that however much we can learn from *Orion aveugle,* and particularly from its preface, this is a very different work from *Conducting Bodies,* and its lessons are only partially applicable to the later text. A new process may well be at work here, but so is the old; the preface implies both a new start and continuity with the old. For the novel exercises that conscious and articulate control (even over what might loosely be termed "autobiographical" data) which the art book preface appears to deny, and it does so without sacrificing that intensity of commitment which characterizes each of Simon's previous novels. Moreover, this tortured portrait of the artist who turns his own body and blood into universal history—an image derived from *Finnegans Wake*—is as appropriate to Simon as to Joyce, both voyagers exploring inexhaustible landscapes.

The immediate landscape of *Conducting Bodies* is that place "unknown to geographers" which is spoken of by O. This is not quite the same as saying that it is purely imaginative, however. As Barcelona and Perpignan emerge as sites more of the mind than of the atlas, so we discover with O. that Pharsalus is not even a recognizable place, that its reality is a matter of time (of history and memory) rather than of space; it is the metaphoric Pharsalus that we seek for so blindly. The issue is compounded in *Conducting Bodies*, in which Simon's hero journeys for the first time to the New World. Certain scenes of the novel are set unmistakably in New York City, most likely on the Upper West Side of Manhattan. (No subway system in the world can be so mistaken for the West Side IRT.) But these are most likely remembered scenes from an earlier trip (made perhaps to study Poussin's *Orion* at the Metropolitan Museum of Art).[34] Present action takes place in Latin America—at least this is probably the present—and there are many clues to the specific site. The clues, unfortunately, are all contradictory: the murals in the assembly hall seem to allude to Mexico, the jungles seen from the plane to Central America in general, the carnival to Brazil; there are even hints of Cuba or Chile or Argentina, differing points on a political spectrum. It is not impossible that Simon is confusing us willfully, playing an ironic post-Modern game of misleading detective stories and atlases (a game that begins with Robbe-Grillet's *Erasers*).

But the metaphor of the New World is traditional and constant: "Our world hath of late discovered another," it reads, "and who can warrant us whether it be the last of his brethren. . . ." The quote is from Montaigne's essay "On Coaches" as it is made manifest in Butor's *Degrees*.[35] It speaks, obviously, of the interconnections between continents of geography and of mind, of the effect on the Old World of the conquest of the New, of the myths of renewed hope, and of the disappointed hope implicit in America. It represents, finally, a new manifestation of that blind search for political and artistic idealism and for personal awareness that is at the core of *Conducting Bodies*—and, indeed, of every other work by Simon.

The most evident failure chronicled in *Conducting Bodies* is the political. But this loss achieves none of the dignity or stature of those earlier betrayals of ideals (the political assassinations in Loyalist Barcelona, the death of Blum in the prisoner-of-war camp, the shock of riding to battle on horseback against tanks and machine gun emplacements). The issue here, by contrast, seems trivial, almost parodic; the precise wording of a resolution to be passed by an international conference of writers: ("The translator leans over and whispers: The writer defines himself politically by his active participation in the revolutionary struggle, whether by way of his spoken words, his writings, or his acts"—pp. 105–6.[36]) For the individual writer, the issue is real and significant; we see this throughout Simon's canon. What makes it suspect here is its official status, as if the passage of such a resolution would be binding on every writer. In those earlier novels, we feel the narrator's loss directly through his heightened language and intense emotional reactions. Here we are presented solely with words, heard in part in translation from the Spanish without authorial comment or reaction by the narrator: simply the meaningless verbiage of irrelevant resolutions (there are several variants), the interminable droning on of arguments heard in a foreign tongue in a foreign city, the petty intellectualizing of writers who have never themselves been in battle, who can so easily ignore the constant warfare surrounding them.

Yet the ultimate failure chronicled in *Conducting Bodies* is neither political nor artistic but personal; not sexual but physiological and moral: the warfare is in the narrator's mind and in his body. His feverish attempt to construct another lover's betrayal (reading into the Picasso engraving of the aged king spying on his young wife and her lover) is one more mask for his own pain and decay. He merges in his mind with the faltering members of a jungle expedition (conquistadors or modern guerillas, drawn alike from a magazine article read on the plane and from the heroic murals in the conference hall);[37] identifies with the cuckolded old king in his grief and his pain ("the round, highly magnified eye contemplates with an expression of calm desolation the tangled jumble of interwined limbs"—p. 110); becomes one in his fruitless, blind search with Orion ("With one of his arms stretched out in front of him, fumbling about in the void, Orion is still advancing in the direction of the rising sun. . . . There is every indication, however, that he will never reach his goal . . ."—p. 187). The various charts of the body point, finally, to his own diseased organ; the gray mass which covers the floor of the doctor's examining room, which spreads to the conference hall and follows him back to his hotel room, is his own decomposing substance: "forms of the animate and the inanimate world that are indistinguishable from each other," as he thinks of Poussin's great landscape (p. 63).

Perceptions blur as a result of his illness; normal separations of time and space disappear; unrelated scenes are juxtaposed without evident order or logic. We appear to have before us another Robbe-Grillet, a perfect technical exercise in the limited consciousness of a mind made feverish by illness, a further denial of the possibilities of human emotion in favor of the (distorted) physical perception of unfeeling, unsignifying "things"—in short, another *The Voyeur* or *In the Labyrinth*. We should not be surprised by now, however, that this is not in fact the case.

The narrative of *Conducting Bodies* is not an aimless recording of (and reacting to) arbitrarily given images, as if the eye of the viewer were a malformed camera eye with no substance behind it but the physical. It is, instead, the most thoroughly sustained example of the pure stream of consciousness since the major works of Faulkner, a meticulously structured progression of images and scenes which are subjected to a most rigorous logic,[38] a work which reveals with great force the disabling potential of unexpressed emotion. There is no conscious attempt to mystify (and perhaps to delight), as in Robbe-Grillet, no sense that the images being observed exert mastery over their observer. The close observation of detail, an effort to mask the narrator's pain, makes us aware of that pain. Human emotion is implicit throughout, remaining extremely close to the surface level of observed detail. (Even when he collapses at the end of his narrative, he can record only the view from the floor and not what he feels. But we have some sense of the feeling involved.) As the narrator's diseased body merges in his perception with the doctor's abstracted chart of the body, the result is ·increased, not lessened humanity. Unlike Robbe-Grillet, who will dehumanize even human objects, Simon finds human potential even in the inorganic, as if all those bodies represented by the chart were capable of such individualized suffering.

As its title announces, *Triptych* (1973) represents a further expansion by Simon of the working metaphor of art and art criticism, an opening outward from his typically artful scene into three separate yet interrelated tableaux, an altarpiece of narrative art, in effect. The novel provides in the process additional evidence for the new text-oriented approaches to the fiction of Simon. And so critics speak now not only of the effect of the text on the act of reading: "If *La Bataille de Pharsale [The Battle of Pharsalus]* deals with the action of the text upon itself and *Les Corps conducteurs [Conducting Bodies]* with the variety of interrelated structures it can accumulate, *Triptyque [Triptych]* can be considered as an examination of 'text-ure,' that is, the use of the 'weave' of a text to influence the reading of a novel."[39] They speak as well of a text that is virtually autonomous—self-involved, self-generating, even self-critical: "As the momentum of the text grows, so will its capacity to invent. . . . The novel's plot is, on one level, the composition of its representational mosaic. In another, it is the very *activity* of creating this structure. In previous novels the composition was the real plot. Here the efforts to discover this composition creates it and is the ultimate coordinating force of the fiction."[40]

It is difficult to deny that *Triptych* does indeed make increased demands on the reader and that the process of reading may need to be rethought as a result. But the issue is not quite as shiny and new as some of the text- and reader-oriented practitioners appear to believe. For this is an historical demand, made first in the implied contract which Henry James formed with his readers almost a century ago and manifested in the generations which followed by the responsibility that the Modernists placed on their readers to become active participants in the creation of a continuously evolving, if often ambiguous fiction. What is new here is the emphasis on reading as an art in itself. But even this does not necessarily mandate an entirely new critical vocabulary. The familiar Modernist discussions of narrative technique—and, in particular, of the reflexive workings of a fiction whose central subject is its own creation—might provide at least a starting point for this current discussion and lead us to those other writers who have for many years been engaged in a similar pursuit. The new vocabulary may have the virtue of providing new emphasis to the critical colloquoy; its danger is that it seems to deny at least part of the continuity which is vital to an understanding both of Simon's own evolving canon and of the entire fictional context from which he evolves and within which he continues to create. Even in the stylized and often artificial *Triptych*, the familiar human concerns do somehow emerge.

In this spirit, then, the really significant change of *Triptych* is in point of view. The familiar limited consciousness of the previous novels, which reaches its peak in the stream of consciousness of *Conducting Bodies*, becomes here almost no consciousness at all. There is no recognizable person or consistent group of persons to mediate the events of *Triptych*, no accepted body of facts or impressions, however ambiguous, to serve as their source, no unified community to provide them with background. Instead, there are several prisms—partial, inconsistent, sometimes overlapping, often contradictory—through which the events are revealed. Loubère is certainly correct when she speaks of Simon's challenge in *Triptych* to "our weakness [as readers] for story telling," our urge (to extend Simon's own metaphor) to join together the pieces of a narrative puzzle as if we were detectives and the deciphering of the plot were our primary mission. Yet the pieces of this puzzle, however cleverly we extrapolate, will simply not fit together. For there may be more than one puzzle here—or perhaps less; more than a single focus of character, setting and time—or no focus at all; more than one metaphor through which to approach technique and theme in this novel. The narrative lacks not merely a beginning and end but a realizable center as well. But it does have a history of sorts, and it may be within this context that we can discover the author's full goals and our complete function as readers.

Reading *Triptych*, we are reminded less of other novels[41] than of certain aspects of film technique, as in the fictions of Robbe-Grillet: several of the narrative sources are literally films or film strips or advertisements for films; there are even scenes of films being produced, sequences which form in their turn an additional source for the narrative. Such scenes are viewed through what seems a true camera eye, distant, impartial, unselective in what it chooses to shoot and to screen, and operating before an equally undiscriminating audience. And so characters in one film may suddenly appear in another or emerge in new guises outside the film or enter again as figures in a novel or in an engraving, aspects of the *mise en scène* of still some other film. Some drunken projectionist is surely at work here, mixing reels from different films, projecting images from one onto another. Or perhaps some deranged editor has simply spliced together passages from different but related films to be shown by the unwatching, unthinking projectionist. But we know as readers that this cannot be the case, that no controlling intelligence operates here—not even a drunkard or madman or one of Robbe-Grillet's psychotic seers. For this is, finally, the fiction promised in

the preface to *Orion aveugle*—unplanned, unstructured, almost accidental, growing by some narrative parthenogenesis, starting from nothing
"except an unformed magma of sensations . . .," to be mediated by no
one: chastisement perhaps for Modernist author and reader alike, for
those who believe in a world that is at least potentially knowable, in
which certain human values, at least, remain constant.

Nothing in *Triptych* is constant, nothing finally knowable. One of the
characters does complete a puzzle, but, as the film ends, he immediately
scatters its pieces. "Their meandering edges have been deliberately cut in
such a way that none of them, viewed individually, shows the entire
image of a person, an animal, or even a face" (p. 171).[42] The several
sets of lovers, the several voyeurs, even the several landscapes are pieces
of a puzzle that the rational reader can very nearly construct to his own
satisfaction: the servants who make love in a barn as two boys spy on
them belong to the country village, the drunken bridegroom and the
barmaid in the alley to the industrial town, the middle-aged woman
protecting her son in her luxurious bedroom to the seaside resort. The
triptych seems complete, the metaphor fulfilled. But we may have had
to force some of the pieces, or perhaps there are too many of them, for
this seems not one puzzle but several, with compulsively interlocking
parts and gaping voids. There is evidence to indicate that the woman's
son may be the bridegroom and/or the sheep-faced actor in one of the
films, perhaps the one about the drunken bridegroom who abandons his
bride on their wedding night to seek out an old lover in town. The
woman herself may be a character in the film (a film about making a
film?) shown in the cinema alongside the alley (or in the barn), as well
as in the filmstrips put together without sound by the boys. The boys,
too, seem characters in some other film, and the servants seem figures
in an engraving which decorates the wall of a luxurious bedroom,
perhaps as background for one of these films. (This almost seems to be
the engraving of *The Flanders Road.*) Even the different landscapes blur
into one, "at once urban, industrial, and rural" (p. 21), "crossing each
other, wandering off obliquely for no discernible reason, forming a
complicated labyrinth within the sort of chaotic, cancerous proliferation
stretching out beneath the low sky on the surface of the flat land . . ."
(pp. 44–5). Lured into assembling the narrative puzzle as a rational
exercise, the reader is betrayed; the exercise alone remains. We are left
like "the spectator" contemplating "the pathetic face of the clown" who
performs for us (in a film? in the barn?—p. 13), the same clown seen

on one or more of the posters, his face "frozen" beneath his makeup, contributing to "this impression of dehumanization" (pp. 119–20).

The way of life recorded in *Triptych* is like a movie set: "the entire décor leaves one with an impression of emptiness, impersonality, and desolation, as though the protagonists were merely passing through, staying for only a short time in a temporary and artificial ambiance that has nothing to do with them, set up the day before by stagehands standing ready to take it down and isolated from the rest of the world by floodlights, like a minuscule and ephemeral little island of light in the vast emptiness of the cosmos, or, more simply, that of a vast movie studio, equally black and equally empty" (pp. 130–1).

Viewed in this bleak light, such a reader-oriented approach to *Triptych* seems to negate the humanistic impulses which link Simon to the Modernists (including, ironically, the impulses of the reader) and to posit instead a perfect post-Modern critical solution: all theorizing and no emotion, but effected with great ingenuity and skill. There is pain in these events, according even to this approach, but no one to experience the pain; it is an abstract emotion apparently, a vestigial reminder of the suffering which informs all of Simon's previous novels and which singles out their protagonists. Even the reader's involvement is elicited, in this view, so that it might be betrayed. Surely Simon has repudiated here his own fictional past: there is no political import in *Triptych*, only the suspicion of a betrayal (but no single culprit) and no real love—merely some lovers to be described as frozen, geometric forms, as in a Robbe-Grillet tableau, fit solely for a pornographic film in a sleazy theatre. It is difficult to recall, when viewed from this critical perspective, that the distant recorder of the events of *Triptych* was once the creator of Georges and Blum and those other suffering (and involving) consciousnesses of the major novels. And it has not been necessary for the post-Modernist readers to invent this Simon; the evidence is undeniable: he seems determined to shape his latest work precisely to fit this latest of critical forms.

But there is more: Simon rejects our involvement and then leads us on once again. For there are palimpsests upon palimpsests in this ostensibly autonomous text, from "the layer upon layer of superimposed posters" (p. 6) which announce and then become the several performances that constitute so much of the narrative, to the filmstrip which the boy at his desk holds up to the light of the window, superimposed upon the world outside. The woman in the bedroom—the actress

portraying the middle-aged woman—is Corinne de Reixach; the official
who promises to aid her son is Lambert, Georges's old friend from
Histoire ("But what wouldn't I be willing to do for the ravishingly
beautiful cousin of my best friend from school!"—p. 36); the father of
her rebellious son is unknown ("I imagine, must have, father somewhere, frightfully rich too"—p. 41). Could it be Georges? Why does
Simon even induce us to raise the issue? Is this autonomous text, after
all, part of his slowly evolving, continuously involving personal
universe?

The boy sitting at his desk and pondering his geometry lesson recalls
the artist Simon at work at his desk. The figures that he draws, a study
of certain and potential relationships, might conceivably serve as a
metaphor of the narrative relationships seen in *Triptych*. The postcard
lying on the kitchen table, with its view of palm trees along the arc of a
tropical bay, echoes those postcards denoting foreign scenes and a
missing father in *Histoire*. (There are older women in this household, but
no men are evident.) This will become the setting of the scene played by
Corinne in the seaside resort. These seem to be the images on the
filmstrip held up by the boy to the light; the scene outside his window
is of a rabbit being skinned; when we first see Corinne, she is unusually
vulnerable, lying before Lambert, her "body sprawled out with its legs
apart, too pink in certain places, . . . naked, stripped bare, . . . like the
body of a skinned animal" (p. 36). The image may also suggest the
imagined fetus among the palm trees in the final scene of *Histoire*—the
narrator visualizing, perhaps even creating himself, although uncertainly.

There are further connections. The boy's youthful voyeurism when he
spies on some lovers in a barn (the girl's "pink tongue" linked directly
to the "pink body" of the dead rabbit—p. 63) recalls that of the
protagonists of *Conducting Bodies*, and there may be a hint here too of
the homosexuality with his childhood companion seen in the stream of
that older consciousness. The implicit act of betrayal is the death of a
child (his younger sister?) abandoned by her nursemaid (occupied now
in the barn) as well as by all those others delegated to care for her. The
boy himself is not a betrayer but is somehow involved in the act (first
associations of sexuality and guilt), and thus he will likely assume
responsibility for the betrayal: this is, after all, the paradigm established
in each of the novels from *The Palace* to *Histoire*. Does this mean that the
boy, one of the few identifiable centers of consciousness in *Triptych*, is
somehow related to Georges or to O. or to those other unnamed

narrators who are so much like Georges and O.—perhaps even, in certain respects, a younger Georges, a still more impressionable O.? The fact that we can ask such a question is a sign, will-he, nill-he, that Simon has not totally abandoned his old technique, his own history, his humanist needs and concerns.

There can be little doubt that a new Simon is operating in these later novels and that the new post-Modern, reader-oriented critical approach provides useful insights into these works. We are less moved now by the rhythms of the prose, less profoundly affected by the accretions of past history as they influence the characters, more aware of the act of writing as a significant theme in itself. Like Robbe-Grillet and Butor and those others who have made this difficult transition into a new literary age, Simon continues to play on and perhaps to expand Modernist advances in narrative technique (witness the beautifully sustained stream of consciousness in *Conducting Bodies,* and what might be called the implied consciousness of the boy in *Triptych.*) The expression of emotion in these later novels is increasingly indirect; but emotion remains. Simon does not abandon in these new narrative interests the old humanistic concerns of his Modernist forebears.

To be sure, there is nothing in these books to equal the emotional depths of our discovery of Georges in *The Flanders Road,* left alone by Corinne in his hotel room, as he continues his monologue to the long-dead Blum. There is nothing as concentrated as the pain of those who have been betrayed or who have been betrayers, nothing of the suffering—imagined perhaps, but no less intense—of the "Seeing ear" waiting outside the lovers' door, nothing even of the implicit agony of the (dying?) foreigner in a chamber a hemisphere away from his ancestral home. But we recognize even in this divided narrative many of the same old emotional strands that have involved us throughout the ever-developing canon, many of the same old humanistic concerns. For Simon retains the ability to involve us in the lives of his people, however fragmented they may have become, and to remind us through them of the accretions of our own history, of the discontinuity of our lives. His fictional career remains an assertion of human potential in a diminished age. We have not lost even now, he shows us, our capacity for feeling, our compulsion to endure despite our feelings, our ability perhaps to prevail. No text, Simon shows us in the end, can be more basic than life. Through the window of his art, as a continuing function of the Modernist endeavor, he looks outward still to the world.

The critical expectation that once accompanied the Nouveau Roman has vanished along with its novelty. The Modernist possibilities that it seemed to promise in the late 1950s and early 1960s—at the same time that the British were sure that Modernism had died and had left no issue—have not, on the whole, been realized; that hoped-for, fruitful progression will have to come from a newer culture and continent. The French have followed Modernism's example as they understood it— mandating a continuously expanding narrative technique as a means of capturing a new and ever-shifting reality. But it has brought them, for what may be uniquely French reasons, to a sometimes sterile practice: it is not technique but theory, not the Modernist example but the French propensity for serious, intense, theoretical exploration that has led them along this fictional cul de sac. These theories may have their validity— although I must confess that they mean little to me; but I am confident that they have little to do with literature and that no significant fiction can be built from materials so extraneous to art and to life.

Robbe-Grillet, Butor, and Simon represent strikingly different points on the spectrum of French reactions to Modernism. Robbe-Grillet has been most faithful of them all to Modernist technique, but he has used it in an effort to establish a new, distinctly post-Modernist vision. It is not a vision that I, for one, find very attractive, and it both contradicts the Modernist worldview and provides seeming support for those who have argued that Modernism is inherently anti-humanistic. There is a real integrity to Robbe-Grillet's career as novelist and critic (even as filmmaker), but his work, of necessity, has more critical than human interest, and so I do not expect that it will survive.

Butor is more varied and more interesting. His reading of the Modernist—more specifically, Joycean—experience is that it demands not consistency but change, and so he has shifted forms and moved from the novel into new genres. Always interesting, always challenging, motivated throughout by the perspectives and insights of the writer of fiction although not always fictions, Butor's protean output demonstrates the possibilities of both form and function opened by the Modernist novelists to their successors. We must respect the daring and depth of his later work, but it remains his early, explicitly Modernist novels that I continue to admire most.

With his roots in Faulkner and Proust as well as in Joyce, Simon is the most demanding and rewarding of contemporary French novelists and, I believe, along with García Márquez and Fuentes, one of the great novelists of our time. His latest novels are perhaps unfortunate in their links to the now popular (yet still arcane) theorizing, which truncates their rhythms, vitiates their message, and lessens our emotional involvement in the lives of the characters and the larger patterns of life that they suggest. There is some reason to hope that Simon in his most recent work is returning to the Modernist-inspired rhythms and themes which informed his earlier fictions. However, he has produced already an extraordinary body of work, throwing light on the modern predicament, affirming our ties to the past—convincing proof of the rich legacy left by the Modernists to their willing inheritors.

5 "THE FORTUNATE EXPLOSION"

Contemporary Fictions In Latin America

James, Proust, Faulkner, Joyce, Virginia Woolf, Mann, Céline . . . yes, very well, there they were, far away. The reading of Spanish American novels, on the other hand, not only got under my skin and entered my bloodstream but also, I think, permitted me, when I opened I have no idea which sluices, to incorporate the European and North American masters as something of my own. . . .

The novelists I have known are for the most part the Spanish American novelists of my own and other generations, whether or not they belong to the Boom, which may or may not exist.

—José Donoso
The Boom in Spanish American Literature

Latin American fiction, in the minds of most North American readers, is hardly more than a decade old. It was in 1967, in the well-known essay "The Literature of Exhaustion," that John Barth paid homage to the Argentine poet, essayist, and writer of short stories Jorge Luis Borges, suggesting for the first time that here was a literature mature enough and significant enough to influence our own. This was followed in 1977 by the English translation of José Donoso's *The Boom in Spanish American Literature: A Personal History,* the Chilean novelist's account of the forces and friendships which had led to that presence now known widely as the Boom: a public relations phenomenon equivalent to that of the so-called Nouveau Roman a decade or so earlier. But this was more than a case of a disparate group of novelists linked merely by a shared publisher or language or continent; this was an explosion of some creative substance. After two generations of conflict between those writers who emphasized the native origins of their art (the *Criollistas* and *Costumbristas* and other Local Colorists and Realists) and those whose inspiration came principally from foreign borrowings (as in the Symbolist movement known as *Modernismo* at the start of the century), the writers of

the Boom have effected a union of these indigenous and alien sources—
of tradition and innovation—whose result is the most vigorous and vital
and challenging fiction of our age: a fiction truly Latin American, yet
recognizably Modernist; not an import a generation late and not
Modernismo reborn, but an extension and elaboration of European
Modernism that is in the spirit at once of Joyce and his fellows and of
this new continent. Reading the novels of Fuentes, García Márquez, and
Vargas Llosa, of Cortázar, Puig, Cabrera Infante, Arenas, Callado, and
Donoso himself, among many others, we may learn that an insistence
that Modernism is dead is merely a sign of provinciality.

The Modernist presence in Latin American fiction, largely derivative at
first, goes back at least to 1938, with Eduardo Mallea's *Fiesta in
November*, an Argentine rendering of Woolf's *Mrs. Dalloway*. Its protagonist is a woman at the heart of, yet not quite at home in, her
society; its central event is a party held at her home to celebrate her
place in this milieu but accenting, finally, otherness; she has a daughter
who rejects her way of life and who asks, echoing Clarissa Dalloway,
"What is this strange thing, life?" (p. 20).[1] The role of Peter Walsh is
played here by an artist who assaults the reactionary social attitudes of
the partygoers. The Septimus Smith of this narrative is a poet taken
from his home and executed by soldiers, an intrusion which those at the
party do not yet perceive—although some there do recognize, "In the
midst of this luxury, this brilliant and aristocratic play, . . . the tragic
suddenness with which life might intrude upon the comedy . . ." (p.
50). But there is no potentially positive epiphany to be drawn from this
death. In the Argentina of the late 1930s, political realities are too
oppressive to allow for even that affirmation which Woolf, for all the
social injustice in her England, can provide her individuals. Mallea uses
Woolf—at times seems to copy her—in order, in part, to show the
differences between her world and his: the royal automobile which links
the events and people of Clarissa Dalloway's day becomes here the
headlights of the car taking the poet to his death.

These same political realities, in a society whose forms are still in flux,
remain in the background thirty years later in José Lezama Lima's
Paradiso (1968). Yet the result is much the same. Begun apparently
before the Cuban Revolution but written largely during the Castro years,
at once derivative and idiosyncratic, *Paradiso* is *A la recherche du temps
perdu* set in the Havana of 1910–1930—but with no metaphor comparable to that of the Dreyfus Affair. The connections to Proust are

unmistakable: this, too, is a chronicle of a bourgeois family life dominated by a mother and grandmother (but with the ever-present ghost of
a prematurely dead father); the hero is asthmatic, and many of his
friends are homosexual; much of his life is derived, it would seem, from
the life of his creator, although they are ultimately kept carefully
separate. The spontaneous, affective memory which dominates José
Cemí's account of his life is similarly Proustian (standing at Morro Castle
as an adult, he recalls contracting asthma there as a child, "a reminis-
cence that would not have curved back to him had he not been
standing right there in its strong presence"—p. 240).[2] But the progression of his memories is less ordered than Marcel's; his dreams seem
more fanciful, his erudition more strained; and his prose is far more
ornate and less functional (the baroque, we are told, "is what has real
interest in Spain and in Hispanic America . . ."—p. 239). For this is an
explicitly Cuban affair; the narrator speaks continuously of Cuban
manners, Cuban Spanish, the Cuban "tendency toward digression" (p.
131), the "pleasant Cuban resourcefulness" (p. 166) and the "lordliness
of the Cuban bourgeoisie" (p. 166). And the Cuban air before Castro,
before even Batista, empty of political realities, seems almost surreal.
Thus Cemí sees—not imagines, but sees—accompanied by Roman
maidens and a genie, an enormous phallus on the streets of Havana (p.
269). The surreal imagery, the baroque prose, the sense of time as not
merely subjective ("time crisscrossed horizontal, vertical, and time now
made for man. A vertical shape of time that is hurried, a shape acquired
in flight and a shape that uses man as an intermediary, wiping him out
afterwards"—p. 51), the point of view which weds author and protagonist, the life in fiction and the life that has seemingly become a
fiction—all serve to connect Lezama Lima to Proust and the Modernists
and then to set them apart. Like *Fiesta in November, Paradiso* is perhaps
too derivative to be truly convincing, yet even here, in these early efforts
of an older generation—these endeavors to adapt Modernist modes to
Latin American realities—we can see beginning to emerge the unique
landscape, history, and vision of life which will come to characterize the
novels of the Boom.

The Joycean presence is similarly revealing. From direct references to
him and his works (Juan Filloy's *Op Oloop* [1934], a day in the life of a
Finnish resident of Buenos Aires, a lesser, Argentine *Ulysses;* Leopoldo
Marechal's *Adan Buenosayres* (1948), in which the city itself, like Dublin,
becomes a protagonist; and Gustavo Sainz's *Obsesivos días circulares*

[1969], whose Mexican narrator reads *Ulysses* and uses it to shape his own fiction) to more generalized borrowings and adaptations (the blending of naturalism and Classical myth in *El sueño de los héroes* [1954], by Adolfo Bioy Casares, Borges's friend and sometime collaborator; the flexibility and inventiveness of the language of *Three Trapped Tigers* [1967], by the Cuban Guillermo Cabrera Infante) to claims by critics of influence where perhaps none can really be found, Joyce seems almost omnipresent in the Latin American fiction of the past two generations. But we must be wary of such seemingly universal and undifferentiated acceptance; influence so generalized may not be functional influence at all. We see something of this in the frequent critical claim that the novels of Gabriel García Márquez, the great Colombian author, have been profoundly affected by his early reading of Faulkner, and the counterinsistence by Norman Thomas DiGiovanni, Borges's translator, that the Spanish translations of Faulkner then available to García Márquez were inaccurate and unrepresentative.[3] The direct influence of Joyce may be similarly superficial: something in the air, known to all, assimilated concretely and imaginatively by only a few. Yet this is not to deny the true Joycean presence in Latin America. The aura of Joyce and the Modernists has been profoundly important to the development of what Donoso has termed "the fortunate explosion."[4] It has been the catalytic force—in technique, vision, example—which has enabled this new generation of writers to transform their separate, local literary inheritances into fictions which are truly universal. It is the aura of Joyce which has enabled these disparate novelists, from countries throughout the continent, to convert what had seemed a limited tradition (a series of separate limited traditions) into the unique idiom and vision that today characterize their art. "Through Joyce," says Carlos Fuentes of current Latin American fiction, "we came into our tradition; how wonderful to discover we have a tradition."[5]

The peculiar genius of Latin America has from the start been its ability to transmute alien patterns into indigenous art. Thus, when eighteenth-century Spanish baroque architecture reached Latin America, as Guillermo de Zéndegui notes, "Latin America did not limit itself to receiving the new style with open arms and propagating it, but was capable of taking possession of it and impregnating it with value and characteristics from native tradition and then returning it to Iberia in what has been called 'the architecture of the return.' "[6] The analogy to contemporary fiction is obvious. The writers of the Boom, "which may or may not

exist" as a movement, as Donoso warns us,[7] have built upon the
Modernist advances in style and technique, have learned from the
Modernist insights into the nature of man and his limited life and have
added to them a sensibility drawn from the experience of a new and
powerful continent, a vision of human potential and life that could
hardly have derived from the more settled cultures of Western Europe or
North America. And they have done so at a time when critics and
writers in France, England, and the United States, speaking of art,
architecture, and fiction alike, have trumpeted the demise of Modernism. Their perspective, their very idiom, and the "magical realism"[8]
which they create in their fictions, are surely unique. Yet it is equally
certain that their art represents not the abandonment or denial or
remaindering of the Modernist masters but their continuation and
expansion. The current fiction of Latin America is unmistakable proof
that, there at least, Modernism remains very much alive, developing still
in the spirit of innovative technique and humanistic impulse through
which it first started to thrive in alien Dublin on that lovely spring day
in 1904.

II

Hopscotch (1963), by the Brussels-born, Paris-resident Argentine novelist
Julio Cortázar (who died at the height of his power in 1984), is the first
work of fiction from Latin America—aside from the stories of Borges—
to be acclaimed beyond Latin America. In its shifting points of view and
time sequences, its shifting sense of what constitutes reality, its highly
ordered yet shifting structure, and its themes of exile and the search for
identity (shifting residence and shifting personae), it appears to encom-
pass perfectly that union of Modernist and native concerns which has
come to characterize the fiction of the Boom.

Horacio Oliveira, an Argentine intellectual living in self-exile in Paris,
details his experiences there in the first part of this narrative, "From the
Other Side." The second part, set in Argentina, is viewed "From this
Side." Part three, which begins after the close of the narrative proper—
or, at least, what seems a proper, more or less conventional Modernist
narrative—is labeled, "From Diverse Sides": these are titles of perspective as well as geography. The chapters in "From Diverse Sides" are the
"expendable chapters" which, the Table of Instructions informs us, must

now be read interspersed with those chapters which we have already
read, in a new, unpredictable, sometimes unfathomable order, to wit:
73—1—2—116—3—84—71—5, and so on. These new chapters,
forming a kind of interlinear[9] with the first fifty-six but also providing
new characters and episodes, offer additional points of view, some more
objective than Horacio's and potentially more reliable (his friend Traveler, "a stern and impassive witness"—p. 202);[10] some almost mystical
(the aptly named La Maga, whose unschooled ability to see with clarity
contrasts sharply with Horacio's straining, dense intellectuality); and
some outside this narrative entirely but paralleling its views on art and
its reading of life (the notebooks of the old novelist named Morelli
whom Horacio has witnessed, in Paris, being hit by a car). There is also
the possibility, of course, that these other perspectives are also Horacio's,
his endeavor to progress beyond a limited personal vision, to discover
how others might see. For the narration functions throughout, no matter
who speaks, as an aspect of his witness and search. There is even the
self-reflexive sense that the future novel which "I will never write"
(p. 21) is the novel which we are reading.

As we reread the narrative following the hopscotch pattern set out
before us, we not only learn about characters and events previously
unexplained but perceive as well the workings of time in the lives of
these exiles: time becomes not merely an external measure of their
activities but a vital force within them, a cyclical inevitability which
traps all men in the present, "a present in which he felt himself placed
and obligated" (p. 228), a notation of fatefulness. Horacio attempts to
evade its force by denying his future; one of his friends escapes
momentarily by winding and rewinding a tape recorder, which "goes
against time" (p. 244); only the primal La Maga is truly above it, for
"time falls apart in her hands" (p. 271). She, naturally, "was always
reaching those great timeless plateaus that they were all seeking through
dialectics" (p. 30). Yet even these others achieve some little freedom
from time in America: in America—especially in La Maga's Montevideo,
across the river, but even in Horacio's more cosmopolitan Buenos
Aires—there is a feeling of timelessness, of freedom from the history
and culture which envelop even Americans in Paris.

Reality in this New World is forever in flux; in each new world that
he discovers, Horacio discovers also the likelihood of its illusoriness. Yet
he continues to search; "searching," he says, "was my symbol" (p. 15).
He searches in La Maga for that "inconceivable" center (p. 48) which

represents unity; he will not be content, he insists, with seeming external order, "the false order that hides chaos" (p. 86). He searches through art, through an elaborate pattern of myth and ritual and literary allusion, through images of mirrors and the game of hopscotch, "those childish rites of a pebble and a hop on one leg to get into Heaven, Home" (p. 26). His search—his reality—is as involved and as shifting as is his narrative. There is no true home for him in either narrative or life, no heaven in New World or Old.

Although Cortázar at times treats his hero's compulsive search, his constant seriousness and occasional posturing, with irony, we sense in him the same intellectuality, the same distancing from his creations, the same aloofness. His people may well be based on observation and experience, yet they seem intellectualized rather than felt. As an artist, Horacio is remote and emotionally uninvolved; he seems removed, as narrator, even from himself; he—like his creator—practices the aesthetic distancing which the young Stephen Dedalus advocates (and which the mature Joyce treats with some irony). Even the earthy La Maga, designed as symbol to set off Horacio's intellectual remoteness from life, is herself unrealized except as artifice, and thus she demonstrates Cortázar's remoteness. As for the novelist Morelli, with whom Horacio—and perhaps Cortázar also—comes to identify, he is progressing in his vision of fiction "towards what has been poorly termed abstraction" (p. 389), building his reality from fragments of life, abandoning traditional characterization. Horacio's characters are real, he assures us (as does Cortázar), and he is part of their lives, yet he treats them all—including himself—as if they were Morelli's abstractions. In his own profoundly reflexive "paravisions," as he terms them (p. 334), he will come to create, finally, himself, what Morelli calls "The strange self-creation of the author through his work" (p. 329), another abstraction. The intellectual process of *Hopscotch* is compelling throughout, but it leaves us emotionally uninvolved. In this respect it seems more a French than a Latin American novel, for it cannot command from this distance the unique, immediate reality of the Americas.

Born in Europe and resident there for much of his adult life, Cortázar captures wonderfully the sense of loss experienced by Americans exiled in Europe. And he is a fine and challenging craftsman who has put to good uses the lessons of the Modernist masters. But he is not quite the ideal "representative of the Boom" as he has been called.[11] He seems, in the end—removed from his characters and their social setting, distanced from Latin American reality and writing about that distancing, in his language, his narrative perspective, his vision of a reality that is not quite magical—he seems more European Modernist than Latin American. Yet he provides a unique entry into that phenomenon known as the Boom: Modernist borrowings, however expertly and imaginatively assimilated, are not enough in themselves to form a new fiction and world.

III

The immediate, localized context of Manuel Puig's *Betrayed by Rita Hayworth* (1968),[12] as the title suggests, is not local at all. The staple of cultural life in Puig's Vallejos, the primary source of imagery and ideas for its residents, is Hollywood. Films alone provide respite for them from the dreariness of Argentine provincial life in the 1930s and 1940s. The prevalence and centrality of foreign films is a sign for Puig of the immaturity of their viewers and of the stunted development of the society as a whole. By the end of this narrative, Peron has come to power in Argentina. (Just as a junta controlled the nation while Puig wrote, to be followed again by Peron, to be followed by another military junta.) But this is not a political novel: political news, too, like virtually all other news, comes to us indirectly in the provinces, as if in a newsreel. The movies provide our angles of vision as well as our source material and our metaphors.

Recent demographic data have revealed that Argentina is even more a nation of immigrants than is the United States. Most of the inhabitants of Vallejos—it is a young town, and most of its people are young—are descended from families bred in Spain, Italy, or Eastern Europe. Even some of the native-born Argentines are emigrants from larger cities. This is a land of material opportunity for them all, but it is also a cultural desert, hence the significance which popular films assume in their lives.

For Mita Casals, for example, having been raised and educated in the university town of La Plata makes living in Vallejos irretrievably dull; movies and children and smalltown gossip are now her sole pleasures. She attends nearly every film shown at the Select and other local theatres and infuses Toto, her son (with his name drawn from the movies), with their peculiar reality. They become the principal imaginative force in his life. We see him grow from infancy to adolescence, his mind filled with film scenes and film stars, and we know that he will never become emotionally mature, that he cannot outgrow the shallow, romanticized vision of life provided him by his mother and Hollywood and virtually mandated by his milieu: so, too, his classmates and townsmen—even though they may not be so addicted to films as he is—and the whole of underdeveloped Argentina.

Betrayed by Rita Hayworth is, on one level, a novel of regional life in the manner of *Winesburg, Ohio*. But it is more. It makes use of multiple points of view—the repeated internal monologues of Toto and his mother and the occasional monologues of others, the commonplace book of a clearsighted spinster piano teacher, the diary of a disillusioned young romantic who will surely become a Peronist; the narrative opens with two long, involved conversations (with the speakers only partially identified), setting the Argentine scene, and closes with a letter written by Toto's father to his brother in Spain in 1933 and never mailed, telling us alone of his disappointments and preparing us for those of his family and neighbors. Underlying all are the movies: we feel frequently as if we were seeing through the camera's eye or hearing through a theatre's sound system; we see in the movies, even for those not shown at them, both source and symbol of Argentine provinciality—a metaphor and a self-reflexive narrative technique—suggesting the deeper frustrations of life in the American provinces: the failed promise of the new land. This is the immediate reality, we know, of those regions in which Puig himself was raised, but it reaches as well toward universal experience in an age made common by the movies. There is no reference at all to Joyce or to Modernist concerns in this novel. But then we recall that Joyce was the manager of the first movie theatre in Ireland in 1909 and the first to perceive the value of this new art form for the novelist.

IV

The most explicitly Joycean of contemporary novels is Guillermo Cabrera Infante's *Three Trapped Tigers* (1971).[13] The title derives from a popular Latin American tongue twister, *tres tristes tigres en un trigal* (p. 123), "three sad tigers in a wheatfield." "I used it," says the author, "because I wanted the book to have the fewest possible literary . . . connotations . . . and this was the nearest thing to an abstract title. . . ."[14] It is also one of those novels most devoid of an immediate social and political context. We are shown much of Havana nightlife, to be sure—the clubs, the music, the incessant talk, the activity on the streets as viewed from a speeding automobile, the emigrés from the country, the whores and intellectuals—but virtually nothing, in these final years of Batista's dictatorship, of the rebellion already forming in the Sierra Maestra. The seven narrated versions of the death of Trotsky, "the New Wandering Jew" (p. 238), in the styles, among others, of José Marti, José Lezama Lima, and Alejo Carpentier (both narrators and killer are Cuban), are more parody than politics. The insensitive North American tourists shown in a vignette are as much a joke (shaggy dog) as a commentary (anti-imperialist). And the character who speaks of going off to join the rebels— a prominent actor—is probably sincere but also acting. And that, aside from some complex puns (Marx and Marcuse and their excuse for ideology become "Marxcuse"—p. 288) and some passing observations on the quality of life in Havana, is virtually all. The lack of a more direct political context is, in a sense, of course, a political comment, in the spirit perhaps of Stephen Dedalus's refusal to sign the peace petition addressed to the Czar or Leopold Bloom's fantasy of becoming the new Parnell: in a milieu in which reasonable political movement has been made impossible, in which idealism and involvement seem futile at best, an active withdrawal from politics may be for some the only political act possible. Cabrera Infante left Castro's Cuba in 1965 and today lives in England.

   The literary context of *Three Trapped Tigers* is far less reticent than this. The prominent Cuban novelist Alejo Carpentier is almost invited to a party (p. 118); Borges is present in his example and characters (*e.g.,* p. 357); bad translations of Faulkner are cited (pp. 335-6); and Joyce is everywhere. He is the "megaesoteric J'aime Joys" (p. 232), the inspirer of the central but absent character called Bustrófedon, whose very name comes from *Ulysses:* Bloom's secret code is described in "Ithaca" as a "reversed alphabetic boustrophedonic punctuated quadrilinear cryptogram (vowels suppressed). . . ."[15] He is literally a "bull turner," a figure of the artist sacrificed (according to the imagery of *A Portrait*) for his art. Two young ladies of the (night)town are named by the punsters who pick them up *"Anna and Livia Pluralbelles"* (p. 140); and they speak of Bloomsday, "the anniversary two weeks back of the day when Bloom's moll sitting on the bog had let flow a long stream of unconsciousness which would become a milestone, a millstone . . . in literary history . . ." (pp. 150–1). To Bustro, as to the denizens of Barney

Kiernan's pub or the Ormond Hotel in Joyce's Dublin, "literature is no more important than conversation" (p. 277). Yet his friends, after his death, attempt to immortalize him, too, in literature—a literature of conversation.

Their narrative is the book of "Bustro's magic nightwords" (p. 232). It is a world of punning (a flying napkin is a "servjette"—p. 214), of languages twisted irrevocably together (becoming alternately "Espanglish"—p. 399—and "Spunnish"—p. 453), of the Cuban mind hard at its assumed intellectual task ("the Gulf Stream of Consciousness"—p. 367), of the linguistic ascension of a politically downtrodden people: a Joycean work indeed. Cabrera Infante has criticized the language of *Finnegans Wake:* "the creation of a unique and therefore hermetic language, full of multiple and secret associations exclusive to the writer and elaborated in a work of literature, as is the case in *Finnegans Wake*, exhibits language as it is *not*. . . . [This is] contrary to communication: that failure of language which represents any writing that is deliberately hieroglyphic."[16] And one of his characters explicitly rejects the Joycean vision of the artist as monumental creator: "You're just a writer," he says to a friend. "A spectator, a tepid soul" (p. 383). Yet it is clear that Joyce is the essential starting point of this novel, whether in emulation or repudiation or not-so-simple elaboration, or some combination of them all.

"What I set out to do," says Cabrera Infante,[17] without mentioning Joyce or the Stephen of *A Portrait*, "was not the grandiose forging of any old race's uncreated conscience, but rather a petty forgery to create a consciousness: to take the raw but malleable material of mediate reality (also called immediate memory) in *el habla de los cubanos* and to strike with it a *counterfeit* koine that Cubans could take for their change and pass it on as their own verbal currency." Yet this is a novel to be read now as much in English—American English—as in Cuban Spanish. The novelist has spoken in some detail of the translation of *Tres Tristes Tigres*[18] and compared that act, " 'in *closelaboration* with the author,' " to the work of Joyce and Larbaud and others on the "remarkable rendering into French of that complex, composite, collated, elaborate, labored English that reads like Irish in the original *Ulysses*."[19] Like Joyce's "Irish" English, Cabrera Infante's "Cuban" Spanish is directed from the start—not merely in translation—to alien readers: "dear reader," repeats one of the narrators on occasion, with some strong indication that some of those readers at least are North American ("by the fish tank . . . there was a horny ray swimming around in circles eternally. It was what we call an *obispo*, a bishop, and you—yes, *you!*—call a devilfish"—p. 347). It is not simply that English has invaded Latin American Spanish (Bustro "expound[ed] his theory that contrary to what happened in the Muddle Edges, when seven (7) languages all different came out of a single language like Latin or German or even Slav, in the tense future these twenty-one . . . languages would turn into one single long language based on or sticking to or on a guided turn with English, and man (and/or woman) would speak at least in this partition of the world and till eternity do us part an enormous lingua frangla, a sensible, possible, stable Babel"—p. 230), or even that the novelist knows with Charles de Gaulle and the unthinking American tourist that language is power: language here is everything: not simply power, but identity; not simply our connector in space, but as universal as history and myth.

"As I've said many times," says the author,[20] "the book is a gallery of voices." Voices singing on impossibly high notes, voices ringing changes on words, voices confessing or lying to a psychiatrist or to a friend or to oneself, voices in love with their own sounds: there are at least four distinct narrators in *Three Trapped Tigers*, barely differentiated, revolving around Bustrófedon, aspects of a single Cuban character. "All these names do not conceal character but a voice, a different texture among the different voices that make up the book, and, at times, as protagonists in a play which may or may not be their own game."[21] They are as diverse and as ultimately uniform as the voices of *Ulysses* and those (nightvoices) of the *Wake* (with one dream perhaps, but many voices to expound it). Bustro dies, ironically, of a lesion on the brain "(he, poor guy, would have called it a lesson) [formed] since he was a kid, or earlier, from birth, or before he was even formed . . . , which pressed on his brain and made him say all those marvelous things and play with words so he ended his life as a new Adam, giving everything a name as though he really was inventing language . . ." (p. 231).[22] For Bustro, as for Joyce and perhaps for Cabrera Infante, "Whenever he made a pun a pain was hidden" (p. 388).

It is possible to speak of *Three Trapped Tigers*, as one of the narrators does, as "aleatory literature" (with a dictionary rather than a score for the writer and, for the reader, "along with the book . . . an anagram to make a title out of and a couple of dice. With these three elements anyone would be able to make his own book"—p. 357)[23] or, as the author does as "baroque" "—and by baroque I precisely mean its idle

imitations, its tricky travesties, its embezzled embellishments to con-
form/form voluptuous volutes. . . ."[24] The baroque, we are told by a
voice of (perhaps false) modesty, is "the art of honest plagiarism" (p.
321). This might also be a comment on, and homage to, the art of
James Joyce, not often called baroque.

What book, then, could be more self-consciously literary, more obviously apolitical than this aleatorical, baroque, derivative yet highly
original account of the desultory events of a day in (late) June in the
capital city of an undeveloped land? "However, in Fidel's Cuba, my
book is not merely banned, it is considered anathema."[25] *Three Trapped
Tigers* is, finally, paradoxically, a political work after all: political not
merely in the sense of the foreign tourist who would not deign to learn
his hosts' language or of the head of state inveighing against the
invasion of his language by an ally's. Freedom of speech, Cabrera
Infante insists, is more than the freedom to speak one's mind; it is the
freedom to speak at all—for the artist, the ultimate freedom. For all its
literary context, *Three Trapped Tigers* was intended from the start as
political comment, as memorial to the last free Cuban speech. "When I
began writing the book in Havana, Summer of '61, I already suspected—suspected hell! I *knew* that the lives and the language depicted,
reproduced in it, those talkative specimens and their spoken habitat,
were condemned to disappear into silence, not in the course of
time . . . but rather to be abolished by history—that is to say, condemned to vanish by the revolution through an immediate catastrophe
by decree: a loquacious people reduced to laconism."[26] For all the vigor
of its literature, its sense of impending force about to burst upon the
world in a generation to come, much of Latin America remains today
politically undeveloped, unfree. In such a milieu, it may be meaningless
to attempt to sort out politics and art, to separate language and
literature from life. The rise of the Latin American novel in this
generation is irremediably a political fact, whatever the immediate
subject of any individual novel. As Carolos Fuentes has put it, "The
Counter Reformation destroyed the modern opportunity, not only for
Spain, but also for its colonies; however the new Latin American novel
presents a newer founding of the language, one opposed to the calcified
prolongations of that false and feudal founding of our continent with its
equally false and anachronic language."[27] With his new language, in his
old but new land, the Latin American novelist of our day, like Cabrera
Infante, cannot not be political.

V

When Stephen Dedalus rejects the appeals of "universal brotherhood" and "universal peace"[28] and declines to add his name to the petition addressed to the Czar, he seems to be setting the pattern for all subsequent Modernist novelists: involvement in politics is necessarily harmful to the cause of art. "—My signature is of no account, he said politely. You are right to go your way. Leave me to go mine."[29] An artist at this point in sensibility alone, Stephen will not allow his classmates even to think of him in political terms; he refuses to be labeled as either radical or reactionary; he perceives that politics and religion are inextricably linked—the most faithful of his classmates are among the most politically involved—and not only in imperial, Catholic Ireland; he understands that both are death to the artist.

But Stephen is not in all regards a reliable spokesman for Joyce. Joyce, of course, devoted his own life to his art and carefully avoided overt involvement in politics. But Leopold Bloom, who is so much closer to Joyce than is Stephen, is in his way a most political figure: he identifies with Parnell, "the fallen leader" of Ireland;[30] he offers a program of political reform that is vaguely Socialist and distinctly confused but also idealistic and not unadmirable;[31] he is rumored (falsely, no doubt) to be somehow involved with the nationalist resistance. Bloom knows from his own experience the stupidity of the chauvinist, yet he is a patriot, and he becomes in imagination the scapegoat who bears the sins of his people and thereby redeems them. Joyce treats Bloom's fantasy with irony but also, I feel, with some sympathy. Political affairs should not be the concern of the artist perhaps, but even in democratic lands they may well provide some significant part of his subject matter.

It is hardly surprising, then, given the history of despotism in Latin America, that politics should provide a major theme for the novelists of the Boom. (As of this writing, at the close of December 1981, there are only three or perhaps four reasonably representative governments among the twenty republics of Latin America; fewer than one-fourth of the quarter-billion inhabitants of the continent and its environs live in what might even loosely be considered democracies.)[32] It is hardly surprising as well that politics in these fictions are almost always revolutionary and almost always veiled. The realities of the place dictate the radicalism; the forms of Magic Realism provide the screen of perception behind which the novelist may, for a time, disguise his possibly unrealistic vision. And so we may speak of *Three Trapped Tigers* as a political work even though Batista and Castro alike are absent from its scenes—because, paradoxically, they are so blatantly left out. Cabrera Infante's novel, by this reasoning, is more characteristically a product of the place and time than is that more direct expression of Cuban political life, Alejo Carpentier's *Explosion in a Cathedral* (1962).[33] Still more characteristic, in this sense, is Reinaldo Arenas's *Hallucinations* (1966).[34]

Hallucinations, or *El mundo alucinante*—"The Hallucinatory World"—seems a strange novel to have come out of Castro's Cuba in its early years: a revolutionary novel with critical implications for the revolutionary process. It is not surprising, perhaps, that it was published originally in Mexico, or that it purports to be a chronicle of a much earlier time, or that its political surface is veiled by its near-magical, hallucinatory vision. There is no single reality, either objective or psychological, which can be firmly identified and named within Arenas's narrative. "Of my arrival and non-arrival at Pamplona, and what happened to me without happening to me" is the title of one of his chapters (p. 111), reflecting only in part the blur of imagination and fact, history and legend, inner vision and outward event which characterizes the book. The "I" of the narrative—referred to also at times as "he" and as "you"—is Fray Servando Teresa de Mier, an eighteenth-century Mexican memoirist. His *Memorias* are allegedly historical, yet their historicity can today only be guessed at. To his original, Arenas adds the further distancing of this narrative, which encompasses not merely Fray Servando's adventuresome life but also his book.[35]

Arenas's Fray Servando travels through Europe and the Americas in search of personal vindication and national independence. He is a learned country boy, naive and honest, who is continually thrown into prison by archbishops and nobles who recognize him as a threat—because of his honesty and innocence, in New World or Old—to their own vested interests. The foolish idealist is thus made a revolutionary. He escapes from prisons and from towns by flying over their walls; he is treated so miserably by his captors (tortured, starved, gnawed at by rats, assaulted by visions of unforgiving foes and lustful women) that it would seem that he must have died many times; his experiences are rendered so matter-of-factly, so blandly (he swims under water from England to America in two short sentences: "This was one of the worst sea journeys I ever made . . ."—p. 188), that they seem somehow more than surreal: idiosyncratic, dreamlike, and perhaps a bit magical.

Fray Servando survives his ordeal to return to a revolutionary Mexico that is as unmindful of individual freedom as was the Old World regime which it replaced. He refuses to be honored now as a patriot as he refused in the past to be stilled as a rebel.[36] He has been disillusioned by Royalist Spain, by Papal Italy, by Revolutionary France, by the mercantile Democratic United States, by a Free Latin America: disillusionment has become vested within him. Because Arenas's account incorporates passages from Fray Servando's original and echoes from histories about him, we may be inclined to view its perspective as largely historical: a criticism of European colonialism in the New World. Yet we sense a current political import as well (although the only scenes set in Cuba are in a Spanish prison): do all revolutionary regimes inevitably betray the revolutions which brought them to power?[37]

Fray Servando is a mixture of Candide and of medieval legends of miraculous saints' lives, of Dante (the Spanish king himself guides him, in a vision, through the Spanish hell—pp. 94 ff.) and of more modern anti-Realistic works (he is befriended in England by Woolf's Orlando—pp. 177–87). There is also a touch of the picaresque in his adventures and of Rabelais as well. But his tradition is more than literary; he is the young man from the provinces and something more. He will lose his innocence as a matter of course, but he will not accept the inevitability of his initiation into the world of political experience. And he will never lose his idiosyncratic perspective, his belief (Arenas's belief, that is, and not the original's) that liberty remains possible if difficult, that life is tragic yet livable, "that even the most painful situations are touched with both irony and brutality, and this turns every real tragedy into a grotesque and hilarious calamity" (pp. 126–7): a hallucinatory world indeed.

Unlike his countryman Carpentier's work, which seems almost European in its tone, its detached political perspective, and its reading of historical reality, Arenas's narrative borrows from European traditions but is indisputably American—excessive, fantastic, close to objective reality but never quite of it—in its vision of the world. Its principal starting point is the Old World view of America as the New World Garden, innocent, honest, filled with potential. Its conclusion is that American experience, human and political, has disproven that view. In Fray Servando's experience, America has become the Old World.

El mundo alucinante is more overtly political than most of the contemporary fictions of Latin America, yet even its politics purport to be historical and not current: some small part of Joyce's strictures survive.

It is because we know something of the history of the times in that politically unhappy continent that we may feel in the novels of Mallea, Cortázar and Puig, Lezama Lima, Arenas, and Cabrera Infante, the unstated presence of a Peron or of a Batista or Castro. We may infer as well from this absence of statement the totalitarian force which constricts normal political life and deters political reference, even in art. The problem is not confined to Argentina or Cuba: novelists throughout the continent have been imprisoned or exiled in recent years for their political beliefs—even for the potentiality of belief. It is no coincidence that so few of the novelists of the Boom continue to live in the countries in which they were born and of which they write. Behind the shifting structures and time schemes of *Hopscotch*, the multiple points of view of *Rita Hayworth*, the exploding language of *Three Trapped Tigers* and the surreal vision explored by Arenas—hidden behind the multiple styles and techniques of Magic Realism—lurk the unaccepting, uneasy, perhaps radical, even revolutionary politics imposed on the novelists by the politicians and their bitter reality.

VI

The politics of *Quarup* (1967) and *Don Juan's Bar* (1971), by the Brazilian newspaperman-turned-novelist Antonio Callado, are overt: marked by narrative inventiveness, to be sure, but not hidden behind it: not subtle or indirect but immediate, concrete. Very close to the surface of these fictions are the inescapable realities of public life in modern-day Brazil: the generals ruling the land; the Catholic Church co-opted by its desire for order; the business community distorted by greed; the public servants serving themselves and a select public only; the intellectuals proclaiming loudly their liberal beliefs but unable to put them into action; the professional revolutionaries (the amateurs are quickly disposed of) cut off from all hope of change. The Amazon jungle is officially opened up to "civilization" and "progress," and the Indian Protection Service serves its charges by practicing their genocide. The Indians' insistence on following their old ways is an implied comment on the new, and so, like all those who resist, they must be removed. The Indians and insurrectionists are equated in their resistance and in their ruin. In his open-ended first novel, published in Brazil three years after the military coup which ended constitutional government there,

Callado appears to suggest the possibility of growth, through myth, for nation and individuals alike. By the time of its sequel, virtually all hope has gone. The Indian myths—the source of potential redemption—have been diverted and the land and most of its people disenfranchised.

Callado's novels are both regionalist and symbolic, set in particular locales but directed toward the nation as a whole, concerned both with the social and spiritual aspects of Brazilian life. They are in this respect part of a long native literary tradition, dating from 1902 and Euclides da Cunha's *Rebellion in the Backlands (Os Sertões)*. Begun as a sociological report of a late nineteenth-century rural rebellion against the newly formed republic—da Cunha was a field engineer who accompanied the conquering army expedition—told from the dispassionate viewpoint of the urban observer who, like the coastal cities of his homeland, looks to Europe for his culture, *Os Sertões* turns suddenly inward into a novel whose admiration and respect are all for the rebels. In the *sertão*, the vast arid inhospitable backlands, the racially mixed *sertanejos* have learned to adapt to the diversity of their environment and have made it the source of their strength. By refusing to acknowledge and accept its own diverse peoples and cultures, da Cunha argues, the nation as a whole loses strength, suffers spiritually as well as politically.

The other major works in the tradition—Jorge Amado's *The Violent Land (Terras do Sem Fin*, 1942) and João Guimarães Rosa's *The Devil to Pay in the Backlands (Grande Sertão: Veredas*, 1956), which are comparable unions of social background and fiction—make essentially the same point: the nation which denies its identity, which turns against some central aspect of its own inheritance—the mestizo backlands, the Indian jungles, political reality or myth—can never realize its potential. In the late nineteenth century, soon after its establishment as a republic, "Some saw Brazil as the potential rival of the United States in America; at the same time, it was obvious that the South American state had not the sense of identity and mission which the northern power had."[38] Its identity today, Callado would argue, is as confused, its sense of mission more brutally perverted.

Quarup is clearly rooted within this Regionalist/political Brazilian tradition, although it moves beyond its source in the intensity and specificity of its political message and in its broad symbolic approach. It calls not just for awareness but for action; it deals not just with one but with all the major regions of Brazil. Callado endeavors to recreate the whole, vast panorama of the land through the personal odyssey of a single character: Father Fernando, a learned priest who longs for the glorious past (represented by the Guaraní Indian empire founded by the Jesuits in the eighteenth century)[39] and who becomes Nando, sensualist and man of affairs, companion of the Xingu Indians and member of the first expedition to reach and map the center of Brazil. Like his nation, presumably, Nando suffers—potentially virile as he is—from premature ejaculation. (He wastes his strength as Brazil spends its own in obeisance to the Yankees.) As the heart of the land, however, he experiences perfect love for the first time with Francisca, one-time fiancée of a dead revolutionary named Levindo. Back again in the city, he becomes active in the legal revolution of the underclass fostered by President Jânio Quadros, and he is imprisoned and tortured when the military takes power. Like Moses, he kills a particularly vicious soldier and so is prepared to become a guerilla in the sertão, to be recast as Levindo for a Brazil turned Francisca. The final images of the novel are of the *quarup*—an ingathering of Indian tribes to celebrate the death and resurrection of an old chief—in which the priest-sensualist-revolutionary is himself reborn as a new kind of Christ in what will some day, perhaps, be a new kind of Brazil.[40]

Don Juan's Bar, however, published only a few years later, indicates that such a renewal will not be easy or simply symbolic, certainly not for the sort of dilettante that Nando once was. Don Juan's Bar is a gathering place for the leftist intelligentsia of Rio de Janeiro. Here, they can speak freely of the revolt which they would join and which some of them, stung by their repeated talk and inaction, eventually will join and in which they will die. Their yearning, philosophical discussions (about freedom and justice and power, the identity of a man and his acts, the union of man and nature that may be effected through action) are played out against a backdrop of scenes from the actual revolution; Che Guevara's band advances through the lowlands of Bolivia, ignored by the peasants whom they would save, and pursued by their unseen and unnamed enemies: the American CIA, the Brazilian military dictators, and their right-wing compatriots throughout Latin America. The Brazilian intellectuals, weighted down by the images and experiences of their city lives, will try to join Che in Bolivia and will be destroyed as his band is destroyed, their causes equally futile. But Che at least reaches toward the sort of mythic union of which the intellectuals talk and which they fail to enact; perhaps he will prove to be the fertility figure—fusion of man and action and nature—who will some day redeem them all, those who would join and those who ignore him alike: not a practical hope, however, merely a symbol.[41]

Callado's books are powerful politically, in part because they deal forthrightly with issues which beset the whole continent and which others may consider only tangentially. But they are less impressive as novels. Even a brief summary of *Quarup* seems ludicrously overplotted; the panoramic career of the revolutionary priest may work well as a symbol of diverse Brazilian realities and hopes, but it is so improbable that it is sometimes unintentionally comic. This is not the improbability of magic realism, which involves and carries along the reader in its wondrous flow; this is simply unbelievable in human terms. And *Don Juan's Bar*, with its more restricted narrative approach, is similarly clumsy at times and similarly unconvincing in terms of its characters' lives: their motivations are credible, but they and their actions are not. Put differently, Callado's fictions fail where his politics work—and they fail because of their politics. That *Quarup* and *Don Juan's Bar* together address significant issues—whatever perspective we view them from— must be undeniable: the movement away from democracy in Latin America and toward military dictatorship has spread rapidly, and frighteningly, in the years since Callado first turned to novels.[42] But the literary and human failures of his books raise inevitably the issue of politics and fiction: the issue of their incompatibility. They appear to suggest that those other writers, Arenas and Cabrera Infante, Puig and Cortázar, are wise to avoid explicit contemporary political comment and to allow the realized states of their fictions and nations to speak for themselves—if only inferentially. It remains for the masters of current Latin American fiction, García Márquez and Fuentes, to resolve fully the issue of a demanding politics and a demanding art.

VII

There may be another way still of treating political issues in the novel: neither overtly nor by indirection as theme but as simple subject matter, as one facet only of the society being explored. In *The Obscene Bird of Night* (1970), José Donoso differentiates carefully between what might be termed political and what is actually historic, between the temporal demands of modern Chilean society and the spirit of the people and place as it has developed through time and as it helps to form social institutions and to mold individual lives. This is Chile before Allende and, of course, before Pinochet, and Donoso's intent is neither to advocate revolutionary reform nor to decry totalitarian rule; his concern is not demonstrably political at all, not even political in the unstated manner of Cabrera Infante or the distant allegorical historicism of Arenas. Something further is at stake in Donoso's critique of life in Chile, both ancient and modern. His primary concern, as manifested through his point of view, is with the individual, but his is an individual who cannot be distinguished from his culture. Personal and societal decay in Chile, the novelist shows us, are inseparable. The obscene society of *The Obscene Bird of Night* is viewed through a solitary lens, a single Chilean consciousness, witty, observant, obsessed, perhaps mentally disturbed, potentially unrealiable throughout, representative. It is a brilliant fusion of function and form, of borrowed Modernist technique and native vision, a firm and powerful statement of the new fiction of Latin America as it is grounded in the old.

In *The Boom in Spanish American Literature: A Personal History,* Donoso speaks disparagingly of the *Costumbristas* of an earlier generation and of "the lack of boldness," the "everyday quality" of *Coronation,* his own first novel, "an offshoot of the classic *costumbrismo* of our environment." *Coronation* (1957) is derived from characters and events from the Chilean past, some of them quite obviously autobiographical, those observed surface realities of "the most remote and at that time the most stagnant country of the continent" (p. 52).[43] The novel depicts a world of enfeebled rich and embattled poor, a past without meaning and a present without form, equally powerless to confront and master the harsh and empty facts of Chilean life. The arteriosclerosis of one of the principal characters serves patently as symbol of the malady which afflicts the city and nation as a whole. *This Sunday* (1966), Donoso's second novel, reaches beyond the capital, Santiago, but is concerned with the same basic national themes: the interaction of rich and poor, of rural and urban, of individuals and their society. Again, they are marked uniformly by failure: the now abandoned home of the narrator's grandparents—the home in which he was raised, seemingly the same house as in *Coronation*—serves as symbol of decaying human and social relationships in modern Chile. Both novels are rooted in observable details, and both are, in the end, intrinsically omniscient; Donoso has not yet mastered his heritage and the mechanics of his craft. When he speaks in *The Boom* of the problems encountered by the novelists of his generation, he is speaking clearly of his own early novels: "What shackled the novel most was the impoverishing criterion of mimesis and especially mimesis of what was verifiably 'ours'—social problems, peoples, landscapes—which was transformed into a measuring stick of literary quality since the quality of a work could be appreciated only by the inhabitants of the country or the region described and was relevant only to them" (p. 17).

As Donoso describes the development of the so-called Boom of the 1960s and 1970s, it is the movement beyond the region which made possible the growth of a Latin American literature, as opposed to the separate Chilean or Argentine or Mexican or Cuban literatures which had existed before then. "[M]y generation of novelists looked not only (and almost exclusively) outside Latin America but also outside our own language, toward the United States, toward the Anglo-Saxon countries, toward France and Italy, in search of sustenance, opening ourselves up, allowing ourselves to be contaminated by all the 'impurities' from the outside . . ." (p. 18). Among the Modernists they found a general sense of literary endeavor and seriousness—moral and psychological support—as well as specific models of linguistic freedom and expansive technique. And then they turned inward again. It was not, finally, the distant Modernist masters who made possible Donoso's own breakthrough but his "reading of Spanish American novels . . . [which] permitted me . . . to incorporate the European and North American masters as something of my own" (p. 84). This is surely the process which led to the fortunate explosion of *The Obscene Bird of Night*.

The *donnée* of this narrative may again be autobiographical, but it is its method rather than its subject which derives from and/or parallels the novelist's experience. As a visiting scholar (alien) in the United States, in 1969, after surgery for bleeding ulcers, Donoso "for many hours . . . was delirious with hallucinations, split personality, paranoia and suicide attempts stemming from his inability to tolerate morphine pain killers."[44] He was experiencing in his own mind something akin to the relativity of perception of Modernist narrative modes—and of his own new novel as well. Yet the characters and events of this novel— even the buildings in which most of the action takes place—seem largely invented. The theme is again the inherent decay of Chilean society, but the disease is no longer literal or simply symbolic; the narrative method itself, its hallucinatory perspective, makes manifest the nation's failure of vision and purpose, the rottenness of its institutions, the self-destructiveness of its people. Donoso has at last mastered his Chile, with all its historical and potentially political import, and he has done so by means of a narrative technique whose mechanics are borrowed from North and West yet whose vision seems uniquely South American. He thus points the way in *The Obscene Bird of Night* to that union of subject and method, of vision and theme, of innate and alien, which is popularly called Magic Realism and which has come to characterize for many critics the essence of contemporary fiction in Latin America.[45] The indigenous ingredients have been in place for a generation or more; it is only the addition of the Modernist use of point of view which makes possible this final, original union.

And so it is appropriate that the novel should open with the return to Chile of one of its native sons from Europe. When Jerónimo de Azcoitía comes back to his homeland at the start of the Second World War, he is urged by his uncle, the Reverend Father Don Clemente de Azcoitía, to join the conservative party, to run for the legislature, and to marry and father a son: to perpetuate the family's name and influence, to resist change and carry on as before. Although he scorns politics and has no particular beliefs other than in himself and his family, Jerónimo does run for office; he becomes a powerful legislator, a symbol of his careless, oppressive class; and he marries the beautiful and devout Inés Santillana. But the only son he can father, after years of failure, is the grotesque, even monstrous Boy.

Jerónimo's secretary and aide, Humberto Peñaloza, claims to be the sole narrator of these events as well as a principal actor in them. Yet certain actions appear to be seen through other eyes—through Jerónimo's or Ines's, for instance, or through those of the inhabitants of the institutions controlled by the Azcoitías, the Casa de Ejercicios Espirituales de la Encarnación (for old serving women and young orphan girls), and La Rinconada (The Corner, designed especially for Boy). And Humberto appears now not as the scholar that he claims he once was, the ruler of La Rinconada, but as Mudito, the mute old servant at the Casa de Ejercicios, another grotesque. We cannot even be certain that he was once a scholar and Jerónimo's aide. Humberto-Mudito has no trouble reconciling these apparent contradictions; all their voices are really his, he contends, and his muteness is merely pretense (like his lack of virility), a means of escaping the burdens of his former position. Indeed, he goes further and claims that he has frequently in the past assumed his master's role, that he was the hero of

the famous act which made Jerónimo a symbol of aristocratic force
(overbearing a rebellious mob) and that he may be the father of the
monstrous heir (conceived perhaps on Inés, in a magical rite, or on Peta
Ponce, the old witch who is her servant, or on Iris Mateluna, the
orphaned teenaged virgin whore). He himself is not quite certain, but
his narrative suggests all three possibilities (perhaps, somehow, collectively). He even seems at times to become Boy himself, although his
may also be the ṣhriveled body sewn up in a sack at the end, thrown in
a fire for warmth, and (at the time of Jerónimo's murder at La
Rinconada) overturned into the river: disembodied at last, free of his
lifelong trials. He may even be lesser than this; he may be the
manuscript which he ostensibly writes and which he carries with him to
be dispersed in the end.[46]

The contradictory possibilities of Mudito's (?) narration raise questions
of reliability ("There's no historical record of my shout, because my
voice made no sound. My words didn't pass into history"—p. 166),[47] of
verisimilitude ("I don't want to repeat the scene [of procreation], there
was no such scene, it was a nightmare that produced monsters . . ."—
p. 186), of reality itself (in the world of grotesques created especially for
him, to make him feel that he is the ideal of physical beauty, "Boy was
to grow up believing that things came into being as his eyes discovered
them and died when he stopped looking at them . . ."—p. 197). Questions of relativity within relativity: whose voice(s) is (are) this (these), in
fact? is he (are they) always truthful, or ever truthful? what is the
objective reality of these events, and is that their ultimate reality? We
cannot answer such questions with any certainty—any more than we
can answer definitively similar questions in Joyce's "Circe"—but we do
comprehend the real and discoverable implications of the surreal vision
which they evoke. These unanswerable questions, in their ambiguity, are
their own answer. They are the expected problems of Modernist narration, and Donoso relates them to the most traditional of Modernist
themes, the working out of individual identity; but this is an identity at
once individual and national, decidedly Latin American.

In Donoso's Chile, all life is perceived as a series of horror shows and
ironies, possessing both human and symbolic import. Inés is taken away
from the supposed refuge of the Casa de Ejercicios and thrust into an
insane asylum: her reward for a life of familial pride, religious fervor,
and sexual frustration. Jerónimo is killed at La Rinconada, as he tries at
last to know his son, for threatening to move Boy to the outside world:

his retribution for bringing such an heir into his world. And Boy rejects the real world (alleged), connives at his father's murder, and returns forever—and knowingly—to the world of grotesques in which he is our model and representative figure; "if we don't wear some kind of disguise we're nothing," Mudito warns us all (p. 121). The lives of the Azcoitías are touched throughout by an ancient folk legend of a young girl turned to a witch—a girl of good family, seduced, bearing a son, saving miraculously the Casa—perhaps the ancestor whom Inés would sanctify, or the bride of Jerónimo, or the mother of Boy; she represents "the underside of life" (p. 148) which lurks always beneath their lives, bringing to them something of the complexity and horror and lost dignity of myth. She would speak, it seems, for the nation's past, for its fusion of times and realities, its obsessions and fears, but we do not even know who it is who narrates her tale or which, if any, of its many versions may be most accurate. All identities are blurred, all relationships questionable, in such a realm as this: of the citizen and his State, of the worshipper and her Church, of fathers and sons, of narrators and narrative art. "[I]f you don't escape," Mudito predicts, "you'll have to be a self again, whose identity you no longer remember and that exists you don't know where" (p. 114), and we must wonder whether his narration, like his nation's history, is an effort to seek his identity or to hide it forever.

The political possibilities in so symbolic a fiction are undeniable—particularly in light of our knowledge of recent events in Chile. Yet despite the terrible decade which followed the publication (in Spain) of *The Obscene Bird of Night*, we cannot view this as a political novel, even in retrospect. Donoso's political views are subsumed in his concern for the larger issues of Chilean identity. Thus when Jerónimo de Azcoitía intimidates the rebellious mob outside the conservative Social Club (whose members have just stolen another election), we see the episode not as it reflects the just grievances of the masses but as it focuses on Jerónimo as an individual whose potential is delimited by his class: his apparent political success here foreshadows his greater, personal failure at La Rinconada. To the extent that Donoso does advocate change—and this is available only by inference—it is not for institutional reform that he calls but for individual awareness of the national (hence individual) condition. He speaks not as a reformer but as a type of Juvenalian satirist, holding a moral mirror up to his countrymen.

But, then, the reality reflected in that mirror is so nebulous, so

shifting, so difficult to define with any certainty that we may suspect
that the creation of the mirror itself is the novelist's prime goal: that
he aims not to reform reality or even to reflect it fully in its most
characteristic subjects; that his intent is to build the most telling of
narrative structures and to allow it, in a wonderful union of function
and form, to speak for itself. It is the surreal perspective of *The Obscene
Bird of Night* which enables us to perceive its hallucinatory world. Such
a narrative technique—such a union of theme and technique—derives
directly from the Modernist example. Endeavoring in his early works to
render Chilean reality but still lacking an appropriate point of view,
Donoso could merely reflect back the surfaces which he saw before
him—hence his subsequent dismissal of those books as *costumbrismo:*
local colorist, superficial, and, however indigenous their subjects, ultimately untruthful to his reality. It is only when he has learned to look at
the reality through borrowed lenses that the novelist can see beyond its
surfaces and reveal the truths lurking there. Jerónimo discusses with an
old family retainer Humberto's " 'belief that my life would make a good
biography.' "

> "Yes, he started out by talking about that, but later on he distorted
> everything. Humberto had no talent for simplicity. He felt the need to twist
> normal things around, a kind of compulsion to take revenge and destroy,
> and he complicated and deformed his original project so much that it's as if
> he'd lost himself forever in the labyrinth he invented as he went along that
> was filled with darkness and terrors more real than himself and his other
> characters, always nebulous, fluctuating, never real human beings, always
> disguises, actors, dissolving greasepaint . . . yes, his obsessions and his
> hatreds were more important than the reality he needed to deny . . ."
> "Interesting, Emperatriz. You're a good literary critic . . ."
> "So many years of living close to him." (p. 392)

They are describing, of course, this narrative in which they are characters. Yet for all their closeness to the narrator, neither perceives that his
reality is not theirs; they would have him continue to write local color.
It is not until the Latin American novelist learns to see anew his familiar
reality that he can render it fully, convincingly, in a fiction that is not
local but universal. Magic Realism, so evidently a native growth, in fact
demands a borrowed technique. As Donoso's novels so brilliantly reveal,
Latin American fiction does not become truly Latin American until,
paradoxically, its practitioners begin to build on the Modernist example.

VIII

The fictions of Mario Vargas Llosa are explicitly Peruvian—set in the varied milieus of this surprisingly diverse land, rooted in the social and symbolic facts of its life—but they illustrate brilliantly, at the same time, the development of that contemporary literary mode practiced through-out Latin America and known popularly as Magic Realism, the singular approach to reality which distinguishes this from all other fictions post-Modernism, which links it, indeed, to the Modernists. Robbe-Grillet declares that all literary revolutions are conducted in the name(s) of realism; he speaks as an enemy of the Modernists and posits a reality in which physical objects, devoid of but threatening meaning, overwhelm their viewers—viewers whose very means of perception have been provided by Modernist innovations in narrative technique. We can hardly imagine one of Arnold Bennett's objectively observed pro-tagonists becoming obsessed by the rows of banana trees which he sees from his window or by the stain of a centipede on his meticulously detailed living room wall: this is so even though the passions which activate his characters may be similar to those which possess Robbe-Grillet's. It is not so much the facts of their lives as their very different means of perception—and the differing implications for their viewers—which distinguish the characters, and worlds, of Robbe-Grillet's post-Modernist fictions from those of the Edwardian Bennett, only half a century earlier.

Bennett's tradition, as Virginia Woolf shows us in "Mr. Bennett and Mrs. Brown," externalizes all objects; he avoids much of the omniscient commentary and obvious control of his Victorian predecessors and accentuates their social concerns, but in other respects his world is a simple continuation of theirs. The Edwardians, according to Woolf, "laid an enormous stress upon the fabric of things. They have given us a house in the hope that we may be able to deduce the human beings who live there. To give them their due, they have made that house much better, worth living in. But if you hold that novels are in the first place about people, and only in the second about the houses they live in, that is the wrong way to set about it."[48] There are few major changes in narrative practice or vision in the half-century between, say, *Hard Times* in 1854 and *The Old Wives' Tale* in 1908, and the Victorian-Edwardian line did not suddenly die out with the ascension of Woolf and the Modernists: it is easy to forget that *Riceyman Steps*, one of

Bennett's most characteristic works, did not appear until 1923, the year after *Jacob's Room* and *Ulysses*.

The essentially material world which we find in Bennett is one, so Karl Marx tells us (in evident agreement with Woolf), that dehumanizes its inhabitants and beholders and thus makes a human-centered revolution inevitable. For we create the external world in the process of perceiving it, says Marx, almost as if he were a critic of what is today called "narratology," and in doing so we shape ourselves; man, in Marx' view, "duplicates himself not only, as in consciousness, intellectually, but also actively, in reality, and therefore he contemplates himself in a world that he has created. . . . [Thus,] all *objects* become for him the *objectification of himself,* become objects which confirm and realize his individuality, become *his* objects; that is, *man himself* becomes the object."[49] Marx's description of the individual's status in Victorian society seems equally a description of Robbe-Grillet's close-sighted, post-Modernist protagonists, who are also apparently objective about the world which they view, who attempt to eschew all emotion and who end by objectifying themselves: who become things because they cannot be human. Robbe-Grillet's world has perhaps more in common with Bennett's than he might care to acknowledge—and less in common with Joyce's than some critics have claimed.

By removing the obtrusive author of the Victorians and Edwardians from their narratives, Joyce and Woolf and the other Modernist novelists effect a revolution as profound in its way as Marx's: they make it possible for their characters, for the first time in the history of the novel, to balance outward and inner vision, the world of objects and the realm of emotion, to become fully human; and they induce their readers, for the first time, to share in the process of discovery and thus to become more fully human themselves. All subsequent developments in narration, in novel and criticism alike—whether or not they acknowledge it—have of necessity been reactions to Modernist technique and the Modernist vision of man enduring in an inhumane world. Hence the current British reversion to omniscience and the mistaken critical view which assaults the Modernists through Robbe-Grillet, allegedly their ally and representative. Robbe-Grillet himself demonstrates that those same narrative techniques can be employed to present a very different reality and image of man and to deny the Modernist vision of life.

As for the Magic Realists, so-called, they make use of these same techniques but to yet another, more human-centered end, one that is pointed toward in the example of Joyce and his fellows as well as in the perceived experience of their own continent. The heightened sense of reality which they offer in their novels—what Alejo Carpentier first identified as *"lo real maravilloso americano"*[50]—is surely indigenous, but it connects to and borrows from the Modernist vision and practice. Thus, when old José Arcadio Buendía, in García Márquez's *One Hundred Years of Solitude,* literally becomes part of the chestnut tree to which he has been tied for years, it is not a denial of his human nature, as Robbe-Grillet might have it, but an affirmation that he remains part of the natural process, as Bloom does less dramatically, an integral facet of that larger pattern of myth affecting all of our lives even in an urbanized and disharmonious world, a universal involvement that may give form and meaning still to individual lives: not a mundane realism, to be sure, but reality nonetheless. There is little to prepare us for this in the work of the *Criollistas* and *Costumbristas* of a prior generation; their reality is straightforward, recognizable—if a bit exotic—even to a North American eye. For all their closeness to the lands and peoples of the continent, they are not a significant, inevitable source of Magic Realism. The mode would never have developed had the indigenous been the only source.

It was only from the perspective of his long residence in Europe that Borges, one-quarter English and thoroughly bilingual, discovered his unchanging Buenos Aires. It was at the British Museum that the Guatemalan Asturias first thought seriously of Mayan art and at the Sorbonne that he mastered Mayan literature and myth. And it was in Paris that Carpentier, who was born in Havana of European parents, whose first language was French, and who lived most of his formative years in France, learned how to regard his native Caribbean. It cannot be surprising, then, that their America is not precisely a literal representation of that surface materiality which Local Colorists and Realists have defined as "reality." "There are no boundaries between reality and dreams, between reality and fiction, between what is seen and what is imagined," says Asturias,[51] with his European sensibility, his Jungian perspective, and his Mayan eye. And we sense that García Márquez, writing of his hamlet in the Colombian jungle from his homes in Barcelona and Mexico City, would not allow "reality"—even in so simple a formulation as this—to be opposed to dreams, to fiction, and to the imaginary. To him and to many of his generation, they are all one, all equally "real."

Magic Realism is in large part the product of a continent still living close to its roots in nature and informed still by the life-giving potential of myth; that is, it is the product of the Indian experience of these lands, even if that experience is not shared by everyone and if the Indians themselves are being killed off in some of these lands: at least this is the native experience as it is perceived by writers who themselves share in it only sympathetically. (Asturias boasts of his mestizo blood, but virtually all the novelists of the Boom are of full European ancestry. Only José María Arguedas of Peru grew up among Indians, speaks fluently an Indian language—Quechua—and writes from an Indian perspective.)[52]

Balanced against this (in part imagined) indigenous growth as a source of Magic Realism is a borrowed, purely literary source, the narrative daring of the Modernist novelists of Europe and North America. As displayed, for example, in the "Circe" episode of *Ulysses*, it may cut across customary distinctions in consciousness and point of view and, in the process, reorder traditional concepts of reality. As Leopold Bloom and Stephen Dedalus sit in the reception area of Bella Cohen's whorehouse in the midst of a slum in imperial Dublin—half a century and half a world removed from the Latin American interior—each man moves in and out of surface reality, shifts without warning from wakefulness to dream, from consciousness to preconscious to deepest unconscious. And then, without transition and apparently unawares, they share with each other the separate images of their disparate but touching days. Bloom's old friend, Professor Goodwin, suddenly appears in Stephen's dream—does he know him, too, we wonder, or is this some sort of sympathetic memory? And how do we account for the fact that it is directly out of Bloom's visualization of Virag, his long-dead father, an image that Stephen cannot realistically know, that his own search for a spiritual father materializes? Did Bloom also, earlier in the day, hear Dillon's lacquey ringing his handbell—as we know Stephen did—or does he hear him now through some form of auditory osmosis, borrowing somehow from Stephen's consciousness? Bloom envisions himself now moving through the city with "fleet step of a pard,"[53] and we recognize that this is Stephen's image of Bloom seen in passing that afternoon and that Stephen will soon recapture that image and himself make the connection—but is it merely coincidence that gives the words and image to Bloom, or is it some other, inexplicable source? (Not totally inexplicable: the word "fleet" is Bloom's alone, part of his ideal self-image, but we may still question who or what provided the private text for him to edit.) As lovers of Shakespeare who alike draw analogies between his life and theirs, Stephen and Bloom share, in the same instant, independently of each other, the vision of Shakespeare's face in the mirror, "beardless, . . . rigid in facial paralysis," wearing the horns of Bloom's cuckoldry and Stephen's martyrdom.[54] We can easily understand the thematic significance of the shared image, but we cannot so easily rationalize the psychological and narrative process. In the traditional terms of verisimiltude, none of this movement in "Circe" is realistic; yet it surely works on some deeper level (Freudian or Jungian or some combination of the two), for Stephen and Bloom together share more than either alone can realize, and it is only through such sharing that each can develop fully as an individual. In "Circe," through his manipulation of point of view and consciousness and the indistinct edges of reality, Joyce foreshadows the profound human connections that he will establish more firmly through myth in the "Ithaca" chapter of *Ulysses* and then later in *Finnegans Wake*. In the process, he provides a glimpse of a reality that cannot be fully understood or rationalized in the old logical empirical terms, a reality that—seen through another, still less restricted, non-European lens—may well appear magical.

There are some obvious points here that we should not neglect simply because they are so obvious: realities—at least perceptions of reality—do, of course, shift in time and across cultures, and not only in fiction; all art, whatever it calls itself, is an abstraction from reality; and artists have always interpreted reality to suit their own needs. Writing of "The Neolithic Artist's Reality," the archaeologist Marija Gimbutas concludes that "Art reveals man's mental response to his environment, for with it he attempts to interpret and subdue reality, to rationalize nature and give visual expression to his mythologizing explanatory concepts. The chaotic forms of nature, including the human form, are disciplined. . . . The [Neolithic] artist's reality is not a physical reality, though he endows the concept with a physical form. . . . The primary purpose was to transform and spiritualize the body and to surpass the elementary and corporeal."[55] The specific needs may be different, but we might say much the same for Bennett or Robbe-Grillet or Joyce, or for García Márquez or Vargas Llosa.

The physical reality of *The Green House* (1965), Vargas Llosa's best known novel, is nonetheless convincing: for the reader who knows little of life in Peru—of its geography, its people, its political and moral concerns—this seems the ideal introduction. Lima, the capital, is seen only in the distance from here, as a place to be sent for reward (a promoted police officer) or punishment (a convict). To learn about Lima, we must read an earlier novel of Vargas Llosa's, *The Time of the Hero* (1962), which is set at a military academy in the city (and based on the author's youthful experiences there), or a later one, *Conversation in the Cathedral* (1969), whose setting is a workers' bar and whose subject is the moral morass which afflicts all the city's inhabitants—as revealed by a son in search of his father. But in *The Green House* we see only such jungle villages as Santa María de Nieva and the town of Piura on the edge of the desert, and we are struck by the diversity of the country (a diversity unknown to many Peruvians, apparently). We recognize at the same time that there is a deeper reality here than this social surface, however convicing it may be, a force analogous to Lawrence's "spirit of place" but one that is reached neither through the accumulation of Realistic detail nor through some mystical understanding reserved to an elect. The spirit of this place—its varied physical and social realities, the national character which links the inhabitants in their reactions to their geography and history, their way of seeing and judging—is conveyed to the outsider through a narrative approach that is unmistakably Modernist. It is the joining of place to approach which creates the magical reality of *The Green House*.

The Time of the Hero, with its several voices, its unnamed but eventually identifiable speakers and viewers, its sometimes ambiguous (if melodramatic) events, and its careful tying together of plot at the end (yet its open ending), serves as forerunner of the narrative approach of *The Green House*. It is not easy, in either novel, to sort out—even to identify—what seem to be the narrative loose ends,[56] but we understand at once that "what happened?" or "who did it?" (the earlier novel revolves around a murder) are the wrong questions to ask. They are questions of plot, of the Dickensian surface, and these are novels whose primary interest—despite the appeal of a glittering surface—lies elsewhere. *The Time of the Hero* also anticipates *The Green House* (and the succeeding novels) thematically: in its use of personal materials from the author's own life, in its theme of initiation into the realities of Peruvian life, in its emphasis on the role of circumstance and fate and yet its insistence on assuming responsibility for one's life and one's people, in its social theme of a multi-racial, class-ridden society whose only common tie appears to be the military and whose identity is inseparable from those of its individual citizens. Theme and technique become one: the attentive reader learns what questions to ask; the several plots come together at the end, as do the several points of view and time sequences, as do the people and the varied regions of their land.

Wildflower, the whore of Piura, we learn for certain at the end, is Bonifacia, the Indian convent girl and servant of Santa María de Nieva, and may be the daughter of Jum, the betrayed Indian chieftain. Lituma, her pimp, once her husband, we learn, is also the Sergeant of Police of the earlier scenes; he alone may be found in Nieva (as policeman), in Lima (as convict), and in Piura (as pimp). And Don Anselmo, the impresario of uncertain origin who builds the first Green House, becomes the blind old harpist who plays for the patrons of the second Green House, where Wildflower now works. Their several stories develop with no apparent progression or chronological order,[57] overlapping one another, turning back on themselves, advancing slowly or by leaps, moving off to the side, connected only by the ever-altering yet always objective, unquestioning narrative voice (or voices) and by the country itself. Across them winds, like the great river system along which it is played out, the melodramatic story of Fushía, the Japanese bandit from Brazil, scourge of the district, told to a friend on their journey to the leper colony in which he will slowly and sadly and tediously end his life: a victim of the place after all, one key to a reality that may not be fully mastered by its observers: a reality that is a mixture of religion and magic, of history and myth, of scrupulously realized geographical and physical details and of the spirit of the land which grows out of and inspires such facts, a world in which "reality and desire become mingled" (p. 307)[58] as a matter of course and the act of narration itself may alter or even create reality. The geographer, the historian, the Realist must be lost in such a place as this. " 'People who make maps don't know that the Amazon is like a hot woman,' " says Fushía's friend; " 'she's never the same. Everything is on the move here, the river, the animals, the trees. What a crazy land we've got for ourselves . . .'" (p. 42).

> There has been so much talk in Piura about the original Green House, that first building [declares a more removed narrative voice] that no one knows for sure any more what it was really like or the authentic details of its history. The survivors from that period, very few, argued with and contradicted one another, and they have ended up confusing what they saw and heard with their own inventions. And the witnesses are so decrepit now, and their silence so obstinate, that it is no use questioning them. In any case, the original Green House no longer exists . . . and no Piuran is able to

locate that part of the desert where once it stood, with its lights, its music, its laughter, and that daytime glow of its walls, which from a distance and at night would be converted into a square and phosphorescent reptile. (p. 85)

The story of the Green House, seen from a distance yet intimate, finally unknowable in all its details, phosphorescent, is in a sense an historical tale. The Green House is an actual structure, built in the actual Piura (some fifty miles from the border with Ecuador) and viewed by Vargas Llosa as a child of nine and again as an adolescent of sixteen, when he lived in the town. (A city of several hundred thousand inhabitants according to the atlas, it seems much smaller, more personal here.) It is a place, says Luys A. Díez, "where reality threatens to overshadow the novelist's power of imagination."[59] Yet, the novelist admits, he was unable to capture that reality through memory and imagination alone, for its most authentic details are clearly not those of the Realistic surface, or even of the fictive imagination per se. The role of narrative technique in realizing the spirit of this place is apparent in the history of the novel's construction.

Vargas Llosa began work on his fiction with five separate *données*, two from Piura (his vison of the Green House itself and the slum called Mangachería), the others from the Amazon jungle as he experienced it on two later trips (the stories of Fushía, the Indian chief Jum, and the Aguaruna girl who becomes Bonifacia-Wildflower). Díez recapitulates the novel's development too well to warrant its retelling here, but we should note that many of its details (even some names) are evidently historical (Vargas Llosa observed for himself the degradation of the Indians at the hands of civil and religious authority alike, and he names such characters as the venal Governor of the district, Julio Reátegui, for their originals); that he adapts these realistic details to his fictional needs (his indictment of regional politics is considerably more muted in the finished novel than in earlier versions or in his "Chronicle of a Journey to the Jungle," written immediately after his first trip to the interior); and that he began work initially on two separate narratives. "In point of fact I did not succeed . . . my greatest efforts were directed at keeping every character in its right place. The Piurans were invading Santa Mariá de Nieva; the jungle characters were determined to slip into 'the green house.' . . . I decided then . . . to merge both worlds and write one single novel that would absorb all that mass of memories. It would take me another three years and plenty of tribulations to sort out such a disorder."[60]

In the finished narrations, too, the characters pass from place to place, but they do so now under the artist's control, reflecting not creative chaos but a new, more compelling reality. No more observant of the strictures of verisimilitude than are Stephen and Bloom in "Circe," they too reach toward a kind of universal identity, linking here not so much individual psyches as the regions, attitudes, and personalities of a nation, attributes that the inhabitants themselves have always viewed as disparate: joining man and his institutions to nature. And so Don Anselmo and Bonifacia begin life mysteriously in the Amazon and end it in the Green House, painted green, like the old man's harp, to remind him of the jungle (p. 380); even her town name, Wildflower—*Selvá-tica*—is an echo of her origins, since *selva* means "jungle." With them, as with Lituma and the others, we are induced to discern the pattern of place and time for ourselves, to impose an order on the narratives of their lives that they themselves are incapable of finding, as we exercise our responsibility as Modernist-trained readers. It may be helpful to know the region personally in order to perceive its fictional reality, but experience in reading Modernist novels is absolutely indispensable for this task. It is our responsibility, then, to sort out and organize the ambiguous actions, the uncertain chronology, the shifting identities and names, the differing styles and narrational voices and tones. And from our collaboration with their creator emerges a new, higher, magical reality: the interior of Peru, a place of desert and jungle and great river systems and many races of men; not precisely a heart of darkness but a place where a searcher might find, or lose, himself; a reality that cannot be made available to us, that we cannot discover for ourselves—as the novelist's initial efforts (and the work of the Regionalists) proved—through straight-forward, chronological, conventional narrative true to the old Victorian unities. The spirit of this place, in short—its magical reality—is the product as much of perceived experience, of ways of seeing and ways of showing, of narrative skill, as of the literal experience of the place itself. We need never visit Latin America in the flesh, if this reading is viable, in order to discover the continent's magical reality. Like Joyce's Dublin, the place of the fiction will remain more real to its readers—even to those who might know the literal Peru (or Mexico or Chile or Colombia)—than will its original.

This does not mean, again, that the surface of *The Green House* is

negligible or that Vargas Llosa ignores its more evident implications—
the political, for instance. However muted it may be in this final
version, there remains a powerful political commentary here: on the
well-meaning nuns who kidnap Indian children in order to "save" them
and who see them instead become servants and prostitutes (the novel
opens with a raid on a jungle village and the presumed liberation of two
terrified little girls from their families; Bonifacia's downfall begins when
she frees these children from the convent); on the venal provincial
officials who are in league with bandits against the Indians they are
supposed to protect (Don Julio Reátegui betrays Jum so as to prevent
the formation of an Indian cooperative which might demand fairer
prices for their rubber); on an army and police force, intended to unify
the nation, that operate at the behest of the powerful and that subjugate
the weak. (Vargas Llosa's view of the military is perhaps best seen in a
later, comic novel, *Captain Pantoja and the Special Service* [1978], in
which the best-run institution in the country is a military brothel set up
in the jungle and closed down precisely because it is so efficient and
close to the people.) The several parts of the nation—jungle, city, and
desert town—remain separate in *The Green House*. Individuals may cross
from region to region, but they do so at their peril: whatever movement
there is between places and cultures in Vargas Llosa's Peru is likely to
result in disintegration or loss of identity (the respected Sergeant who
becomes Lituma the pimp, the dying Fushía, Jum, Don Anselmo, and
Bonifacia/Wildflower, whose original Indian name even she does not
know).

Underlying these individual failures is the betrayal of the national
heritage implicit in the betrayal of the Indians. And this is not simply a
political statement. Because they are linked to nature, to mythic potentiality, to the sense of order and harmony which may be active still in
their lives, the Indians in the fiction represent a moral force much
greater than themselves. Whether this is literally true of the Aguarunas,
Huambisas, and Shapras of northwestern Peru is not really the point:
this is the novelist's perceived reality. It is this consciousness which is
the principal native source of what we have called his Magic Realism,
and it is connected to and allied with his prime borrowed source, his
narrative technique. A product, as it were, of the native consciousness,
perceived through differing voices and at varying moments, out of all
chronological and logical order, without beginning or evident end or
organization imposed from without, this magical reality is created in the

very act of its narration. It is in order to reach toward its more universal appeal that Vargas Llosa tempers somewhat his political convictions. The questions that he would have us ask are still more compelling than these.

IX

It was the extraordinary international success of *One Hundred Years of Solitude* (1967) which made "Magic Realism" a popular term and, at the same time, provided the impetus to his publishers to reissue García Márquez's earlier fictions. These were not notably successful when they first appeared—"until I was forty years old," he has said, "I never got one cent of author's royalties though I'd had five books published"[61]— and reading them now makes clear to us how much lesser they are than their more famous successor. Yet these early stories and novels remain interesting to us today because they offer insight into the origins of the mature work—the fabled town of Macondo and some of its best-known residents appear here in embryonic form—and, more importantly, because they reveal something of the roots and nature of Magic Realism as a literary mode. Some critics have argued that the Magic Realism of García Márquez is fundamentally different from that of such other writers as Vargas Llosa—a product, that is, not of "organization" but rather of "pure invention," as Raymond L. Williams has put it.[62] "In the case of *Cien años de soledad*," adds John S. Brushwood, "it is a very strange reality, but it is entirely accessible to the reader since there are no barriers created by difficult narrative techniques. . . . He seems to write from inspiration, using what he remembers combined with what he thinks of during the process of writing. His novel has a high level of spontaneity; it does not have a carefully worked pattern of meaning."[63] Reading these early works now, however, proves rather conclusively how large a role technique does play in the later development of so seemingly natural and artless a form. It speaks also of the subtle interplay of indigenous and borrowed sources in both *One Hundred Years of Solitude* and its still more powerful successor, *The Autumn of the Patriarch*.

In *Evil Hour* (1962), only five years but another lifetime before *One Hundred Years*, begins objectively, early on a hot morning in a town not far from Macondo:

Father Ángel sat up with a solemn effort. He rubbed his eyelids with the bones of his hands, pushed aside the embroidered mosquito netting, and remained sitting on the bare mattress, pensive for an instant, the time indispensable for him to realize that he was alive and to remember the date and its corresponding day on the calendar of saints. Tuesday, October fourth, he thought; and in a low voice he said: "St. Francis of Assisi."

He got dressed without washing and without praying. He was large, ruddy, with the peaceful figure of a domesticated ox, and he moved like an ox, with thick, sad gestures. After attending to the buttoning of his cassock, with the languid attention and the movements with which a harp is tuned, he took down the bar and opened the door to the courtyard. The spikenards in the rain brought back the words of a song to him.

" 'The sea will grow larger with my tears,' " he sighed. (p. 1)[64]

Father Ángel is observed from close by but never very intimately or from within, as it were, over his shoulder. He is seen—as are all the characters of the novel—as essentially a creature of the physical world, appropriately perhaps for Saint Francis's day. Only the last line of his description, " 'The sea will grow larger with my tears,' " and another which follows shortly (and which he does not "sigh" aloud but simply "remembers"), " 'This bark will bear me to your dreams,' " promise something more than the surface realities of a man—a priest—awakening, dressing, thinking of the date, smelling ("He urinated abundantly, holding his breath so as not to inhale the intense ammonia smell which brought out tears in him"—p. 2), speaking aloud to himself, remembering the sounds of the previous night. But even these promisingly metaphoric lines exist solely on the surface; they are drawn not from the priest's imagination or vision after all, but only from a neighbor's new song. They are sentimental, inflated, clichéd in this context, not metaphoric at all. Many of the episodes of *In Evil Hour* give similar promise of a reality higher than mere physical presence, but they too in the end fall back to the quotidian: this is not our familiar daily life, of course, but one just as mundane within its own context. García Márquez's narrative technique is not yet capable of capturing that higher reality which we have learned to call "magical." *In Evil Hour* remains a story of small town Colombian life, in a town beset by poverty, casual murders, periodic floods, sexual tensions, political rivalries, movie theatres, and lampoons posted mysteriously on guarded doorways—some of the same elements, that is, that will soon ascend to the magical in nearby Macondo.

It is primarily a matter of perspective. The movie theatre here, for example, is a business enterprise merely, the single escape aside from politics, sex, and gossip from the pervasive poverty and boredom, but boycotted by the residents when the church bells toll that the current film has not been approved for family viewing. In Macondo, in *One Hundred Years*, the movies seem so full of life to their viewers that they break up the theatre when they learn that they are mere illusion, "for the character who had died and was buried in one film and for whose misfortune tears of affliction had been shed would reappear alive and transformed into an Arab in the next one. . . .The mayor . . . explained in a proclamation that the cinema was a machine of illusions that did not merit the emotional outbursts of the audience. With that discouraging explanation many felt that they had been the victims of some new and showy gypsy business and they decided not to return to the movies, considering that they had already too many troubles of their own to weep over the acted-out misfortunes of imaginary beings" (p. 211).[65] The leap between Father Ángel's boycott and this one is enormous; it goes to the very nature of realism in fiction and to the role of perception in ascertaining and evaluating such a reality. It provides, in a sense, the working definition of Magic Realism. The point of view of *In Evil Hour* is only occasionally omniscient in the broadest sense of the term, but it often feels the need to explain events, particularly those which demand explanation. In *One Hundred Years*, what few explanations there are come not from outside with certainty but from within the community, and they add thereby to the uncertainty of what may be accepted as real and what may remain something else. Fully explained, such phenomena as the mysterious lampoons and motion pictures would become further examples of simple exotica in a strange, distant, isolated town—and nothing more; left as they are, seen solely through the eyes of some resident or even of the town as a whole, largely ambiguous, promising of metaphor, they may reach beyond the normal bounds of the Realistic and toward the universal.

One of the opening images of *One Hundred Years of Solitude* illustrates the point very well. Crossing northward through the jungle as they search for the sea, the founders of Macondo, led by José Arcadio Buendía, pass into a primal world and are "overwhelmed by their most ancient memories in that paradise of dampness and silence, going back to before original sin, . . . like sleepwalkers through a universe of grief . . ." (p. 20). And there, in the midst of the jungle, untold miles from the sea (it later proves to be a four-days' march), "surrounded by ferns and palm trees, white and powdery in the silent morning light, was an enormous Spanish galleon." They do not question its provenance, and there is no rational, definitive voice here to explain it. What it evokes for its viewers is some other reality, a universe of timelessness and myth and the origins of the race, "protected from the vices of time and the habits of the birds" (p. 21).

On one level, this striking scene is a simple matter of vision and voice: we see this threatening, arcadian, unexplained image through the unquestioning eyes of men close to nature and their physical senses but removed from alien intellect.[66] The finders are curious, but they seem never to question the strange presence, and there is no one here to rationalize it for them. After five years of not writing—"I had an idea [after *In Evil Hour*] of what I always wanted to do, but there was something missing and I was not sure what it was until one day I discovered the right tone"—García Márquez has at last developed the narrative voice appropriate to his vision. "It was based on the way my grandmother used to tell her stories. She told things that sounded supernatural and fantastic, but she told them with complete naturalness. . . . I discovered that what I had to do [as a teller of tales] was believe in them myself and write them with the same expression with which my grandmother told them: with a brick face."[67]

On another but connected level, the ship in the jungle serves as metaphor of a way of life that will as suddenly appear and—precisely with the century—as suddenly vanish, inexplicable, perhaps irrational, subject to the forces of nature if not to reason, at once beyond reason and thoroughly human, testimony both to the power of nature over history and to the regenerative power of men within nature. It offers resonances, that is, far beyond those that a rational, external voice could conceivably provide: the "brick face" of the narration is as important to the meaning of the metaphor as is the strange image itself. And we outsiders have little real trouble accepting them as "real" and not merely as "fantasy."

The tendency to consider such an approach as "fantastic"—whether in praise or dismissal—is as limiting as the insistence that it must also be spontaneous and unplanned. "The trouble is," says García Márquez, "that many people believe that I'm a writer of fantastic fiction, when actually I'm a very realistic person and write what I believe is the true socialist realism."[68] The political implications of his comment aside for the moment, there is a certain demonstrable historicity about the events of *One Hundred Years*, although this is obviously not the reality of a Dickens (yet there are echoes here of the Victorian family chronicle) or a Robbe-Grillet. As Mario Vargas Llosa has pointed out in a knowing essay (there cannot be many such cases of a major novelist writing so extensively about the work of a contemporary), the pattern of rise and fall in the fictional Macondo, of prosperity, strife, and collapse, is the historical pattern also of Aracataca, Colombia, where García Márquez was born and where he was raised by his grandparents, "his most solid literary influences." By that time, however, activity in the town "had almost stopped . . . Aracataca—like so many Latin American towns— lived on remembrances, myth, solitude and nostalgia. García Márquez' entire literary work [this was written long before the appearance of *The Autumn of the Patriarch*] is built with this material which fed him throughout childhood."[69] One factual episode may serve as illustration of how the author's creative imagination works in this context. As Vargas Llosa continues, "The grandfather of García Márquez used to sing: 'Mambrú has gone to war/ how painful/ how painful/ how sad.' Years later, García Márquez would discover that this song was a Castilianized version of a French song ('Marlborough s'en va-t'en guerre') [sic] and that 'Mambrú' was in reality 'Marlborough.' Since the only wars his grandfather had known were the Colombian civil wars, García Márquez decided that a Duke of Marlborough had been a protagonist in the Colombian violence. Hence the phantasmagoric warrior who in five of García Márquez' books presents himself at the military camp of Colonel Aureliano Buendía; disguised in tiger furs, claws and teeth, he turns out to be the Duke of Marlborough."[70]

Such incidents in themselves are realistic, even mundane. What raises them to the level of metaphor and the fantastic is, paradoxically, the matter-of-fact tone in which they are told. Theirs is a voice coming, as it were, from within: told not simply with a brick face but from a perspective at once intimate and detached, highly subjective in what it sees, coolly objective in the way it regards it; a point of view capable of presenting both the most simple and the most extraordinary events with the same involved but dispassionate, unexplaining voice, so that all such events become equally fantastic and equally natural. It is a studied, conscious, articulate simplicity, not nearly so artless as it seems, and its model is not the novelist's grandmother alone but his literary experience as well. "One night a friend [at the university] lent me a book of short stories by Franz Kafka. I went back to the pension where I was staying and began to read *The Metamorphosis*. The first line almost knocked me off the bed. . . . I didn't know anyone was allowed to write things like that. If I had known, I would have started writing a long time ago. So I immediately started writing short stories." These early efforts, however, "are totally intellectual short stories because I was writing them on the basis of my literary experience and had not yet found the link between literature and life."[71] His storytelling Colombian grandmother and the European Modernist Kafka are equally essential to the creation of García Márquez's world—a world, like those of its sources, at once so substantial and so fantastic.

The novelist acknowledges certain other debts as well, although somewhat more reservedly. From Joyce, he "did learn something that was to be very useful to me in my future writing—the technique of the interior monologue." (However, "I later found this in Virginia Woolf and I like the way she uses it better than Joyce.") And in Faulkner, so often cited as a primary influence, he found, he says, principally an analogue. "Critics have spoken of the literary influence of Faulkner but I see it as a coincidence: I had simply found material that had to be dealt with in the same way that Faulkner had treated similar material."[72]

With Faulkner, as with Woolf and Joyce and in a certain sense with Kafka as well, García Márquez shares a vision of a world cut off from traditional values yet informed still by mythic potential. Rooted in the reality of a specific time and place (usually a place representative of its time but just outside its center: imperial Dublin rather than London, Jewish Prague instead of Vienna, the stagnant rural American South and not the industrial North or expansionist West), they nonetheless reach beyond their reality toward some other potentially deeper truth. Objective reality is first established (note the comparatively mundane opening chapters of *Ulysses*) and then undercut in this world (note "Circe"), so that "no one knew for certain where the limits of reality lay" (p. 212). We might argue that the assaults on objective reality in *One Hundred Years of Solitude* are principally the products of an unsophisticated, literal imagination (witness the destruction of the movie theatre). But reality in Macondo appears to dwindle of itself. When a siege of insomnia afflicts the town and memory begins to vanish along with sleep, Aureliano Buendía, José Arcadio's son, posts signs everywhere to remind the people of the names of objects and of their functions: *"This is the cow. She must be milked every morning so that she will produce milk, and the milk must be boiled in order to be mixed with coffee to make coffee and milk.* Thus they went on living in a reality that was slipping away, momentarily captured by words, but which would escape irremediably when they forgot the values of the written letters" (p. 53). The seemingly objective eye which views this reality and the detached, seemingly uninvolved voice which reports it merely add to the breakdown of objective reality, undercutting belief in a continuing, universally accepted physical world with its implications immediately apparent to all.

Such a dwindling reality is linked inevitably to time, and diminished further by it: to human and therefore failing memory, to nostalgia for a vanishing past, to the Buendía family's futile efforts to comprehend history and master the future. "Time passes," we are frequently told, but not as it used to. Metaphors emerge that promise momentarily a means of evaluating time's force (a photograph fastening the family "for an eternity"—p. 55; an "innocent yellow train" bringing in the terrible future and uprooting the past—p. 210; a perpetual motion time machine—p. 80), but they too prove ephemeral. Various epochs of time become virtually interchangeable for the Buendías—past and present inescapably confused, the future indefatigably sought after—so that for them a history forms that is "radically opposed to the false one that historians had created and consecrated in the textbooks" (p. 322). Their very family name speaks of their need to incorporate time in their lives, and the mysterious chronicle which several males of the family dedicate their lives to deciphering proves to be the tale of their lives and a prediction that they would spend their lives trying to unravel the parchments rather than living them. The act of deciphering and the act of living become coterminous, so that Aureliano Babilonia, the last male Buendía, after many years of effort, at last "began to decipher the instant that he was living, deciphering it as he lived it, prophesying himself in the act of deciphering the last page of the parchments, as if he were looking into a speaking mirror," recognizing now "that he would never leave that room, for it was foreseen that the city of mirrors (or mirages) would be wiped out by the wind and exiled from the memory of men at the precise moment when [he] would finish deciphering the parchments, and that everything written on them was unrepeatable since time immemorial and forever more, because races condemned to one hundred years of solitude did not have a second opportunity on earth" (p. 383). The last of the Buendías understands at last the interpenetration of reality by time.

Time in *One Hundred Years* is circular, simultaneous, a function of the mind and not of the clock: the familiar Modernist perception and usage. But this time is not a phenomenon of the individual psyche alone, as in Woolf, or of the community at large, as in Joyce, or of the history of a region, as in Faulkner. Time here seems still broader, more inclusive, more Jungian, that is, than Freudian (or Bergsonian or Proustian), connected intimately to nature and to myth. It is in this context that what appears to be the preordained fate of the Buendías may turn out, after all, to be strangely redemptive. For nature remains beyond all in this primal place: as the first José Arcadio becomes part of the chestnut tree to which he is tied, as Aureliano Segundo sleeps with a neighbor so that the animals will be fertile, as the inhabitants of the town are turned almost to plants by a preternaturally long rain ("feeling unbroken time pass, relentless time, because it was useless to divide it into months and years, and the days into hours, when one could do nothing but contemplate the rain"—p. 297), as the Buendía home falls gradually back into the jungle. And we may feel almost as if we have been present at the Creation. For myth, too, remains, sometimes in familiar, almost Biblical manifestations (the great flood, the ash crosses which mark the foreheads of the seventeen sons of Colonel Aureliano Buendía), sometimes in new, strikingly original yet recognizable analogues: in the beginnings of Macondo ("built on the bank of a river of clear water that ran along a bed of polished stones, which were white and enormous, like prehistoric eggs. The world was so recent that many things lacked names, and in order to indicate them it was necessary to point"—p. 11); in the pursuit of knowledge by the male Buendías, encouraged and aided by the gypsy Melquíades (whose tribe "had been wiped off the face of the earth because they had gone beyond the limits of human knowledge"—p. 45—and who had himself "lost all of his supernatural faculties because of his faithfulness to life"—p. 55); in the pursuit of death in this Eden.

All of the Buendías's deeds, including their effort to decipher their fate, are part of and lead to the eventual enactment of that fate. And so they may seem mere victims of their environment, no more in control of their lives than are the inexplicable swarms of dead birds at the funeral of old Úrsula Buendía or the striking banana workers whose bodies are thrown casually into the sea. Yet the Buendías may be redeemed because of the vitality with which they invest their lives, however brief, because they remain so close to nature and to natural myth, because— despite the similarities in their names and sometimes in their deeds—

they remain individuals with recognizably human traits and concerns, and because we react to them and feel for them as fellow human beings whose lives, foreign as they are, may have some bearing on our own. We must not be misled by the distanced, objective narrative voice into assuming that these people are as neutral as the animals around them. Each of the Buendías behaves as if he were responsible for what he makes of his life, and they are all dignified as humans by that responsibility which they so naturally bear. If they are not quite representative of modern, urban, industrial life in the West—as Leopold Bloom or even Gregor Samsa may be thought representative—they nonetheless offer valuable insight into what we have lost and also into our surviving potential.

Equally foreign, equally evocative, as much a product of the historical record as of the novelist's imagination, is the individual life marked out in *The Autumn of the Patriarch* (1975), a compound of images familiar to dreams, of widely known Latin American political realities, and of an exceedingly complex and inventive narrative technique. The title again suggests the pre-eminence of time and myth in this seemingly magical, still primal world, and the theme of human responsibility for human life is again at the center. The Patriarch whose life and name define these events, who is both petty Caribbean despot and archetypal fertility god, serves as a true representative of his people and times, at once source and symbol and principal subject of their less than magical yet somehow inspired lives.

Despite García Márquez's abjuration of the political novel—"I believe that sooner or later the world will be socialist; I want it to be so and the sooner the better. But I am also convinced that one of the things which may delay the process is bad literature."[73]—despite his implication that political literature is necessarily "bad literature," *The Autumn of the Patriarch* is directly and undeniably political. In the tradition of Miguel Angel Asturias's *El Señor Presidente* (1946), its protagonist is a composite of Central American dictators; in the tradition of Estrada Cabrera (Asturias's principal model), of Batista, Duvalier, and Trujillo, his crimes are directed against his own people, and they both fear and revere him: although they may die at his hands, it is through him that they live. There is, says Asturias, an "intuition" about such figures, "a sort of sense of smell or power of divination that dictators have, and which means that it's not everyone who can be one."[74] He moves, says Joseph Campbell of this manifestation of *The Hero with a Thousand Faces*, "in a dream landscape of curiously fluid, ambiguous forms, where he must survive a succession of trials" in his "perilous journey into the darkness. . . ."[75] Like Leopold Bloom before him, he is our truly, ambiguously, paradoxically eponymous hero.

His journey is both mythic and historical, involving factual or potentially factual or at least representative political events in this presumably representative, if fantastic, state. And so the Nicaraguan poet and diplomat Rubén Darío can appear alongside the King and Queen of Babylonia at the Patriarch's court (pp. 179–80),[76] while Columbus, "admiral of the ocean sea," can become his contemporary (p. 166). North American battleships and marines have occupied his land in the past, allegedly to civilize it ("they turned our artists into fairies, they brought the Bible and syphilis, they made people believe that life was easy . . ."—p. 230), and now, like modern conquistadors, they threaten to carry off the sea: "so they took away the Caribbean in April, Ambassador Ewing's nautical engineers carried it off in numbered pieces to plant it far from the hurricanes in the blood-red dawns of Arizona [presumably close to London Bridge], they took it away with everything it had inside . . . with the reflection of our cities, our timid drowned people, our demented dragons . . ." (p. 229). Given the history of United States involvement in Central American affairs over the past century or so, this act seems somehow less than fantastic and largely consistent with the mythopoesis which informs the novel.

The principal failing of North American political life in the novel is not that it is rapacious or supportive of dictatorships in Latin America but that it lacks in itself the life-giving potential of myth available even to the latter. The General, for instance, is obviously a despot, a recognizable contemporary figure and not at all Christlike ("long live the stud," shout his subjects—p. 131), yet he bears with him the burdens and consequences of his Martyr's and Savior's role. Fatherless (because his mother was a whore, and many men might have fathered him), the child of a cult figure who recalls Mary, though hardly a Virgin (the cult, of course, created by her Son), appearing soon after general signs of chaos in the land, and marked by his own sign of divinity ("his right testicle . . . the size of a fig"—p. 126), compared overtly to Christ (by himself), and father himself of a son called Emanuel ("which is the name by which other gods know God"—p. 165), he knows well the price of bearing mythic power and is the prisoner of that power which

he bears. In his great old age, his advisers insulate him from the political
realities of his land, with a

> newspaper which they printed only for you general sir, a whole edition of
> one single copy with the news you liked to read, . . . with advertisements
> that made him dream of a world different from the one they had given him
> for his siesta, until I myself was able to ascertain with these incredulous
> eyes of mine that behind the solar glass windows of the ministries still
> intact were the colors of the Negro shacks on the harbor hills, they had
> built the palm-lined avenues to the sea so that I wouldn't notice that
> behind the Roman villas with identical porticoes the miserable slums
> devastated by one of our many hurricanes were still there, . . . and they
> were not deceiving him in order to please him as had been done in the
> later years of his times of glory. . . or to keep useless annoyances from
> him . . . but to keep him the captive of his own power in the senile
> backwater of the hammock under the ceiba tree in the courtyard where at
> the end of his years even the schoolgirl chorus of the petite painted bird
> perched on a green lemon limb wasn't to be real, what a mess. . . . (p.
> 224)[77]

In the messiest of times—even those created by him—he serves as
measure of continuity for his people, "for the only thing that gave us
security on earth was the certainty that he was there, invulnerable to
plague and hurricane, . . . invulnerable to time . . ." (p. 99). The life and
death of nature are associated with his life and death, as in the "ancient
predictions . . . that on the day of his death the mud from the swamps
would go back upriver to its source, that it would rain blood, that hens
would lay pentagonal eggs, and that silence and darkness would cover
the universe once more because he was the end of creation" (p. 120).
He seems, then, this petty provincial dictator, a true fertility god: a true
force of nature ("the corrector of earthquakes, eclipses, leap years and
other errors of God"—p. 13); the very source of life ("he had ordered
them to take the rain away from places where it disturbed the harvest
and take it to drought-stricken lands"—p. 87). He has "the virtue of
being able to anticipate the designs of nature" (p. 48) and can reverse its
designs: after a great hurricane, "we saw the sad eyes, the faded lips,
the pensive hand which was making the sign of the cross in a blessing
so that the rains would cease and the sun shine, and he gave life back
to the drowned hens, and ordered the waters to recede and they
receded" (p. 98), "because they said I was the all-worthy one who filled

nature with respect and straightened the order of the universe and had taken Divine Providence down a peg, and I gave them what they asked of me . . ." (p. 217). Even an attempt to assassinate him becomes a kind of fertility rite (p. 88).

But he does not die then, perhaps cannot die then when he is merely old, ancient even, but not yet his appointed five or tenscore or more (actually "an indefinite age somewhere between 107 and 232 years"—p. 82). He is no Annual King, according to Frazer's conception,[78] to die for his people when his fertility is spent and thereby to redeem them and bring them new life. He journeys, like Campbell's related archetype, "through a world of unfamiliar yet strangely intimate forces, some of which severely threaten him . . . , some of which give magical aid. . . ." But when he "arrives at the nadir of the mythological round [and] undergoes [his] supreme ordeal," unlike his prototype he will gain no reward: neither union with the Earth Mother nor recognition by the Father nor his own "divinization." At no point does he as hero "re-emerge from the kingdom of dread"; he bears no "boon . . . [to] restore the world."[79]

There is nothing Realistic, of course, about the General's great age, and he is no mythic hero after all to induce our admiration and empathy. The genius of the narrative is that we identify with him nonetheless, despite his despotic acts, knowing that he is no redeemer nor even truly a martyr, because he is a convincing, suffering human being, and in his extreme and perilous condition we may find something of our own. Bearing the burdens and consequences of his position and life, wrapped in mythic expectation even if he is not a true nature god, he seems singled out to learn, as we must all perhaps learn, the ephemerality of our humanity, "when after so many long years of sterile illusions he had begun to glimpse that one doesn't live, God damn it, he lives through, he survives, one learns too late that even the broadest and most useful of lives only reach the point of learning how to live . . ." (pp. 249–50). Only in his great, old, exalted but abandoned age, within the realm of the people whom he serves as a god, terrifying and sustaining, does he learn "of his incapacity for love" and of its significance.

> He had known since his beginnings that they deceived him in order to please him, . . . he had arrived without surprise at the ignominious fiction of commanding without power, of being exalted without glory . . . when

he became convinced in the trail of yellow leaves of his autumn that he
had never been master of all his power, that he was condemned not to
know life except in reverse, condemned to decipher the seams and
straighten the threads of the woof and the warp of the tapestry of illusions
of reality without suspecting even too late that the only livable life was one
of show, the one we saw from this side which wasn't his general sir, this
poor people's side with the trail of yellow leaves of our uncountable years
of misfortune and our ungraspable instants of happiness, where love was
contaminated by the seeds of death but was all love general sir, . . . this life
which we loved with an insatiable passion that you never dared even to
imagine out of the fear of knowing what we knew only too well that it
was arduous and ephemeral but there wasn't any other, general. . . . (pp.
250–1).

In his failed but persistent humanity, the General serves us to affirm
our own.

   Central to this discovery is the interplay between the hero-king-
General and his subjects, between the reader and his narrator(s), among
the shifting narrative voices, a function of the most complex and
evocative point of view in García Márquez's—and perhaps in post-
Joycean—fiction. The narration begins with "we," an eyewitness to the
General's death (p. 7) yet not quite an eyewitness ("because none of us
had ever seen him"—p. 10), revealed finally as a member of the General
Staff (p. 190) and named (but with different names—p. 85—and
perhaps not a general). More significantly, the "me" as witness turns
somehow to "me" as actor, the General himself, speaking and thinking
of himself as both protagonist and outsider, with passionate self-
involvement and a strange objectivity (as "I," "he," and "you"), across a
great span of time, in singular and plural forms, as male and female
alike: his voice seems that of both the General and his people, mutually
involved, an internalized chorus at once national and private. This
constantly shifting, near-universal point of view is a reflection, in part,
of the General's status as a myth-connected figure of great age and
failing memory, free of conventional bonds, acting desperately and
unsuccessfully to order his reality as he has always seemed to order it,
unsure to the end of his own identity ("who the hell am I," he shouts,
"because I feel as if the reflection in the mirror is reversed"—p. 217); in
part also, these shifts are a sign of the political state of affairs. For how
can the hero define himself fully when his principal role is not as
redeemer of his people but as a failed presence, not as man but as

symbol? And how can the citizen-reader, after abiding for so long under so great a shadow, understand who in truth he is? "Commander of time," his people call him (p. 68), controller of history, able to alter time at his will, his own lifespan ordered "not . . . by human time but by the cycles of the comet" (p. 78), an eternal-seeming figure in a land of many presidents for one day, in the end he loses control of his memory (taking "spoonfuls of candlewax to plug up the leaks in my memory"— p. 188), his control over reality, his understanding of what his life has meant or what he has lost. And so he suffers.

But there are uncertainties and problems for us, too: if memory has failed, if history is suspect and mythmaking a fiction, if surface reality has been consciously and consistently amended to suit transient political needs, if mythos turns to senility and the senile General can himself lose control over the world he has made, "where the hell was the truth in that bag of contradictory truths that seem less true than if they were lies" (p. 220)? If there is no objective reality that we can accept as lasting and real, if we have no confidence that some other reality can replace what we have been shown is transient above all, what sort of certainty remains? what part of our humanity survives? We are left—for all our distance and uncertainty and scorn—with the General's narrated experience: with his lifelong sense that he has been the victim of his own power; with his recognition late in his life that he cannot change reality and the nature of life despite his great power, despite his great age; with his discovery and ours that what has seemed most permanent in the face of a changing reality is, in fact, as ephemeral as all that passes for real. His identity is uncertain, his career despicable, yet we are moved by the old man's predicament. We appreciate the truth of the burden he has borne all these years, however false it may be. We perceive that he is at times capable of feeling, enough at least to sense what he has lost. We understand the banal lesson of his life for our own perhaps autumnal age: that we all bear burdens that we cannot understand; that we all experience passions that we cannot control; that none of us can master this life whose reality we cannot comprehend or even name; but that we must continue to feel if we are to be human; and that we remain responsible for our lives. And so we may feel with the General, as we feel with Bloom, caught up in the flow of his narrative and the rhythms of his prose, nurtured by his creator's demanding technique, despite politics, beyond history, outside the re-deeming force of myth. Our ability to feel his pain attests to his humanity and perhaps also to our own.

X

The Mexican novelist Carlos Fuentes—diplomat, man of letters, cited by Donoso and others as godfather of the Boom, as deeply attuned to our culture as he is sensitive to his own—may serve for us as the most representative writer of the most vital and challenging fiction being written today; he is himself one of the great novelists of our time; and he testifies imaginatively to the continuing presence of Joyce: an altered Joyce, to be sure, translated into a new language and a developing new sensibility, but present in his art, his life as an artist, his aura. Joyce knew little of Latin American or Hispanic culture (think of the remote Buenos Aires of "Eveline"). Yet, says Fuentes, "Joyce perceived truths which were latent also in our culture, but which we had to learn to see for ourselves."[80]

Virtually the first word of *Where the Air Is Clear* (1958), Fuentes's first novel, is "paralysis": "Outraged, the unchecked paralysis that stains and dots every dawn," declaims the narrator; "in Mexico City there is never tragedy but only outrage" (p. 3),[81] and we hear clear if culturally distant echoes of *Dubliners* and *A Portrait of the Artist as a Young Man*. But Fuentes's Mexico City has little in common on the social surface with Joyce's Dublin. Here, in addition to the prostitutes, taxi drivers, and servants who exist on a level comparable to that of Joyce's lower-middle and lower classes, we see as well the social elite—businessmen and bankers, the putative intelligentsia, even foreign nobility and pseudo-nobility: the milieu of "After the Race" somewhat magnified. This society, too, is hostile to art, albeit more dramatically: the young artist of this fiction, with his inevitable ties to Stephen Dedalus, is senselessly murdered; a once-serious poet becomes a successful screenwriter of popular, romantic films; and the narrator who tells of them both is himself entrapped within his complex culture, a modern man compelled to act out an ancient ritual of sacrifice and redemption.

For the real differences between Mexico City and Dublin lie beneath the surface. Beneath the modern physical surface of Mexico City, its paved streets and Western veneer, waits the still palpable ancient past: a past less of recorded history than of myth, and of a myth growing out of but very different from Joyce's—not borrowed or intellectualized or used in large part for ironic counterpoint, but lived. Dublin serves Joyce as microcosm of a static world on the precipice of change; Fuentes's Mexico City incorporates within its modern form the images and symbols and thematic echoes of the pre-Columbian past, made still more redolent by the blurred perspective of more than four centuries of apparent change. The differences are profound. Imagine Stephen Dedalus describing his city, as Ixca Cienfuegos does his, as "the swollen city, the center, without memory, . . . city which is the slave and the overseer, which is I myself before a mirror mimicking truth, he who accepts the world as inevitable, he who recognizes someone besides himself, he who loads himself with the sins of the earth, . . . eagle or sun, unity and dispersion, heraldic emblems, forgotten rite, imposed way, beheaded eagle, dust serpent . . ." (pp. 373–4). Imagine Stephen speaking of his fellow citizens as occupants of the mythic and moral center of the earth. " 'Salvation for the whole world,' " says Cienfuegos, " 'depends upon this anonymous people who are at the world's center, the very navel of the star. Mexico's people, the only people who are contemporaneous with the world itself, the only ones who live with their teeth biting into the aboriginal breast' " (p. 299).[82]

Each of Fuentes's heroes bites deeply into that breast; none can escape the pervasive presence of his motherland, at once nourishing and destructive, dominating both social and mythic planes of existence. Cienfuegos is compelled (by his own, literal mother) to abandon his modern detachment, to commit himself to violent and symbolic action, to affirm, despite himself, the mythic potency of his inheritance. His carefully nurtured Western individuality is subsumed within the pre-Western, yet continuing spirit of the land which he inhabits and which is present always within him. The problem expands for his successors. For Felipe Montero, the historian hero of *Aura* (1962), identity itself— Stephen's goal and, indeed, that of all Modernist protagonists—is abandoned in the sort of magical transformation which rationalist Stephen would ridicule but which is possible still, Fuentes suggests, in a land whose reality is not single-edged, in which history and myth remain indistinguishable, whose past is inseparable, finally, from its present. He virtually becomes another man, the long-deceased general whose memoirs he is writing, and he willingly makes love to his widow, the centenarian Señora Consuelo herself and not, as he first thinks, to Aura, her niece, who is in fact her projection. The scholarly historian, long-time resident of France, a man of reason, does not even question reality in this Meso-American household: he easily, naturally accepts the manifestations of a world in which man, nature and dream, history and myth, are inextricably linked. *Aura* contains echoes of both *The Aspern Papers* and "The Wife of Bath's Tale": the disjunction from Jamesian psychological and moral reality, the clear contrasts with Dame Alisoun's wishful little tale of recaptured youth, demonstrate forcefully the unique nature of this Latin American fiction. And then we recall the tranforma- tion sequences in the "Circe" episode of *Ulysses* (in which Bloom changes not only character but sex, and images from Stephen's con- sciousness appear in Bloom's imaginings and images from Bloom's in Stephen's), and we realize that here, too, Fuentes has found in Joyce— with his very different background and his very different apparent approach to nature and myth—at least an analogue if not quite a source for his creation.

A more evident Joycean presence appears in *A Change of Skin* (1967), a work at once Mexican and Modernist. Freddy Lambert, its narrator, who could pass as a North American intellectual, suddenly shifts roles, "changes his skin" and becomes "Xipe Totec, Our Lord of the Flayed Hide" (p. 371),[83] at once observer and cause of his characters' actions. His self-reflexive account is marked by a complex manipulation of narrative perspectives and times, by frequent shifts of character identities and roles (he becomes a character in his own fiction), by the use of the Jew as metaphor of the modern experience: interlocking techniques and themes learned originally from Joyce and transformed in this setting.[84] Through the memories of a Jewish woman from New York (daughter of immigrants and herself an alien in Mexico City—Elizabeth Jonas-Ligeia- Dragoness, as the narrator names her—whose paralyzed brother, Jake, or Jacob or Israel, was murdered in Central Park at the age of thirteen, the age of confirmation and of entrance to the community), through the interior monologue of her husband (Javier, a Mexican novelist—a failure as husband, a failure as artist, but in some ways the narrator's surrogate), through the obsessive images of her Czech lover (Franz, once the architect of Terezin and ever since a penitent), the narrator, who shares memory and consciousness and conscience with his creations, endeavors to bring some order to this surreal modern activity, at once to sort out and to join together these seemingly separate realities. In the end, like the visions of Stephen and Bloom in "Circe" and thereafter, they are inextricably linked; individual dreams, responsibility, involve- ment become universal. Elizabeth's memory of her brother's death— " 'Kike Christ-killer, Christ-killer,' " his murderers triumphantly shout (pp. 281–2)—leads inevitably to Franz's memory of the Jewish cemetery of Prague and its single, modern monument: "Belsec Majdanek . . . Treblinka Auschwitz Bergen-Belsen Buchenwald Dachau . . .

Terezin," it reads (pp. 282–3): images of the collective modern experience not yet turned to manageable, believable, acceptable myth. Above it all sits the novelist, paring his fingernails perhaps, but intensely, humanly involved. Without needing to refer directly to Joyce, *A Change of Skin* is the most Joycean of Fuentes's novels, the one which most evidently makes use of his technique and vision and which most consciously translates them to a Latin American setting and idiom.

Terra Nostra (1975), Fuentes's most ambitious novel, is so characteristically Latin and American in its conception and development that it seems far removed from Joyce and the Modernists. Even its occasional oblique reference to them (*e.g.*, a mysterious map which includes the Liffey and evokes the Plumed Serpent—p. 766)[85] must be measured against its mass of native literary echoes and analogues (including Borges, Cortázar, Vargas Llosa, and García Márquez). Its themes are at once narrowly political and broadly humanistic, reflecting the varied interconnections between New World and Old; its parallel structures are derived alike from history and from myth, both universal and local; its points of view are multiple, forever shifting, highly reflexive; its reality is dreamlike, often surreal, yet recognizably historical throughout; its language and metaphors (among them the Inquisition, the erection of El Escorial, the isolation of the Jews once again) are wonderfully inventive, yet related to and developing out of the author's earlier fictions. With its heightened mix of indigenous and Modernist attitudes and forms, *Terra Nostra* is a novel that no European or North American could possibly have written. Yet here, too, there is a certain Joycean presence: not influence certainly, or even strong echoes perhaps, but the encyclopedic nature and demands of this work are surely in the spirit of *Finnegans Wake;* its daring and inventiveness—more even than its evocation of universal history and myth ("true history is circular and eternal"—p. 652), or its dreamlike reality and complex and ambiguous technique ("every narrator reserves to himself the privilege of not clarifying mysteries, so that they remain mysteries; and who is not pleased, let him demand his money"—p. 655)—are in a way made possible, perhaps even inevitable, by the very presence of *Finnegans Wake*. Both novels reach beyond history to search out and illumine the archetypes of our humanity, "an eternal present" (p. 741), "but always in the same, if transfigured place" (p. 756). If it is not quite as powerful and involving a creation as is *The Death of Artemio Cruz, Terra Nostra* is lesser only in the sense that the *Wake* may be less moving, less immediate, less accessible than is *Ulysses.* It is as history, however, and as myth, as an account of the humanist endeavor made manifest through history and myth, that these fictions of Fuentes, like Joyce's major fictions, function most powerfully. This is, in part, what Fuentes means when he speaks of Joyce's discovery of "truths which were latent also in our culture, but which we had to learn to see for ourselves."

Fuentes's bildungsroman, *The Good Conscience* (1960), recalling *Stephen Hero,* dramatizes the danger to the rebel who remains at home: Stephen's fear, of course, and Joyce's as well. When we meet Jaime Ceballos, its hero, in other novels, he has left provincial Guanajuato but only for Mexico City, where he is already a parvenu businessman and social climber and where, reflecting broadly the movements of Stephen and Bloom through Dublin, his path crosses that of Artemio Cruz. He is seduced by material success, the opportunity to advance into the more modern world, as Stephen, had he remained in Dublin, would have been seduced by failure—the easy pleasures of barroom *bonhomie,* his father's success and death to the serious artist. Fuentes himself has lived much of his life outside Mexico, although he periodically returns there. The mature Joyce, his fear and resentment reaffirmed on each of his early returns to Dublin, stayed away thereafter and made staying away a mainstay of his life and his central literary theme: exile. Mexico for Fuentes serves another purpose, less immediately threatening, more potentially constructive. But then Fuentes was born and educated originally outside Mexico, even treated by his first Mexican classmates as an outsider:[86] a negative experience for the child perhaps—comparable to that fabricated for Stephen in *A Portrait*—but a valuable one for the artist, teaching him distance, affirming his vision formed at a distance. Freed of the Western faith in material progress shared by his class, he was able to construct a history of Mexico which integrates history with myth, present with past. "I had to create my vision of Mexico without living in Mexico," says Fuentes. "I had imagined Mexico as an Indian country. I had imagined Mexico as a colonial country. I had imagined Mexico as a country with a soul divided. . . . The people . . . thought of themselves as modern, Westernized people and did not realize that the country was so much more."[87] If he cannot quite say with Stephen, "This race and this country and this life produced me. I shall express myself as I am,"[88] Fuentes's expression is nonetheless rooted as deeply in the Mexico of his vision.[89]

"Mexico," Fuentes admits, "is not unique." Nor is his own role as chronicler unique: "It is quite natural—and also extraordinary—to tell and retell the history of your country." Still, he goes on, "if I didn't write this history, no one would."[90] He is referring at this point to the lack of a true Latin American historiography, but his fiction reveals that something more is at stake. Fuentes and his narrators may be said, like Stephen in *A Portrait* in one of the rare instances in which that callow young man speaks fully for his creator, to attempt "to forge . . . the uncreated conscience of [their] race."[91] *Where the Air Is Clear,* for all its early ties to Joyce, announces its separateness at the close. It concludes—presaging *Terra Nostra*—with an imagistic history of Mexico, from that time before memory marked by human sacrifice, to the Conquest, the Revolution, and the era of modern development. This vision, these themes—the connections between New World and Old, the Conquest's significance, the Revolution's betrayal, the identity of history and myth—reverberate throughout Fuentes's canon, magnified in subsequent novels by an increasingly rich language and narrative technique, marked by the persistent belief that this land and its people may be known in the present only through their past and that they may speak as well, like Joyce's Dubliners, for universal experience in their time. Fuentes's thematic concerns are different, finally, from those of Joyce and the other European Modernists; his sense of time and myth and his reality (his history) are different as well. But it is through Joyce that he will develop his vision. Mexico in the fiction of Fuentes, like Joyce's Dublin, is both unique and universal.

"Novels are always born of history," Fuentes has said, "but they must transcend history; they must show us the way out of history so as not to be the prisoners, rather the slaves of history . . . ,"[92] and we hear echoes of the still-sleepwalking Stephen's "History is a nightmare from which I am trying to awake."[93] Only at the end of *Ulysses,* in his discovery of Bloom, the Jew who refuses quietly to act as if the Jews were history's ultimate prisoners, does Stephen awaken himself; only in permanent exile and art, he discovers anew, only in living aloof from yet creating his history, can the Irish artist of 1904 escape the historical nightmare which afflicts all Ireland. But the history that Stephen eventually may write, like that of Joyce in *Ulysses,* will not be so much that of his nation—rooted as it may be in the facts of Dublin life—as a history of the modern sensibility, newly emergent. Fuentes attempts both less and more: a specific history of Mexico, encompassing immediate social and political judgments ("We have a conflicted vision of our own past; our past is not solved yet")[94] and an effort to find in Mexican history a movement beyond Mexico into a modern world struggling still to come to terms with its past ("history is the past, the present, and future";[95] "the future will have a future only if we have a past").[96] Both Joyce and Fuentes deny the implicit claim of professional historians that they alone have the means of mastering history; Joyce and Fuentes alike show us in their fictions how we have failed (as nations and individuals) in the past and why we are likely to continue to fail in the future. Yet neither believes that events are predetermined in history. We retain, they insist, responsibility for what we have made of our (national and personal) lives, and it is this which gives us our dignity as humans. Such is the historical realm of "Nestor," "Proteus," "Scylla and Charybdis" and "Ithaca" and of *The Death of Artemio Cruz*.

The immediate context of *The Death of Artemio Cruz* (1962) is modern Mexican history and, in particular, its most persistent, perpetual theme: the betrayal of Mexico's promise by its inhabitants: the betrayal of the Revolution by the ex-revolutionary Cruz; the betrayal of the Indian peasants by Obregón and Carranza, by Santa Ana, and by the conquistadors; betrayal by the Indians themselves in pre-Columbian times ("no one wants to return to the lie of a Golden Age, to illegitimacy, the animal moan, . . . the sacrifice and the madness, the nameless terror of that beginning . . ."—pp. 138–9);[97] and the likelihood of future betrayal in the relationship of Mexican government and business with the hovering giant to the north. The dying Artemio relates to his aide— thinking of himself here as "you"—"the steps by which you gained your wealth: loans at short terms and high interest to peasants in Puebla, just after the Revolution; the acquisition of land around the city of Puebla, whose growth you foresaw; acres for subdivision in Mexico City, thanks to the friendly intervention of each succeeding president; the daily newspaper; the purchase of mining stock; the . . . trusted friend of North American investors, intermediary between New York and Chicago and the government of Mexico; . . . the acquisition of *ejido* farm lands taken from their peasant occupants . . ." (p. 11). In the most immediate sense, *The Death of Artemio Cruz* is a political novel with an easily recognizable political perspective—and thus profoundly different from Joyce's novels.[98] But it is in no sense doctrinaire. It is, indeed, one of the most effective of all political novels because it so convincingly, even movingly identifies the nation with its inhabitants and involves the reader in their mutual fates. The young mestizo peasant Artemio Cruz

testifies to Mexican idealism; the dying old man who tells his own
history is a witness to and active participant in its betrayal. Because, in
part, he understands and acknowledges the ambiguity of his life—
because he perceives that he has betrayed his own promise—and
because of his elaborate, involving narrative technique, we may ourselves identify with Artemio Cruz, as with García Márquez's Patriarch,
and be moved by his life even as we judge it, objectively, with scorn.
Mexican identity, in the historiography of Fuentes, is similarly linked—
similarly ambiguous—with Artemio Cruz.

And the life of the Mexican Artemio Cruz is the product as much of
myth and the mythic process as of actual, but remembered history.
Artemio's account begins, in old age, with an image of failed fertility—
the cold catheter against his inert penis (p. 3). But he recalls another
time, in his youth, when he seemed the very focus of fertility, hands and
body "pounding the earth as if he were having sexual intercourse with
the earth" (p. 280). His penultimate memory, an instant before death, is
of going out into the world, "freed from the destiny of birth and
birthplace," peering wildly "at the new world of the mountain and
night" from the mountaintop, "bound now to a new fate," at one with
the earth and the universe (p. 299). In this extraordinary recreation of
distant memory as fertility myth—private, yet evoking forces beyond his
own; lyrical and full of hope, yet echoing its own past (future)
betrayal—the dying Artemio reaffirms, if not his own life, then at least
the life process. "You, standing, Cruz, thirteen years old, on the edge of
life. You, green eyes, thin arms, hair coppered by the sun. . . . You will
be the world's name. . . . You engage the infinite depthless freshness of
the universe. . . . In you the earth and the stars touch. . . . Upon your
head will fall, as if you were returning from a journey with neither
beginning nor end in time, the promises of love and solitude, hatred and
power, violence and tenderness, friendship and disenchantment, time
and forgetfulness, innocence and surprise" (p. 304). His final memory is
not even his: it is the memory of his birth, suggesting a force of memory
beyond his, the universal potential of human experience.

There is a foreshadowing of this mythic progression in Bloom's lyrical
recreation, in memory, of lovemaking with Molly on the Hill of Howth,
surrounded by images of nature, the center of fertility; in his cold
reminder to himself in the present, "Me. And me now" and his spilled
seed on the aptly named Sandymount; and in the final images of
Bloom's day as he drifts into sleep at the end of "Ithaca," images of

latent fertility. Bloom's unanswered last question, "Where?"[99] is, in fact, answered by Molly in "Penelope," concluding the narrative with her memory of their lovemaking on Howth. Yet Joyce's affirmation, implicit in large part in his elaboration of fertility archetypes, seems more muted than Fuentes's. It is limited among his Dubliners to Bloom: a representative man, to be sure, but not a representative Dubliner. It may be lyrical and convincing and at moments profoundly moving ("Me. And me now."), yet it seems somehow distant, borrowed, intellectualized almost, a product of Joyce's own Modernist sensibility and not his—or his characters'—by inheritance: it is Joyce and Bloom who affirm life in *Ulysses*, and not the life process itself as it is experienced in Dublin at the beginning of the twentieth century. Myth in Joyce, to put it differently, is a reaction to modern life and not an inevitable part of it. His Dubliners— apart from Bloom, whose roots are not fully in Dublin—are too far removed from their ancestral roots to believe in or relate to or be affected by the mythic rhythms that bind humans together through time and within a community. For Fuentes, who may have learned the literary uses of myth from Joyce and whose subject matter is, in truth, far more negative, even despicable (the Citizen's villainy is trivial next to Artemio's), the presence of life-affirming myth seems natural, seems—at least to a North American reader—inborn. It may be the result of the continuing Indian presence in most Latin American countries; its literary source is surely the Modernist novel, but it is the naturalness of its mythopoesis which distinguishes current Latin American fiction from all other Western fictions, present or past. Fuentes's historiography differs from that of the professional historian precisely because it makes room for, is consistently informed by such myth. This is its most marked native element; its principal borrowed source, adapted throughout to this mythic mode, is the Modernist perspective in point of view, the handling of time, and the development of an organic, evocative metaphoric structure.

The time scheme of *The Death of Artemio Cruz* is easily datable (individual sections are headed by their dates) as Artemio turns backward in memory—returning always to the present—turns to past events (although not in chronological order) as a means of justifying his life to posterity and of understanding it himself. His memory is partly affective and spontaneous (and thus Proustian) and partly willed (Bergsonian), but it is willed as if from outside himself: "You will close your eyes and you will see again, but you will see only what your brain wants you to see: more than the world, yet less: you will close your eyes and the real world will no longer compete with the world of your imagination . . . and you will feel yourself split into two men, one who will receive messages and one who will act upon them" (pp. 55–6). Time is a primary force in his narrative and life, a correlate of myth; the dying memorialist is a prisoner of his time and yet outside it. In these final hours, his body failing, his memory works for him as the measure of his time and of his identity. As he remembers toward the end his movement into the world, time becomes for Artemio his creator and creature, at once present and future and past, the life force itself. "Time that fills itself with vitality, with actions, ideas, but that remains always the inexorable flux between the past's first landmark and the future's last signpost. Time that will exist only in the reconstruction of isolated memory, in the flight of isolated desire. . . . Time that is incarnate in the unique being called you, now a boy, now a dying old man, a being who in a mysterious ceremony links together tonight, the little insects glowing against the dark cliff, and the immense stars whirling in silence against the infinite backdrop of space . . . the world opens to you and offers you its time" (pp. 302–3). Such a time scheme is naturally aloof from the usual laws of narrative consistency and progression: he lists at one point—without differentiation—remembered events, events not yet remembered, events not to be remembered perhaps because they never occurred, perhaps because they pale before imagined or reconstructed events, perhaps because there is no time (p. 238); his final memory is of his birth, an event which he cannot, of course, remember in fact (pp. 304–5); his voice goes on even after his death.

Artemio's voice is manifold. He speaks in internal monologue, blurring at times into stream of consciousness; he speaks into a tape recorder, for posterity; he speaks with the voices of others, the voices distinguished from one another at times by roman and italic types. He is split into more than two men, receiver and actor; when he dies, we are told by the continuing voice, he is at least three-fold. "They look at your dilated intestine, deep scarlet, almost black. They say: pulse, respiration, temperature, punctiform perforation. Eaten away, corroded. . . . Hopeless, they say, hopeless, they repeat. The three. The clot breaks loose. Black blood is thrown out. The blood will flow and then it will stop. It stopped. . . . You will not know now. I carry you inside and with you I die. The three, we . . . will die. You . . . die, have died . . . I will die" (p. 306). The three are more than just the "I," "he," and "you" with whom the dying man's narrative begins (p. 7) and ends (p. 305), more than guises of himself at stages of his life, more than narrator, actor, and audience. The voice which goes on, to die after Artemio, which recreates his birth at the moment of his death, is that of some larger force, call it community or the collective unconscious, representing those qualities beyond his individual life for which he stands as representative.

In the most moving scene of his narrative, Artemio himself works at recreating events. This is the reconstruction from small bits of evidence of the last days in the life of his son, Lorenzo, who, much loved and loving, we are told, has gone off to fight for the Loyalists in the Spanish Civil War. Seeing through his dead son's eyes, thinking of Lorenzo as "he"—but a highly personal "he," the same pronoun, with the same distance and immediacy which he applies to himself as a youth— Artemio attempts to live for himself those final hours in the life of his son. His only sources are a single letter "with foreign stamps" and his own experience, a generation earlier, in wartime. But his reconstruction is so definitive, so seemingly factual, that we realize only afterwards that it is a reconstruction:

> ah, I dreamed, I imagined, I knew those names, I remembered those songs, *ay* thanks, but to know, how can I know? I don't know, I don't know what that war was like, with whom he spoke before he died, what the men's names were who were killed with him, nor the names of the women, what he said, what he thought, how he was dressed, what he ate that day, I don't know: I make up a countryside, I invent cities, I imagine names, and now I don't remember: Miguel, José, Luis? Consuelo, Dolores, María, . . . Guadarrama, Pirineos, Figueras, Toledo, Teruel, Ebro, Guernica, Guadalajara; the abandoned corpse, the sun and ice that buried him, the eyes open forever, pecked out by birds:
> *ay,* thank you, because you taught me what my life could be,
> *ay,* thank you, for living that day for me. . . . (p. 235)

This identification of father and son—of the father living through his son, of the son acting out the life of his father—is abetted by the central metaphoric pattern of the novel, the somewhat variable leitmotif, " 'That morning I waited for him with happiness. We rode our horses across the river.' " Repeated throughout the narrative, usually within quotation marks and always out of immediate context, it is revealed finally—after all the scenes of Artemio's maturity have been developed and he is prepared to recall it—as the herald to his memory of his final meeting with his son, when Lorenzo reveals that he is going to Spain.

> You will see him in the distance now and you will tell yourself that he has become the image of your own youth, well-built, strong, dark, with his green eyes set deep behind his high cheekbones. . . . "Some day I will tell you about your father . . . your father, Lorenzo." . . . No . . . he must understand alone and by himself, for even if you wanted to, you would not dare to tell him: you will listen to him. . . . "You would do the same, Papá. You didn't stay out of it, at home. What do I believe? I don't know. You brought me here, you taught me this life. . . . It has been as though you were living your life over again. . . . Now there is a front and I think it is the only front left. I'm going to go to it. . . ." (pp. 217–9)

The irony of his choice cannot be lost on his father, who has repudiated his own youthful idealism by his subsequent acts. That their identification may be ironic, however, that the son's death may prove an unintended commentary on the life of the father, merely intensifies the emotion. Artemio is left with a few words only—"that they must go on, life is on the other side of the mountain, life and freedom, because yes, those were the words that he wrote: they took the letter from his bloodstained shirt . . ." (pp. 232–3)—and with a desperate need, at the end of his life, to recreate the end of the life of his son, as if it too were his own, as if it would make possible his own. "I have a son, I sired him: because now I remember that face: where shall I put it, where, so that it won't escape me, where, for God's sake, where, please, where" (p. 215). The pain of his memory blurs into his bodily pain. He is free now to turn to his own dying.

Lorenzo's repudiation, then, is not simply ironic, as it might be in a European Modernist novel. We mark the irony, perceive its distancing, note its undercurrent of politics (that dichotomy in the Mexican scheme of government which allows for the official avowal of liberal, even revolutionary ideals and, at the same time, for basically conservative practices). But the confused identity of the nation and of its representative son is not wholly negative. We are struck by their ability, even now, as we find them in Fuentes, to create and to live by a viable body of myth and to view their own acts with passionate involvement and surprising objectivity. Scorning the public example of Artemio's life, we are moved nonetheless by him as a man. For we feel with Artemio his loss—of his son, of himself: a heightening of those reactions which we experience toward Bloom. Because of his intense ambiguity about life, because he acknowledges his own duality, because he accepts responsibility for what he has made of his life, we can respect, be moved by, perhaps identify with the man even as we judge harshly his public life. His deathbed identification with his son and his own younger self—the one face that he remembers—enables him, after so many years, to make again an emotional commitment to life. Even at the end, even as its betrayer, Artemio Cruz continues to equal and represent Mexico.

> You could not be more tired than you are [he thinks now]. It's that you have traveled a long way, . . . and the country never ends. . . . It is not one; there are a thousand countries, with a single name. You know that. You will carry with you the red deserts, the hills of prickly pear and maguey, the world of dry cactus, . . . the limestone and sandstone cities, . . . the adobe pueblos, the reed-grass hamlets, . . . the Indians who lack a common tongue: Cora, Yaqui, Huichol, . . . Nahua, Maya; . . . the ruins of the serpent, of the black head, the great nose, the churches and altar-pieces, the colors and reliefs, the pagan faith . . . , the old names . . . ; they weight you down, they have entered your guts, they are your bacilli, your parasites, your amoebas . . .
> the land of your birth. . . . (pp. 266–7).

The voice which recreates his birth at the moment of his death may be that of the land which he carries within him.

The Death of Artemio Cruz shows clearly just how much Fuentes has drawn from Joyce and the Modernist masters and what he has brought of his own to this splendid new fiction. In technique especially, but also in worldview, Fuentes has profited from the Modernist example. In the development of a multi-faceted point of view which expresses both the man at the center and the world around him; in the manipulation of a complex time scheme, at once objective and subjective, which communicates the essence of national and personal history and their interconnection; in the elaboration of a pattern of image and metaphor which both structures the narrative and informs it with feeling; in the use of myth as the measure of man; in the perception of modern man as a potentially worthy, responsible being, capable of evoking our emotion and respect even in a diminished world, even as we view him with irony, Fuentes's fiction echoes Joyce's. But the vision of reality and human experience which makes possible such echoes is not borrowed or alien; the literary techniques of this post-Joycean fiction are perfectly synonymous with Latin American experience. In the end, Fuentes is inspired more by Joyce's presence than by his specific example. And here too he may be thought representative of contemporary fiction in Latin America.

The stars which attend the young Artemio's movement into the wider world of maturity ("the immense stars whirling in silence against the infinite backdrop of space"—p. 303) may perhaps have their origin in "the heaventree of stars" which overlook Stephen's departure from Bloom into art;[100] Molly's final words in "Penelope" are surely repeated in the aged Artemio's memory of youthful lovemaking ("yes, yes, she liked it, yes, she was ready, don't stop, yes, go on, go on, let it never end, yes . . ."—p. 63). The relationship of Artemio and his long dead son, and the continuing fertility latent in the midst of his seeming sterility, reflect Bloom's ongoing relationship with Rudy. The sense in "Circe" that there is a consciousness at work beyond those of Stephen and Bloom is amplified in Artemio's voices. The pattern of history which delimits modern man yet allows him to assume responsibility for his acts, the cycle of myth which ties him to natural process, the hero whose dignity and worth are determined despite (beyond) his public image and career, the vision of a country and a way of life more vital than can be realized by those who live out their daily lives there—these perceptions are shared alike by Fuentes and Joyce. Borrowed in part from Joyce and expanded, in part reached independently, they attest to a vision in Fuentes that is at once continuing and new, Latin American and Modernist, a new perspective from which to view the Modernist accomplishment a generation after its alleged disappearance: in a new setting, renewed.

Examples of Joyce's direct influence may be found throughout current Latin American fiction: in the flexibility and inventiveness of its language, in its blending of naturalism and metaphor, in its application of myth to modern life, in its manipulation of narrative perspectives and time. *Ulysses* itself appears in at least one novel—read by the narrator of Gustavo Sainz's *Obsesivos días circulares* (1969), it helps to pattern his narrative;[101] and it provides inspiration and structure for others—*e.g.*, Juan Filloy's *Op Oloop* (1934), a day in the life of a Finnish resident of Buenos Aires, an Argentine *Ulysses*. But the true Joycean inheritance, I believe, is to be found less in direct, textually traceable influence than in that vision of literature and life shared—across two generations and continents, beyond subject matter, language, and technique—with such Latin American writers as Carlos Fuentes: less in the early "paralysis" of *Dubliners* and *Where the Air Is Clear* than in the complex maturity of *The Death of Artemio Cruz*.

Fuentes's immediate sources in *The Death of Artemio Cruz* are Mexican.

From Juan Rulfo's *Pedro Paramo* (1955) comes the story of the Revolution's betrayal by its former adherents, told through an ambiguous point of view and time sequence, rooted in a dreamlike, almost surreal reality, evoking peasant lives and the natural process as they persist beyond politics and local history. And from the poet and social critic Octavio Paz comes the assurance that beyond the irony of such stories lies an inherent native acceptance of self-contradiction, the recognition of human duality at the heart of Mexican—and Latin American—experience. "Duality," says Paz in *The Other Mexico,* "is not something added, artificial or exterior: it is our constituent reality. Without otherness there is no oneness."[102] From Joyce and the Modernists comes the further recognition, with all its literary and human ramifications, that within such immediate, local perceptions we outsiders too may find a powerful and timeless affirmation of universal experience: duality, in our era, is present in each of our lives, and the role of the novelist—European Modernist or contemporary Latin American, Joyce (who first named that duality) or Fuentes—remains to show us that we may yet be whole.

As we reconstruct with Artemio Cruz his movement out into the world—a world made in part, as we know it, by Leopold Bloom—we attest to his central role in that world; we measure him by the world, but also the world by him. Despite the disjunctions in his life, as in Bloom's, there is a potential harmony there, an enveloping pattern of natural rhythms which speak to his humanity and celebrate through him the centrality and continuing worth of human experience. These are the rhythms not only of our literary, our Joycean heritage, not only of our concern for language, our dependence on myth, and our need to remain close to natural process. They are inherent in Fuentes's Latin America, as in the Modernist sensibility which he, like so many of his compatriots, inherits and adapts. They are the rhythms of life in our time, and they affirm, under the aura of Joyce and *Ulysses,* our connections to the rhythms of past human life and of life in the future.

6 THE GENERATION AFTER

Modernist Literature in a Post-Modernist World

The novel as a form no longer carries conviction. Experimentation, not aimed at the real difficulties, has corrupted response. . . . The novelist, like the painter, no longer recognizes his interpretive function; he seeks to go beyond it; and his audience diminishes. And so the world we inhabit, which is always new, goes by unexamined, made ordinary by the camera, unmediated on; and there is no one to awaken the sense of true wonder.

—V. S. Naipaul, "Conrad's Darkness"

The humanist outlook is pre-eminently a pledge of solidarity.

—Alain Robbe-Grillet, *For A New Novel*

Stephen dissented openly from Bloom's views on the importance of dietary and civic selfhelp while Bloom dissented tacitly from Stephen's views on the eternal affirmation of the spirit of man in literature.

—James Joyce, *Ulysses*

When I was a graduate student of literature in the early 1960s, reading as widely as I could but already with a pronounced interest in twentieth-century fiction, I at no time encountered, so far as I can recall, the term "Modernism." Perhaps I was simply unobservant, or perhaps my failing was my long-standing preference for reading novels rather than the comments of readers like myself on the novels. My own experience aside, what seems fairly certain is that the term "Modernism"—in literature at least—was not very much used until that time when critics began generally to declaim its demise. Today it is everywhere, in the popular media as well as the critical texts, if only as an adjunct to that still more prevalent, if more nebulous term, "post-Modernism."[1] (I seem to recall studying only "modern" and "contemporary" literatures, with the narrowest and most arbitrary of lines distinguishing them. Today, when I teach a course labeled "post-Modernist" fiction, it is always in reference to that far greater age which precedes the present and which, I believe, continues to inform it; but it is the post-Modernist courses, so seemingly up-to-date, that students and schedule-makers appear these days to prefer.) Before we have begun fully to understand the central cultural phenomenon of our century, we are told that we no longer need consider it—except, if we insist, as historians of the past—that our attention for the present can be directed more profitably elsewhere (and an elsewhere without even a proper name of its own).

As the critical context for the study of Modernism narrows, so evidently do its dates and its accomplishments. When Harry Levin first published "What Was Modernism?" in 1960, he was reacting to a movement, international in its scope, whose force (as he saw it, regretfully) had finally been spent but which had formerly possessed enormous vigor and variety—not of the limited, even provincial focus which more up-to-date commentators now tend to speak of; Levin's confidence in Modernist expansiveness remains undiminished, as we see in his latest book, the somewhat nostalgic *Memories of the Moderns* (1981). Compare to this the comment of the poet Mark Strand on the poetry of his American generation: "By 1940 the revolution we call Modernism had run its course; the battle against the ninetenth century had been won with time's help, and the poetry of experimentation was so secure that it had become a new academicism."[2] The editors of a recent text on *Spatial Form in Narrative* are even more delimiting: " 'Modernist,' " they write, "refers to works written between the end of the nineteenth century and World War II—works that are experimental and often involve spatial form."[3] There is none of the hysteria here of a Cooper or a Snow, but the limiting pejoratives "academic" and "experimental"; the certainty that no new Modernist developments are possible in our own (or in the previous) generation; the chronological limits that would unthinkingly lump *Sister Carrie*, published in 1900, with the contemporary (and differing) novels of Conrad and James, and the works of Bennett with those of Woolf; the certain sense that Modernism is a movement to be measured in time alone, limited most likely to those languages with which we are familiar, without a true, consistent, informing vision—all this is implicit, it seems to me, in these representative remarks.

The central argument of this book is that Modernism survives, and so I may well be reading too much into these comments. Mark Strand, after all, is a poet who is speaking here of poetry and not of the novel, and we must be aware that literary Modernism cannot be quite the same or have the same history in all of its genres—indeed, there may be different Modernisms in the different arts. The term itself appears to derive initially from architecture, and it is in this field that the revolt against Modernism—against academic imitations of its once-inspired forms, against distortions of its intent—is the most forceful and articulate. But the revolt has spread—in a kind of academicism of its own—to all the other arts.

The so-called International Style of Modernist architecture, developed in the wake of abstract art, emphasized simplicity and rationality of function, linearity of form, a certain starkness of design. It endeavored to capture the spirit of its time by using the materials and technology of the time, and if it rejected much of the architectural past and at times created buildings in which the human scale might be lost, its aim was inherently humanistic: to elevate the level of our perceptions and the quality of our lives within its new structures. Great Modernist buildings continue to rise in our generation,[4] but it is their imitators—the inhumane, clichéd, glass-box skyscrapers of the 1960s—which have caused the rebellion against architectural Modernism. The new Postmodernist school of architecture—which can be dated from Robert Venturi's *Complexity and Contradiction in Architecture* in 1966—emphasizes decorative elements of design, a concern for the past, the revival of those aspects of the art abandoned by the Modernists; the new art has been described by one critic as "romantic, eclectic and fiercely intellectual."[5] The Postmodernist architects do appear at this point to represent a true movement, although time may prove that they are closer to the Modernist masters than they are likely now to want to admit. Their revolt, moreover, parallels and perhaps helps to predict a certain movement in the other arts: a revived interest in representational painting and sculpture, a new Romantic music, newer forms of dance at once freer and more rigid.[6]

In poetry too, especially in the United States, there has been a very strong reaction against Modernist forms and concerns. Following the example of William Carlos Williams, a contemporary of the Modernists Eliot and Stevens, American poets in recent years have abjured metaphor, have sought for newer and freer poetic structures and consciously smaller subjects, have endeavored to develop an idiom that is particularly and recognizably American. Theirs is an art that is not international but intentionally local, even personal, as seen, on the one hand, in the confessional verse of Robert Lowell among others and, on the other hand, in the theories of Charles Olson, perhaps the most powerful influence in American poetry today. In his concern for the direct, unmediated, almost intuitive perception of life and for the openness of form which can best communicate it, Olson comes to advocate a poetry devoid of all human intercession, including that of the poet. In his hands, the famous dicta of Pound ("Make it new"; "Poetry must be as well written as prose") and Williams ("The language is worn out"; "No ideas but in things") become the theory of "objectism," a poetic way to dispose "of the lyrical interference of the individual as ego, of the 'subject' and his soul, that peculiar presumption by which western man has interposed himself between what he is as a creature of nature . . . and those other creations of nature which we may, with no derogation, call objects. For a man is himself an object. . . ."[7] The contemporaneous echo of Robbe-Grillet is unmistakable, and if the vision of life in the *Maximus* poems of Olson is not nearly as bleak as that of *The Voyeur* or *La Jalousie,* if the American's world is as rich in history and event as in things, if in the end he is more concerned with creating a new sense of human perception than with denying our presence, endeavoring to "restate man [in order to] repossess him of his dynamic,"[8] he is nonetheless reacting against the same Modernist reading of man as is Robbe-Grillet. It may well be that Olson too will survive in literary history more as theoretician than as artist, a sign of the changing times. But such a delimiting judgment about its principal figure can in no way deny the very real presence of a post- (that is, anti-) Modernist movement in contemporary American poetry.

There is no comparable movement in American prose. What there is, instead, is an isolated case with seeming symbolic overtones—the short fiction of Donald Barthelme, short in length and short in intent, with the now-familiar emphasis on objects, on perception, on the reduced scale of vision and potential available today, as these post-Modernists see it, to our generation. Barthelme's city life is very different from Joyce's. His New York is "complicated" (p. 149)[9], to be sure, but it is essentially a small town with few connections among its inhabitants, made up of trivial individuals and their trivial, portentous, object-filled lives: New York (Manhattan, that is) as seen by a non-native resident. It is a representative city, we are told ("Our muck is only a part of a much greater muck—the nation-state—which is itself the creation of that muck of mucks, human consciousness. Of course all these things have a touch of sublimity . . ."—p. 167), and it is presented with humor, through a most observant eye and in an often engaging style. But its art, like its vision, is intentionally minimal. The New York of our time, Barthelme tells us, is of necessity much smaller than Joyce's Dublin; to write about it truly, the artist must exile himself to it (Barthelme is from Philadelphia and Houston; the native New Yorkers—Malamud, Baldwin, and Mailer among them—no longer seem to need to write about the city). More importantly, the reader—that exile from Modernism—can no longer expect to emulate even Bloom, not to speak of Odysseus.

Fuentes's Mexico City, Butor's Bleston (Manchester), even Pynchon's New York are similarly places of profound unease, where life is difficult and the human spirit is constantly threatened, places of exile for their own inhabitants. But they are not, like Barthelme's metropolis, simple reductionist depositories of trivial acts and trivial signs; they are not, in other words, post-Modernist. In reacting against the richness, the artifice, even the opulence of Modernist fictive designs, a post-Modernist writer such as Barthelme—like Charles Olson denying the art of Wallace Stevens—is reacting as well against the Modernist view of the world. In the richness of Joyce's prose, in the artifice of his design (as in Proust, Mann, Faulkner, Woolf, and even, I believe, in Kafka), there is room still for a human presence: no longer commanding perhaps, but capable of asserting itself nonetheless; not in every way estimable, but worthy of notice and at times of respect; acknowledging in the worst of places and times our continuing humanity. For all its good humor and charm, this world of Barthelme's is infinitely bleaker than that of the Modernists, echoing Robbe-Grillet in his denial of life, recalling Cooper and Drabble in the sterility of their art. It serves to remind us, ironically, how profoundly humanistic Modernist fiction has been and how profoundly humanistic it remains.

It reminds us as well that there are different Modernisms: that Balanchine or Ashton, for example, as distinct as they are from each other, can only tangentially be related to Schoenberg or Brancusi, or to Eliot or Joyce; that Eliot, whatever mythic and moral connections he may claim, is antithetical to Joyce; that the art and vision against which the Postmodernist architects have rebelled are very different from those of the Modernist novelists.[10] The linearity of Modernist architecture, with its respect for technology and its rejection of the past, has no real parallel in Modernist fiction. What the Postmodernist architects are searching for, it seems to me, is actually an art not unlike that of the Modernist novel, with its sense of history, its decorative but integral details, its human presence. (The new architectural movement, moreover, however we name it, is directed less against the Modernist masters than against their uninspired followers, who have misunderstood their intent and misused their forms: we recall Robbe-Grillet and the literary critics who have confused him with Joyce.)

Modernism is not a question of chronology, then, or of simple and exact parallelism in the arts, but of something much deeper, and if we intend to apply the term to all the major art forms of this revolutionary era—to music, dance, painting, sculpture, architecture, poetry, and fiction—we must be as aware of their differences as of their broad similarities. We have derived both troublesome terms, "Modernism" and "Postmodernism," from architecture; we have automatically adopted the former in reference to all the other arts. But this does not mean that we are obliged to do so once again with the latter.

I have no desire to offer here a new definition of Modernist fiction or to provide yet another list of its principal characteristics. Such actions are more likely to confuse than to clarify any literary issue and to satisfy no one but their proposers. But I obviously do have strong feelings about the matter, especially in those areas that seem to me to be too often misunderstood: in the interconnection of narrative technique and theme in Modernist fiction, in the relationship of the Modernist novelists to their antecedents and audience, and in the issue of humanist survival: areas which seem to me to go to the heart of Modernist survival. I reject the term "experimental"—with all its English-borne pejoratives—when it is applied to Modernist narrative innovations, for I agree with B. S. Johnson that these are not experiments at all but knowing efforts to comprehend and realize a new reality. There is nothing sacrosanct about narrative omniscience or about the characterization and plotting that traditionally accompany it; there is nothing inherently realistic or moral about such an approach. To think otherwise—and on this ground to decry the Modernists' daring endeavor—is ludicrous; even worse, it is to misunderstand, almost willfully, the very tradition of the novel that it is meant to defend. It is surely a truism that every age must develop its own art forms in order to communicate its own vision of the world. The strength of the novel as a form is that it has always been able to change with its times, to reflect and sometimes to announce them. As omniscience served the secure Victorians so accurately and so well, so more limited forms of narration (more limited in the absolute truths they convey, far more daring in their technique) represent more truly our own ambiguous world. In the process of developing such forms, the great Modernists created a fiction more closely realized, more tightly structured, more intensely developed than had ever before been written. They thus placed on the reader a new burden, one that I believe to be representative of the age: we must now read Modernist novels with all the attention and seriousness that we once reserved for the Shakespearean sonnet. Some readers—and some novelists and critics as well—may recoil from so heavy a responsibility, and so we have in our time, for the first time, a cleavage between the serious novel and the popular novel.

But the Modernist masters did not intend to be elitist and to write for a select and limited audience of enthusiasts. I am convinced—twenty years of reading and teaching their work has convinced me—that they honestly expected to create through their work a new genre of reader, who would discover for himself the rewards of involvement in the narrative and who would thus honor the creators, as they have honored us, with his deepest attention and concern. (It is because it best demonstrates that concern that I continue to value an eclectic New Criticism, open to other sources but putting the text above all else. Of course, if we believe that Modernist fiction persists, even thrives in our time, then there is little need for us to replace its critical technique with some newer, more modish approach.) In so ideal a world, Joyce, like Dickens before him, would be not only the best and most representative novelist of the day but also the most popular. (His novels do sell well, incidentally, but not enough to prevent Harold Robbins from claiming that he is the world's greatest novelist because he is the most widely read—and most promptly forgotten, I suppose.) But we have refused as readers to fulfill our part of this implied contract with the novelists, and so the cleavage has grown—although the patient, good-willed, attentive reader of *Ulysses* or even of the *Wake* will happily attest to the rich rewards that he earns for his labor. It is only those who refuse to involve themselves in the Modernist narrative, to meet its demands and thereby to reap its rewards, who can so knowingly deny its humanist presence.

In "The Dehumanization of Art" (1925),[11] considering "all the arts that are still somewhat alive in the Western world—that is, not only music, but also painting, poetry, and the theater" (p. 4), Ortega y Gasset concludes that Modern Art "will always have the masses against it. It is essentially unpopular; moreover, it is antipopular" (p. 5). It is inherently dehumanized as well. This is because of its manifest concern for style and form, since "style involves dehumanization" (p. 23), and "a tendency toward a purification of art," of necessity, "would effect a progressive elimination of the human, all too human, elements predominant in romantic and naturalistic production" (p. 11). The dichotomy, to Ortega y Gasset, is inescapable: "preoccupation with the human content of the work [of art] is in principle incompatible with aesthetic enjoyment proper" (p. 9). In 1925, three years after the publication of *Ulysses*, one year after *The Magic Mountain*, the year of *Mrs. Dalloway, The Trial*, and the penultimate volume of *A la recherche du temps perdu*, the great Spanish philosopher neglects to include the novel among the arts "still somewhat alive in the Western world."[12] But it is evident that his remarks relate equally to the novel form; to those critics who insist that Joyce and the others have followed Flaubert away from humanity and into abstraction—into pure form— these remarks must relate especially to the Modernist novel.

It may be evident as well, however—at least it is to me and, I suspect, to many other attentive and caring readers of Joyce and his contemporaries—that it is precisely their concern for "style" which makes possible their revelation of humanity, and that "aesthetic enjoyment proper" and human discovery are the same in the great Modernist novels. It is because of the demanding narrative technique of *Ulysses*, not at all abstract but leading us within Bloom and also perhaps within ourselves, that we are able to discover Joyce's hero in his manifold forms, to realize his curiosity, his decency, and even his courage, to become involved in the details of his life, not at all sordid as some once thought but "all too human," to be moved by his predicament and to respect his resolution, and perhaps within the complexities and ambiguities of his humanity to find something of our own.

Ulysses—and the Modernist novel for which it may stand as emblem—is profoundly humanistic because it involves us with characters whose solidity we recognize as comparable to our own; because it engages our emotions over the predicaments of other human lives; because it evokes our concern in a human cause we had long thought lost, enabling us to learn for ourselves about ourselves. Its concern for narrative technique is not for the sake of "experiment" but to effect this involvement. Its realism is that of modern urban life, wandering and disjointed—our reality, however much we may fear it and yearn for the old. Its emphasis on myth is not merely ironic, as we once thought, but also traditional, offering us a means of making connections to our past; providing a place for man lost in urban society—helping to humanize Bloom's life, as it once humanized the processes of nature for our

distant ancestors; establishing the potential for ties among errant individual lives. Man in Modernist fiction is no longer at the center of the
universe; he may no longer control his own destiny. But Leopold
Bloom, HCE, Proust's Marcel, Mrs. Dalloway and Mrs. Ramsay, Quentin
Compson in the face of his ancestors, Hans Castorp and the Biblical
Joseph, even Joseph K. become aware of and sensitive to the complica-
tions of their lives, responsible for their own lives. And because the
reader's involvement is integral to their narratives, we too may become
more sensitive to life—to our own as well as to theirs. Their narratives
are not quite human-centered perhaps, but they remain human-revealing: for all the irony of modern existence, for all the negative changes
which may have taken place in the facts of our lives and, especially, in
our perceptions of those facts and of their implications—Bloom, after
all, is not Homer's Odysseus, and some of his descendants may not even
aspire to be Bloom—for all this, man remains the measure in them of
modern existence. Modernist fiction may well be oriented inward to
individuals rather than outward to the larger society, as its detractors
have often claimed; but it is directed through its heroes to the whole
course of human values, noting what has been lost, reasserting what
may remain, what we may need to survive in a world not of their
making.

To the extent that their narratives may end—a major problem for
some readers, of course—they end in reaffirmation: Bloom falling into
sleep, having completed his accounts, surrounded by fertility archetypes;
Hans Castorp re-emerging into the world—it is the terrible world of
World War I, but he at least can confront it, having confronted himself;
Marcel understanding at last the significance of his divided life and able
at last to reintegrate it in his art; Clarissa Dalloway, before her mirror,
truly seeing herself and her world, and Lily Briscoe with her vision;
even Joseph K. glimpsing for an instant the responsibilities attendant on
living. And because of the reader's involvement, because we too,
through them, must confront ourselves, that reaffirmation—in a world
of diminished potential—may become ours as well. From the perspective of the most self-destructive half-century in human history, their
work, as strongly as the acknowledged humanism of the past, seems to
me profoundly moral as well as emotional, even spiritual: humanistic,
in a word. "All the doubts cast upon the inspiration of those pioneers
may be justified," writes Ortega, "and yet they provide no sufficient

reason for condemning them. The objections would have to be supplemented by something positive: a suggestion of another way for art different from dehumanization and yet not coincident with the beaten and worn-out paths" (p. 50). It is just such an art, I believe, that Joyce and the Modernist masters have created, just such a model that they have provided for their followers. Of Joyce and these others we may say what the anthropologist Loren Eiseley has said of Darwin, who similarly disrupted his comfortable world: "Philosophically Darwin may have removed us from a privileged position in the universe but he brought us, at the same time, back into the web of life."[13] At the center of the Modernist web we may perhaps find ourselves.

Ortega's "art of the young" (p. 6) seems today, to some, to be the old art. Hence all the claims for a newer, more modish, less threatening, post-Modernist art. Certainly the provenance of Modernist fiction is old: the cataclysm of the First World War, with its destruction of values, of certainty, of the past itself, of all the old humanistic connections that the Victorians and Edwardians could take for granted and that we would so much—so naturally—desire to assume for ourselves. But we cannot reconstitute that old world—a world which may never have existed in reality, in any event. And the Modernist provenance remains current as well, for we in our time have had our own cataclysms, equally unresolved: in the Holocaust and the Second World War, in Hiroshima and Vietnam, in the recurrence in our generation—almost the banality in our lifetimes—of genocide, even of self-genocide, our novelists may find a reality not unlike that which faced the first Modernists.

In such a mad world as ours, all of us are like the Latin American novelists to whom García Márquez refers in his Nobel Prize speech, "all creatures of that unbridled reality, we have had to ask but little of imagination." In spite of this madness, García Márquez declares, "we, the inventors of tales"—speaking alike for the artists of his continent and generation, following the example of the Modernist masters[14]—"in spite of this, to oppression, plundering and abandonment, we respond with life." The "second opportunity on earth" for which the novelist now calls—reversing the history of the Buendías, in response to "this awesome reality that must have seemed a mere utopia through all of human time"—must seem now, speaking practically, no more than an illusion. But to call for that second chance now, to call for it knowing that it must seem an illusion, to call for it as Joyce and his contemporaries had done in the reality of their time, to devise a new language and mythos in the Modernist spirit (in narrative forms similarly inspired, with a similar sense of human values and presence) is to affirm not simply the survival of the Modernist literary example but perhaps our own survival as humans as well.

NOTES

Chapter 1

1. Richard Ellmann, *James Joyce* (New York, 1959), p. 307.
2. Anthony Trollope, *Barchester Towers*, Zodiac Press edition (London, 1962), pp. 121–2. Trollope singles out Mrs. Radcliffe as principal malefactor, but it is clear that he is speaking also of Dickens and Thackeray.
3. See my own essay, "A Hero for Our Time: Leopold Bloom and the Myth of *Ulysses*," in Thomas F. Staley, ed., *Ulysses: Fifty Years* (Bloomington, 1974), pp. 132–46.
4. Perhaps the best-argued and best-known such listing is Maurice Beebe's "*Ulysses* and the Age of Modernism" in Staley, pp. 172–88.
5. José Ortega y Gasset, *The Dehumanization of Art and Other Writings on Art and Culture* (Garden City, 1956), p. 12.
6. James Joyce, *A Portrait of the Artist as a Young Man*, Viking Press edition (New York, 1956), p. 215.
7. Alain Robbe-Grillet, *For a New Novel: Essays on Fiction*, trans. Richard Howard, (New York, 1965), pp. 19, 53.
8. Ortega y Gasset, *The Dehumanization*, p. 21.
9. But there is a hint of such an admission in the essay "Nature, Humanism, Tragedy": "That there is no more than a rather loose parallelism between the three novels I have published up to now and my theoretical views on a possible novel of the future is

certainly obvious enough"
(Robbe-Grillet, *For a New Novel*, p.
50).

10. T. S. Eliot, "Ulysses, Order and
Myth," in *James Joyce: Two Decades
of Criticism*, ed. Seon Givens (New
York, 1963), p. 201.

11. Robbe-Grillet, *For a New Novel*, pp.
158, 157.

12. Ortega y Gasset, *The
Dehumanization*, p. 23.

13. The particular quote is from
Bernard Bergonzi, "The Advent of
Modernism 1900–1920," in *The
Twentieth Century*, ed. Bernard
Bergonzi, Vol. VII of *The Sphere
History of Literature in the English
Language* (London, 1970), p. 45,
but the concept may be found
throughout contemporary British
novel criticism.

14. Henry W. Sams, "Satire as
Betrayal," *ELH*, 26 (1959), 38–41.
For a comparable critical view of
some of the newest critical modes,
see David H. Hirsch, "Penelope's
Web," *Sewanee Review*, 90 (1982),
119–131.

Chapter 2

1. Stephen Spender, *The Struggle of
the Modern* (Berkeley, 1963), pp.
77–8.

2. Spender, *The Struggle*, p. 76.

3. "[N]o one single novel of Virginia
Woolf's seems to get beyond the
feminine fragility of her
sensibility," writes the usually
more sensible Malcolm Bradbury
("The Novel in the 1920's," in *The

Twentieth Century, ed. Bernard
Bergonzi, Vol. VII of *The Sphere
History of Literature in the English
Language* [London, 1970], p. 191);
she "not only tends to poeticize
modernism, but also to feminize
and domesticate it. . ." (Malcolm
Bradbury, *Possibilities: Essays on the
State of the Novel* [London, 1973],
p. 130). For an earlier version of
this same sexist foolishness, see
Herbert V. Muller, "Virginia Woolf
and Feminine Fiction," in *Modern
Fiction: A Study of Values* (New
York, 1937).

4. For a fascinating account of the
Woolf-Bennet controversy—and of
the basic connections between
them—see Samuel Hynes, "The
Whole Contention Between Mr
Bennett and Mrs Woolf," in
Edwardian Occasions (New York,
1972), pp. 24–38.

5. Angus Wilson, *As If By Magic*
(New York, 1973), p. 63. " 'I'm
not asking you to accept all
Joyce's verbal fireworks,' "
exclaims one of the characters,
" 'but the basic common humanity
of Bloom!' " It is more common to
assume that such fireworks of
necessity preclude humanity.

6. T. S. Eliot, "Tradition and the
Individual Talent," in *The Sacred
Wood* (London, 1960), pp. 49–50.

7. "Once I planned to make a survey
of Kafka's precursors," writes
Jorge Luis Borges. "At first I
thought he was as singular as the
fabulous Phoenix; when I knew
him better I thought I recognized
his voice, or his habits, in the

texts of various literatures and various ages" (Jorge Luis Borges, *Other Inquisitions, 1937–1952,* trans. Ruth L. C. Simms (Austin, 1964), reprinted in Peter F. Neumeyer, ed., *Twentieth Century Interpretations of* The Castle [Englewood Cliffs, N.J., 1969], p. 101). It is precisely the unfamiliarity of the Kafkan narrative voice, heard as it is in such unfamiliar surroundings, which makes for the singularity of Kafka. Thus, both the tone (as in Gogol or the Yiddish writings of Eastern Europe in the late nineteenth century) and the ostensible subject matter of *The Castle* (*e.g.,* the quest motif, as in *Pilgrim's Progress*) are common enough; it is their strange juxtaposition which is so idiosyncratic.

8. Virginia Woolf, "Modern Fiction," in *The Common Reader,* First Series (New York, 1953), pp. 152–4.

9. Woolf, "Modern Fiction," p. 154.

10. This final sacrifice appears to have been made, at least to the satisfaction of Woolf's detractors, five years afterward in Woolf's well-known essay, "Mr. Bennett and Mrs. Brown."

11. Cf. Harold Bloom's suggestion, relative to the relations between Romantic and Modernist poetry, that such misreadings may well be intentional, that the poet misreads his predecessor in order to be free of him. "Poetic influence," as Bloom conceives it in this neo-Freudian view, "is a variety of melancholy or an anxiety-principle. It concerns the poet's sense of his precursors, and of his own achievement in relation to theirs. Have they left him room enough, or has their priority cost him his art? More crucially, where did they go wrong, so as to make it possible for him to go right?" (Harold Bloom, *Yeats* [New York, 1970], p. 5). We may wonder, however, whether it is possible to "go right" merely by returning to still older forms.

12. John Bayley, *Tolstoy and the Novel* (London, 1966), p. 59.

13. Virginia Woolf, *To the Lighthouse* New York, 1955), p. 189.

14. Woolf, "Modern Fiction," pp. 155–6.

15. Virginia Woolf, "Mr. Bennett and Mrs. Brown," reprinted in *Approaches to the Novel,* ed. Robert Scholes (San Francisco, 1961), p. 227. In *Afterjoyce: Studies in Fiction After* Ulysses (New York, 1977), p. 68, Robert Martin Adams claims that Woolf "was jealous of Joyce and afraid of him," afraid as she was writing *Jacob's Room* "that Mr. Joyce must be doing the same thing at the same moment, and doing it better, . . . oppressed by the sense of Joyce's giant egotism, and frightened by the hard surface of that scholastic structure which he offered in place of the traditional intrigue. She must have felt uneasy about replacing one rigidity, one formalism, with another. And so she absorbed Joyce slowly." Part of the point, I

think, is that Joyce and Woolf alike, and D. H. Lawrence as well, were inherently conservative both about many social concerns and about those literary issues which did not activate them directly.

16. John Bayley, *The Characters of Love* (New York, 1960), p. 285.

17. Such readings of Modernist art, fostered in part by the Modernists themselves, are by no means confined to the British or to those hostile to the movement. To the Americans Richard Ellmann and Charles Feidelson (eds., *The Modern Tradition: Backgrounds of Modern Literature* [New York, 1965], p. vi), this is "the great age of the century's literature," although it "has already passed into history." Yet they agree with its enemies that "Modernism strongly implies some sort of historical discontinuity, either a liberation from inherited patterns, or, at another extreme, deprivation and disinheritance. . . . Committed to everything in human experience that militates against custom, abstract order, and even reason itself, modern literature has elevated individual existence over social man, unconscious feeling over self-conscious perception, passion and will over intellection and systematic morals, dynamic vision over the static image, dense actuality over present reality. . . . These are the two forces, positive and negative, of the modern as the anti-traditional: freedom and

deprivation, a living present and a dead past."

18. "The dominance of alien talents in the Modern Movement, whether Continental or Celtic or American, has given weight to recent attempts to erect an anti-modern native tradition, even though a major aspect of English literary culture has always been its eclecticism and openness to outside influences." Bernard Bergonzi, "The Advent of Modernism 1900–1920," in *The Twentieth Century*, ed. Bernard Bergonzi, Vol. VII of *The Sphere History of Literature in the English Language* (London, 1970), pp. 21–2.

19. Hence such productions as Graham Hough's *Image and Experience* (Lincoln, Neb., 1960), which argues, as Bergonzi puts it ("The Advent of Modernism," p. 19), "that much of the poetry of the Modern Movement was merely a detour from the true English tradition. . . ." A similar contention is implicit in much of the recent fiction in Britain.

20. See, for example, Malcolm Bradbury, "The Novel in the 1920s," p. 74.

21. Among others, see David Lodge, *The Novelist at the Crossroads* (Ithaca, 1971), p. 254.

22. "If there is a persistent world-view [within Modernism] it is one we should have to call apocalyptic; . . . At such times there is a notable urgency in the proclamation of a break with the

immediate past, a stimulating sense of crisis, of an historical license for the New" (Frank Kermode, *Continuities* [New York, 1968], p. 2). "Flaubert, Henry James, Proust, Joyce and Virginia Woolf have finished off the novel," says Cyril Connolly. "Now all will have to be re-invented as from the beginning" (Cyril Connolly, *The Unquiet Grave* [New York, 1945], p. 21, as cited in Bernard Bergonzi, ed., *The Situation of the Novel* (London, 1970), p. 14.

23. This is among the most persistent of all the charges brought against the Modernists. Denis Donoghue, for example, argues that *Ulysses* is not what it seems on the surface, "rich, dense, earthy, a Dublin book; . . . Joyce has begun to ask, as he did not ask in *Dubliners*, where is reality, what constitutes the real? Increasingly, as the book proceeds, the answer has more to do with the autonomous imagination and less with the density of the world." This presumed shift has high moral overtones (although its roots are in the Dublin street view which rejects *Ulysses* outright but admires *Dubliners* because "I know people like that in Dublin"). "I am also arguing," says Donoghue, "that Joyce became more and more interested in these possibilities [of a new philosophy and language], less and less in the human reference." In *Finnegans Wake*, "Joyce, like Kafka, becomes a modern hero; turning away in

distaste now from the phenomenal world, they represent the Nietzschean imagination, virtually identified with the will (Denis Donoghue, *The Ordinary Universe: Soundings in Modern Literature* [New York, 1968], pp. 63–4). Yet we are badly mistaken if we go on assuming that realism in the novel, as it developed through the eighteenth, nineteenth, and early twentieth centuries, is perforce the same as reality today. The failure to perceive this has led to what Northrop Frye calls "stupid realism": "In this context we can see that realism of form has changed sides; it is no longer a liberalizing and emancipating force. . . . Stupid realism depends for its effects on evoking the ghost of a dead tradition: it is a parody of the realism which was organic a century or two ago" (Northrop Frye, *The Modern Century* [Toronto, 1967], pp. 62–3). The results have been disastrous: "it is difficult to avoid associating the restoration of traditional literary realism with a perceptible decline in artistic achievement" (Lodge, *The Novelist at the Crossroads*, pp. 7–8).

24. The American Harry Levin is frequently said to have been the first to announce Modernism's demise (Harry Levin, "What Was Modernism?" in *Reflections: Essays in Comparative Literature* [New York, 1966]—the essay itself was written in 1960). Like such other American critics as Irving Howe

(ed., *The Idea of the Modern in Literature and the Arts* [New York, 1967]), Richard Chase ("The Fate of the Avant-Garde," in Howe, above), and Richard Ellmann and Charles Feidelson (eds., *The Modern Tradition*), Levin reacts to this passing with a certain ambiguity and even regret. "[N]o literature of the past matched the literature of our time in power and magnificence," Lionel Trilling comments for them all; although it is marked by "the bitter line of hostility to civilization which runs through it," "No literature has ever been so intensely spiritual as ours" (Lionel Trilling, "On the Modern Element in Modern Literature," in Howe, pp. 60–4). The British reaction is dramatically different: few critics even bother to speak of Modernism's death, assuming, it would seem, that Modernism for the British was never really alive. Or they may assume that it died several generations ago, even before others noticed that it had been born: "Indeed one could argue that by the 1920's the heyday of modernism [in Britain] was already past; that its culminating phase was between 1908 and 1915, when London was for a while the international capital of what was after all an international tendency . . ." (Malcolm Bradbury, "The Novel in the 1920's," pp. 182–3).

25. Arnold Bennett, "Why A Classic Is A Classic," in *Essays,* ed. Fred L. Bergmann (Dubuque, Ia., 1975), p. 122. There is a fascinating echo here from the charge of elitism against the Modernists: "The term 'modernism' (or 'modernness') has, for some of the Marxist critics, the pejorative secondary meaning of bourgeois disintegration, decay, decadence . . ." (Miklos Szabolcsi, "Avant-garde, Neo-avant-garde, Modernism: Questions and Suggestions," *New Literary History,* 3 [1971], p. 50). Accused simultaneously of being elitist and bourgeois (but in both cases decadent), the Modernist movement has been a useful whipping boy for both conservatives and radicals.

26. In *Unofficial Selves: Character in the Novel from Dickens to the Present Day* (New York, 1973), Patrick Swinden lists Bennett, V. S. Naipaul, and Richard Hughes as the most praiseworthy novelists since Dickens. Leavis himself says of Bennett that he "seems to me never to have been disturbed enough by life to come anywhere near greatness" (F. R. Leavis, *The Great Tradition* [New York, 1967], p. 7). But cf. Margaret Drabble's biography, *Arnold Bennett* (New York, 1974).

27. Leavis, *The Great Tradition,* p. 2.

28. Leavis, *The Great Tradition,* pp. 7–8, citing Lawrence's review of *Death in Venice,* in *Phoenix: The Posthumous Papers of D. H. Lawrence,* ed. Edward D.

McDonald (London, 1936), p. 308. This judgment—that the Modernist novelist is more concerned with his art and his artistry than with life—appears to many British critics to be the most damning commentary of all on Modernist fiction. " 'I feel that my work is more real than reality itself,' " John Bayley quotes Joyce. "Could Shakespeare possibly have said such a thing?" (Bayley, *The Characters of Love*, pp. 278–9). I am inclined to believe that he might have.

29. Leavis, *The Great Tradition*, p. 26, citing *The Letters of D. H. Lawrence*, ed. Aldous Huxley (New York, 1932), p. 260.

30. Leavis, *The Great Tradition*, p. 26.

31. Lodge, *Crossroads* p. 271.

32. Founded in 1932, *Scrutiny* survived as a stimulating and controversial journal of criticism until 1953. The subtitle of *Culture and Environment* (London, 1934) speaks directly to its pedagogical intent, to wit, *The Training of Critical Awareness*.

33. See, *e.g.*, Stephen Spender, *The Struggle of the Modern* (Berkeley, 1963), p. 241): "When we arouse ourselves from the superiority complex of Great Traditional thinking, we see that we do not and cannot transport ourselves through the study of literature into the past organic community spiritual life, because to do so would mean our living in that time, which is unthinkable."

34. See my essay, "A Hero for Our Time: Leopold Bloom and the Myth of *Ulysses*," *in Ulysses: Fifty Years* ed. Thomas F. Staley (Bloomington, Ind., 1974), pp. 132–46.

35. C. P. Snow, *London Sunday Times*, 27 December 1953, as cited in Lodge, *Crossroads*, p. 18. There is a clear pattern to the frequent reviews which Snow wrote for the *Sunday Times* in the late forties and early fifties. "Snow's critical formula is too predictable: any warm, human, readable novel which displays no experimental tendencies is approved of. Using this formula Snow praised many mediocre books and rejected many that were worthwhile; nevertheless Snow's theories were, on the whole, approved of in England" (Rubin Rabinovitz, "C. P. Snow vs. The Experimental Novel," *The Columbia University Forum*, 10 [1967], p. 40).

36. Kingsley Amis, *The Spectator*, (2 May 1985), p. 565, as cited in Rubin Rabinovitz, *The Reaction Against Experiment in the English Novel, 1950–1960* (New York, 1967), pp. 40–1.

37. William Cooper, "Reflections on Some Aspects of the Experimental Novel," *International Literary Annual*, No. 2, ed. John Wain (New York, 1959), pp. 29, 36.

38. "[W]e may point to the presence in the twentieth-century arts of two contrasted functions. One is art in its liberal function; the artist is essentially the humanist. . . . The other tendency is art in its

formalist function; it believes in the distinctiveness of its own way of knowing and may be seriously concerned for the fortunes of civilization, but it postulates an anarchistic environment in society in which certain aspects of the traditional activity are no longer possible. . . . There is little doubt that the liberal function of art in our century has been reduced" (Malcolm Bradbury, *The Social Context of Modern English Literature* [New York, 1971], pp. 104–5). My own sense is that the major Modernists are not only not responsible for any failure in our century of "the liberal function" of art, but also that their work almost never lapses into mere formalism (although this may well be the case with some of their lesser imitators and followers of subsequent generations). This may be only a difference in emphasis, but it is an important one, I believe.

39. Kermode, *Continuities*, p. 10.

40. See Gabriel Josipovici, *The Lessons of Modernism* (Totowa, N.J., 1977), p. x.

41. "But the consequence of this [New Critical] procedure was not to increase literature's role in shaping the individual's self-realization in society; instead it proved a means for avoiding or neglecting such roles. The subtlety of literary analysis of individual poems was surely increased, but the insistence on the purely literary function of the analysis served to heighten rather than control the crisis it was meant to resolve" (Ralph Cohen, "On a Shift in the Concept of Interpretation," in *The New Criticism and After*, ed. Thomas Daniel Young [Charlottesville, Va., 1976], p. 63). This may perhaps be true of the purist form of New Criticism, which may never stray beyond the text. But this has not been the basic use of the mode in America; it has served instead as the focus of all other critical modes—historical, psychoanalytic, mythic, and the like—so long as they recognize the primacy of the text. The very term "formalist" begs the question; it is no more useful, or honest, in this context than that other pejorative "experimental."

42. "It remains that Modernism in art, if not in literature, has stood or fallen so far by its 'formalism.' Not that Modernist art is coterminous with 'formalism.' And not that 'formalism' hasn't lent itself to a lot of empty, bad art. But so far every attack on the 'formalist' aspect of modern painting and sculpture has worked out as an attack on Modernism itself because every such attack developed into an attack at the same time on superior artistic standards" (Clement Greenberg, "Necessity of 'Formalism,'" *New Literary History*, 3 [1971], p. 173). At the least, one might argue, the parallels between painting and literature have been sometimes

simplistic: Andy Warhol, Roy Lichtenstein, and even Marcel Duchamp are not the appropriate parallels to Modernist fiction among twentieth-century painters. To raise their names in this context, as Peter Ackroyd does *Notes for a New Culture: An Essay on Modernism* [New York 1976], pp. 134–5), rather than those of Picasso, Matisse, and Klee, is yet again to beg the question.

43. Bradbury, *Possibilities*, p. 194.

44. See, *e.g.*, Robert K. Morris, ed., *Old Lines, New Forces: Essays on the Contemporary British Novel* (Rutherford, N.J., 1976), p. xviii, which also names Kingsley Amis's *Lucky Jim*, and see also Maurice Cranston, "The New Novelists, an enquiry," *The London Magazine*, 5 (1958), p. 31, and Bradbury, *Possibilities*, p. 193.

45. William Cooper, *Scenes from Life* (New York, 1961), p. 252. All further references to this text, which includes both *Scenes from Provincial Life* and *Scenes from Married Life*, are in the body of the chapter.

46. In "An Interview with Margaret Drabble," conducted by Nancy S. Hardin, *Contemporary Literature*, 14 (1973), p. 282.

47. One critic has written convincingly of the shift in point of view in *The Waterfall*—from third- to first-person narration—as a means of delineating character development: "Narrative technique thus helps define heroine and conflict" (Virginia K. Beards, "Margaret Drabble: Novels of a Cautious Feminist," *Critique*, 15 [1973], p. 44). Drabble herself speaks of this shift as coincidence, as almost an accident. See Hardin, "An Interview with Margaret Drabble," p. 293.

48. All references to *The Waterfall, The Realms of Gold*, and *The Ice Age* are to the American editions published by Alfred A. Knopf (New York, 1969, 1975, and 1977).

49. Thus, although Drabble's fiction might well be labelled pre-Modernist, such a book as Cooper's *Disquiet and Peace* (1956) is not so much an evocation of an Edwardian novel as it is an Edwardian novel. Its perspective is entirely from outside; its characters are seen primarily as part of their social setting; its political frame is indistinguishable from those of Disraeli or Maurice Edelman; its psychological development is nil. Cooper's characters are early contemporaries of Freud who are ignorant of, but would surely be hostile to, Freudian ideas; instead of psychological development in any pre-, post- or simply Freudian sense, they are made subject to changes announced from on high, changes of which they are themselves unaware and which have no effect on their actions. Whether through ignorance or choice, in subject as in technique, Cooper seems determined to

restore one of the least
distinguished of all the moments
in the history of the British novel.

50. All references are to Anthony
Burgess, *Re Joyce* (New York,
1966). The British edition,
published in London in 1965, is
entitled *Here Comes Everybody* and
contains an index omitted from
the American text.

51. Anthony Burgess, *The Novel Now*
(New York, 1970), p. 23.

52. In an interview with Anthony
Lewis, " 'I Love England, But I
Will No Longer Live There,' " *The
New York Times Magazine* (3
November 1968), p. 61.

53. In *Books and Bookmen* (July 1970),
p. 8, Burgess goes on to specify
his particular inheritance from
Joyce and from an earlier love,
Hopkins: "What I ended up
learning from Joyce as well as
from Hopkins was the importance
of the ear, the essentially auditory
nature of imaginative prose. . . . It
was a help to me that I'd trained
myself in an art that meant much
to both Joyce and Hopkins—
music. If you're a writer who
knows something of music you
won't make the error of confusing
the boundaries of the two arts."

54. Robert Nye, *Falstaff* (Boston,
1976), pp. 159–60.

55. A temptation impossible to resist
for long: in 1963, Julian Mitchell
[the novelist] published his third
novel, entitled, strangely enough,
As Far As You Can Go.

56. All references are to Julian
Mitchell, *The Undiscovered Country*
(New York, 1968).

57. The character Julian Mitchell's
introduction to *The New Satyricon*
comments implicitly on the
Robbe-Grillets and Sollerses of the
critical/artistic world: "The sheer
unreadability of many writers, not
all of them French, their obvious
concern to baffle and daze the
reader, their private snickering
and deliberate nonsense, have not
always been seen for what I
believe they are—gestures which
are primarily aggressive and only
secondarily artistic. Most *avant-
garde* manifestoes, for instance, are
a good deal more interesting as
protesting social documents than
the poems and pictures which
subscribe to them are valuable as
literature or painting" (p. 173).
Charles himself comments on
Joyce and, implicitly, on his own
life and work: " 'There's nothing
to be learnt from James Joyce—
he's *sui generis,* like Richard Dadd.'
(Dadd, I discovered later, was a
mad nineteenth-century painter
who killed his father and spent
the rest of his life in an
enlightened lunatic asylum)" (p.
160).

58. A Reuters dispatch of 20 January
1978 (*Philadelphia Inquirer,*
Section A, p. 3) reported that a
white woman in South Africa is
suffering from a brain tumor that
darkens her skin and thus subjects
her to discriminatory practices:
such an incident might almost
have been a *donnée* for *Out.*

59. All references are to Christine
Brooke-Rose, *Out* (London, 1964).

60. All references are to B. S.

Johnson, *Aren't You Rather Young to be Writing Your Memoirs?* (London, 1973).

61. "Most of what I have said has been said before, of course; none of it is new, except possibly in context and combination. What I do not understand is why British writers have not accepted it and acted upon it" (Johnson, *Aren't You Rather Young,* p. 30). Johnson's relationship with Drabble seems instructive in this respect. They are obviously at opposite ends of the Modernist/anti-modernist spectrum, and so it is fascinating to discover that they acted as co-editors of a book, entitled *London Consequences* (London, 1972), which consists of twenty novelistic chapters by twenty different writers, compiled as a promotion on behalf of the Greater London Arts Association (for one hundred pounds, guess the authors of the individual chapters). Plot remains reasonably secure in such a frame; technique tends to be lost. But I feel reasonably secure in suggesting that the first chapter is in Drabble's narrative style, the reflexive twentieth in Johnson's.

62. "In some ways the history of the novel in the twentieth century has seen large areas of the old territory of the novelist taken over by other media, until the only thing the novelist can with any certainty call exclusively his own is the inside of his own skull: and this is what he should be exploring, rather than anachronistically fighting a battle he is bound to lose" (Johnson, *Aren't You Rather Young,* p. 12). The purpose of all narrative art, Proust writes in *Contre Sainte-Beauve,* is to enable the writer to reach "a particle of himself, the only material of art" (as cited in George D. Painter, *Proust: The Later Years* [Boston, 1965], p. 130).

63. All references are to B. S. Johnson, *Travelling People* (London, 1963).

64. "[T]he incomprehension and weight of prejudice which faces anyone trying to do anything new in writing is enormous, sometimes disquieting, occasionally laughable. A national daily newspaper (admittedly one known for its reactionary opinions) returned a review copy of *Travelling People* with the complaint that it must be a faulty copy for some of the pages were black; the Australian Customs seized *Albert Angelo* (which had holes justifiably cut in some pages, you will remember) and would not release it until they had been shown the obscenities which (they were convinced) had been excised . . ." (Johnson, *Aren't You Rather Young,* p. 31).

65. All references are to B. S. Johnson, *Albert Angelo* (London, 1964). It is here, Johnson writes, that "I broke through the English disease of the objective correlative to speak truth directly if solipsistically in the novel form, and heard my own small voice" (Johnson *Aren't You Rather Young,*

p. 22). The reflexivism thus counts for much more than mere narrative playfulness; it is the key to the author's discovery of his voice, to his creative identity, to his reaching for "truth."

66. The "Table of Instructions" to *Hopscotch* informs us that we are to read the first fifty-six chapters in order and then to re-read, in a carefully calculated if not always coherent succession, the entire one hundred and fifty-six chapters of the text (with the sole exception of #55). The goal is to achieve a simultaneity which will enrich our understanding of the characters and of their milieu. The results, however, seem sometimes strained and gratuitous. (For more on *Hopscotch*, see chapter 5, part 2 of this book.) *Composition No. 1,* at the other extreme of control, consists entirely of unbound and unnumbered pages in a box, which are designed to be shuffled and re-shuffled through various readings. The mechanism seems strange and radical, almost anti-novelistic; but the result, as my colleague Philip Stevick points out, is "remarkably traditional." Some years age, I loaned my copy of the text to a friend, who left it on his living room table when guests were present and who returned from filling drinks to find one of his guests on his knees, the scattered pages of the text around him on the floor. "I think I've got it all in the right order now," the guest said after a moment.

67. Called in the original *6 810 000 Litres d'eau par seconde, étude stéréophonique,* Butor's novel skillfully makes use of various type faces and positioning on the page to suggest a stereophonic reading that may actually be more flexible and richer than stereophonic sound: a most Joycean use of other media.

68. B. S. Johnson, *House Mother Normal* (London, 1971), p. 204.

69. All references are to B. S. Johnson, *Christie Malry's Own Double-Entry* (New York, 1973).

70. All references are to B. S. Johnson, *See the Old Lady Decently* (New York, 1975). The structure and layout of the novel, not surprisingly, are quite complex, with a series of different headings and characters to differentiate among the sources (GB for Britain, BB for the Empire, 16(8) for Emily's eighth year of life in 1916, N for Neumann, and the like) and to involve the reader as an almost reflexive participant himself in the act of unifying the text.

71. Beyond the question of immediate influence, there are certain ties among these novelists and their works. As Lucien Daudet said early of *A la recherche du temps perdu,* in "an image worthy of Proust himself, . . . 'every masterpiece is the cry of a precursor, and rallies beyond time, in the black frost of eternity, its companions yet to come'" (cited in Painter, *Proust,* p. 201).

72. " 'Experimental' to most reviewers

is almost always a synonym for 'unsuccessful.' I object to the word *experimental* being applied to my own work. Certainly I make experiments, but the unsuccessful ones are quietly hidden away and what I choose to publish is in my terms successful. . . . Where I depart from convention, it is because the convention has failed, is inadequate for conveying what I have to say" (Johnson, *Aren't You Rather Young*, p. 19).

Chapter 3

1. Myth is significant throughout Murdoch's canon, in fact, but hers seems a different sort of myth from Joyce's: Jungian, to be sure, but analytic rather than narrative or natural, one further tool to help us comprehend the individual psyche in a confused environment, rather than a means of linking together all individuals.

2. Reprinted in Seon Givens, ed., *James Joyce: Two Decades of Criticism* (New York, 1963), p. 202.

3. Malcolm M. Willcock, *A Companion to the Iliad* (Chicago, 1976), p. 282.

4. Hazel E. Barnes, "Greek Mythical Figures as Contemporary Images," *The Key Reporter*, 41 (Summer 1976), p. 2.

5. C. G. Jung, "Ulysses," *Europäische Revue*, 9 (1932), pp. 547–68, as reprinted under the title "Ulysses—A Monologue," in *Nimbus*, 2 (1953), pp. 7–20.

6. See my article, "A Hero for Our Time: Leopold Bloom and the Myth of *Ulysses*," *James Joyce Quarterly*, 10 (1972), pp. 132–46.

7. All references are to Thomas Pynchon, *V.* (New York, 1964).

8. "If there were, as some doctors of the mind were beginning to suspect, an ancestral memory, an inherited reservoir of primordial knowledge which shapes certain of our actions and casual desires, then not only [Victoria's] presence here and now between purgatory and hell, but also her entire commitment to Roman Catholicism as needful and plausible stemmed from and depended on an article of the primitive faith which glimmered shiny and supreme in that reservoir like a crucial valve-handle: the notion of the wraith or spiritual double, happening on rare occasions by multiplication but more often by fission, and the natural corollary which says the son is doppelgänger to the father. Having once accepted duality Victoria had found it only a single step to Trinity" (Pynchon, *V.*, p. 183).

9. Profane "told her about the alligators; Angel, who had a fertile imagination too, added detail, color. Together on the stoop they hammered together a myth. Because it wasn't born from fear of thunder, dreams, astonishment at how the crops kept dying after harvest and coming up again every spring, or anything else very permanent, only a temporary interest, a spur-of-the-moment

tumescence, it was a myth rickety and transient as the bandstands and the sausage-pepper of Mulberry Street" (Pynchon, *V.*, p. 128).

10. "To go along assuming that Victoria the girl tourist and Veronica the sewer rat were one and the same V. was not at all to bring up any metempsychosis: only to affirm that his quarry fitted in with The Big One, the century's master cabal, in the same way Victoria had with the Vheissu plot and Veronica with the new rat-order. If she was a historical fact then she continued active today and at the moment, because the ultimate Plot Which Has No Name was as yet unrealized, though V. might be no more a she than a sailing vessel or a nation" (Pynchon, *V.*, p. 210).

11. All references are to Thomas Pynchon, *Gravity's Rainbow* (New York, 1973).

12. Washington Irving, "The Legend of Sleepy Hollow," *Selected Prose* (New York, 1961), pp. 182–3.

13. "Let human beings go free amid nature," as the Puritans' Anglican opponents urged, "and what will be the result? The same old chronicle of meanness and cruelty, bloodshed and robbery, hatred and betrayal, blunder and stupidity, which passes under the name of history. . . . no matter how unintelligible the world might seem to a Puritan, he never lost confidence that ultimately it was directed by an intelligence.

Yet even with this momentous difference in our imagination of the controlling power, the human problem today has more in common with the Puritan understanding of it than at any time for two centuries: how can man live by the lights of humanity in a universe that appears indifferent or even hostile to them?" (Perry Miller and Thomas H. Johnson, eds., *The Puritans*, vol. I [New York, 1963], pp. 50, 63).

14. Hugh Honour, *The New Golden Land: European Images of America from the Discoveries to the Present Day* (New York, 1975), p. 3.

15. See Joseph W. Slade, *Thomas Pynchon* (New York, 1974), pp. 187–90.

16. C. G. Jung, "The Collective Unconscious and Archetype," in *The Modern Tradition: Backgrounds of Modern Literature*, eds. Richard Ellmann and Charles Feidelson, Jr. (New York, 1965), p. 645.

17. Mircea Eliade, *The Myth of the Eternal Return* (Princeton, 1971), p. 18.

18. From Ronald Sukenick's *98.6*, a novel whose characters are prey to the disintegration of modern society and whose efforts to organize their lives fail because of their inner disorder: "Still rocking with the motion of the sailboat he's overcome with an appreciation for gravity you might say he falls in love with it. He loves the way it hugs him firm against the ground like a mother.

He loves the way he has to press back erect against it his force against its force in balance. He loves the steady pressure of it on the soles of his feet. . . . People who grow out of the earth and never get too far away from it never forget they're getting back into it lesson of the pyramids pressing down" (Ronald Sukenick, *98.6* [New York, 1975], p. 5).

19. *"Gravity's Rainbow* demonstrates more clearly than any other work of modern fiction how science can be incorporated as a tool for metaphor and style. Science illustrates the struggle to understand life and death. . . . The fundamental choices between belief in order and determinism versus a belief in disorder and lack of control, are expressed in scientific images. Yet these two extremes are sterile for mankind. . . . Science in *Gravity's Rainbow* is not an escape from human problems, but rather a valuable tool with which the novelist reflects those problems. *Gravity's Rainbow* presents the unifying view that all our pursuits are common responses to the same problem—how to regard a universe which demands coexistence between extremes" (Alan Friedman, "Science and Technology in *Gravity's Rainbow,"* unpublished ms.).

20. As a representative man, Slothrop speaks to our slipping humanity: "He's looking straight at Slothrop (being one of the few who can still see Slothrop as any sort of integral creature any more. Most of the others gave up long ago trying to hold him together, even as a concept—'It's just got too remote's what they usually say)" (Pynchon, *Gravity's Rainbow,* p. 740).

21. All references are to Robert Coover, *The Origin of the Brunists* (New York, 1967).

22. All references are to Robert Coover, *The Universal Baseball Association, Inc., J. Henry Waugh, Prop.* (New York, 1969).

23. All references are to Robert Coover, *Pricksongs and Descants* (New York, 1970).

24. All references are to Robert Coover, *The Public Burning* (New York, 1977).

25. Joseph Campbell, *The Hero with a Thousand Faces* (New York, 1962), p. 384.

26. In the introduction to his collected correspondence with Thomas Mann, Karl Kerényi observes that "whoever opened men's eyes to the great teachings that emanate from the human-divine play of mythology also purified and humanized." And Mann concurs: "Indeed, in my case the gradually expanding interest in myth and religious history is a 'sign of old age.' It corresponds to a taste that has, in the course of years, moved away from the bourgeois-individualistic toward the typical, the general, the universally human." The Joyce of *Ulysses,* in part through the use of myth,

succeeds in merging these disparate concerns. The Joyce of *Finnegans Wake,* however, might have agreed with Mann, who writes toward the end of his life, citing *"the old Aristotle"*: " 'The more I am alone and thrown back on myself, the more I become attached to myth' " (Karl Kerényi, *Mythology and Humanism: The Correspondence of Thomas Mann and Karl Kerényi,* trans. Alexander Gelley [Ithaca, New York, 1975], pp. 28, 37, 190).

27. Campbell, *The Hero,* p. 384.
28. This situation would later be appropriated for William Goldman's popular thriller, *Marathon Man.*
29. All references are to E. L. Doctorow, *The Book of Daniel* (New York, 1979).
30. James Joyce, *Ulysses* (New York, 1986), p. 525.
31. "Why did Bloom experience a sentiment of remorse" at the memory of his long-dead father?

    "Because in immature impatience he had treated with disrespect certain beliefs and practices.

    "As?

    "The prohibition of the use of fleshmeat and milk at one meal, the hebdomadary symposium of incoordinately abstract, perfervidly concrete mercantile coexreligionist excompatriots: the circumcision of male infants: the supernatural character of Judaic scripture: the ineffability of the tetragrammaton: the sanctity of the sabbath.

    "How did these beliefs and practices now appear to him?

    "Not more rational than they had then appeared, not less rational than other beliefs and practices now appeared" (Joyce, *Ulysses,* pp. 595).
32. Joyce *Ulysses,* p. 571.
33. Joyce *Ulysses,* p. 544.
34. In a review of *Giles Goat-Boy* (1966), B. S. Johnson, who had admired the "wonderfully enjoyable send-up of both history and literature" in *The Sot-Weed Factor,* objected to Barth's academicism. *"Giles Goat-Boy* is essentially a book made out of other books. It does not represent any advance in the novel form; it merely tells where we are, instead of taking us some of the way towards where we shall be: it recapitulates without innovating" (B. S. Johnson, "Giles FitzWESAC FitzEnglit," *Books and Bookmen* [April 1967], pp. 60–1).
35. All references are to John Barth, *The End of the Road* (New York, 1969).
36. John Locke, *Of Civil Government* (London, 1953), p. 141.
37. Jorge Luis Borges, *Labyrinths: Selected Stories and Other Writings,* ed. Donald A. Yates and James E. Irby, trans. James E. Irby (New York, 1964), pp. 40–41.
38. Borges, *Labyrinths,* p. 42.
39. Borges, *Labyrinths,* p. 44. In the well-known essay called "The Literature of Exhaustion" (*Atlantic,* Aug. 1967, pp. 29–34), Barth has said of "Pierre Menard"

that Borges "writes a remarkable and original piece of literature, the implicit theme of which is the difficulty, perhaps the unnecessity, of writing original works of literature. His artistic victory, if you like, is that he confronts an intellectual dead end and employs it against itself to accomplish new human work." It is obvious that this intended paradox helps to explain what sometimes seems the dead ends of Barth's later fiction. "I myself have always aspired to write Burton's version of *The 1001 Nights*, complete with appendices and the like, in twelve volumes, and for intellectual purposes I needn't even write it" (Barth, "Exhaustion," p. 31). What he has written, of course, is the "Dunyazadiad." Barth has also commented informally that he spent some hours in a library attempting to verify Menard's listed canon and was able, finally, neither to prove nor to disprove the existence of such works.

40. Borges, *Labyrinths*, p. 18. Citing the " 'contamination of reality by dream' " in "Tlön," Barth comments that "it turns the artist's mode or form into a metaphor for his concerns, as does the diary-ending of *A Portrait of the Artist as a Young Man* or the cyclical construction of *Finnegans Wake*" (Barth "Exhaustion," p. 32). Both of these endings appear in "Autobiography," one of the tales in *Lost in the Funhouse*.

41. Borges, *Labyrinths*, p. 18.

42. All references are to John Barth, *The Sot-Weed Factor* (New York, 1964).

43. James Joyce, *Finnegans Wake* (New York, 1974), p. 185: 32–6.

44. All references are to John Barth, *Lost in the Funhouse* (New York, 1969). "I saw the best minds of my generation destroyed by madness," Allen Ginsberg says at the beginning of *Howl* (1956). Ginsberg is speaking, of course, of one lost generation and not of lost generation, the end of creation.

45. Campbell, *The Hero*, pp. 245–6.

46. James Joyce, *A Portrait of the Artist as a Young Man* (New York, 1956), p. 253.

47. It is no coincidence, then, that in "The Literature of Exhaustion" Barth speaks only of *A Portrait* and the *Wake* and not of *Ulysses*. In a certain sense, these stories of his of procreation owe more to Sterne or Pirandello or the Beckett of *Krapp's Last Tape* than to Joyce—even in technique. "Autobiography," for example, is subtitled "A Self-Recorded Fiction," and it speaks via the medium of its mother, the tape recorder, and in the unspoken presence of its father, the author, presumably young Ambrose, or the father of Ambrose.

48. Barth, "Exhaustion," p. 34, citing Borges, "Kafka and His Precursors," *Labyrinths*, p. 201. Borges explains that "The early Kafka of *Betrachtung* is less a precursor of the Kafka of somber myths and atrocious institutions

than is Browning [as in the poem "Fears and Scruples"] or Lord Dunsany [in the story "Carcassone"]."

49. Barth, "Exhaustion," p. 33. In response to the "misreaders of my earlier essay," wrote Barth in "The Literature of Replenishment," in 1980, that it was "the aesthetic of high modernism" that had become "exhausted" in our time—not narrative itself—and that a newer fiction, "more democratic in its appeal," was currently being worked out: "not . . . the next-best thing after modernism, but . . . the *best next* thing: what is gropingly now called postmodernist fiction; what I hope might also be thought of one day as a literature of replenishment." But he does not, he reminds us (presumably more careful readers), repudiate Modernism: "I deplore the artistic and critical cast of mind that repudiates the whole modernist enterprise as an aberration and sets to work as if it hadn't happened" (John Barth, "The Literature of Replenishment: Postmodernist Fiction," *Atlantic*, Jan. 1980, pp. 71, 70).

50. All references are to John Barth, *Chimera* (New York, 1972).

51. Robert Graves in *The White Goddess* (New York, 1958, pp. 243 ff.) interprets the myth of Perseus and Medusa as an iconographic summary of the invention of an early Greek alphabet, a reading strangely consonant with Barth's.

52. Barth, "The Literature of Exhaustion," pp. 29, 30.

Chapter 4

1. Vivian Mercier, *The New Novel from Queneau to Pinget* (New York, 1971), pp. 9–11.

2. All references are to Alain Robbe-Grillet, *For a New Novel: Essays on Fiction*, trans. Richard Howard (New York, 1965).

3. Wayne C. Booth, *The Rhetoric of Fiction* (Chicago, 1961), p. 384.

4. Erich Heller, "The World of Franz Kafka," in *Twentieth Century Interpretations of* The Castle, ed. Peter F. Neumeyer (Englewood Cliffs, N.J., 1969), p. 76.

5. Charles Neider, "*The Castle:* A Psychoanalytic Interpretation," in Neumeyer, *Interpretations*, p. 42.

6. Henri Daniel-Rops, " 'The Castle of Despair,' " in Neumeyer, *Interpretations*, p. 18.

7. Max Brod, *Franz Kafka* (New York, 1947), p. 178.

8. Cited in Gustav Janouch, *Conversations with Kafka* (New York, 1971), p. 80.

9. Cf. the very different use made of the Jews by such Modernist poets as Eliot and Pound.

10. Franz Kafka, *The Castle*, trans. Willa and Edwin Muir (New York, 1966), p. 337.

11. All references are to Alain Robbe-Grillet, *The Voyeur*, trans. Richard Howard (New York, 1958).

12. Cf. John Barth's early novel, *The End of the Road* (1958), in which a

psychoneurotic English professor is made to teach prescriptive grammar and told to avoid emotional involvement as a means of ordering his psyche. The therapy, naturally, fails, and he falls into catatonia, a state not unlike that of Mathias.

13. Alain Robbe-Grillet, *Topology of a Phantom City*, trans. J. A. Underwood (New York, 1977), p. 72.

14. *The Erasers* is perhaps the first novel to make use of the detective story as a metaphor of truth's inaccessibility, but it has become by now a paradigm of post-Modernist fiction. Michel Butor in *Passing Time* (1957), Robert Pinget in *The Inquisitory* (1962), Mario Vargas Llosa in *The Time of the Hero* (1963), Mark Smith in *The Death of the Detective* (1974), Don DeLillo in *Running Dog* (1978), and, of course, Pynchon are among those who have elaborated this initial little perception of Borges's.

15. Virginia Woolf, *The Years* (New York, 1965), pp. 192–93.

16. Michel Butor, "Esquisse d'un seuil pour Finnegan" (Sketch of a threshold for Finnegan), in *Essais sur les modernes* (Paris, 1964), pp. 291, 297, 296.

17. This occurred at the Fourth International James Joyce Symposium in Paris, in 1975, when Butor was chairman of a panel with Nathalie Sarraute, Philippe Sollers, and others. See "Joyce et l'aventure d'aujourdhui"

(Joyce and the adventure of today), in J. Aubert and M. Jolas, eds., *Joyce et Paris 1902 . . . 1920–1940 . . . 1975* (Paris, 1979), p. 59.

18. Michel Butor, *Passing Time*, trans. Jean Stewart (New York, 1960).

19. All references are to Michel Butor, *A Change of Heart*, trans. Jean Stewart (New York, 1959).

20. The French term for timetable, *l'emploi du temps* is also the French title of *Passing Time*.

21. All references are to Michel Butor, *Degrees*, trans. Richard Howard (New York, 1961).

22. Michel Butor, "The Novel as Research," in *Inventory*, ed. Richard Howard, trans. Gerald Fabian (New York, 1968), p. 28.

23. Michel Butor, *Histoire Extraordinaire: Essay on a Dream of Baudelaire's*, trans. Richard Howard (London, 1969), p. 170. Cf. Eliot's citation of Baudelaire in *The Waste Land:* " 'You! hypocrite lecteur!—mon semblable,—mon frère!' "

24. Something of this emphasis can be seen in my essays, "Disillusionment and Epiphany: The Novels of Claude Simon," *Critique*, 12 (1970), pp. 43–71, and "The Burden of History: Claude Simon's *Histoire*," *Kenyon Review*, 31 (1969), pp. 128–34.

25. Salvador Jiménez-Fajardo, *Claude Simon* (Boston, 1975), p. 191.

26. J. A. E. Loubère, *The Novels of Claude Simon* (Ithaca, 1975), pp. 228, 227.

27. The earliest novels of Simon—*Le Tricheur* (The trickster, 1945),

Gulliver (1952) and *Le Sacre du printemps* (The rite of spring, 1954)—remain untranslated; they are interesting but unsuccessful attempts to find a voice and a technique. A more significant work is *La Corde raide* (1947), part fiction, part essay, which lays out many of the major themes and subjects of Simon's subsequent books. It too is untranslated. The major novels, from *The Wind* to *The Battle of Pharsalus*, have been beautifully translated into English by the fine American poet Richard Howard; they are notable even in an age of great translations. The most recent novels have been translated by Helen R. Lane, and it might seem at first that the change in style is due to the change in translators. The French text quickly reveals, however, that the new prose is Simon's and not his translator's. It parallels the dramatic shift in Beckett's prose—and in his vision—when he abandoned English and the influence of Joyce and became a writer in French, perhaps the first conscious act of a post-Modernist literature.

28. It is something of a shock for a reader familiar with Simon's fictions but not with his life to encounter the photographs in *Entretiens*, No. 31 (1972), and to find there the images so prevalent in the novels: the derelict reaper from *The Battle of Pharsalus* seen near Pharsala; Simon in Barcelona in 1936; Simon in a German

prisoner of war camp. The confluence of fiction and autobiography is partially explained by *La Corde raide* (The tightly drawn cord), but we may wonder still about the extent to which one obtrudes into the other. The temptation to read the fiction in order to discover the life is obviously a temptation to be resisted, yet Simon does continue to tempt us.

29. All references are to Claude Simon, *The Flanders Road*, Richard Howard, trans. (New York, 1961), p. 87.

30. Only the first of his books on painting, *Femmes (sur vingt-trois peintures de Joan Miró)* (Women: on twenty-three paintings by Joan Miró) (Paris, 1966), appeared between the publication of *The Palace* in 1962 and that of *Histoire* in 1967.

31. All references are to Claude Simon, *Histoire*, trans. Richard Howard (New York, 1968).

32. All references are to Claude Simon, *The Battle of Pharsalus*, trans. Richard Howard (New York, 1971).

33. More than a third of the novel (the first eighty-six pages of the French text, the first seventy of the American, plus some passages in the conclusion) is drawn virtually unchanged from the 146-page Skira edition, published in Geneva in 1970 but never translated. (All references to *Orion aveugle* are to this edition.) What changes there are, are minimal, a

matter of stylistic or thematic emphasis. Thus a sentence from *Orion aveugle* which reads, "The gigantic body thrusts or plunges in accord with its parts in that Nature from which it never detaches itself" (p. 127) becomes in *Les Corps conducteurs* (*Conducting Bodies*), "The gigantic body thrusts or plunges in accord with the lights and shadows of that Nature from which it never detaches itself" (p. 77). The only significant alterations in this section of the text are the omission of the opening sentence, which identifies Orion as the principal subject, and the elimination entirely of the author's preface.

34. It is unfortunate that he could not have delayed for a time, since the Poussin has only recently been cleaned, and by a technique whose name and character would surely appeal to Simon. Called "reforming," it is designed to reconstitute a surface whose pigments have broken down over the years into separate particles. As a result of the process, "The microscopic particles coalesce. Poussin's wonderful, philosophic landscape is largely recovered. . . . The annihilation of space by dominating intelligence has never found a better metaphysics." [Thomas B. Hess, "Unvarnished Truths," *New York*, January 17, 1977, p. 61).

35. Michel Butor, *Degrees*, trans. Richard Howard (New York, 1961), p. 286.

36. All references are to Claude Simon, *Conducting Bodies*, trans. Helen R. Lane (New York, 1974).

37. There may be, in fact, two separate articles: one more or less historical which deals with the Conquest and is probably found in some popular history which serves the narrator as background reading for his trip, the other found in the newsmagazine. (A strange wedding of Orozco and *Time*.) To them are added many other sources, for he is by no means limited to the twenty images of *Orion aveugle*. Encyclopedia essays and museum catalogues, advertisements for films in local newspapers, pictures in shop windows, signs in the street and posters in the subway, a painting in a doctor's office—from each of these he abstracts details necessary to his construction. Even a toy store provides him with useful images of war.

38. In one brief sequence, as the narrator leans against a fireplug on the sidewalk in an effort to recover from an attack (kidney? liver? gall bladder?), he watches an old woman through a hotel window as she reaches over to pick up her boa, sees a young mother in Bermuda shorts reach to the sidewalk to lift her child's fallen toy (a wheeled rabbit on a string), envisions the limbs of lovers, recalls a model of the human body, moves finally to Orion in perpetual motion just as the old woman begins to move

forward. The associations are free but under strict, logical control: connected by images of motion and of the body, by hints of organic (especially sexual) capacity (and incapacity), even by the sudden sun in his eyes, which connects to an earlier moment on the plane when, with the sun "striking his eyes and his burning eyelids with such force as to be actually painful," he first imagines the lovers. He has, after all, flown over great distances and several time zones, and he has experienced much pain. He is entitled to a few shortcuts and thus to expect us to provide the links that are missing. But it is obvious that there is nothing accidental or haphazard about his creation. The intensity of this organization of the stream of consciousness is akin to that of the classical Modernist efforts of Faulkner and Joyce (Simon, *Conducting Bodies*, pp. 53–6).

39. Loubère, *The Novels*, p. 221. More specifically, she writes, "In *Triptyque* Simon demonstrates our weakness for story telling by getting the process going in the reader and then leaving him to carry on by himself. . . . To such a reader, Simon proposes that he revise his reading habits, his opinion concerning the function of the text, and the function of the reader himself" (p. 218).

40. Jiménez-Fajardo, *Claude Simon*, pp. 176, 190.

41. But cf. Mauriac's *L'Agrandissement* (Blow up), which reverses the narrative procedure of *Triptyque* by limiting the focus of *The Marquise Went Out at Five* but "blowing up" the images being perceived there. Mauriac's purpose, of course, is to make us more, not less, aware of the perceiver.

42. All references are to Claude Simon, *Triptyque*, trans. Helen R. Lane (New York, 1976).

Chapter 5

1. All references are to Eduardo Mallea, *Fiesta in November*, trans. Alis De Sola (London, 1969).

2. All references are to José Lezama Lima, *Paradiso*, trans. Gregory Rabassa (New York, 1974).

3. Personal conversation with Norman Thomas DiGiovanni, Philadelphia, May 1978.

4. José Donoso, *The Boom in Spanish American Literature: A Personal History*, trans. Gregory Kolovakos (New York, 1977), p. 4.

5. Personal interview with Carlos Fuentes, Philadelphia, December 1980. Referred to hereafter as Philadelphia interview.

6. Guillermo de Zéndegui, *Introduction to Colonial Art in Latin America*, undated supplement to *Américas* magazine, p. 11; de Zéndegui cites the Carthusian sacristy in Granada, La Cartuja, as "an excellent example of the inverse influence that America exercised on Spain."

7. In a sense, Latin American literature is hardly more than a decade old: Donoso speaks of that process by which national literatures, Argentine or Mexican or Colombian, became continental within the phenomenon known as the Boom. The irony is that knowledge and acceptance of the Boom has become widespread now that it has ceased to exist, as Carlos Fuentes has told me, as a group. Donoso speaks now of exile as the central "collective experience" of the writers of Latin America. "It is sure to become the great theme of the novels of the eighties. . ." (José Donoso, "Ithaca: The Impossible Return," *The City College Papers,* 18 [1982]. p. 7).

8. See Donoso, *The Boom,* p. 78, among others.

9. The term comes from Lawrence Durrell's *Balthazar,* second of the volumes of *The Alexandria Quartet.* The interlinear is Balthazar's commentary on Darley's narrative—the first volume, *Justine*—and its function is to suggest the relativity of knowledge, especially a narrator's knowledge of events in which he has been a participant. (Unfortunately, Durrell undercuts this point in the omniscient third volume, *Mountolive.*)

10. All references are to Julio Cortázar, *Hopscotch,* trans. Gregory Rabassa (New York, 1967).

11. See, *e.g.,* John S. Brushwood, *The Spanish American Novel: A Twentieth-Century Survey* (Austin, 1975), p. 212.

12. Manuel Puig, *Betrayed by Rita Hayworth,* trans. Suzanne Jill Levine (New York, 1971).

13. Published originally as *Tres Tristes Tigres.* The English translation (New York, 1978) is by Donald Gardner and Suzanne Jill Levine "in collaboration with the author"; all references are to this edition.

14. Rita Guibert, "The Tongue-Twisted Tiger: An Interview with Cabrera Infante," *Review,* 4–5 (1971–72), p. 13.

15. James Joyce, *Ulysses,* (New York, 1946), p. 706.

16. Guibert, "Tongue-Twisted," p. 16.

17. Guillermo Cabrera Infante, "Epilogue for Late(nt) Readers," *Review,* 4–5 (1971–72), p. 25.

18. See, *e.g.,* Guibert, "Tongue-Twisted," p. 12.

19. Guillermo Cabrera Infante, "Epilogue," p. 28.

20. Guibert, "Tongue-Twisted," p. 14.

21. Guibert, "Tongue-Twisted," p. 14.

22. "And it was at the phone, by a casual or causal chance of life, that Bustrophoneme, Bustromorposis, Bustromorphema began really to change the names of things, really and truly, for he was already sick . . . as from gotan, which isn't Gotham but the reverse of tango, he derived the barum which is the opposite of the rumba to be danced in reversed gear, with the head on the floor and moving the knees instead of the hips. . . . and

Scotch Fitzgerald and Somersault Mom and Julius Seizure . . . and Georges BricaBraque . . . and wanting to write a roman a Klee, about a painter that lost its tale . . ." (Cabrera Infante, *TTT,* pp. 228–9).

23. Cf. John Cage's vision of the *Wake, Writing Through Finnegans Wake* (Tulsa, 1978), a clever and arid constriction.

24. Cabrera Infante, "Epilogue," p. 24. The author's wish that *TTT* had been "written in the late 17th Century or early 18th Century" so that it "would be taken then *cum grano salis* but without scandal," may remind us of the narrator of Borges's "Tlön, Uqbar, Orbis Tertius" who, with the world dissolving around him, "pay[s] no attention to all this and go[es] on revising . . . an uncertain Quevedian translation (which I do not intend to publish) of Browne's *Urn Burial*" (Borges, *Labyrinths,* p. 18).

25. Guibert, "Tongue-Twisted," pp. 14–5.

26. Cabrera Infante, "Epilogue," pp. 25–6.

27. Carlos Fuentes, "On TTT," in *Review,* 4–5 (1971–72), p. 22.

28. James Joyce, *A Portrait of the Artist as a Young Man,* Viking Press Edition (New York, 1956), p. 197.

29. Joyce, *A Portrait,* p. 198.

30. Joyce, *Ulysses,* p. 532.

31. "I stand for the reform of municipal morals and the plain ten commandments. New worlds for old. Union of all, jew, moslem and gentile. Three acres and a cow for all children of nature. Saloon motor hearses. Compulsory manual labour for all. All parks open to the public day and night. Electric dishscrubbers. Tuberculosis, lunacy, war and mendicancy must now cease. General amnesty, weekly carnival, with masked licence, bonuses for all, esperanto the universal language with universal brotherhood. No more patriotism of barspongers and dropsical impostors. Free money, free love and a free lay church in a free lay state" (Joyce, *Ulysses,* p. 399).

32. And two-thirds of them live in Mexico, with its unique one-party system; the other, smaller, persisting Latin American democracies are Venezuela and Costa Rica, with Colombia promising to revert to democracy. Revising now in December 1986, it is wonderful to see how the situation has, again, changed.

33. Alejo Carpentier's *Explosion in a Cathedral* is an historical novel which relates the coming of the French Revolution to the New World and the betrayal there of its ideals. Although its Caribbean settings include Guadeloupe and Guiana as well as Cuba, most of its principal characters are Cuban, and it requires but a small leap to perceive its Cuban significance.

34. Reinaldo Arenas, *Hallucinations* (subtitled "Being An Account of the Life and Adventures of Friar Servando Teresa de Mier"), trans. Gordon Brotherston (Baltimore,

1976). All references are to this edition.

35. For his heretical views which undermined the claims of the Spanish Church "to a providentially assigned role as missionaries to the indigenous peoples [of the Americas], . . . Fray Servando was sent to Spain for trial [in 1795]. . . . For the next twenty-odd years, he was forced to live in Europe, persecuted by the Church and the omnipresent Spanish bureaucracy, imprisoned in all kinds of dungeons, escaping from one only to be recaptured and immured in another, in an endless succession of adventures that took him not only to all parts of Spain, but also to France, Italy, and England. Those two decades saw the collapse of the Spanish Empire in America, the first wars of independence in Mexico and South America, and the redesigning of the map of Europe by the Napoleonic armies. . . . Wrongly cast into the role of heretic and revolutionary, Fray Servando was actually a very conservative man who was pushed to excesses by his own exalted sense of the dramatic. He was a true creature of his time—a time when every young man thought he could reach the highest places, the time of Napoleon and Bolívar" (Emir Rodríguez Monegal, *The Borzoi Anthology of Latin American Literature* [New York, 1977], I, pp. 175–6).

36. His principal modern memorial is a major avenue named for him in traffic-clogged, smog-ridden Mexico City.

37. "Dear Servando," Arenas writes in his preface. "Ever since I discovered you in an execrable history of Mexican literature, . . . I have been trying everywhere to find out more about you. . . . The amount of facts about your life that I assembled was actually quite large; but getting to know and love you was not made easier by those wearisome, all too precise encyclopedias, or by those awful essays which were never precise enough. It was far more useful to discover that you and I are the same person. So that all the material I gathered before making this momentous and unbearable discovery has come to seem superfluous and I have hardly used any of it . . . ; your memoirs and nothing else appear in this book, and they appear not as quotations from another text, but as a fundamental part of this one. . . .

"You will not appear in this book of mine (and yours) as a perfect man with the insignia of evangelical purity, or as a blameless hero who is incapable of making a mistake or of occasionally wanting to die. You remain, dear Servando, as you are: one of the most important (and most neglected) figures of the literary and political history of America: *un hombre formidable*. And that is enough for some people to consider that this novel ought to be censored."

38. Jean Franco, *The Modern Culture of Latin America: Society and the Artist* (Baltimore, 1970), p. 56.

39. On the day that this was written, 27 February 1982, Pope John Paul II ordered the Jesuits, who have once again become active in liberal political causes in Latin America, to remain aloof from politics.

40. In 1963, the Brazilian air force bombed the *quarup* of the Cintas Largas tribe of Xingu Indians. This is the origin of Christopher Hampton's powerful play, *Savages,* which was produced in London in 1973.

41. Cabrera Infante's view of Che "is so unfashionable and inopportune that my friends consider it a form of madness to make it public. As a revolutionary Guevara is a dubious figure and only after fifty years, when it is possible to judge him impartially, shall we see him as he really is: the avatar of the myth of the warrior, self-created. . . . Somewhat as we see Lawrence of Arabia today. . . . The *Diary,* a captain's log of the carrying out of a fictitious theory, is the testament of a colossal failure, because it is evidence of a disaster that couldn't happen. It is the gospel of a redeemer rejected by those he tried to save. It is the story of a professional guerrilla general who planned the most disastrous campaigns and was routed by amateurs. . . . Finally, it is the program of an active revolutionary more concerned with his *image* as a revolutionary . . . than with his revolutionary *activity!*" (Rita Guibert, *Seven Voices,* trans. Frances Partridge [New York, 1973], pp. 362–63).

42. It is fascinating that Callado was able to publish *Quarup* and *Don Juan's Bar* in Brazil. Novelists appeared to enjoy considerable freedom under the military régime there. On the other hand, Callado the journalist was deprived of his political rights in 1969. "The leeway given to novelists—taken away when they turn to writing soap opera serials for television and often when they write plays—reflects the narrow range of their readership." *Financial Times* (London), 8 November 1977, p. 19. It must also reflect something of the nature of Brazilian society, however, since Collado's refusal to go into exile as ordered was supported by friends and by the *Jornal do Brasil,* for which he continued to write.

43. All references are to Donoso, *The Boom.*

44. George R. McMurray, *José Donoso* (Boston, 1979), p. 24.

45. For Donoso's description of the process, see *The Boom,* pp. 77 ff.

46. For only papers are found in the sack. Cf. a similar identification of narrator and manuscript in John Barth's "Life-Story" from *Lost in the Funhouse* and in his "Bellerophoniad," as well as the

similar death scene in Samuel Beckett's *Murphy.*

47. All references are to José Donoso, *The Obscene Bird of Night*, trans. Hardie St. Martin and Leonard Mades (Boston, 1979).

48. Virginia Woolf, "Mr. Bennett and Mrs. Brown," reprinted in *Approaches to the Novel*, ed. Robert Scholes (San Francisco, 1961), p. 225.

49. Karl Marx, *The Economic and Philosophic Manuscripts of 1844*, ed. Dirk J. Struik (New York, 1964), pp. 114, 140, as cited in Minna Doskow, "The Humanized Universe of Blake and Marx," *William Blake and the Moderns*, eds. Robert J. Bertholf and Annette S. Levitt (Albany, 1982), p. 393.

50. In the Prologue to *El Reino de este Mundo* (1949), which is omitted from the English edition, *The Kingdom of this World*, trans. Harriet De Onís (New York: 1970).

51. Quoted in Guibert, *Seven Voices*, p. 136.

52. Although as a child Asturias visited Indian villages with his grandfather, he was never allowed to learn Indian languages. "We grew up at a period when it was necessary to appear to be European, when it was thought wrong to speak the native language, behave as a native, or show that one was in contact with Indians. . . . My generation had to wait until the year 1920, when the great Mexican mural paintings began, . . . for our eyes to be opened by archaeological discoveries, and for us to begin wondering how we could go on thinking about Europe, when we had so much that was admirable in our natives" (Guibert, *Seven Voices*, pp. 127–28).

53. Joyce, *Ulysses*, p. 478.

54. Joyce, *Ulysses*, p. 463.

55. Marija Gimbutas, *The Goddesses and Gods of Old Europe* (Berkeley, 1982), p. 38.

56. Vargas Llosa's concern for the sort of narrative innovation associated with the Modernists is apparent throughout his canon. Thus, *Conversation in the Cathedral* is built around a long discussion-confession in which we hear voices other than those of the speakers (a reconstruction, that is, of these absent voices) and which continues on after one of the participants has left the bar (both echoes of Claude Simon's *The Flanders Road*). A later novel continues the pattern. *La tía Julia y el escribidor* (*Aunt Julia and the Scriptwriter*) (1977) is highly self-reflexive and autobiographical, with its novelist-protagonist shown at work on a novel of his life, this novel which we are in the process of reading (recalling Simon's *Triptych*, among other recent works).

57. For a very detailed analysis of this order, see Michael Moody, "A Small Whirlpool: Narrative Structure in *The Green House*," *Mario Vargas Llosa: A Collection of Critical Essays*, eds. Charles Rossman and Alan Warren

Friedman (Austin, 1978), pp. 15–35.

58. All references are to Mario Vargas Llosa, *The Green House*, trans. Gregory Rabassa (New York, 1973).

59. Luys A. Díez, "The Sources of *The Green House:* The Mythical Background of a Fabulous Novel," in Rossman and Friedman, *Vargas Llosa: A Collection*, p. 37. Díez bases his reading on several interviews given by Vargas Llosa (notably with Elena Poniatowska and Emir Rodríguez Monegal, on the "writer's log book" *Historia secreta de una novela* (Barcelona, 1971) and essay "Crónica de un viaje a la selva" (1958), and on his own visits to Piura and Santa María de Nieva.

60. Vargas Llosa, *Historia secreta*, pp. 51–3, cited in Díez, "The Sources," p. 49.

61. "The Art of Fiction: Interview with Gabriel García Márquez," *Paris Review*, 82 (1981), p. 69.

62. Raymond L. Williams, "The Narrative Art of Mario Vargas Llosa: Two Organizing Principles in *Pantaleón y las visitadoras*," in Rossman and Friedman, *Llosa: A Collection*, p. 86.

63. Brushwood, *Spanish American Novel*, pp. 288, 291–2.

64. All references to Gabriel García Márquez, *In Evil Hour*, trans. Gregory Rabassa (New York, 1980).

65. All references to Gabriel García Márquez, *One Hundred Years of Solitude*, trans. Gregory Rabassa (New York, 1971).

66. Cf. the similar image in the final scene of Werner Herzog's powerful and demanding film *Aguirre, the Wrath of God*. The conquistadors who pass the ship in the trees without even noticing it are outsiders, alienated from the land by their (European) expectations of mastering it and thus defeated by it. The ship serves in the film— borrowed almost certainly from the novel—as a sign of the Spaniards' alienation and defeat.

67. "Interview with Gabriel García Márquez," *Paris Review*, pp. 55–6.

68. "Interview with Gabriel García Márquez," *Paris Review*, p. 59.

69. Mario Vargas Llosa, "García Márquez: From Aracataca to Macondo," *Review*, 1 (1970), p. 130.

70. Vargas Llosa, *Review*, p. 131. Many such references, García Márquez admits, are "private allusions . . . which only my most intimate friends can discover: that each date corresponds to someone's birthday, that a character has the same spirit as my wife's, that someone wants to give his children the names of mine. . ." (Armando Durán, "Conversations with Gabriel García Márquez," *Review*, 1 [1970], p. 113.) Vargas Llosa adds (p. 130) that the name of Macondo is taken from a banana plantation which the young García Márquez used to explore near Aracataca.

71. "Interview with Gabriel García Márquez," *Paris Review*, p. 51.

72. "Interview with Gabriel García

Márquez," *Paris Review,* pp. 52–3. The matter is obviously not quite as straightforward as this. "I would have written what I did anyhow," says García Márquez, "without Borges and Carpentier, but not without Faulkner." The North American novelist seems to have provided some necessary affirmation if not quite an influence. "And I also believe that after a certain moment—by searching for my own language and refining my work—I have taken a course aimed at eliminating Faulkner's influence, which is much in evidence in *Leaf Storm* but not in *One Hundred Years*" (Guibert, *Seven Voices,* pp. 327–28).

73. Quoted in Durán, "Conversations," p. 114.

74. In Guibert, *Seven Voices,* pp. 133–4.

75. Joseph Campbell, *The Hero with a Thousand Faces* (New York, 1962), pp. 97, 101.

76. All references are to Gabriel García Márquez, *The Autumn of the Patriarch,* trans. Gregory Rabassa (New York, 1977).

77. It is said that during the final months of the long reign of the Portuguese dictator Antonio Salazar, cabinet meetings were held at their regular times and orders taken, although none of the orders was fulfilled and some of the ministers were no longer members of the effective government. But no one could manage to tell Salazar that he no longer ruled.

78. "[T]he king's life or spirit is so sympathetically bound up with the prosperity of the whole country, that if he fell ill or grew senile the cattle would sicken and cease to multiply, the crops would rot in the fields, and men would perish of widespread disease. . . . when he has ceased, whether partially or wholly, to be able to reproduce his kind, it is time for him to die and to make room for a more vigorous successor" (Sir James George Frazer, *The Golden Bough* [New York, 1958], pp. 312–3).

79. Campbell, *The Hero,* pp. 245–6.

80. Philadelphia interview. Joyce chooses Buenos Aires for its distance from Dublin, for the freedom that it promised from the paralysis of Dublin, and for its name: the pervasive image of "Eveline" is dust, and there can hardly be such dust in a city named for its fine air. To a writer residing in Buenos Aires, however, even if he was born on the Continent, the air here may be as dust-ridden and life-threatening as the Dublin atmosphere. As the narrator of Cortázar's "Casa Tomada" (1947) puts it: "Buenos Aires will be a clean city, but that is due to its inhabitants and to nothing else. There is too much dust in the air," and it settles everywhere, pervasive, unsettling. (Julio Cortázar, "Casa Tomada," in *Espejos,* ed. Donald A. Yates [New York, 1980], p. 54).

81. All references are to Carlos

Fuentes, *Where the Air Is Clear*, trans. Sam Hileman (New York, 1960).

82. Recalling *Finnegans Wake*, the city and its environs are described as a huge human body: "from the armpit of Puerto Isabel to the toepoint of Catoche, from the thigh of Cabo Corrientes to the teat of the Panuco, from Mexico City's navel to the ribs at Tarahumara" (Fuentes, *Where the Air*, p. 373).

83. All references are to Carlos Fuentes, *A Change of Skin*, trans. Sam Hileman (New York, 1970).

84. When I asked Fuentes about his literary interest in the Jews—who are central not only to *A Change of Skin* and *Terra Nostra* but also to his recent entertainment *The Hydra Head* (1978)—he spoke, among other things, of *La Celestina* (1499), by the *converso* Fernando de Rojas, and described it as the first urban novel, a foretaste of the world to come and a sense of what had been lost in 1492 with the expulsion of the Jews from Spain. And, he added, referring to the *Crónica general*, compiled under the aegis of Alfonso X of Castile (1221–1284), "The Jews gave us our language." As he explained, when the king wished to compile the history and humanistic knowledge of his age, he turned not to the monks but to the Jewish scholars associated with his court, and it is their language—like Chaucer's English and Dante's Italian—which

determined the shape of modern-day Spanish (Philadelphia interview).

85. All references are to Carlos Fuentes, *Terra Nostra*, trans. Margaret Sayers Peden (New York, 1976).

86. Stated in a taped interview broadcast (*Fresh Air*) over public radio station WUHY-FM in Philadelphia, 16 December 1980, at precisely the hour Fuentes and I were meeting in his office. I am grateful to the staff of *Fresh Air* for providing me with the tape. Referred to hereafter as WUHY interview.

87. WUHY interview.

88. Joyce, *A Portrait*, p. 203.

89. Fuentes's recent work includes a play, *Orchids in the Moonlight*, written in both Spanish and English and produced originally in the United States. " 'My work is probably becoming less and less "Mexican," ' "says the author. " 'I've been living outside my country for a long time. Maybe I've paid my nationalistic dues by now' " (Arthur Holmberg, "Carlos Fuentes Turns to Theater," *The New York Times* [6 June 1982], Section 2, p. 12.)

90. Philadelphia interview.

91. Joyce, *A Portrait*, p. 253.

92. WUHY interview.

93. Joyce, *Ulysses*, p. 28.

94. WUHY interview.

95. WUHY interview.

96. Philadelphia interview.

97. All references are to Carlos Fuentes, *The Death of Artemio*

Cruz, trans. Sam Hileman (New York, 1966).

98. Political concern, Fuentes suggests—disagreeing with Joyce and with Stephen in *A Portrait*—is a natural concomitant of being a novelist. He speaks of "breaking the silence" and "bringing the news—the etymology of 'novella.'" "The demand," he adds, "has been with us forever, and the worse the situation gets, the greater the demand on the novelist." This is but part of the novelist's quest for "universals," for "knowledge achieved through imagination." Yet, he admits, putting it all in a personal perspective that Joyce could easily accept, "I'm not writing about anything but fear and identity, my own obsessions." Philadelphia interview.

99. Joyce, *Ulysses,* pp. 144, 300, 607.

100. Joyce, *Ulysses,* p. 573.

101. Sainz's *La Princessa del palacio de hierro* (1974) is an extended monologue by a Mexican Molly Bloom.

102. Octavio Paz, *The Other Mexico: Critique of the Pyramid,* trans. Lysander Kamp (New York, 1972), p. 75.

Chapter 6

1. The Sunday Entertainment section of *The New York Times* serves as a particularly accurate barometer of public knowledge and taste in the arts; for a public that may never have heard of Modernism, it has brought, in recent years, news that the movement has been supplanted. What follows is a random selection of headlines, all of them, unless otherwise noted, from this section of our so-called newspaper of record. On dance: "The 'Post-Modern' Choreography of Trisha Brown" (Roger Copeland, January 4, 1976, p. 1), "Notes on Post-Modernism" (Anna Kisselgoff, October 25, 1981, p. 16; note that the quotation marks are no longer needed) and "Postmoderns by Werkcentrum" (Jennifer Dunning, November 23, 1982, p. C12; even the hyphen has now been dropped). On popular music: "Count Basie—the Explosive Catalyst" (on "Jazz modernism"; Robert Palmer, August 15, 1982, p. 1). On architecture: "Brash, young and post-modern" (Paul Goldberger, *The New York Times Magazine,* February 20, 1977. p. 18), "The Japanese New Wave" (Ada Louise Huxtable, who speaks of herself as "a survivor of modernism," January 14, 1979, p. D27) and "Modernist Villa in Ohio" (Paul Goldberger, *The New York Times Magazine,* December 28, 1980, p. 36). On areas related to architecture and outside New York: "Modernism Is Dead, Long Live Regionalism" (Ellen Edwards, *The Miami Herald,* April 2, 1978 p. 26; speaking of "Post-Modernism, Radical Eclecticism, Regionalism—

call it what you will . . ."), even a discussion of "post-modern colors" (Ellen Kaye, "Design," *The Philadelphia Inquirer Today Magazine*, August 8, 1982, p. 20). Perhaps my favorite is from the newsletter of the National Trust for Historic Preservation: "Once the bane of preservationists, the minimalist movement seems rather passé now and is sure to be the subject of future defense efforts. (We can imagine the headlines: 'Turreted postmodern building set to replace glass tower.')" ("Modernism is 50," *Preservation News*, August 1982, p. 2).

2. Mark Strand, ed., *The Contemporary American Poets: American Poetry Since 1940* (New York, 1972), p. xiii.

3. Jeffrey R. Smitten and Ann Daghistany, eds., *Spatial Form in Narrative* (Ithaca, 1981), p. 14. In the collection called *Modernism* (Harmondsworth, Middlesex, 1976), editors Malcolm Bradbury and James McFarlane use the still more limited dates 1890–1930.

4. "Now, the success of modernism in our culture is total and complete—and not only in the museums, of course. In the big world beyond the museum, in the workaday environment of our daily lives, we live in a universe decisively shaped by the grammar of modernist design. It is there in the shape of the chairs we sit on, in the colors of the walls that enclose us, in the look of the objects we covet and of the advertisements that entice us into spending our money on them, not to mention the very cityscapes we inhabit. So sweeping has been the triumph of modernism in our culture that a great many people who have never consciously looked at a Mondrian or a Matisse now live, whether they know it or not, in the visual world bounded by the distant offspring of ideas first adumbrated in the work of these and other modernist masters" (Hilton Kramer, "Beyond the Avant Garde," *New York Times Magazine*, November 4, 1979, p. 43).

5. Ada Louise Huxtable, "The Gospel According to Giedion and Gropius Is Under Attack," *New York Times*, 27 June 1976, Sec. D, p. 1.

6. Compare these reviewers' comments on Sir Frederick Ashton's *A Wedding Bouquet* (1937) and Alwin Nikolais's *Tribe* (1975) and *Somniloquoy* (1967): "The result [in the Ashton] is an archetypal modernist ballet, strong on free association, Surrealist touches and a juxtaposition of words [from Gertrude Stein] with images that illustrate the same or just the opposite. This fragmentary structure builds and builds. And suddenly the nonsensical business accumulates into something very deep. The scene is a French provincial wedding. But beneath the merriment, 'Bitterness is entertained by all,' as the text puts it." (Anna Kisselgoff, "Ballet," *New*

York Times, 6 Nov. 1980, Sec. C, p. 22). And, "Nikolais puts the human form in quotation marks— or maybe parentheses. . . . No persons emerge from the strict composition, and when hands touch, it is with the click of circuitry. . . . [*Somniloquoy*] was a dance for characters standing with one foot in mechanistic systems and one foot still in the world of dancers" (Daniel Webster, "Nikolais at the Walnut: Iconoclasm revisited," *Philadelphia Inquirer,* 5 March 1977, Section A, p. 5). What is interesting here, of course, is that the post-Modernist Nikolais is the spare and linear, impersonal ballet, while the Modernist Ashton is romantic and full of metaphor and depth.

7. Charles Olson, "Projective Verse" (1950), in *Selected Writings* (New York, 1967), p. 24.

8. Olson, "Human Universe" (1965), in *Selected Writings,* p. 59.

9. All references are to Donald Barthelme, "City Life," the title story in his collection *City Life,* (New York, 1970).

10. There is nothing very surprising in this. If we include among the Romantics—the English Romantics, that is, not to speak of the French or the Germans—the visionary Blake, Wordsworth the sentimentalist, and ironic Byron; if we join to them Tennyson and Browning, the sensuous young Yeats and the intellectual Stevens, as well as Walt Whitman and Allen Ginsberg; then we are obviously dealing with something other than a single, unified tradition. But this does not mean that we cannot speak of the Romantics as a group—although it may suggest that we need to be wary of Eliot's claim that the Modernists had rebelled against and supplanted them. Literary and artistic movements, whatever their parallels and connections, however symbolic the events with which, from a distance, we date their origins and ends, are always rather messy affairs: the Classical Greeks, too, like their Alexandrian followers, painted their statues and temples in gaudy colors and were inclined at times to monumental excesses: where, then, the clarity and grace of ancient Greece—its Classicalness—and where the line between "Hellenic" and "Hellenistic"?

11. All references are to José Ortega y Gasset, *The Dehumanization of Art and Other Writings on Art and Culture* (Garden City, New York, 1956).

12. The equation is balanced somewhat in a companion essay, "Notes on the Novel," published in the same volume. Here Ortega does speak of the novel as "one of the few fields that may still yield illustrious fruits, more exquisite ones perhaps than were ever garnered in previous harvests." Even this late crop, however—and he singles out only Proust among the Modernist novelists—may

attest to the general decline, for "the works of highest rank are likely to be products of the last hour when accumulated experience has utterly refined the artistic sensitivity." And the issue of dehumanization remains unresolved; it is only what Ortega calls "imaginary psychology" that can lead to a future humanist revival in the novel (Ortega y Gasset, *The Dehumanization*, pp. 91–5).

13. Loren Eiseley, *Darwin and the Mysterious Mr. X: New Light on the Evolutionists* (New York, 1979), p. 218.

14. García Márquez refers directly in his speech to "my master William Faulkner," just as thirty-two years earlier Faulkner had done implicitly, I believe, to his master James Joyce (Gabriel García Márquez, "The Solitude of Latin America," *International Herald Tribune* [9 Feb. 1983], p. 7).

INDEX